The Red Man's on the Warpath

R. Scott Sheffield

The Red Man's on the Warpath: The Image of the "Indian" and the Second World War

UBCPress · Vancouver · Toronto

09 08 07 06 05   5 4 3 2

Printed in Canada on acid-free paper

Library and Archives Canada Cataloguing in Publication

Sheffield, R. Scott
   The red man's on the warpath : the image of the "Indian"
and the Second World War / R. Scott Sheffield.

   Includes bibliographical references and index.
   ISBN-13: 978-0-7748-1094-4 (bound); 978-0-7748-1095-1 (pbk.)
   ISBN-10: 0-7748-1094-7 (bound); 0-7748-1095-5 (pbk.)

   1. World War, 1939-1945 – Indians. 2. Indians of North America – Canada –
Public opinion – History – 20th century. 3. Stereotype (Psychology). 4. Indians
of North America – Canada – Government relations – 1860-1951. 5. Public
opinion – Canada – History – 20th century. I. Title.

D810.I5S47 2004   940.53'089'97071   C2004-902698-4

Canadä

UBC Press gratefully acknowledges the financial support for our publishing program of the Government of Canada through the Book Publishing Industry Development Program (BPIDP), and of the Canada Council for the Arts, and the British Columbia Arts Council.

This book has been published with the help of a grant from the Canadian Federation for the Humanities and Social Sciences, through the Aid to Scholarly Publications Programme, using funds provided by the Social Sciences and Humanities Research Council of Canada.

A reasonable attempt has been made to secure permission to reproduce all material used. If there are errors or omissions they are wholly unintentional and the publisher would be grateful to learn of them.

Printed and bound in Canada by Friesens
Set in Stone by Artegraphica Design Co. Ltd.
Copy editor: Robert Lewis
Proofreader: Kate Spezowka

UBC Press
The University of British Columbia
2029 West Mall
Vancouver, BC V6T 1Z2
604-822-5959 / Fax: 604-822-6083
www.ubcpress.ca

Contents

Acknowledgments

In producing a work such as this over the course of many years, I have incurred a variety of debts. The research on which this work is based was conducted with the aid of scholarships and funding from the Ontario Graduate Scholarship Program, the Social Sciences and Humanities Research Council, and the Department of National Defence, Security and Defence Forum.

I was fortunate to become part of the Tri-University Program in History at Wilfrid Laurier University, the University of Waterloo, and the University of Guelph. I benefited from the stimulating intellectual environment provided by many excellent faculty members and students in the three departments. My work in race, slavery, and imperialism with Jim Walker at Waterloo were especially important for opening my eyes to new approaches and sparking new questions in my own work.

Above all I was blessed with a great friend and mentor in the person of Terry Copp. His energy and boundless intellectual curiosity pushed me onward, but his sharp questions never let me lose my focus and purpose. In many ways, this project was as much an intellectual journey for him as it was for me, and I remain thankful that he joined me for the trip.

Subsequently, I have moved on to assignments at the Centre for Military and Strategic Studies at the University of Calgary, run by the industrious David Bercuson, and in the Department of History at the University of Victoria. Both these institutions and the conversations with colleagues helped me to further develop my ideas for this study. Special thanks are due to Whitney Lackenbauer and Donald Smith in Calgary and to John Lutz, Brian Dippie, Susan Ingram, and Hamar Foster in Victoria, all of whom saw a form of the manuscript, in whole or in part, and offered comments and criticisms that helped strengthen the final product. Finally, I am greatly indebted to the anonymous reviewers whose conscientious and thorough review of the manuscript forced me to face its inadequacies, to buttress its adequacies, and to derive encouragement from its strengths.

I would be remiss if I did not mention the support I have received over the years from the office staff at Wilfrid Laurier, Calgary, and Victoria. Without their help this already absent-minded academic could never have negotiated the Byzantine bureaucracy that is part and parcel of the university experience as student and faculty. In addition, I must mention the gracious hospitality of Lee and Tammy Windsor, John Walsh and Karen Rayburn, and finally Ian Miller and Liisa Peramaki, all of whom helped to make my research trips to Ottawa a pleasure.

Finally, I must thank my family. My parents, Bob and Irene Sheffield, have been a constant support throughout my academic career. So too have Bob and Elaine Olafson, my "other" parents. I also thank my boys, Jordan and Liam, and my standard poodle, Loki, for reminding me that a walk at the end of the day is *always* more important than a deadline. And lastly I thank my wife, Kirsten, who keeps me going when my drive fails me and with whom I celebrate life's successes. This is her accomplishment too.

This book has been improved by the efforts of all those named above, but of course responsibility for any errors or omissions rests with me alone.

Abbreviations

DND	Department of National Defence
DNWS	Department of National War Services
IAB	Indian Affairs Branch
NAC	National Archives of Canada
NAIB	North American Indian Brotherhood
NBBC	Native Brotherhood of British Columbia
NRMA	National Resources Mobilisation Act
RCAF	Royal Canadian Air Force
RCN	Royal Canadian Navy
RG	Record Group
SJC	Special Joint Committee of the Senate and of the House of Commons appointed to examine and consider the Indian Act, 1946-48

Introduction

On the 24th of May 1941, the *Winnipeg Free Press*'s Saturday magazine section carried an article under the stirring headline: "Red Men Dig Up the Hatchet."[1] It opened with a melodramatic flourish:

The red man's on the war path! From the loghouses [sic] of the once mighty Six Nations, ancient allies of the "King George Men"; from the prairie lodges of tall and stately Blackfeet west to the Rocky Mountain haunts of nomad Stonies, and north to the smoke-stained tepees of caribou-hunting Chipewyans and Dog Ribs in the Land of the Little Sticks, the moccasin telegraph has carried word that the children of the Great White Father are threatened by the mad dog Hitler and his iron-hatted braves. That the time has come for the red men to dig up the hatchet and join his paleface brother in his fight to make the world safe for the sacred cause of freedom and democracy. And Canadian Indians, whose forebears fought encroaching palefaces in their conquest of the New World, are rallying around the Great White Father to protect embattled Britain and stop the spread of Naziism to North America.

The previous autumn, Samuel Devlin, the Indian Agent in Parry Sound, Ontario, had complained to his superiors about the impact that the call-up for compulsory military training was having on his agency.

Only three cases have been so far brought to my notice in this agency of Indians being called to report for medical examination, but that was enough to create a furore and I have been beseiged [sic] by delegations who want me to stretch out a long arm and halt all the functions of government. The Department's circular just received makes it clear that Indians are subject to call the same as other citizens, which I think is no more than right. I have explained at some length to the Indians that there should be no reason why their young men, many of whom have at the moment nothing else to do, should not be willing to put in thirty days of military training to fit them for their part in the defence of Canada which should be just as much their obligation as it is their white brethren. I expect that they will benefit by it both physically and mentally.[2]

These two quotations abound in rich imagery and complex layers of meaning on the subject of the "Indian" participating in Canada's national war effort during the Second World War.[3] The concerns expressed and the tone differ profoundly, yet both view First Nations military participation in the conflict alongside their "paleface brethren" as noteworthy and proper.

Both documents, and a host like them, came to my attention while I was conducting research into government policies on recruitment and conscription of Aboriginal people during the Second World War. The symbolism and significance associated with First Nations military service were particularly striking. Why did their participation seem to matter so much to English Canadians, both in the public realm and among Indian administrators, and why did those in both realms seem to view First Nations military service in such a different light? These queries could not be deciphered without first answering two more fundamental questions: What image had English Canadians developed of the "Indian," and how had the Second World War affected that image, if at all? This was the intellectual genesis of my study, and these questions provide the overarching purpose for the analytical journey that follows.

The original inhabitants of the North American continent have long been a subject of interest, fascination, neglect, and derision for Europeans and later for Canadians. From the time of contact, Western cultures have contemplated, discussed, and mythologized Aboriginal cultures, societies, and physical attributes.[4] In the words of Sherry Smith, identifying and articulating "the meaning of Indianness had pre-occupied non-Indians since the sixteenth century. From that point on, Europeans who visited American shores and those who chose to stay, contemplated 'Indian' and used those deliberations not only to define Native Americans but also themselves."[5] Prior to the voyages of Christopher Columbus in 1492, the world was a known place for Europeans. At its heart was their own continent, with the African shores to the south and to the east the vast steppes of the Russian Empire and the exotic lands of the Orient: India and China. This comfortable Mediterranean-centred worldview was profoundly disrupted by the discovery of the New World. The impact of Columbus's discoveries on late-fifteenth-century Europe might be comparable in many ways to how contemporary humankind would react to discovering extraterrestrial life. Finding new continents was remarkable in its own right, but the lands were also inhabited, and incorporating these new beings into Europe's suddenly expanding understanding of the cosmos was not a simple matter.

Once the initial sensationalism had subsided somewhat, there began a process of determining the nature of these novelties, discovering their capabilities, and determining where they ought to fit in the world Europeans knew. Intellectual and spiritual questions arose that significantly influenced how the colonizing powers conducted themselves in the Americas. Were the *indios,* as Columbus casually termed them, rational beings?[6] What manner of technologies did they possess? How were their societies organized? From whence had they originated? Were they a lost tribe of Israel? Were they even descendants of Adam, possessing a soul and thus capable of conversion to the Christian faith? Europeans, however, did not ask such questions in a vacuum; instead, they learned about, judged, and defined the inhabitants of the New World based on their own criteria and within their own frame of understanding.[7] They did not ask "what manner of people are they?" but rather "how are they different from us?" Europeans measured the indigenous peoples of the Americas against what they viewed as the Old World's greatest virtues: "the twin criteria of Christianity and 'civilisation.'"[8]

These unresolved questions so troubled King Charles V of Spain, whose subjects had been making war upon and enslaving *los indios* for more than fifty years, that in 1550 he suspended all colonial expeditions until the matter could be resolved by the country's greatest thinkers and theologians.[9] A great debate was held at Valladolid with the intent of constructing Christian laws to govern Spain's interaction with the indigenous peoples. The issue under discussion was whether it was just and proper for the King of Spain to wage war against the indigenous nations of the New World in order to bring them under his rule and begin instructing them in the Christian faith. Two great theologians presented contending perspectives before a panel of ecclesiastical judges. Arguing for the humane treatment of the indigenous population of the Spanish colonies was the Dominican friar Bartolomé de Las Casas, who believed that the "Indians" were sufficiently rational and virtuous to be instructed in the Christian faith without violence and cruelty. Opposing Las Casas in the debate was Juan Ginés de Sepúlveda, who portrayed the New World's inhabitants as depraved and uncivilized. He proclaimed that Spain's conquest and enslavement of *los indios* were not only just measures, but necessary preconditions for the education and conversion of such barbarians.

For Sepúlveda, the bestial nature of the New World's people was enough to condemn them, but, to further strengthen his case, he drew on Aristotle's theories of natural slavery. This classical doctrine claimed that part of humanity was born to be slaves and that it was right and indeed good for them to be so. Therefore, in conquering and enslaving the Aboriginal inhabitants of the New World, the Spanish were helping them to see and fulfil their true destiny. Even Las Casas argued his case within an Aristotelian framework, primarily differing over the necessity of violence and brutal labour in Spanish colonial mines. Despite the erudite pleas of the debaters, the judges were unable to reach a definitive conclusion, and, in practice, Spain used both approaches in its interaction with the New World's *indios*. Of significance for this study, however, is that no "Indian" appeared before the ecclesiastical court, either as witness or evidence, and that the entire conceptual, philosophical, and intellectual framework in which the discussion was conducted was European. Spain had judged the "Indian" by the yardsticks of European religion and civilization and had found the "Indian" wanting.

Europeans did not universally condemn the indigenous people of the New World. For some there was much to admire in the people whom the French and English referred to as *sauvages,* or savages. Through the latter half of the seventeenth century and extending up to the early nineteenth century, this savage became increasingly idealized and romanticized by thinkers, writers, painters, and travellers. Though the "noble savage" is most commonly associated with Jean-Jacques Rousseau in the mid-eighteenth century, he was simply the best known publicist for what was by then a long-standing and widely recognized notion across Europe.[10] The concept came in many forms but essentially articulated the notion that human beings had once lived in a state of wild grace, free from the corruption of civilized society. The noble savage, as with Spain's Aristotelian *indios*, was developed and constantly reconfigured by Europeans to fill their own needs, frequently having little to do with the New World. In the seventeenth and early eighteenth centuries, the noble savage helped to revive faith in the inherent goodness of human nature and its potential for progress.[11] By the latter half of the eighteenth century, with the French Revolution on the horizon, it served as a useful whip with which to flog European societies for their decadence and inequities, while at the same time providing a model democrat. In the postrevolutionary period, itinerant high-born Europeans travelling to the New World saw in the noble "Indian" warrior and hunter a reflection of the inherent and natural aristocracy they yearned to see rekindled in the Old World.[12] Though its popularity among the intellectual, artistic, and literary elite waned during the nineteenth century, the idea of the "Indian" as a noble savage would remain an enduring element of popular notions of First Nations people in Western cultures.

The colonial societies that developed in North America owed much of their image of the "Indian" to this European intellectual and cultural lineage. However, their ideas would also increasingly reflect the greater intimacy of contact and conflict with the First Nations from the late eighteenth century onward. The sometimes-bloody skirmishes between settlers and indigenous people did not endear the "Indian" to Euro-Americans, yet the newcomers developed a grudging respect for Native warriors, both as allies and as adversaries. While the First Nations remained militarily potent and politically significant, they were able to force Euro-American people and governments to negotiate the nature of the relationship with them. Richard White's seminal work, *The Middle Ground*, reveals how this process worked in the region of the Upper Great Lakes and the Ohio River, where a culture developed that was neither distinctly indigenous nor European but a unique hybrid built through accommodation by both parties.[13] As the fur trade and settlement frontier moved west, this middle ground would be replicated again and again, although as Ted Binnema has argued, this process occurred within what he calls the "common and contested ground" of broader intra-ethnic and inter-ethnic relations.[14] After the War of 1812, the First Nations never again had the power to maintain the middle ground with the newcomers for so long a period. Without this power, Americans and Anglo-Canadians were freed to define First Nations people as "Indians" and to force them to live with the consequences.

The noble savage was much less prevalent in the United States and British North America throughout the latter half of the nineteenth century. In both jurisdictions, the expansion of settlement across the continent provoked war with the Aboriginal peoples of the West. Clashes between the American army and Plains tribal groups, in particular, rekindled North Americans' perceptions of the "Indian" as bloodthirsty and savage. Such characterizations helped to legitimize the seizure of Aboriginal lands. These processes were paralleled, albeit to a lesser degree, in Canada by the Northwest Rebellion of the Métis and the reluctant involvement of the Plains Cree. As a result of the high-profile nature of Plains First Nations resistance in the later decades of the nineteenth century, their physical attributes, cultural activities, and modes of dress came to dominate popular conceptions of the "Indian" in North America. As a result, all "real Indians" invariably appeared tall and physically impressive, with piercing eyes and a hawklike nose, dressed in buckskins and eagle-feather headdresses.

With the extinguishing of the frontier and the shunting of the defeated tribes onto reserves, the threat to civilization's domain over the whole continent receded. As it did, hate and fear gave way to pity among North Americans. The noble savage returned, riding upon a wave of nostalgia for a great people seemingly fading into oblivion – a vanishing race. The entire history of Euro-American interaction with Aboriginal people "increasingly proved to Whites ... that civilization and Indianness were inherently incompatible."[15] The notion that the "Indian" was dying out had been a pervasive aspect of Canadian and American common sense about the "Indian" for so long that it required "no justification apart from periodic recitation."[16] The idea had been based on very real demographic decline resulting from the ravages of war, deprivation, and disease; however, contrary to popular belief, the population of the First Nations reached its nadir around the turn of the century in both the United States and Canada and then began to rebound. Nevertheless, data to the contrary rarely dented the armour of myth and the potent sentimentality that infused the trope of the vanishing "Indian."[17]

The first few decades of the twentieth century in North America witnessed the rise of mass media to a prominence and diversity previously unimagined. By the Great War, the print media reigned supreme, benefiting from a concomitant rise in literacy rates in Canada and the United States, and would not be superceded until well after the Second World War. To the printed word was added the immediacy of radio broadcasts and the remarkable visual impact of motion pictures, first in silent form and later in sound and colour. All three would become powerful vehicles for the articulation and dissemination of political thought and socio-cultural norms. Newspapers and movies proved most important for keeping the image of the "Indian" a common, if irregular, visitor to the cultural landscape in Canada during the first half of the twentieth century.

This investigation takes up the story of English Canada's image of the "Indian" as the country and world began its freefall into what would become known as the Great Depression. By the 1930s the idea of the "Indian" had become such a familiar aspect of Canadians' experience that even those who had never seen "real Indians," let alone experienced their diverse cultures, could draw on an extensive mental framework of visual impressions, assumptions, and stereotypes at the mere mention of the word. This mental framework had been shaped from childhood by school textbooks, dime-store novels, Wild West shows, and Hollywood's steady stream of silent films and "talkies." It was refashioned, promulgated, and reinforced through experience and hearsay in day-to-day conversation and in the mass media. This framework was immediately accessible and contained a profusion of potent, yet frequently ambiguous and contradictory, ideas. It is the evolution of this framework in English Canada, along with the impact that the Second World War had upon it, that forms the central purpose of this book.

Part of the rationale for examining this subject is that it does not fall neatly within any one field of history, but rather between several different fields, and has thus been largely overlooked in Canadian historical literature. Though the study of Canadian history has become increasingly rich and sophisticated in recent decades, its practitioners have also become somewhat fractious and ghettoized. This process has not gone unnoticed within the discipline and was in fact the cause of some passionate, and even rancorous, debate through the 1990s.[18] I do not accept the notion that the discipline is hopelessly sundered, let alone dead, as Jack Granatstein contends.[19] Nevertheless, the boundaries between fields of study have ossified, and intercourse across them has withered to varying degrees. As a result, between many fields there remain voids, rarely trodden, where subjects that do not fit comfortably within the boundaries languish.

The image of the "Indian" in Canada during the 1930s and 1940s is just such a subject. It falls within a void at the intersection of three historical fields: war and society, Native studies, and race/ethnicity. The war-and-society historiography in Canada has shown a recent interest in broader trends toward the study of the image, perception, and memory of war, with such excellent works as Jonathan Vance's *Death So Noble* and Ian Miller's *Our Glory and Our Grief*.[20] Unfortunately, this approach has not yet spilled over into the Second World War nor into matters of ethnicity and Native people. Indeed, apart from the prominent body of writing on the internment of Japanese Canadians in the Second World War, the war's impact on ethnic minorities and the First Nations is still very limited. Although there are some works available on the Great War,[21] one of the only works available on ethnicity during the Second World War is a collection of essays entitled *On Guard For Thee: War, Ethnicity, and the Canadian State, 1939-1945*, which contains nothing about First Nations people.[22] Several good articles have been published on the First Nations during the Second World War, but each is relatively narrow in focus and does not explicitly or systematically investigate the attitudes of the dominant society.[23]

Historical writing on Canada's First Nations has focused heavily on the contact and fur trade periods, leaving the twentieth century relatively underrepresented. Ken Coates and Robin Fisher, in the introduction to their collection of essays, *Out of the Background*, lamented that, "despite the proliferation of fine writing in the field, enormous historiographical gaps remain. Academics have documented comparatively little about twentieth-century developments related to First Nations (particularly the post-Second World War period), despite the fact that there is no shortage of detailed government and other records relating to the era."[24] They might have included the war years with their emphasis on the post-Second World War period, but the oversight is in keeping with the general neglect in the historiography. This omission seems all the more remarkable considering the tendency of scholars in the field to treat the Second World War as an important watershed. J.R. Miller set the tone in his major survey, *Skyscrapers Hide the Heavens*, where the war marks the end of the "era of irrelevance."[25] Yet those who acknowledge the conflict in this fashion largely gloss over the event itself, offering little examination of the characteristics and historical processes that made it a significant turning point in Native history.[26] Two recent doctoral dissertations, by John Leslie and Hugh Shewell, have thankfully begun to give shape to these neglected years.[27] However, both focus primarily on the development and implementation of Canadian Indian policy and social welfare into the postwar period and generally downplay or ignore the larger context of a country at war and even Native military service.

Sadly, there has been little interaction between the study of the history of race and ethnicity and the study of Native history, and the former's greater theoretical sophistication has had a negligible impact on the latter. Steve High notes that there has been "an implicit understanding that Amerindians are somehow outside the conception of 'ethnicity.'"[28] In many regards, this is fitting given the profoundly different historical experience of First Nations people, their distinct constitutional status, and their relationship with the dominant society. However, it is unfortunate that this topical division has impeded conceptual cross-fertilization. The outcome, according to High, is that, "from its biological origins, the concept of ethnicity has expanded to include socially constructed identities. Despite the general acceptance of ethnicity as a social construct, historians have been slow to explore its meaning. They have been even slower to locate Amerindian peoples within its boundaries ... Ethnic studies has, therefore, not yet become a major player in the study of aboriginal peoples."[29] There remains strong potential for the theoretical and methodological fertility found in the race and ethnicity historiography to enrich our understanding of Canada's relationship with the First Nations, especially in the twentieth century.

In this respect, works that examine the construction and application of notions of race and imperialism, such as Edward Said's classic monograph, *Orientalism*, are perhaps most pertinent.[30] His influential and controversial book explored how Europeans constructed the Orient through academic study, imaginative creation, and the colonial bureaucracies developed to administer and exploit the relationships between the West and the East. The process of creating the Oriental other was fundamental to western Europe's burgeoning sense of itself and its power, as well as to defining the region as an exotic but subordinate place amenable to Occidental rule. Closer to home, similar approaches have been used to good effect by Kay Anderson in examining how race and the spatial location of an internal other have been imagined and shaped. In *Vancouver's Chinatown*, she argues that

"Chinatown" is not "Chinatown" *only* because the Chinese – whether by choice or constraint – have lived in enclaves. Rather "Chinatown" is in part a European creation. Like the idea of a Chinese race, "Chinatown" has possessed a tradition of imagery that has lodged it firmly in the popular consciousness of Europeans (and indeed of the Chinese themselves). Moreover, the premise of a uniquely Chinese race and place has shaped and justified practices that have inscribed it further in European society and space. For more than a century in cities such as Vancouver in Canada, assumptions about Chinese "difference" have informed the policies of powerful government institutions towards the Chinese enclave and its inhabitants, in ways that demonstrate the considerable material force and effect of beliefs about a Chinese race and place. In an important and neglected sense, the "Chinatown" belongs as much to the society with the power to define and shape it as it does to its residents.[31]

More recently, James W. St. G. Walker's subtle case-study approach, entitled *"Race," Rights and the Law in the Supreme Court of Canada*, explored the intersection of cultural notions of race with Canadian society's institutional legal and court structures.[32] Walker destroys the myth of "the law" and the judiciary as external, impartial umpires, revealing their intimate relationship to broader cultural currents like race – to ideas so basic and self-evident to members of Canadian society as to be common sense. Though examining divergent topics, these studies presume that the mental framework of knowledge and assumption was designed and created by the dominant society for its own consumption and to meet its own requirements. It enables the members of this society to make sense of the world around them, to impose meaning and order on chaos. However, such beliefs were not benign abstractions because imagining the other as inferior and subordinate was simply the first step in realizing their subjugation and control. These and other such works sparked questions about the power, pedigree, and pervasiveness of the idea of the "Indian" in English Canada and about how the dominant society imagined, represented, defined, and ruled First Nations people in the twentieth century.

There is a small body of literature that explicitly deals with Euro-Canadian attitudes toward, and images of, Aboriginal people in Canada, but it remains very limited and all but nonexistent for the twentieth century.[33] The writing on Canada is not nearly as extensive and well developed as it is on American and European images of the "Indian," where such classic works as Robert F. Berkhofer's *The White Man's Indian* and Brian Dippie's *The Vanishing American* mark only the starting point of a rich field.[34] By far the best work to date in this genre dealing with Canada is Elizabeth Vibert's meticulous *Trader's Tales: Narratives of Cultural Encounters in the Columbian Plateau, 1797-1846*.[35] Vibert unpacks the jumble of culture, gender, class, and race assumptions evident in the writings of early European fur traders in the continent's northwestern interior, producing a nuanced understanding of the encounter relationship.

There are two Canadian works that overlap with my study chronologically, conceptually, and methodologically. Daniel Francis's *The Imaginary Indian* is the better of the two and introduces many of the issues discussed herein.[36] His important study, which takes Canadians' imagined Indian as its focal point, is a fascinating trek through the long construction and use of the image. His book is structured in four sections based on the progression of the "Indian" image from its seizure and presentation by the dominant society to its eventual appropriation and implementation. Unfortunately, this structure produces an ahistorical and overly rigid impression of the imaginary Indian that is largely divorced from its historical context. Moreover, *The Imaginary Indian* covers such a broad sweep of time that it can only skate across the surface of a deep and complex process. The complexity and nuances of English Canada's image of the "Indian" can be best understood in light of the historical particularities in which it existed because only thus did it have meaning.

The second noteworthy study is a short monograph by Ronald Haycock entitled *The Image of the Indian: The Canadian Indian as a subject and a concept in a sampling of the popular national magazines read in Canada, 1900-1970*, which was published in 1971.[37] This interesting study examines a select group of prominent magazines read by Canadians, including American periodicals, to determine the attitudes expressed about Native people and to trace the changes in those views. He arbitrarily divides the seventy years at 1930 and 1960 but argues that the "changes were ... evolutionary" and tries to maintain a chronology within each period.[38] Unfortunately, he chooses to define all the articles examined within a cumbersome framework of five categories that he finds suitable to his evidence for 1900: religion, customs and manners, travelogue, popular history, and contemporary Indian affairs. The explanatory value of this structure proves limited once he moves beyond his first time frame. Haycock's findings, though vague and restricted by his approach, are in several respects similar to my own.

This book builds upon the foundation of this historiography, while pushing off in some different directions. It examines the notions of First Nations people prevalent in English Canada during eighteen difficult years of depression, war, and peace. There are more than just historiographical reasons for doing so. First, much of the work published to date examines such issues across broad chronological landscapes. A sharper concentration makes possible a disciplined examination of an extensive base of primary source material, both published and archival. Moreover, it enables an intensive and deep reading of this material and thereby a gateway into the complexities of the dominant society's image of the "Indian." This construct can then be located within its peculiar historical context, which is essential for something so intricately interconnected with English Canada's cultural landscape. Second, the hardships, challenges, and threats that the Great Depression, the Second World War, and postwar reconstruction represented for Canadians provide an often highly charged crucible in which to explore their discussions of First Nations people. Societies under strain are often forced to reexamine and reimagine themselves, their values, and their wider world. The image of the "Indian" provides a window onto this process and is most useful therefore not as a means of revealing indigenous peoples, cultures, and experience but of understanding the desires, anxieties, conceits, and assumptions of Canadians. In defining the "Indian," English Canadians were also defining themselves, and when delineating where the First Nations should fit in their society, English Canadians were trying to articulate the kind of society they believed they possessed or hoped to achieve.

In this sense, then, this book is not a work of Native history even though First Nations people form the subject of much of what is discussed. Rather, it is an examination of an aspect of English Canada's cultural history. Therefore, the emphasis remains on the dominant society's perception of the "Indian" or of various events, rather than on the First Nations' experience, except where indigenous people enter the story to directly affect English Canadians' "Indian" image. Nor is the perception of the *indigène* among francophone Canadians examined. The pattern of interaction between French-speaking Canadians and the First Nations has been influenced by a very different historical relationship and a unique intellectual and cultural milieu. It requires its own analysis by someone with the linguistic and cultural fluency to comprehend its subtleties. Henceforth, the term Canadians refers to English-speaking Canadians unless otherwise indicated.

The present work draws a distinction between the images of the "Indian" articulated by English Canadians in the administrative structures of the state and those expressed in the broader public realm. Each of these two mental frameworks, or images, was separated from the other by differing needs and intimacy, but both operated within a single cultural system of knowing, defining, and ruling indigenous peoples. Within the larger public or administrative image of the "Indian," a broad range of representations, stereotypes, and assumptions emerged. In some cases the patterns of characteristics, temporal setting, visual imagery, and cultural utility of these representations coalesced into fairly coherent subimages or archetypes, such as the persistent "drunken-criminal" image common to the public realm. These are noted and designated with quotation marks for ease of reference where they occur, but such distinctions are of necessity somewhat arbitrary, and the boundaries of these archetypes were rarely sharply defined. Tracking the development, waxing, and waning of these images is a prominent part of this book.

The public and administrative images are not the sum total of distinct discursive threads that might be explored in the Canada of this or other periods, but they do provide an entry into what are arguably the two most critical. Exploring how the "Indian" was discussed by those responsible for the state's management of Native people, among the most heavily administered segments in Canadian society during this period, is self-evidently necessary. But comprehending the larger national cultural environment in which Canada's relationship with the First Nations was created or allowed to exist is also essential. At least in theory, the civil servants of Indian Affairs laboured on the behalf of Canadians to achieve goals with which the wider society agreed.

The working image of the First Nations developed by the officials of the Department of Indian Affairs (Indian Affairs Branch, or IAB, after 1936) will be referred to herein as the "Administrative Indian." This agency was not the sole government body involved in Indian administration in Canada during this period, but it was the single most important actor, functioning almost like a mini-government in the breadth of services it provided and powers it exercised. Moreover, it was responsible for the overall direction of Canadian Indian policy, subject only to the intermittent and fleeting interest of Parliament and the public. Officials of the Indian Affairs Branch developed an image of their charges that was unique unto themselves and not representative of all government departments. Similarly, though somewhat interrelated with broader public notions, the working image of the First Nations evident in the IAB was distinct from that of English Canadian society. Indeed, the gulf between the two may never have been wider than it was during the period under investigation.

The material utilized for the analysis of the "Administrative Indian" was derived from a range of Indian Affairs records during the period. For instance, the first chapter covering the 1930s examines the internal correspondence in the school files of Record Group 10, the archival group holding material on Indian administration at the National Archives of Canada. In later chapters on the official image of the "Indian," the focus shifts to correspondence files dealing with Status Indian enlistment and conscription, Indian policy reform, and the postwar Parliamentary review of the Indian Act. In reality, the "Administrative Indian" might successfully have been extracted from virtually any substantial file in Indian Affairs records. Even relatively mundane matters – like appointing teachers to Indian schools, ensuring that Native men and women received national registration cards to avoid losing their jobs, or contemplating the establishment of indigenous advisory councils to supervise the use of community centres on reserves – offer avenues into the official image of Indian Affairs' charges. The emphasis is on internal memos and letters between IAB headquarters' personnel and field staff. Such correspondence was less likely to be guarded than public-policy statements, and in any event, the focus is on the distinct corporate language used in conversation between Indian Affairs officials in the 1930s and 1940s.

Alongside the "Administrative Indian," this book examines the image of the "Indian" in the nation's print media: the "Public Indian." Newspapers and magazines can be fruitfully mined for the common sense of the day because they "purport to deal in fact, not fiction."[39] This was not the only site in which the "Indian" was publicly constructed and negotiated, but it was one of the most important alongside the older medium of literature and the newer forums of radio and cinema. Nevertheless, during this period the print media had yet to be surpassed in significance by film, radio, or television and remained the principle forum for public discussion. In addition, both film and literature sources reflected a relatively small intellectual elite and have already been the subject of scholarly attention.[40] There is another advantage to periodical sources: They appear regularly and predictably in a structured format, unlike film and literature, which tend to be episodic, occasional, and eclectic. The consistency of dailies, weeklies, and monthlies establishes a baseline, thus providing a continuity that is essential for measuring change over time.

Traditionally, historians in Canada have viewed newspapers in a relatively narrow and limited fashion – as fonts of a particular political perspective and perhaps as enclaves of the usually white, male, middle-class journalists and their values. Historians tended to focus primarily on the editorial content and occasionally scanned the principal news page for the headlines, selectively checking small periods of time to find press response to particular events. I view and use the print media in a more holistic fashion. In the first instance, much of the material was not produced by journalists or editorial boards but comprised letters from concerned citizens, essays written by academic or self-styled specialists, poems submitted by amateur writers, and artwork produced by illustrators for advertisements or satirical cartoons. But more fundamentally, newspapers were not simply sources of opinions. They were also reflections of the cultural values and norms of the society in which they operated; they not only shaped and reinforced opinion, but also drew from an existing cultural toolbox, employing language and imagery that their readership would recognize. At their core, the print media were about communication. To be successful, dailies, weeklies, and monthlies had to engage their readership in a meaningful and mutually intelligible dialogue.

This communication went on at many levels, from consciously opinion-driven editorials to the more subconscious responses evoked by advertising, photos, and satirical cartoons. Unpacking this diverse and complex communicative process required an intensive examination of the periodicals selected. For this book, I canvassed each daily paper from cover to cover for significant time periods: typically one to two months several times within a year. Similarly, every single issue of all weeklies and monthlies was examined for entire years. Throughout, careful attention was paid to the context of national and international events and moods. Every single reference to Native people in editorials, letters to the editor, news stories, cartoons, poems, photo essays, short stories, and advertisements was noted and copied. A broad sampling of newspapers and monthly magazines was used as the source base for analysis of the "Public Indian" to compensate for any idiosyncrasies of one periodical. The periodicals sampled were selected from different regions of English Canada and ranged from major urban dailies and rural weeklies to academic quarterlies and popular monthlies, such as *Saturday Night*.[41] Some, such as the weekly *Cardston News*, were chosen from communities in close proximity to Indian reserves where interaction with the local indigenous population was significant, and others, like Toronto's *Globe and*

Mail, were chosen from populations with little contact. The result was literally thousands of pieces of evidence from which to reconstruct the image of the "Indian" as it was publicly discussed in Canada during the 1930s and 1940s.

When read together, this mass of material provides a remarkably rich source for extruding the prevailing common sense about the "Indian." The starting point is the content of the various pieces of data, which are fascinating and informative in and of themselves. But reading more deeply, a series of patterns becomes observable. The frequency, relative to other news, with which "Indian" topics appear hints at the waxing and waning of public interest. So too does the salience of their placement within the periodical: Did "Indian" stories warrant a large headline on the front page, or were they buried in the minor stories on the ninth page? The type of story in which the "Indian" appeared can also be informative. Frequently, the "Indian" was the subject of amusing, exotic, or educational human-interest pieces, the fluff that helped fill the paper on slow news days. At certain times, however, Native people and topics became worthy of hard news stories in the primary or secondary headlines. Even more occasionally, editors turned their pen to pontificate about the "Indian" in an editorial. Finally, there are patterns in the tone of the language used in discussing indigenous people or issues that reveal a great deal about the dominant society's conceptualizations of Native people and their place in Canadian society. Stories and editorials might be sympathetic or derogatory, examine the "Indian" in a serious light, or make them the butt of droll humour. News and editorial content are augmented with the equally rich, evocative, and often visually dramatic material derived from cartoons, photographs, and advertising. How "Indian" subjects were utilized to make Canadians laugh, how they were visually represented, and how "Indian" characteristics were capitalized upon to sell products say a great deal about the dominant society. Layering these distinct patterns one on top of the other enables a remarkably three-dimensional reconstruction of the "Public Indian."

A few final comments must be made about the methodological use of newspapers in this book. First, extensive use is made of quotations from the evidence in reconstructing the image of the "Indian" because in many cases the tone, tempo, emphasis, meaning, and double meaning can only be conveyed through the words used at the time. Second, no American or British publications were considered in the sampling. This decision does not imply that English Canadians were free from the intellectual and cultural influence of their imperial parent or the colossus to the south. Far from it, common sense about race had long been shaped by ideas imported from abroad, particularly by the British experience of empire and the American struggles over race. Some of the most commonly read periodicals in Canada during this time were American, including *Reader's Digest, Time,* and *Life.* Nevertheless, this book treats the material in the Canadian print media as part of a conversation among and between Canadians. Therefore, only periodicals generated in Canada for consumption by Canadians have been considered. Any foreign contributions made to that dialogue will no doubt be reflected therein. Finally, though undoubtedly there were regional and rural/urban differences, this book does not investigate them. Much more intensive comparative research would be required to draw any such conclusions. Instead, the focus is on the commonalities in language and imagery that cut across regional boundaries. It is this overlap in the depiction of the characteristics, imagery, stereotypes, and assumptions that provides a view of the core elements of the "Public Indian," a figure recognizable to the majority of English Canadians during the 1930s and 1940s.

1
The Image of the "Indian" in English Canada, 1930-39

The 1930s were difficult years for Canadians. Internally, the people and their governments wrestled with a crippling depression from which the country would not finally emerge until the early stages of the Second World War. Rampant unemployment, wilting export markets, a collapse in the world price of grain and the worst drought in western-Canadian memory formed the everyday fodder of public and private discussion. Social and labour unrest, always riding the coat-tails of such conditions, spread across the country, most noticeably in the "On-to-Ottawa Trek" of 1935. Numerous political movements were spawned in response to what seemed to many to be the bankruptcy of the Western capitalist system, among them the Social Credit Party of Alberta and the Co-operative Commonwealth Federation. Canadians spent most of these ten years looking inward, consumed with their own problems. However, when they did shift their gaze to the wider world, the news was not exactly heartening. The world was not a happy place in the 1930s, as Canadians anxiously noted the similarly depressed conditions elsewhere during the early part of the decade and the increasingly aggressive expansionism of the totalitarian states of Germany, Italy, and Japan in the latter half.

The 1930s were also hard years for much of Canada's indigenous population. In many cases they felt the contractions of Canada's economy immediately, as they were unable to get jobs off reserves when so many Euro-Canadians were unemployed. Even those remote from the country's economic centres felt the Depression's pinch in slumping fur prices. First Nations farmers on the Prairies, whose reserves were often on marginal land, were affected, as were other farmers, by the drought and the depressed price of grain. Most of the Native political organizations that had formed during the 1920s in response to various government actions had folded before the Depression, leaving no organized voice to carry their plight to Canadians.[1] Not that Indian Affairs officials would have been inclined to hear them if they had done so. In 1933 the department placed an administrative ban on

First Nations delegations coming to Ottawa to lay their grievances or land claims before senior officials.[2] The combination of hard economic times, political powerlessness, and the still-prevalent ravages of disease made many First Nations people dependent on relief payments from an Indian Affairs Branch whose budget had been cut to the bone.[3] In short, their situation verged on desperate.

The effect that federal administrators and legislation had on the lives of First Nations people resulted from more than the provision of relief. By the 1930s the Indian Affairs organization was a rigidly structured, hierarchical institution with an autocratic central office in Ottawa. From there, a handful of senior bureaucrats, the deputy superintendent general (or director), the superintendents of various divisions (Education and Training, Reserves and Trusts, etc.), and the departmental secretary remained in constant contact with the field offices maintained by the branch across the country. The field structure was directly supervised by provincial inspectors of Indian Agencies but effectively revolved around the nearly one hundred Indian Agencies across the country. Each of these agencies, which could encompass a single large reserve or dozens of reserves scattered across ten thousand square kilometres, was ruled by an Indian Agent. The agent was the IAB's man on the spot, who was at the same time granted wide-ranging powers and responsibilities and tightly constrained in his decision making by Ottawa. The agency office might have had other sundry personnel attached, such as an administrative assistant or farm instructor, but the Indian Agent, backed by Ottawa, was the administrative constant in the lives of Native people.

As a result of the Indian Act, the IAB and its personnel had the authority to insert themselves into the political, social, economic, and even moral activities of First Nations communities. The height of directed civilization, or "coercive tutelage" as it has been termed by some scholars, occurred in the early 1920s under Superintendent General Duncan Campbell Scott.[4] He remained in this post until 1933, and his legacy arguably lasted much longer.[5] While historians have argued that Indian administration "drift[ed] into a state of flux" and "ad hoc decisions" after Scott's departure, this should not be taken to mean that it was motionless.[6] The ultimate goal of eliminating the "Indian" as an entity apart from the mainstream of Canadian society remained the raison d'être of Indian Affairs throughout the 1930s.

In contrast to the continuity in Canada, Indian administration in the United States was going through profound changes during the 1930s. There, the General Allotment Act of 1887 had pried away reserve lands and enfranchised American Indians with even more ruthless efficiency than had Canadian Indian policy in the same period. Increasingly articulate by the 1920s, a loose movement of liberal, antimodern intellectuals, led in part by John Collier, popularized the idea of Indian policy reform.[7] So effective did this critique become that President Franklin D. Roosevelt decided to make Collier the commissioner of the Bureau of Indian Affairs in 1933. What followed was a remarkable and dynamic era of reform that came to be known as the Indian New Deal.[8] Built on the Indian Reorganization Act (1934), the New Deal attempted to reaffirm tribal identity and reinvigorate traditional Native cultures, while ending land allotment and establishing some measures of self-government. It would prove only partially successful because the program was created and driven by Collier's idealized and romantic views of indigenous life and culture as he tried to impose his own "notion of welfare – a collective democracy – upon a reluctant Indian population."[9] By the late 1930s, Collier's program was already beginning to unravel in the face of Congressional resistence and Native political activism. The monetary constraints of wartime and the increasingly assimilationist stance of the American public and government led to his resignation in 1945 and in effect to the death of the New Deal, although it would take until the early 1950s before a new policy was articulated and implemented. Interestingly, in Canada there was seemingly no such interest in the plight of the indigenous population; indeed, a cartoon printed in the *Winnipeg Free Press* seems to suggest that there was some sympathy with Americans who were skeptical about civilizing the "Indian" (see Figure 1.1).[10]

This chapter explores the ways English Canadians discussed Native people and issues during the 1930s in order to better understand the relationship between the First Nations and the society and state in which they resided: Specifically, it examines the administrative and public images of the "Indian." This approach is not meant to imply a simple cause-and-effect linkage between public or official attitudes and specific policies. Such a link would be difficult to establish conclusively and too crude to explain an exceedingly complex relationship. However, the Canadian image of the "Indian" formed the context in which policy and reserve conditions were created or allowed to exist. This analysis provides the essential precursor to the rest of this study, but the decade of the 1930s is noteworthy in its own right. The dramatic domestic and international events in the news during the decade provide a competitive context in which the relative significance of Native issues can be measured. In addition, it is worth discovering whether the gyrations in Indian-policy reform going on in the United States had any influence on Canada's Indian Affairs Branch or the Canadian population.

This chapter, as with those that follow, should be conceived of as an explorative journey in search of answers to significant questions. How did Canadians construct the "Indian" in both the public and official domains? Where did these images arise, and what were their meanings? Were there differences or similarities between the IAB and the "Public Indian"? Finally, what purpose did these images serve for their creators? Out of this analysis a broad range of perceptions of First Nations people emerges, each distinct

1.1   "Aboriginal Uplift for the US Indian," *Winnipeg Free Press*, 18 August 1930, p. 13.

from the others and often contradictory. In the end, these various conceptions of the "Indian" help to make sense of the state of Canadian Indian policy, as well as Canada's varied relationships with the First Nations during the Depression years.

Crucial to any understanding of the period is determining how the Indian Affairs Branch administration articulated and constructed the image of their charges. The officials in Ottawa and in the field had formulated a fairly cohesive view of the "Indian" over the many years of administering such matters as land sales, relief payments, agriculture, and education. The research for the "Administrative Indian" focused on internal correspondence in the school files of the branch between senior officials in Ottawa and the agents, inspectors, principals, and superintendents across the country. Education-related correspondence is advantageous, as it contains discussion of not only what the "Indian" was perceived to be, but also what it was hoped the "Indian" would become. Given the government's goal of assimilation, education was the front line in the bureaucratic battle to civilize the "Indian." Everyday matters of evaluating teacher performance, constructing buildings, deciding what to do with graduates of Indian schools, and determining whether "Indian" students could visit their parents provide a glimpse behind the facade of benevolent paternalism that marked the public persona of the branch.[11] What emerges from this wealth of material is an antagonistic and often demeaning image of the wards under their jurisdiction. The "Administrative Indians" of the 1930s were, in the words of one teacher, "lazy, shiftless, indolent, liars, all stomach and cunning."[12]

One of the most common assessments of First Nations people by IAB personnel was that they shied from work, preferring to do nothing – in short, that they were lazy. As one instructor from the Chehalis Indian Day School complained, "it is noted that the Indian Residential Schools in this section of British Columbia are turning out an exceptional class of young Indians, that is to say if indolence, laziness and uselessness can be said to be exceptional."[13] While the sarcasm of the preceding statement was rare, the sentiment was not. Even when educators assumed that they had improved their pupils, many principals of Indian residential schools wished to keep students past the sixteenth year mandated by the Indian Act because they feared the influence of lazy parents when the children returned home. A Saskatchewan Anglican principal, in his effort to extend the careers of several boys at his school, appealed to Ottawa, stating confidently that "the Parents [are] all too eager for them to leave the School, the father becomes less energetic than ever, [and] sends the boy out to cut hay or wood."[14]

In the eyes of Indian Affairs administrators, worse than being lazy was the irresponsibility they saw in the indigenous population. In the context of the school files, it was the officials' views on parental responsibilities that were most evident, and those of the "Indian" were usually found wanting.[15] For instance, the Indian Agent in New Westminster, BC, advised the secretary that local day schools should be maintained, instead of sending the children to residential schools, despite the mobile existence of their families, which kept the children from school for much of the year. In his opinion, the parents merely wanted "to shelve the responsibility of the upkeep of their families onto us, and as long as they have a Day School on the reserve they find it difficult to do so."[16] Even if they were not viewed as wilfully negligent, Native parents were still viewed as unhelpful in the effort to turn their older children into the type of "Indian" the IAB wanted to see. The agent in Gleichen, Alberta, argued that "very few parents of Boarding School children have the slightest idea of parental responsibility. This is not his fault but rather the curse of the whole educational system. As a result, you cannot put dependence on the average parent to constructively help to build a responsible character out of the boys and girls from an institution."[17] Although he conceded the influence of systemic factors, even this Indian Agent deemed Indian parents irresponsible and unreliable.

Considering the view of the "Administrative Indian" as uncivilized, primitive, and even "semi-barbar[ous]," this is hardly surprising.[18] An inspection report for the Burnt Church Indian Day School in New Brunswick spoke warmly of the work done by the teacher, claiming that "in the next four or five years this Reserve should be well civilized."[19] This was a high compliment in the language of the Indian Affairs Branch. Even within Ottawa, such phrasing crept into official memos. Discussing a provincial report that linked economic conditions to immorality and delinquency in the general Canadian population, the superintendent of welfare and education informed Dr. Harold McGill, deputy superintendent general after 1933, that "if such conditions exist amongst the white population, the task of correcting them amongst primitive and semi-primitive people, such as our Indians, is going to be exceedingly difficult work."[20] In some cases, officials did not even wish to force their personnel to live among such backward people on remote BC reserves without "Whites for society."[21] The "Indian mode of life," as it was termed, was an inferior remnant that needed to be supplanted by more advanced Euro-Canadian cultural values and social norms.[22]

Even the intelligence of indigenous people was questioned and decried. Teachers generally assessed their pupils' intellectual abilities below those of their Euro-Canadian counterparts – "about two years below," according to the Oblate Catholic Indian Missions Board.[23] Few went as far as the following individual: "Teachers may explain and expound and give the very best that is in them, but they can't be expected to bridge the void left by Nature in the Indian child – a receptive brain. Memory they have not, and the germ of impulse of Intelligence insofar as educational matters are concerned has not been born in them. There are a few exceptions, but the exceptions are so rare that they arouse and excite curiosity. But even in an Ape jungle exceptions will be found."[24] Branch correspondence rarely demonstrated this degree of racist animosity, but the widespread belief in the inferior capabilities of indigenous people fostered fatalism among, and sapped the morale of, IAB personnel.

Even when education improved the "Administrative Indian," there was always the danger that they would "revert to type" due to moral weakness and susceptibility to unsavoury influences.[25] Such concerns were not limited to Indian-school graduates but extended during the interwar years to the increasing anxiety about the growing social freedom and perceived idleness of Canadian, and especially immigrant, youth.[26] In Indian schooling, this was the primary motivation for keeping young people in residential schools after age sixteen. "Our Indian girls are exposed to a great many dangers when they are dismissed from Schools at the age of sixteen. They are too young to marry and the home environment does not contribute to their moral well-being."[27] Nor did IAB personnel view Native youth as the only ones vulnerable to such negative influences. An inspector from Antigonish, NS, recommended a First Nations man for a teaching post in an Indian day school, noting that his "only concern [was] that his conduct [would] be what it should be when he is living with other Indians."[28] Indeed, like sheep, "Indian" students were expected to regress under the influence of their parents, and whole communities were believed at risk from contact with the bad sort of white man or half-breed.[29]

Ironically, these malleable creatures were also considered intractable and proudly stubborn in their dealings with Indian Affairs officials and policies. First Nations peoples' resistance to the often intrusive and oppressive measures of the government was interpreted by administrators as being "hauty [sic] and exacting."[30] One example from Prince Edward Island is worth mentioning. Parents of children attending the Lennox Island Indian Day School refused to send their children to school unless the teacher, a brother of the band chief, was removed. Officials debated whether to open the school at all in September 1938, to leave it open with no students attending, or, finally, to replace the teacher in the face of a continued stalemate. While the correspondence did not reveal the exact nature of the dispute within the community, this is less important than the assessment given by the agent and his superiors in Ottawa. They boiled the grievances of the parents down to petty spite and attributed the lack of a resolution to their "obstinate attitude."[31]

Indian Affairs personnel often assumed the worst about the "Administrative Indian" during the 1930s. Officials distrusted their charges, despite the Indian's supposed lack of intelligence, and saw complex schemes and nefarious goals in the actions of indigenous people. This emerges clearly in the school files on the question of whether children could leave residential schools for home visits on holidays. Due to the infrequent visits allowed, Native parents were often keen to keep their children home, although officials usually made light of this reaction to the policy. In one case, a man was accused of having incited his son to misbehave at school so that he would be sent home.[32] On the Indian Agent's recommendation, the department reduced the man's relief money by a dollar a week to dissuade others from trying the same thing. In another case, the Indian Agent in Summerside,

PEI, requested a medical exam for a little girl who was not returned to school after the summer. The acting superintendent of Indian education was suspicious and thought that "it [was] very likely that the parents have reported to you that she is ill in order to keep her at home."[33] The "Administrative Indian" was a shifty individual, too cunning to warrant trust.[34]

Underlying the character traits of the IAB's "Indian" during the 1930s was a tone, both patronizing and paternalistic, that emphasized not only Native peoples' subordinate status as wards, but also their perceived cultural and intellectual inferiority. The inspector of Indian Agencies for Alberta wrote condescendingly "that the Indian parents have a strong and parental desire to have their children home for a few days during the Christmas festivities. Such a feeling is quite natural and to be highly commended."[35] Yet in the same letter he declared that "academically, ecclesiastically, officially and personally," he could not agree to the children going home for the holiday. At Norway House and Shubenacadie Residential Schools, the children were not even allowed to return home for the summer holiday for fear that they would not be returned except at department expense.[36] When parents attempted to keep their children home, their reasons, such as having insufficient clothing for the children, were dismissed as "trivial."[37] Usually, Indian Affairs officials claimed to be acting in the "best interests of the pupils themselves," by which they meant "the progress of the residential schools" in contributing to the ultimate goal of assimilation.[38] However, there was a noticeable slackening of the faith that this could be achieved through academic education, and during the 1930s Indian education became increasingly vocational to better "prepare them [Indian students] for their future life."[39] In this acceptance of the likely future for First Nations youth, IAB administrators in effect conceded that assimilation was not proceeding, nor could it as long as opportunities were denied them in mainstream Canadian society at the time. However, threaded through the initiative was a self-fulfilling racist perception that this was all "Indians" could accomplish anyway.[40] Whether young or old, the "Administrative Indian" was conceived of as a constitutional, technological, intellectual, and cultural child.

Cloaked as their charges were in the prevailing negative characteristics of the "Administrative Indian," officials did not view them as benignly infantile but rather as juvenile delinquents. As such, they required discipline and supervision, as did any unruly young person, and the correspondence between Ottawa and its field officials constantly emphasized the need for control.[41] Robin Brownlie has argued that during this custodial period of administration, maintaining departmental authority became the central feature of Indian Affairs' daily activities.[42] This predilection comes through clearly in the school files during the 1930s. Usually such concerns about control were couched in paternalistic terms like those in the following quotation:

"Education increases ones potential either for good or bad and that the educated 'crook' is the one concerning whom the police are most apprehensive. If we are going to increase the Indians' scope of action without seeing that he has a wholesome respect for authority, are we doing him a kindness or are we doing more harm than good?"[43] However, when children were truant from school, particularly if the Indian Agent believed the parents were encouraging them, the branch had an established system for escalating the state's coercive pressure. One agent was informed by Ottawa that "the Department suggests that moral suasion be used as far as possible; but, when it is wise to make an example, you should commit the child to school, using the service of the R.C.M.P., if necessary. Only in extremities should a parent be proceeded against under this section of the [Indian] Act. The Department considers that the arresting of the child, after due warning, is all that is usually required."[44] Adopting the administrative equivalent of gun-boat diplomacy – that is, prosecuting a child as an example to others – betrays the fact that behind the mask of paternalism lay officials' fear of dissension and loss of control over their charges.

The degree of anxiety about threats to branch authority was evident in the correspondence pertaining to the refusal of Mi'Kmaq parents to send their children to the Lennox Island School, mentioned previously. The branch refused to back down because "if the Indians ... are permitted to dictate terms to the Department in this case, it is difficult to say where such insubordination may end."[45] The memo forwarded from the director (deputy superintendent general) to the deputy minister on the matter is revealing. He argued that "under the circumstances I think it would be very unwise for the Branch to make the concessions asked for. This would amount to practically yielding to the threat of force and withdrawal as it were under fire."[46] The military terminology and analogy is striking: Indian Affairs personnel viewed the "Indian" in an adversarial and even hostile manner. In effect, the "Administrative Indians" were the enemy in the war to assimilate them.

The working image of the "Indian" articulated by administrators was of a profoundly negative, unappealing, and antagonistic figure. Within the bureaucracy there appeared a remarkable consensus on the "Indian's" prominent elements and characteristics, while the tone remained paternalistic, patronizing, and dominated by the language of control. This cohesion is remarkable given that the majority of Indian Agents and field personnel never spoke to each other but only to their superiors in Ottawa. Not until after the Second World War would Indian Agents actually meet in conferences to share experiences. The branch was not a completely monolithic structure manned by automatons, however, and there were variations in the attitudes exhibited and in the assumptions on which they were grounded. But, while there were individual exceptions, expressions of pity, and occasionally a recognition of flaws in the system, there was no agreement on any single redeeming feature in the character of the "Administrative Indian."

Though most Canadians would have recognized some elements of the "Administrative Indian," their own preconceptions and assumptions about the First Nations were usually more innocuous and equivocal. The Canadian population had long demonstrated a profound fascination with First Nations people, customs, and history; they thus believed that they knew a great deal about the "Indian." This commonsense knowledge was discussed with surprising frequency in the public forum. Newspapers printed letters to the editor, satirical cartoons, advertisements with visual representations of Native people, and stories about local "Indian" history, archaeological finds, criminal behaviour, and a host of other topics.[47] These representations differed little regardless of the political affiliation of each periodical due to the nonpartisan nature of Canadian Indian policy.[48] A careful reading of the print media allows one to construct an image of the "Indian" as it was publicly discussed across Canada, both in major urban centres and in smaller communities.

The popular conception of the "Indian" in the 1930s contained a broad range of positive, negative, and ambiguous elements, and it was common for contradictory images to emerge even within a single story or advertisement. A 1935 advertisement for cigars provides a good example. It tells a typical tale of a man fishing in the North with an indigenous guide. The fishing is poor and the guide unhelpful until the fisherman gives him a cigar, after which they move and the man catches numerous fish. The anecdote finishes on a sagacious note, stating that "the early traders used to bribe the Indians with beads and kind words, but the Indian of today is a different gent. He has acquired a sense of values."[49] A multitude of conflicting meanings are evident here. "Indians" were foolish to have been duped by "beads and kind words" but had improved by developing a sense of values, meaning Euro-Canadian materialism. Even the circumstances of the tale itself implied stereotypes of the "Indian" as knowledgeable and inscrutable, seemingly positive, but also as devious and untrustworthy for not showing the fisherman the good fishing spot until bribed. There existed a broad range of public conceptions of the "Indian" encompassing everything from the "lazy drunk" and the "licentious squaw" to the "wise elder" and the "brave warrior." In the discussion that follows, it should be remembered that, while there existed distinct images of the "Indian," these images were neither monolithic nor rigidly sustained.

Within this context, the "Indian" most commonly appeared as colourful and alien in the public print media of the 1930s. They formed the romantic and outlandish attractions in advertisements for cruises up the Pacific Coast to Alaska and up the Atlantic Coast to Labrador. The prospective tourist was enticed with the opportunity to see exotic lands "conquered by a song,"

with their "quaint Indian villages" on "totem poled isles" inhabited by "nomad Indians."[50] During the decade, no other writer published as prolifically
on the subject of the "Indian" or pressed the themes of exoticism and the
inherent nobility of the savage so strongly as did ethno-historian Marius
Barbeau.[51] For him, "Indians" were fascinating, "a colourful field," and rife
with mysticism.[52] These themes emerge strongly in his description of a chief
from Alert Bay, BC:

> His stately demeanor was one never to be forgotten. He was more impres-
> sive than a king on a throne. He did not look at us. We moved aside to let
> him pass. His features were massive, his complexion like reddish copper.
> There was something of the grizzly-bear in him – the grizzly-bear of his
> mountains which he must have hunted many times. Yet he was distinctly
> Mongolian. He was thick and squatty. I thought of Buddha, after he had
> gone – a Buddha that had journeyed all the way from Manchuria, across the
> Siberian wastes and the strait of Bering, then down the West Coast to the
> country of the American Natives.[53]

Barbeau's repeated linkages of the First Nations of the Pacific Coast with
Asia, another powerful exoticism in Canadian popular culture, served only
to enhance the otherness of the "Indian."[54] Of one trip to the British Columbia Coast he waxed dramatic, stating that "more than ever it seemed we
had already gone over the border, from America into the realm of the mystic dragon, beyond the sea."[55]

Often the fascination with the exoticism of the First Nations revealed
itself in an emphasis on the pageantry of traditional dress at ceremonies,
country fairs, and other events.[56] For example, in the coverage of the Royal
tour of Canada in 1939, almost every publication examined carried at least
one story, and some many more, highlighting the participation of the First
Nations, their alien behaviour, and their picturesque appearance.[57] Inevitably, mention was made of the "native costume" of the "Indians." One reporter noted that when the Stony, Cree, and Chippewa bands came to Calgary
and Banff to meet Their Majesties, "all had new wardrobes: new beaded
headdresses complete with feathers, fancy vests, mocassins, gauntlets, belts
and coats," while a second was impressed by the Six Nations who met the
Royals in Brantford, Ontario, where "the chiefs, in war paint, feathery headdresses, buckskins and beads and carrying hatchets, wampuns [sic], and a
pipe of peace, captured the imagination of the children."[58] Judging from
how frequently observers and commentators made note of the "regalia" of
the First Nations, these events and the splendour of "Indians" appearing in
traditional clothing captured the imaginations of more people than just the
children in Canada.

The "Public Indian" was usually the human-interest story for slow news days. First Nations people became newsworthy either when they did something that captured the essence of the Canadian idea of the "Indian" or when they acted in ways that seemed at odds with the dominant society's assumptions and stereotypes. Thus the operatic excellence of baritone Chief Os-Ke-Non-Ton as he performed at Varsity Arena in Toronto seemed a poignant example of the clash of the ancient and primitive with the modern and civilized.[59] Similarly, the *Cardston News* printed a picture of an "Indian" chief in full regalia trying his hand at the bagpipes, while a Highland piper in his own regalia leans back laughing at his efforts.[60] A final example demonstrates both expected behaviour in the expressions of loyalty as well as the unexpected in a rendition of God Save the King in Cree during the reception of the king and queen in Edmonton on 2 June, where "Indians of the Winterburn Reserve chanted 'God Save the King' in the strange Cree language to the throbbing beat of tom toms when their Majesties stopped today outside the Red men's encampment here. Cree words fit none too readily to the tune, and war whoops are more natural to the tribesmen, but they paid homage gallantly to the King and Queen from across the 'great water.'"[61] For newspapers' editorial staffs, "Indian" stories provided their otherwise drab recitation of the day's events with a little spice and flash or comic relief.

Despite a colourful flair, the discussions of the "Public Indian" reflected little understanding of the cultural or physical diversity among First Nations people. The "Indian" had a distinct and consistent appearance that drew largely from Plains Native culture and dress as well as stereotyped physical traits. The Plains tribes, particularly the Dakota (Sioux) and the Blackfoot in Canada, came to represent the "Indian" in North America during the latter part of the nineteenth century.[62] The last and greatest of the Indian Wars, the Wild West shows, and Hollywood conspired to make the eagle-feather headdress, buckskins or breech cloth, aquiline nose, and tall powerful physique the dominant impression of the "Public Indian" in Canada. Few traded as explicitly or graphically in the image of the "Indian" as did the McColl-Frontenac Oil Company with advertisements that ran in the *Globe*, the *Brantford Expositor*, and *Saturday Night* during the first half of the decade.[63] The aura of physical prowess, endurance, silence, and speed were evident in the pictorial representation of the befeathered "Indian" paddling his birch-bark canoe (see Figure 1.2). Moreover, it was epitomized by the ever-present logo of two lithe "Indians" in silhouette running effortlessly in perfect synchronization (see Figures 1.3 and 1.4).

Even nonphysical traits were stereotyped across indigenous cultures. First and foremost, the "Indian" was assumed to be courageous. In one instance, an "Indian" man broke his leg after a fall from his wagon but managed to capture his horse and ride two miles into town for help. This tale gained the notice of the local paper, which claimed that "Indians have always been credited with having an abnormal share of 'grit' and tales of their bravery have often been told by the pioneers."[64] A play advertised for the Strand Theatre in Calgary, which included "Real Danger, Real Indians, Real Romance," spoke to the intensely masculine nature of the "Public Indian,"

1.2 "Speed ... silence ... smoothness on the Red Indian trail!" McColl-Frontenac Oil Company advertisement, *Toronto Globe (and Mail)*, 2 April 1930.

1.3   "Unflinching Protection!" McColl-Frontenac Oil Company advertisement, *Toronto Globe and Mail*, 4 July 1935, p. 7.

1.4 "Matchless Fidelity." McColl-Frontenac Oil Company advertisement, *Saturday Night*, 25 May 1935, p. 10.

promising its audiences a "Powerful Drama of Actual Life of Strong, Silent Manhood."[65] Once again, however, it was an unusual series of ads for the McColl-Frontenac Oil Company's Red Indian Oil that attempted to capitalize most aggressively on the commonsense knowledge of the "Indian." Each of the advertisements contained a different melodramatic story of "Indian" life, with striking visuals to grab the readers' eye and drive home the message. In one, an "Indian" woman taken captive by enemies after her village was attacked gains vengeance at the cost of her life by guiding the canoes of foolish enemy braves over a waterfall. In another, a young brave and a maiden from opposing tribes have fallen in love, but when the brother of the young woman catches up with them, intent on killing his sister to expunge "the dishonour done his tribe," her young lover steps in front of the fatal arrow. These advertisements and the other bloodthirsty episodes suggested that the company's oil was, like "Indians," "Faithful to the Task" and "Loyal to the Last," while providing "Matchless Fidelity" and "Unflinching Protection" (see Figure 1.3).[66] The "Public Indian" was a dramatic and positive figure, embodying courage, integrity, loyalty, and stoicism. All of these representations of the "Indian," both physical and nonphysical, harken back to the glorified period in history when the First Nations were great and powerful.

Indeed, the "noble savage" formed the central tenet of Canadians' image of the "Indian" well into the twentieth century and predominated during the 1930s. Though the "noble savage" image had once formed a potent tool for social criticism, he became increasingly romanticized, particularly by American writers of the nineteenth century.[67] Romanticism dominated the 1930s' manifestations of the "noble savage" in Canadian newspapers. Commenting on a stirring speech made by a Native man in a Sault St. Marie courtroom in response to charges against him for hunting out of season, the editor of the *Globe* waxed eloquent: "This man must have in his veins the blood of the famous Chiefs of his race whose eloquence thrilled the explorers at the dawn of Canadian history ... The dignity and force of this language removed the Indian from the class of men who shoot game out of season, and made him a splendid figure pleading the ancient right of his race to live on what nature has prepared for him."[68] A literary review of a novel that appeared in the *Canadian Forum* in 1931 echoes similar, if more introspective, imagery.[69] In considering a murder committed by the primary character, who is an Inuit man named Mala, the reviewer argued that "it is so appropriate that Mala should murder, so necessary, it would seem, to his incredibly primitive self-fulfilment, that it appears almost a virtue in him. I would no more sit in judgment on the fury of Mala than on Ajax or Achilles." Declaring the book a masterpiece, the reviewer made an interesting comment: "It is more than a century since Romantic-minded writers began to idealize 'the noble savage' and it is nearly as long since men argued the fallacy of it. And now when you would have thought that we had heard the last of the idea, there comes a realization of this supposedly fictitious creature at once more savage and certainly more noble than anything Rousseau ever dreamed of. Here is 'the noble savage' made classical." Even though demonstrating an awareness that the character of Mala is an idealized entity, the reviewer "never questioned [the] utter veracity" of "this starkest of books."

In light of Canadians' assumptions about the "Indian," the odd phenomenon that was Grey Owl at the height of his fame during the 1930s makes some sense.[70] He was in every respect the perfect "Indian" for Canada, as indeed he was also for America and particularly for Great Britain, where he made several lecturing tours to great acclaim. His physical features matched the stereotypes: his long black braided hair, tall lean physique, hawklike nose, penetrating eyes, and the "forest costume" of buckskins that he typically wore.[71] Moreover, Grey Owl's demeanour was that expected of an "Indian": He was stern, wise, inscrutable, attuned to nature, and honourable, as well as a passionate orator.[72] Grey Owl combined all that was best, most exotic, and engaging about the "noble savage" with the ability to convey it to a modern audience through his articulate writings, motion pictures, and popular speaking engagements. The result was that he became the most famous "Indian" during this decade as well as a very effective spokesperson for the conservation of Canada's wildlife and wilderness. The great irony was that Grey Owl knew how to capture the imaginations of Europeans and North Americans because he was himself an Englishman and not of Aboriginal descent. His name was Archie Belaney and he had been born and raised in Sussex, where as a lonely child he had himself been enraptured with the mystique of the "Red Indian." Even when his facade was exposed after his death in 1938, Canadians did not begrudge the deception because his cause had been an admirable one, and they accepted that the masquerade had lent his message a legitimacy and impact that it would never have had otherwise.[73]

Hand in hand with the romanticized "noble savage" was the certainty that the Native race, diminishing in numbers and vitality, was doomed to an inevitable demise. Indeed, the sentimental tone and tragic language of the 1930s convey the sense that indigenous people were already gone.[74] In one lyrical and sad essay published in *Saturday Night* under the title "Gone Is the Old Trail," the author concluded with an aching requiem:

I have to say good-bye to the old narrow trail. At night the cry of the coyotes – or is it the lamenting voices of the Indian dead? – still echo against my cottage door, and the sob of the loons is a soul in pain. But they [the Indians] do not come to me as formerly across the old living trail. Never again at bud of leaf, or at mournful rustling of dying leaves shall I wander idly adown it, reliving its glorious but tragic pageant. The old trail is gone forever. Yesterday, government engineers tore it up and built a gravel highway.[75]

The metaphor of the "Indian trail" formed a powerful expression of the inevitable extinction of First Nations people, or at least their "Indianness," before the irresistible force of modernization and assimilation.

Two advertisements by Canadian Pacific – one in 1931 announcing the fiftieth anniversary of its founding and the other in 1935 celebrating the fiftieth anniversary of the driving of the last spike – demonstrated these sentiments in visual form. The first contains a drawing of the Banff Springs Hotel against a mountain backdrop, but overhanging all is the ghostly, fading apparition of an aging, proud Plains chief astride a horse (see Figure 1.5). Even more poignant was the celebratory advertisement of the anniversary of the railroad's completion (see Figure 1.6). The picture symbolized Canada's march of progress according to Canadian Pacific. Proceeding from left to right, the image encapsulates fifty years: The train changes from an early steam locomotive to a more modern diesel engine; the dress of the people, from all walks of life, changes to reflect the passage of time and the variety of people that the railway brought to this new land. This march of progress heads off the page to the right, with an industrial city of high-rises and an airplane in the background showing how far Canada has come. Almost missed in this busy picture is the figure of a Plains warrior sitting forlornly on his horse at the far left edge of the page, having already partially slipped from the picture into historical oblivion.

The inevitability of the "Indians'" extinction tinged the discussions of Native rights and issues with fatalism. One editorial summed up a long discussion of the "noble savage" rather abruptly, saying "anyway, the forests are gone, and so is the noble red man. So what's the use in talking about it?"[76] In another describing the devastation of migratory-bird stocks around Moose Factory on Hudson Bay by Canadian hunters and the resulting starvation among local indigenous groups, the editor closed on an apathetic note:

The dominant race will take what it needs; that is the way of the world. But a pitiful consequence of this is that the tribes which ruled supreme on this part of the continent a few hundred years ago cannot now retain a bit of good hunting territory even as far north as Moose Factory. The white hunter must have his wild ducks and geese; consequently his red brother, who needs the food, must go without. An old adage might in this case be revised to say that one man's wild fowl means another man's starvation.[77]

1.5   This image was used in a Canadian Pacific advertisement, titled "In the Heights of the Rockies," commemorating the fiftieth anniversary of the establishment of the corporation in 1881. The ad claimed that "Where only the Indians had hunted on the mountains, now the great hotels at Banff and Lake Louise arrest the eye." *Canadian Forum*, April 1931, p. 273. *Canadian Pacific Railway Archives BR184*

1.6 "1885 – Fifty Years of Canadian Pacific – 1935." Canadian Pacific advertisement commemorating the fiftieth anniversary of the driving of the last spike. *Saturday Night,* 9 November 1935, p. 20. *Canadian Pacific Railway Archives NS25975*

Commonsense wisdom of this nature was indicative of the indifference that such fatalism fostered.

Even when the media portrayed Native people in a positive, if often inaccurate, manner, there was a tendency to belittle and trivialize through the language and tone of the editorial or news story.[78] For instance, a front-page story of several men from the Six Nations Reserve in Brantford who went to Kitchener to greet the Royal train in 1939 bore the headline, "Chiefs Use Wives' Lipstick as 'War Paint' to Meet King."[79] In a parody of the terms Canadians believed typical of "Indian-speak," Euro-Canadians became "Palefaces," the king became "the Great White Father," and the "Indians'" abodes inevitably "tepees" or "wigwams." First Nations people were denied a sense of humanity in terms that referred to men as "chiefs" or "braves," women as "squaws," and children as "papooses." For instance, the *Halifax Chronicle* ran a front-page picture bearing a caption that read, "In full regalia hundreds of Indian chiefs, braves, squaws and papooses converged on Calgary to offer a warm and loyal welcome."[80] An article in the *Brantford Expositor*, a paper that generally refrained from this type of characterization, ran an article about the Six Nations that concluded by saying, "evidently when war paint is worn by braves, a woman's place is in the tepee."[81] Even more mocking was a *Vancouver Sun* editorial describing a meeting between the Royals and "Indians" in Calgary: "Most of the Indians spoke English which was just as well – the King and Queen could not speak a word of Indian, although His Majesty's 'Ugh' when he saw the dirty old pipe of peace was passable Indian."[82] The droll tone of such stories reduced First Nations people and their cultures to a caricature, one that did not need to be taken seriously.

Though hardly an unambiguous figure, this image of the "noble savage" was the dominant articulation of the "Indian" in the public realm and was generally constructed in a positive, if comical, manner by Canadians during the 1930s. Because the "Indian" was overwhelmingly male, he was strong, wise, and honourable. However, the combination of the conglomeration of ideas that made up the "noble savage" with the trope of the "disappearing red man" meant that the principal manifestation of the "Public Indian" was a largely historical figure. Grey Owl's appeal rested on his ability to present himself as the embodiment of this historical mystique in a modern setting. Even when discussed in a contemporary story, journalists couched their terms and context in some distant and glorious past that had long since faded away. In a sense, consigning First Nations people to the past denied them a present, and fatalism denied the possibility of a future. The "noble savage" of the 1930s was a heroic, but tragic, shadow.

The "noble savage" image was not the sole manifestation of the "Indian" in the public forum during the 1930s. Canadians had been defining and mythologizing indigenous people for far too long for even such an ambivalent figure as the "noble savage" to capture the complexity of the "Public Indian." Underlying the historical and positive image of the "Indian" was another antithetical image, distinctly unappealing and resident in the present. Though much less prevalent than the "noble savage" image, this articulation of the "Indian" was a constant presence in the public media during the decade, with examples in almost every publication examined. When discussing the "Indian" in this framework, Canadians emphasized the negatives that they saw in contemporary First Nations people and their living conditions. This image of the "Indian" had no redeeming qualities: It exhibited a host of vices and character flaws ranging from drunkenness to cultural backwardness and from infantile irresponsibility to a lack of intelligence. This "Public Indian" was often either inebriated or committing a crime and frequently both. The presumption of blame for this state of affairs lay squarely with the wretched "Indian." Overall, Canadians constructed a loathsome contemporary counterpart to the "noble savage."

One of the more common contexts in which the negative "Public Indian" appeared was in the crime stories that filled the pages of the papers, then as now. Here was the blood and violence that titillated, shocked, and, most important, sold newspapers. Regularly, the language or tone of these stories suggested that "Indians" were naturally violent or even enjoyed such activity. One *Calgary Herald* article told of two "Indian" men who "were very glad to see a policeman Thursday afternoon, at 6:30 o'clock. They had been fighting each other for an hour, causing damage to furniture in the process, and were growing weary. The arrival of the constable revived interest in the battle. They went to work on him with vigor and enthusiasm."[83] Even when the events were reported in more neutral language, inevitably the headlines gratuitously identified the accused or victim as "Indian."[84] Highlighting the racial other in headlines was customary. The practice produced an exaggerated sense of the degree of crime and violence among the First Nations in Canada. Canadians did not need to even read the stories because the headlines alone told them that it was merely another tale of what they already expected of the "Indian."

Whether intermingled with crime stories or on their own, the public representations of Native people revealed one of the pervasive assumptions about "Indians": They could not resist liquor, were usually drunk, and became violent when intoxicated.[85] In one story about a flood in the Sumas Valley of British Columbia, the reporter managed to find "undercurrents of drama and humor."[86] One of the elders was quoted as saying, "Ugh ... I'd like drink of whisky," at which point the reporter departed from the subject of the flood, stating that "it transpired that the Indians had been getting relief orders for emergency clothing from the provincial government. They had been selling the new clothes to unscrupulous whites in return for whisky and a mild tribal drunk had ensued." The relief supplies referred to were part of an ongoing governmental welfare provision, not relief supplies in response to the flood. Whether the allegations were accurate or not, the anecdote had nothing to do with the flood and was inserted into the story for no other reason than to evoke a knowing snicker from readers. It made a mockery of people whose homes were flooded, not only denying them their humanity, but also robbing them of any sympathy for their predicament. References to alcohol, or "fire water" as some journalists liked to call it, were frequently expressed in a snide manner, such as in one article about a fight that broke out in a home on a reserve where a wedding was being celebrated "with a dance and it is alleged with something else – that goes to the head besides the feet."[87] Such derisive and droll humour applied to these subjects erected a barrier that made it difficult for Canadians to empathize with Native people and their plight.

Crime and alcohol were merely vices on the surface of this image of the "Indian" that hinted at the depravity and weakness within. Inferences and vague comments in stories, editorials, and comics suggested that the contemporary "Indian" was plagued by a wide range of character and cultural flaws. Among the more widespread stereotypes was that the "Indian" was lazy, that "they can lay any lesson or task aside if a trip is in prospect."[88] As with the "Administrative Indian," it was assumed Native people were unintelligent. So pervasive was this assumption that it became part of a parable used by the *Cardston News* to encourage more advertising: "Remember the old story of the Indian who heard about feather beds and thought he would try one. He took one feather, laid it on a plank and slept on it all night. In the morning he woke up with a crick in his back and growled: 'White man say feather bed heap soft. White Man big fool.'"[89] The moral was that the businessman ought not to be as foolish as the "Indian" because "it takes more than one [feather] to make a feather bed." In addition, the contemporary "Indian" was infantilized, as demonstrated by a pair of editorials in the *Kamloops Sentinel* that seem to echo the basis of the "Administrative Indian." The editors had argued consistently that "bottom of all the Indian problems ... is the fact that the reserve is too close to the bright, shining lights of the city, with all its glitter and appeal to the childish Indian imagination."[90] The solution, as they saw it, was to "treat them as the juveniles they are: protect them from the evils which they cannot abhor when they are close at hand."[91] Given their handicaps and the poverty in which they lived, the modern-day "Indian" might have been an object of pity for Canadians. However, the drunkenness and violence expected of them as a result of their racial flaws meant that little such sentiment appeared in the language and imagery of the "Public Indian" during the 1930s.

This debauched and pathetic creature, the "drunken-criminal" image of the "Public Indian," was in almost every way the opposite of the "noble savage." Whereas one was contemporary, the other was historical. Whereas one was despised, the other was admired. It seems strange that, throughout the decade, English Canada could construct such dichotomous images when First Nations people, issues, or cultures were discussed. Yet the two seemed to coexist despite their inherent contradictions. Having said this, the dualistic images were alike in two ways. First, both were extremes that bore little resemblance to the vast majority of indigenous people. Second, both the "noble savage" and the "drunken criminal" were objectified and trivialized through comedy. But whereas the humorous treatment of the "noble savage" was bemused and light in tone, the representations of the present-day "Indian" evinced a more derisive and sardonic edge. Nonetheless, the effect was the same: It satirized First Nations people and the difficult social problems that many faced with substance abuse, poverty, and violence.

This exploration of English Canadians' images of the "Indian" during the 1930s reveals very different conceptions of the First Nations. The official view of the "Indian" differed profoundly from the dominant image of the "Public Indian," both in form and in substance. The image of the "noble savage," though ambivalent and often contradictory, was that of a largely positive and dignified figure. How is it possible to reconcile, within the span of a single decade, such disparate images of what Canada considered a single racial group? Perhaps more important, how did these various "Indian" images develop and what do they mean for our understanding of the period? Essentially, both the IAB and the Canadian public developed and constructed a different "Indian" because each had different requirements and perspectives in their relationship with the First Nations. Moreover, Canadians of various stripes defined the "Indian" as they wished because they could, largely irrespective of Natives' sense of themselves. The power within the relationship rested securely with the dominant society and government at this point in Canadian history.

The most cohesive and distinct construction of the "Indian" was that developed by the federal department responsible for administering the Status Indian population. Uniformly negative and derogatory, the corporate language of the IAB reflected an antagonistic relationship with its charges. Unlike the public, Indian Affairs officials did not have the luxury of ignoring First Nations people: Their raison d'être was to think about and interact with real indigenous people on a daily basis. Nor could administrators avoid viewing their charges in the present tense, rather than as historical entities. Moreover, they were responsible for implementing policies designed to destroy the culture of the First Nations and supplant it with an idealized version of English Canadian culture. In order to legitimize and rationalize such work and their own existence, administrators needed a potent, overt feeling of both their own superiority and their wards' degeneracy and backwardness. Their conceptualization of their relationship with the "Indian" as a hostile and combative one was accurate if the significant historiography on Native resistance to this aggressive assimilation is any indication.[92] The cohesive image presented by the IAB can, in part, be explained by its own peculiar nature and by the influence of the man who had ruled it as his fiefdom for almost twenty years.

The IAB of the 1930s was Duncan Campbell Scott's creation. He had crafted its ethos in his own "narrow vision" and had selected its personnel over two decades as the senior bureaucrat in charge.[93] To a remarkable degree its officials stayed within the branch in one capacity or another for very lengthy periods, benefiting from what Harold Hawthorn termed a "grass-roots pattern of career mobility."[94] This trend was likely reinforced by the economic conditions of the Depression, during which the lack of other options would have encouraged IAB personnel to cling to their jobs. Scott himself was involved in the work of the Department of Indian Affairs from the late nineteenth century, but the tenures of other prominent personnel such as R.A. Hoey, T.R.L. MacInnes, G.H. Gooderham, W.M. Graham, and John Daly demonstrate that such longevity was not unique.[95] Thus a long period of indoctrination and selection ensured that those who excelled and gained promotion under Scott were those who shared his vision.[96] There would be very little turnover of IAB personnel until after the Second World War, especially after 1950. The result was a strangely cloistered group of civil servants, almost monastic in nature, that maintained a highly conservative, nineteenth-century view of the "Indian."

The "Public Indian" of the 1930s was a complicated and conflicting duality composed of a tragic and noble resident of the past, soon to be gone from this earth, and a miserable remnant that existed in the here and now. Canadians, through their media, and as a result of the segregation of the First Nations on remote reserves, had the luxury to think of the "Indian," or not, in whatever way they wished. In this sense it was more pleasant to conceive of the "Indian" in a romantic and positive manner, an impulse that was probably stronger in the public media given its goal of entertaining as well as informing. In doing so, Canadians were partly attempting to cope with a sense of collective guilt, or at least obligation, resulting from the dispossession and devastation of the First Nations. Many editorials, news stories, and literary pieces frequently mentioned that the responsibility for the "Indians'" decline belonged to Euro-Canadian/American society, as did the obligation to do something. As one writer summed up, "This Indian problem is strictly of the white man's making – and the white man alone can remedy it."[97]

Several mechanisms can be seen in representations of the "Indian" for managing the pain of guilt. One is the construction of the "Indian" as a historical figure, a useful buffer against considering the harsh contemporary conditions on reserves in the 1930s. In addition, Canadians, with some legitimacy, tended to include themselves within a broader white race responsible for the decline of the original inhabitants of the continent, thus diluting their own culpability. Even when they did turn their gaze on the contemporary "Indian," what they saw was the pathetic "drunken criminal" with whom they could not empathize; this creature did not deserve their pity or concern. The repeated trivialization of indigenous issues, culture, and people through language and a tone that were demeaning and comical helped Canadians by further reducing the "Indian" to manageable proportions. Finally, the canon of the "vanishing Indian" provided a last line of fatalistic defence; the decline of the "Indian" was viewed as inevitable and, in a social-Darwinian sense, natural. There was nothing that Canadians could do but speak prosaically of some romanticized past and the tragic harsh truth of the survival of the fittest.

The various images of the "Indian" that existed at this time formed the intellectual and conceptual environment in which policies pertaining to Native people and the conditions in which they lived were created or allowed to exist. Following the retirement of Duncan Campbell Scott as director of Indian Affairs, and with him his zealous sense of purpose, the department was left with little but an infrastructure and its authority. If anything, the IAB's need to maintain its control was augmented by the conceptualization of the "Indian" as a wayward delinquent child in need of rules and a firm hand. The attempts during the decade to gain legislative amendments that would strengthen the intrusive powers of the department similarly make sense in light of the intransigence expected from "Indians" and the combative view of the relationship held by administrators. The public image of the "Indian" is useful for understanding the roots of Canadian indifference to the plight of the First Nations. "Indians" were historical entities, not contemporary human beings; they were objects of trivializing comedy, not of serious concern. Even when unpleasant modernity was discussed, there was little impulse to do anything because common sense told them that "Indians" were a doomed race nearing extinction.

This indifference left the Indian Affairs Branch with an almost free hand to pursue assimilation in whatever manner it saw fit. There was no popular movement as in the US, even among radical intellectual and socialist elites, to reform the manner in which the country treated its indigenous population. Sadly, First Nations people, neither as noble nor as depraved as Canadians' extreme images of them suggested, were caught somewhere in between, struggling to maintain their cultural existence against the onslaught of the government and the indifference of Canadians.

2

The "Administrative Indian" as Soldier and Conscript, 1939-45

On 10 September 1939, a special session of the Canadian House of Commons passed its declaration of war against Nazi Germany, and the country officially entered the greatest conflict of its history. The armed forces had already begun quietly guarding strategic points and sending out orders for militia units to begin assembling even before hostilities broke out. In the wake of the declaration, the rest of the government began mobilizing its human and material resources for the trials to come. Initially, the process was conducted in a measured way. The government of Prime Minister William Lyon Mackenzie King, haunted by the spectre of conscription with all its threats to national unity, remained dedicated to a limited war effort until the changing war situation in 1940 forced its hand. Thereafter, Canada pursued something closer to a total national commitment.

Along with the Canadian population and the First Nations, the Indian Affairs Branch and the rest of the government bureaucracy went to war in September 1939. Like everyone else, the IAB was utterly unprepared for the new strains and demands that the war would place on its infrastructure, on its charges, on its jurisdiction, and on its image of the "Indian." The war would increase the frequency and degree of government interference in the daily lives of First Nations people as well as the number of government ministries and agencies involved. For instance, the Department of National War Services (DNWS) was responsible for including Native people in the National Registration of all Canadians over sixteen years of age from 1940 onward. National Defence took charge of First Nations men once they were recruited or conscripted, and its Dependant's Allowance Board administered the distribution of the allowance moneys and assigned pay that was due First Nations dependants of service personnel. The National Selective Service and, later, the Ministry of Labour mobilized the domestic labour force to maximize wartime production. Native men and women were generally included alongside the rest of the population in these national programs.

The overlapping jurisdictions of these various government agencies complicated the work of the Indian Affairs Branch (IAB), whose personnel generally considered themselves responsible for virtually everything to do with their charges. Out of this administrative morass, a series of confusing policies emerged, some of which were then reversed, only to be reinstated. The IAB's network of field personnel was ill-equipped for transmitting rapidly changing policy to the country's indigenous population, which remained uninformed or misinformed about regulations that had significant bearing on their day-to-day lives.[1]

The most serious challenge to the branch's corporate image of the "Indian" was presented by the voluntary enlistment and conscription of thousands of First Nations men. The attitudes of IAB administrators concerning Native military service and conscription provide an excellent vantage point from which to examine the "Administrative Indian," the relationship between the IAB and its charges, and any influence exerted by the Second World War. Indeed, it would be meaningless to study the impact of the Second World War on the official image of the "Indian" without understanding something so symbolically significant as indigenous military service. American historiography is agreed on the point that the Native American record of enlistment and participation in the US war effort became one of the central catalysts for policy reform after both world wars.[2] Even though the American involvement in the First World War was relatively brief, the thousands of Native Americans who enlisted generated public and governmental interest in their people's status, administration, and standard of living. In 1924 Congress declared all indigenous people citizens, with the concomitant rights and responsibilities, although not all American Indians were happy to be recast as Native Americans.[3] As mentioned in Chapter 1, during the 1930s a significant and controversial change in American Indian policy took place, which is usually referred to as the Indian New Deal. The Second World War, historians argue, accelerated the decline and demise of the New Deal by 1945. Approximately 25,000 Native American men and women served in American forces around the globe and again gained prominent exposure. Particularly significant was the well-publicized example of Ira Hayes, a Pima Indian marine who helped raise the American flag over Mount Suribachi on Iwo Jima, a moment immortalized in one of the most recognizable photographs of the war.[4] Americans, who viewed Native participation as proof that they were ready for full equality, wished to reward the Native population by getting the government off the "Indian's" back. According to Tom Holm, "American Indians marched off to war for various reasons; yet, Whites took the tribes' participation as an unquestionable act of loyalty to the United States. Whites looked upon it as an American Indian effort to prove themselves worthy of 'mainstream society.'"[5] The result was another major upheaval in Indian policy in the early 1950s, when the notorious policy of termination was instituted as "a liberal, democratic method of solving Indian problems."[6] Termination, for those Native tribes considered sufficiently advanced, meant a removal of special status and a severing of their relationship with, and support from, the US government. For many its effects were disastrous, arguably a dubious reward for services rendered. Given the importance of the World Wars and Native military service in the US experience, the First Nations' record and its impact on administration warrant examination in the Canadian context.

As with the image of the "Indian," military service in Canadian society was rich in meaning and symbolism. Jonathan Vance has ably demonstrated in *Death So Noble* that the icon-laden memory of First World War soldiers and their sacrifices deeply affected Canadians during the interwar years.[7] Serving one's country in wartime was both the highest honour and the most profound duty for a young man. It demonstrated his willingness to assume the most demanding and dangerous obligations of citizenship and created a debt of gratitude owed by the society he had fought to protect. Voluntary enlistment was preferable to compelling a person to fight; it marked the pinnacle of one's democratic right to choose and was more valued because it was freely undertaken. Nonetheless, Canada has demonstrated a willingness to suspend some of the freedoms associated with democracy when a threat to the whole has been perceived as sufficiently serious. Ian Miller has shown how this process worked for Torontonians in the Great War, when the privilege of defending the country, initially granted only to those deemed most worthy, was transformed into a duty that might legitimately be demanded of everyone.[8] However, even if conscripted, the soldier was owed something by the state and society for his sacrifices. These multiple layers of meaning and significance would have important implications for the First Nations during and after the Second World War.

The Indian Affairs Branch was the traditional voice for Native people and issues in Ottawa and was, at least in theory, the agency responsible for protecting their interests and administering government policies pertaining to them. At times the branch was intimately involved in establishing policy in concert with the military and mobilization authorities vis-à-vis the First Nations. However, for the majority of the conflict, the senior IAB officials voluntarily abdicated any role in how military service and conscription would apply to the First Nations. Nonetheless, a significant correspondence exists between the field staff and Ottawa because the IAB infrastructure was put at the service of the mobilization authorities to facilitate the registration, call-up, and medical examination of potential First Nations enlistees as well as the prosecution of those unwilling to comply. In addition, the IAB communicated repeatedly with the RCMP and the Departments of National War Services, Labour, National Defence, and Justice. The language of these communiqués is revealing, as are the policy decisions, actions, and in some respects conspicuous lack of action by the IAB during the war.

Taken as a whole, the significant correspondence speaks volumes about the strength and resilience of the official image of the "Indian." This chapter will focus on the interaction between the "Administrative Indian" and the policies affecting Native military service. In order to maintain any kind of narrative cohesion in treating the complex policies and administrative decisions, chronology has been sacrificed to a more thematic organization in this chapter. Of concern is how IAB officials conceptualized military service by "Indians." What significance and meaning did conscription of First Nations men have in the minds of administrators? How did the negative and hostile "Administrative Indian" image shape IAB policy and actions during the war? Finally, did Native military service alter the overall image of the "Indian" in IAB circles?

Before exploring the official view of the "Indian" in military service, it is necessary to describe briefly the development of recruitment and conscription policy as well as the IAB's role in this process during the Second World War. Voluntary enlistment by the First Nations was governed by the recruitment dictates of each of the three branches of the armed forces, with little input from Indian Affairs. As a result of a racial ban in Royal Canadian Navy policy, only people who were "of Pure European Descent and of the White Race" were accepted until the "colour line" was revoked in 1943.[9] The Royal Canadian Air Force (RCAF) had its own colour line but specifically decided to accept "North American Indians" from the beginning of the conflict.[10] Nonetheless, the especially stringent health and educational standards of the RCAF were hurdles that very few Native men or women were able to get past, especially given the abysmal state of health care and education provided them prior to the war. Jean Barman, Yvonne Hébert, and Don McCaskill, in their important study, *Indian Education in Canada,* Volume 1: *The Legacy,* detailed the low average level of education acquired during the interwar years, the period when those who would attempt to enlist were being educated; only one in four Native children progressed beyond Grade 3.[11] As for the health concerns, any of the annual reports of the Department of Indian Affairs/Indian Affairs Branch during the 1930s demonstrates the widespread nature of serious communicable diseases ravaging Native communities. Tuberculosis and trachoma were those most likely to have caused rejection of would-be First Nations recruits. The various restrictions meant that the only avenue left to the First Nations was the army, which accepted several thousand into its ranks, many of whom served with distinction.[12]

The Indian Affairs administration was involved, at least initially, in applying the National Resources Mobilisation Act of 1940 (NRMA) to the indigenous population. This important piece of legislation would provide the foundation for Canada's national organization of its human resources, although in practice policy "was characterized by gradualism, compromise, conciliation and decentralization."[13] It made provision for an immediate national registration of all Canadians over sixteen years of age, for the compulsory medical examination and military training of all young single men, and for the organization and direction of labour and industry to maximize war production. There was some initial confusion as to whether Native people would be registered with the rest of the country. However, representatives of the Department of National War Services, a new department created by the NRMA to administer the registration and initial call-up of conscripts, conferred with Dr. Harold McGill, the director of Indian Affairs, in September 1940 and agreed that the First Nations should also register. Getting the majority of Status Indians on the national list would take much of the next year to accomplish, as many bands living in remote regions could not be located until treaty time the following summer. However, once registered, Native men became liable to thirty days' compulsory military training. The IAB realized this only when the call-up notices were received on many reserves across the country and immediately sought clarification of the legal issues raised.[14] The branch's legal counsel assured McGill that there was nothing written in the NRMA that might preclude conscripting Status Indians.[15] Convinced that conscription of the First Nations for home defence was legal and content to disclaim any jurisdiction or responsibility in the matter, the senior officials of Indian Affairs left the formulation of conscription policy to the mobilization authorities for most of the duration of the war.

First Nations leaders and communities protested vigorously, but to no avail, as the branch refused to do anything about their eligibility. The branch remained deaf to Native concerns even when the training period for NRMA conscripts was lengthened to four months, followed by mandatory enlistment in the militia for the duration of the conflict. Nor did this indifference change when home defence was redefined to allow service in Newfoundland, the Carribean, and the US, including the potentially hazardous amphibious assault on the Aleutian Island of Kiska. Virtually unanimous in their concerns about conscription and wartime taxation and frustrated at their inability to gain a hearing in government halls, Native leaders in many parts of the country were galvanized to organize. Wartime issues provided the catalyst for Native political organization, but the grievances articulated bespoke longstanding concerns about their relationship to Canada.[16] The most important organization to arise was the North American Indian Brotherhood, which emerged from national conferences of Native leadership held in Ottawa in October 1943 and June 1944 at the behest of the outspoken and dynamic Jules Sioui, John Tootoosis, and Andrew Paull.[17] But this was only a beginning, as the end of the war would see a proliferation of new regional and provincial organizations across the country in response to the postwar Parliamentary review of the Indian Act.[18] Despite organization, protest, and resistance, First Nations people were only marginally successful in shaping the national agenda and conscription policy in particular.

In the interim, the mobilization authorities determined the fate of Native conscripts. Michael Stevenson has demonstrated that this bureaucracy failed to establish consistent and coherent policy toward First Nations conscripts during the remainder of the conflict.[19] The IAB might have brought some clarity, but it was not until the conscription crisis of November 1944 that it again decisively entered the policy-making arena. Once conscripts could be sent overseas into combat, the legality of conscripting First Nations men was called directly into question. During the negotiations of several treaties with western and northern indigenous groups in the late nineteenth and early twentieth centuries, verbal promises had been given that the queen "would not ask her Indian children to fight for her unless they wished."[20] At the urging of IAB officials, T.A. Crerar, the minister of mines and resources, requested that the Cabinet War Committee agree to provide a limited exemption for the minority of First Nations covered by these treaty promises.[21] Those who fell within the region concerned amounted to approximately one-sixth of the Status Indian population. All others were still available to be shipped overseas. In practice, however, few, if any, were likely included in the 16,000 conscripts sent to Europe in the winter of 1944-45.

Generally, Indian Affairs personnel were keen to encourage the enlistment of their charges. This eagerness sprang in large part from the unusual meaning that Native military service came to have in the language of the department. Where the Canadian public beheld "Indians" fighting for their king and country and demonstrating tremendous patriotism, administrators saw a useful tool for furthering the assimilation of the First Nations. What is striking in the IAB correspondence is the virtual absence of the symbolism and significance of Natives fighting the Axis in the cause of freedom. For the vast majority of IAB personnel, military service was merely a pragmatic means to the ultimate end of eliminating the "Indian problem" from Canada. While Native military service was generally viewed as beneficial for the "Indian," officials were not so certain about the benefits and value for the national war effort. This ambivalence arose from the negative and combative image of the "Indian" with which administrators had entered the war. Some of the contradictory policies pursued by the branch during the war begin to make sense in this light.

The internal correspondence of the IAB was overwhelmingly centred on the pragmatic utility of army service for First Nations men throughout the Second World War. For most officials, having "Indians" serve in the armed forces fulfilled two utilitarian objectives: (1) it facilitated the long-term, eventual assimilation of the First Nations, to be discussed below; and (2) it met the short-term needs of Native people who were unemployed or under-employed. As J.P. Ostrander, the Indian Agent in Battleford, Saskatchewan, noted in September 1941, he had "been advising the Indians to enlist, where possible, as a means of providing a living for their families for the coming winter, if for no other reason."[22] It was not clear whether he considered that the men who did enlist would be soldiers for longer than just the next winter. Similar reasoning was behind the original decision to include indigenous people in the national registration in August 1940 at the last minute, only after it became clear that they would lose their jobs if they did not hold registration cards. Generally speaking, the traditionally underfunded and pecuniary department was pleased to have the "Administrative Indian" off the relief roles; indeed, this was the most immediate and practical value to branch personnel of First Nations enlistment.

More significantly, the enlistment and military service of Native men was viewed as highly beneficial to the IAB's mission of civilizing and assimilating the stubborn and backward "Administrative Indian." It is not hard to see why Indian Affairs would view military training and service as well suited to the task of altering the "Indian's" values and cultural norms. For centuries, one of the purposes of basic training in armies the world over was to take raw recruits and break down their sense of individual identity and their civilian cultural values, replacing them with a new group-centred identity and a new set of social norms. Such a system was not in fact much different from the residential schools set up in many parts of Canada, but the army could be more forceful and wielded greater moral authority in demanding compliance. In both cases, a highly regimented day – combined with hard labour, strict discipline, group punishment for individual infractions, and corporal punishments – was designed both to destroy, or at least to suppress, the existing cultural traits and to inculcate a new set in their place. Western military establishments wished to turn individuals into group-oriented team members amenable to discipline and subservient to authority, a task achieved consistently and effectively. Canada's residential schools, by comparison, took First Nations children, who came from more collectively based cultures, and attempted to turn them into individuals with notably less success and often with destructive consequences for the people involved.[23] In addition, individual Native men would be immersed in a massive organization that was predominantly Anglo-Saxon in orientation, denying them the cultural support of their fellows. Under these circumstances they would face considerable pressure to conform in order to attain the respect of their comrades in arms and to become effective soldiers.

Certainly, administrators hoped that experience in the military would teach young First Nations men proper Western values. The Indian Agent in Parry Sound sarcastically dismissed the opposition to compulsory military training of the First Nations in the area, who wanted him, in his words, "to stretch out a long arm and halt all the functions of government."[24] In any event, he was disinclined to interfere because he expected "that they will benefit by it [military training] both physically and mentally." In a similar vein, the agent on Christian Island, Ontario, was asked to make a recommendation as to whether a young Native man should receive a compassionate exemption from military training. He reasoned that the boy's father was an unsavoury influence, and "taking all this into consideration and the fact that Solemon is receiving training in the army which should make him a more valuable citizen when he returns after the war, I cannot recommend his exemption from military service." Perhaps most important, given the notorious irresponsibility and other negative traits attributed to the "Administrative Indian," officials hoped that First Nations men and women serving in the armed forces would learn responsibility and discipline. Indeed, the inspector of Indian Agencies in Quebec was of the opinion that "compulsory military training is the best thing that could ever happen, to give the young indians [sic] some knowledge of discipline."[25] Underlying this hope was the lingering commitment to the eventual assimilation of their charges.

The Indian Affairs Branch, believing military training and service to be positive for the "Indian," often attempted to aid the mobilization authorities and expedite the recruitment of Native men and women throughout the Second World War. In this manner the field agents of the branch fulfilled a number of important official and unofficial roles. Immediately after the outbreak of hostilities, T.R.L. MacInnes, the secretary of the Indian Affairs Branch, issued a circular letter to all agents and inspectors cautioning them against initiating any enlistment proceedings among their charges, but stating that it would "be in order for you to give any information or assistance that may be desired to the proper authorities."[26] Once the NRMA came into effect in the summer of 1940, the director volunteered the services of his personnel to the Department of National War Services; this offer was accepted, and the Indian Agents were sworn in as registrars for their agencies. However, the IAB stopped short of having its personnel act as official recruitment officers for the Department of National Defence, as it feared that this "would be inappropriate, and indeed might place them [Indian Agents] and the Department too, in a somewhat invidious position."[27] Nonetheless, the role of IAB personnel was crucial, and senior officials exhorted field staff to do their utmost to aid recruiting.[28] However, seeing their chance to do something for the national war effort, most of the field agents did not need the encouragement. Most would have agreed with the sentiments expressed by R.L. MacCutcheon, the Indian Agent in Fredericton, NB, who assured Ottawa in his March 1940 report that he "along with every other member of your staff have a job to do to bring about victory and peace. No assistance shall be asked for Indians during the coming year, only in cases of dire need."[29]

In contrast to the exuberance about the benefits of military training and service for the "Administrative Indian" was a contradictory doubt that the "Indian" was capable of contributing to the national war effort as a soldier, sailor, or airman. Such skepticism grew out of the limited expectations and generally negative opinion that IAB personnel had developed of their wards. One agent from Alert Bay, BC, was "inclined to feel that the Indians could best serve their country by being exempted from active military service and kept home in the fishing industry."[30] Nor was this an isolated example. The IAB concurred with the Department of National War Services and the RCMP when it decided that it was a waste of time trying to conscript indigenous men from remote areas.[31] Official doubt also manifested itself on the question of organizing all-Indian military units, a notion raised several times during the conflict and at least partly employed during the Great War.[32] In response to one such request in 1942, McGill replied that the consensus among his officials was that, "from the standpoint of the Indian himself and the effectiveness of his service in the Armed Forces, we are not at all sure that an Indian battalion would be of much value."[33] This comment expresses all the ambiguities and contradictions of the IAB's view of Native military service. Clearly, McGill and his staff were not confident that a segregated Native combat unit would perform well, fearing that it might hamper the "effectiveness of his [the "Indian's"] service in the Armed Forces." However, the statement can also be read as concern that putting First Nations soldiers together would negate the assimilative potential of military service, thereby preventing the "Indian" from getting the full value from the war and his military service.

In part, this doubt about the value of Native military service might have been symptomatic of a growing loss of confidence that assimilation of the "Indian" was ever going to be achieved. In this light, military duties were less likely to be of use to First Nations people on a reserve after the war than more applicable skills developed by continuing in agricultural or fishing pursuits on the home front. By March 1944 the Kwawkewlth Agency on the British Columbia Coast had recorded 106 deferrals for essential service in the fishery, only obtainable with the support of an Indian Agent, with six men serving in Canada and only one overseas.[34] Another option was raised by Victor Webb, the Indian Agent for the Peigan Agency of southern Alberta, who suggested that he would like "to see a battalion of Indians raised for non-combatant duties, that is as a labour battalion for road building etc, as such with white men officers they could do a lot of good work, and the training etc would be beneficial to them."[35] The implication was that whereas frontline duties might prepare the "Indian" for assimilation, labour skills like road construction would be more useful in a continued life on the reserve. This seeming loss of faith in the IAB's mission does not appear to have been widespread but helps to explain the contradictory stance of some Indian Affairs personnel on the issue during the war.

The conscription of Native men raised a number of problems for the Indian Affairs Branch during the Second World War, particularly in light of the sustained and widespread protest by First Nations communities from all parts of the country. Compelling men to serve clashed with the essentially voluntary nature of military service in most First Nations cultures as well as with their sense of their place in Canada. Even more than voluntary military service, the conscription of an individual was linked closely to his membership in the society requiring his service. In order for the defence of the state to be viewed as a duty demanding compulsory measures, those called had to belong and to have a stake in the society and the state. Voluntary enlistment and military service in general were seen as a positive for the "Indian," but compelling them to fight raised new questions about their constitutional and social status. Could Indian men, who were wards of the state and legal minors, be enlisted forcibly? Did they have the same obligation to defend the state as did those with full citizenship? Finally, if they could be conscripted, was this only for service in Canada, or could they be sent overseas despite their indigenous roots? The Indian Affairs Branch wrestled with these difficult questions for much of the war, retreating behind a wall of jurisdictional and legal confusion. In the end, they decided that Native men were liable to conscription, but this decision was not made out of a sense of egalitarianism.

Status Indians were considered wards of the state under the Indian Act (1927) and legal minors. They possessed none of the rights of citizenship, most conspicuously the franchise, but were still considered British subjects. This status left them in something of a constitutional no-man's-land in relation to conscription because, as British subjects, they were legally in the same position as other Canadian citizens.

The senior officials of the IAB quickly sought legal clarification when the issue of conscription first raised its head in September 1940. Rather than request clarification on the principles of the issue, McGill phrased his question to the branch solicitor in a manner reflecting more narrowly legalistic concerns: He wondered "whether you consider this thirty-day training by Indians would constitute military service."[36] McGill's interest was in the applicability of the precedent established in the First World War of giving Status Indian men an exemption from compulsory combative service. That the branch sought an answer to such a narrow legal point is noteworthy. Only a direct legal imperative would have forced the Indian Affairs Branch to involve itself in pursuing an exemption for the First Nations, something it could probably have obtained at any point if senior officials had decided to press the matter. Instead, they determined that there were no legal impediments to their encouraging conscription of the "Indian," an indication of their keen desire to see First Nations men in uniform.

The branch's legal council clarified the issue with the Departments of Justice and National War Services in September 1940. The deputy minister of the latter, Major-General L.R. LaFlèche, seems to have made the initial decision that, as British subjects, the First Nations should be liable to conscription along with everyone else. The Indian Affairs Branch quickly bowed to his authority on this matter.[37] The Department of Justice and the courts repeatedly confirmed that there was nothing in the wording of the Indian Act or the NRMA to preclude Native conscription.[38] Buttressed by the claim to jurisdictional authority by the Department of National War Services and legitimized by the rulings of the Department of Justice, branch officials declared themselves irrelevant on the issue of First Nations conscription. In this way, Indian Affairs protected itself from the difficult moral and philosophical issues raised by "Indian" conscription, despite the scores of forceful and often eloquent appeals and accusations received from First Nations communities and leaders in all parts of the country.[39]

Although there were variations among indigenous groups, in general the First Nations questioned their liability to conscription on four grounds: (1) in the case of the Six Nations, that the Canadian government had no authority to conscript them, as they were still allies of the British Crown, not British subjects; (2) that in the First World War they had been granted an exemption from conscription; (3) that it was morally wrong to compel wards, bereft of citizenship, to protect their guardian; and (4) that in several of the treaties signed with the First Nations, verbal assurances had been given that they would not be conscripted. The branch declared the Six Nations' claims of allied status ridiculous, quickly examined and verified the inapplicability of the 1918 exemption as legal precedent, and largely ignored the First Nations' status as wards, content in the knowledge that before the law all that mattered was that they were British subjects.[40] The senior officials in Ottawa refused or were unable to respond to the First Nations' arguments on moral grounds. Instead, they loudly and repeatedly disclaimed any role or responsibility.

The average Indian Agent or Ottawa bureaucrat cared little about the constitutional niceties of Indian status, which played little part in their reasoning on the question of whether "Indians" could be made to serve.[41] For instance, Samuel Devlin, the Indian Agent in Parry Sound, argued "that there should be no reason why their young men, many of whom have at the moment nothing else to do, should not be willing to put in thirty days of military training to fit them for the defence of Canada which should be just as much their obligation as it is of their white brethren."[42] Devlin provided no justification behind why the "Indian" should bear the same obligation as his "white brethren," something common in the branch's correspondence. In effect, officials believed that the "Administrative Indian" ought to be conscripted. If there was any question for the IAB it was not "why should they be liable to conscription?" but "why shouldn't they be?" And "the conclusion reached was that no good reason existed for the special exemption of Indians"; the burden of proof lay with the "Indian," and virtually all their arguments were either ignored or legally circumvented.[43]

Only the matter of the verbal promises of exemption from compulsory military service that were extended at some treaty negotiations held sufficient legal or moral claim on the branch to impel it to act. However, this did not occur until conscripts were to be sent overseas for combat in November 1944. Prior to this, administrators were legally certain that the "Indian" could be forced to serve inside Canada. Only in December 1944 did IAB administrators feel compelled to seek an exemption from conscription for some Status Indians, but even here they requested the minimum required. Included were only those men covered by Treaties 3, 6, 8, and 11, where written records existed of explicit promises being made by the Crown's treaty negotiators. This distinction provided exemptions to only about 20,000 of the Status Indian population of 125,686, covering large portions of the Prairies, northwestern Ontario, northeastern British Columbia, and the southern portions of the Territories.[44]

Curiously, at no stage of this debate did the idea that the First Nations' indigenous roots freed them from the obligation to defend Britain make an appearance. Among many British Canadians there was a widespread and strong emotional tie to the motherland and a sense of obligation to aid in the defence of the empire. Many Anglo-Canadians assumed that others must feel, or at least ought to feel, the same way. From this supposition sprang the arguments used to encourage French Canada to support the war effort for France, if not for Britain. It mattered not that the francophone population felt little or no connection to its old imperial parent nor much desire to save it from fascist aggression. Similar assumptions were made, often legitimately, about Canadians whose roots were in now-occupied Europe. However, the anomaly of forcing a people who had no emotional or historical connections with the Old World to fight and die in its defence seems never to have raised any eyebrows in the Indian Affairs Branch during the war.

From the beginnings of the conflict, the Indian Affairs Branch scrupulously wished to avoid any policies or actions vis-à-vis military service and the NRMA that would set their charges apart from the population at large. Only days after Parliament declared war, MacInnes issued the branch's first circular to its field personnel on the matter of Native service in the armed forces.[45] He ordered the Indian Agents not to initiate the enlistment of First Nations men because "in this regard, [they] are free agents and not differentiated from other members of the community." Such concerns with equality before the law may appear out of character given the prevailing negative image of the "Administrative Indian," but a secret letter sent from Ottawa in 1942 to the provincial inspectors and the Indian Commissioner in BC revealed the rationale behind the policy.[46] The senior officials in Ottawa sought their opinion regarding a new policy proposed by the National Selective Service, which would in effect ignore the failure of Native men to report for service if they lived on remote reserves. What was intended was not an amendment to the NRMA regulations to specially exempt "Indians," "as such action obviously might establish an embarrassing precedent," but rather a special administrative solution.[47] Thus official attempts to avoid differentiating "Indians" from the rest of the population did not spring from a deep commitment to egalitarianism. Administrators feared that doing so might provide the First Nations with a precedent that they could later use to impede the assimilation mission of the IAB.

The irony of this obsession with making the "Administrative Indian" just like everyone else was that it required a whole range of special legal, legislative, and bureaucratic measures that either existed already or were set up during the war.[48] These distinctions had the effect of utterly setting the First Nations apart from Canadians on the question of conscription. An example was the working arrangement set up between the Indian Commissioner for British Columbia, D.M. MacKay, and the divisional registrar, C.G. Pennock, in January 1942, which was later adopted across much of the country. By this accord, the mobilization authorities would notify the Indian Agent concerned before sending a call for a medical exam to any First Nations man.[49] The agent would then inform the registrar if there were geographical or medical reasons why the man should not be sought for conscription. In addition, the registrar would avoid calling up coastal First Nations who would likely claim deferment for essential work in the fishery. In cases where a Native man wished to gain deferment from military training or service, the application would be forwarded through the Indian Agent. The agent attached his own recommendation on the suitability of the claim, which generally determined the outcome of the request. MacKay informed the secretary of this arrangement when he received the confidential circular in April 1942, arguing:

> It would, of course, be out of the question to defer any particular calls on the Indian population from the provisions of the National Resources Mobilisation Act as the Act stands, nor, is it considered desirable to ammend [sic] the Regulations to exempt our Indians. The working agreement made here does not interfere in any way with the purposes of the Act, but was designed to insure that, action compelling Indians to report for service would only be taken in the case of those medically fit and otherwise in a position to obey the law.[50]

MacKay felt no need to justify his attitude toward an exemption from military service for the First Nations population. The problems of the embarrassing precedent such a decision would create were so obvious to both the secretary and himself that "of course" it would be out of the question. So instead the branch instituted this bureaucratically cumbersome system to avoid creating even the perception that they were differentiating the Native people from anyone else.

This reluctance to allow the creation of a legal precedent, or even the perception of special treatment on conscription, remained paramount in the minds of IAB administrators for the duration of the conflict. Even in 1945, with the war winding down, appearances had to be maintained as much as possible. In February the acting director, R.A. Hoey, informed all personnel about the decision to provide a limited exemption from overseas service to those Status Indians covered by Treaties 3, 6, 8, and 11. He recognized that those First Nations not covered by the ruling would be outraged but rationalized the ruling by saying: "It has been decided ... that only in the case of treaty Indians aforementioned [covered under the four treaties] would the government be justified in differentiating between Indians and other of His Majesty's subjects in the matter of military service, and then only in fulfilment of a verbal commitment made by Commissioners representing the Crown at the time the treaties were negotiated."[51] The acting director closed the circular letter with the stock phrase that "Indians" were "subject to the NRMA Regulations in the same manner as other people." However, despite the too-shrill claims of IAB officials, the "Administrative Indian" was far from being in the same position as other people – constitutionally, legally, administratively, and certainly conceptually.

While the IAB was usually keen to see its "Indians" enlisted or conscripted, this feeling was not always shared among Canada's First Nations. Native leaders and communities across the country usually supported and encouraged the voluntary enlistment of their young men and women. They also vigorously supported the war effort through other avenues, such as working in wartime industries, buying war bonds, and donating to the Red Cross. However, most First Nations were also strongly opposed to the application of conscription to their people. Their prolific and consistent protest, combined with resistance by many First Nations men, caused the IAB difficulties throughout the conflict. How IAB personnel articulated and responded to this resistance demonstrated the dependence upon authority and control in their day-to-day interaction. It also made clear how withered the IAB's sense of mission was by the war years; there was little left but their power, and this they fought to maintain. Underlying these themes, the IAB's response to Native resistance suggested an image of the "Administrative Indian" little changed from that evident prior to the conflict.

The records of the Indian Affairs Branch are filled with letters and petitions received from leaders and band councils from across the country, all expressing their anger and distress at being subject to conscription.[52] Beyond issuing protests, however, active and passive resistance became commonplace on many reserves. First Nations men and women refused to register under the NRMA in many communities, but civil disobedience was prevalent even in other communities that did register. Most commonly, young men refused to report for medical examinations or for military training, sometimes with the encouragement and aid of their communities and elders. Some living close to the border slipped over into the United States to avoid conscription, which worked until that country enacted its own draft legislation. Others on northern and more remote reserves simply vanished into their hunting territories and were rarely found. In the most extreme incident at Caughnawaga, a large disturbance erupted when the RCMP seized three draft dodgers from a restaurant on the reserve in 1943.[53] The police, their tires flattened, were forced to retreat under a hail of stones from a large and angry crowd. One officer, who was separated from his colleagues, shot three of his assailants before making good his escape. While violence was rare, Native determination to defy the government's efforts at conscription was a constant thorn in the side of the Indian Affairs Branch.

Once removed from the policy-making process on military service and conscription in 1940, the IAB only rarely reentered that arena until late in the war. Its personnel did so only when they felt their authority over their charges threatened. One such incident occurred in 1942 over the question of whether the mobilization authorities should pursue Natives from remote reserves who failed to report, particularly given the high cost and difficulties involved and the number of them who subsequently failed the medical exam. The Department of National War Services and the RCMP simply wanted to ignore such cases but asked the IAB for its views prior to instituting the policy. This decision precipitated a confidential circular from Ottawa to the senior field personnel, canvassing their opinion on the utility and ramifications of such an approach.[54] The replies are revealing. C. Schmidt, the inspector of Indian Agencies for Alberta, thought that ignoring delinquents was a good idea because if the authorities could not apprehend the fugitives, "it will start gossip in the various neighbourhoods, when insinuations will no doubt be made that the Indians 'are getting away with it.'"[55] IAB officials were loath to let this sentiment fester, as the inspector for Manitoba, A.G. Hamilton, expressed in a letter to the secretary:

Personally, I think it would be better not to call the Indians unless the call is followed up. I find a growing feeling "that they [the Indians] are not obliged to obey the Government, nor the Army, and so, why should they even notice instructions issued by the Indian Agent or Inspector" ... Allowing the Indians merely to disregard their notices is not good – they assume it to be their right and the notices are treated more or less as a joke. There is an underlying feeling of defiance which is becoming more and more evident; and is already showing its effect in our general administration of reserve matters.[56]

Defiance and insubordination were a slippery slope to chaos and irrelevance that had to be avoided at all costs.

Indian Agents, inspectors, and senior bureaucrats explained the resistance of indigenous communities to conscription in order to diminish and disarm its legitimacy, falling back on the stereotypes of the "Administrative Indian" for support. Often intransigence was ascribed to ignorance on the part of the "Indians." To some extent this was a legitimate issue because the limitations of communications technology and the IAB's infrastructure severely hampered its attempts to disseminate information quickly and accurately to a widely scattered population.[57] Frequently, however, IAB personnel simply belittled their charges. For instance, the agent in Birtle, Manitoba, forwarded the protest of the Rolling River Band Council over conscription to Ottawa, relegating its opposition to the fact that "neither the Chief or Councillor were at school, and they do not realise the meaning of the war to the Indians."[58] However, not all were convinced that a lack of information was the problem. McGill told the agent in St. Regis, Quebec, that he was of the opinion "that Indians in organised districts frequently ignore the regulations, not because of ignorance, but because of their stubborn refusal to admit that the laws of the country apply to them."[59] Either way, the legitimacy of Native concerns was undermined within the government.

Most commonly, however, IAB personnel blamed the First Nations' intransigence on the influence of agitators and troublemakers, scapegoats that had long been used to explain difficulties.[60] The "Administrative Indian" was a notoriously sheeplike character, easily misled by nefarious individuals, and the IAB assumed that agitators were behind a good deal of the difficulties encountered in conscripting the First Nations. However, the problem was not just with Native troublemakers. The Indian Commissioner of BC was of the opinion that the ignorance of the "Indian" had "undoubtedly permitted certain white subversive elements of foreign extraction to capitalize on the subject and create a considerable doubt in their minds."[61] Given the wartime conditions, such claims took on an added resonance. Under no circumstances could the IAB's understanding of the "Indian" allow for acceptance that the First Nations' opposition might be based on logical concerns and a considered decision to resist government actions that they believed illegal and immoral. Accepting such a premise would have involved a profound change in the concept of the "Administrative

Indian," particularly in their perceived intellectual and cultural inferiority. But more fundamentally, it would have called into question the very purpose of the branch.

The IAB developed several methods to combat and suppress the First Nations' resistance to conscription. As discussed previously, the branch deprived the indigenous population of its traditional voice in government by withdrawing from policy formulation on conscription and abdicating one of the central tenets of Canadian Indian policy: protection. Moreover, the branch constantly ordered its agents to explain the policies and their importance to their charges in the hope that opposition could be overcome through persuasion. In the Okanagan, the Indian Agent spent over five months repeatedly trying to convince one elder, "an old agitator," to register, but to no avail.[62] In the last letter on the subject, the agent indicated his intention "to give this man another opportunity to register and if he still refuses to do so, to advise the authorities to take action, as a number of Indians have stated that Timoyakin is 'beating the law.'"[63] The threat of prosecution was the third stage in the IAB's escalating pressure on resistant "Indians."[64] A 1943 circular letter encouraging all agents to overcome the resistance of their "Indians" is illustrative of the overall procedure:

> The question of compulsory military service by Indians, of course, is not under the jurisdiction of this Branch and, therefore, the Indian Agents have no official status in connection with it. It is nevertheless, a matter in which the Indian Agent can use his good offices with advantage as the friend and natural advisor of the Indians. The subject is one which should be approached with tact, discretion, and patience. Where, through ignorance or subversive influence, Indians show a disposition to avoid or evade the call-up, a mere curt warning that they must obey or be punished may result only in more obstinate resistence and ill-will on their part. It is felt that in many cases, better results might be obtained by careful explanation to them of their duties and appeal to their pride, self-respect and loyalty. If reasonable persuasion fails, however, then, of course, the law must take its course, and this fact should be clearly explained to the Indians, where necessary.[65]

Strong doses of condescending paternalism were served up with each stage of this process. Despite their best efforts, however, many Native men continued to resist until prosecuted and forced to register or to report for medical exams or for military service.

The registration of the Six Nations population demonstrated all elements of the IAB's penchant for jealously guarding its authority and the degree of anger generated when that control was challenged. Many within the Six Nations, such as the Hereditary Chiefs and other organizations, believed that their ancestors had never surrendered their independent status and were not British subjects covered by the laws of the Dominion of Canada but allies of the British Crown. The Canadian government had always declared this position absurd, but the issue had persisted for generations. When the IAB scheduled the registration of the Six Nations Reserve in Brantford for 25 September 1940, Arthur Anderson, secretary of the Hereditary Chiefs, posted a public notice claiming that all Indians need not register.[66] Significant portions of the community were already predisposed against registering, but the fact that Anderson so brazenly signed the public notice and the subsequent failure to register much of the population caused quite a stir in official circles. D.J. Allen, the superintendent of reserves and trusts, was livid and notified the director of the incident immediately, arguing that:

> This incident at the Six Nations Reserve at Brantford presents an opportunity of declaring the whole Long House Group, the Mohawk Workers' Organisation, and all organizations harbouring the theory that they are not British subjects illegal organizations, and definitely and finally putting them out of business. This in the judgement of the writer should be followed by a seizure of all their books and records on all reserves, and particularly in the case at Brantford the arrest of Anderson and possibly all members of the hereditary council on charges to be preferred under The Defence of Canada Regulations.[67]

Cooler heads prevailed in this case, and the draconian reaction put forward by Allen was not pursued, but the severity of his response to a relatively minor incident demonstrates how seriously IAB personnel took their authority.

The issue did not go away, as a longer-term conflict developed over how the Six Nations would fill in Question #7 on the registration form. This question pertained to nationality. Many within the Six Nations community refused to sign as British subjects and insisted on registering only if they could note their separate Iroquois nationality, to which the IAB was strongly opposed. In a memorandum to his superiors in February 1941, the director said: "I am now apprehensive, however, that if the Six Nations Indians are permitted to register other than as British subjects they will treat that fact as a recognition – and concession to – their allied status claim by the Government of Canada. On that basis they would try to re-open the whole question and I may add that they are particularly apt and pertinacious in making use of any precedent or foothold which might strengthen their argument in any way."[68] The standoff posed a difficult dilemma for the branch. If they followed their usual procedure to its logical conclusion, the authorities would be prosecuting and incarcerating large portions of the Six Nations population. The associate deputy minister of the Department of National War Services, T.C. Davis, assured McGill that the Ontario government did not have adequate "gaol facilities to deal with the ensuing problem."[69] However, if they had simply tried to ignore the problem, they would have run the risk of losing face and could have found themselves losing control of the largest First Nations group in the country.

Neither option appealed, so instead, in collusion with the DNWS, they decided on subterfuge. They would let the Six Nations answer Question #7 with "Canadian-born member of the Six Nations Indians" because "this description cannot mean anything else but a British subject."[70] Regardless of what the Six Nations might have put down as their nationality, the IAB decided that their status would not be altered, but by allowing them to think that it would be, the crisis could be overcome. Although the branch recognized that "a concession to the Indians in this matter may cause trouble" down the road, the alternatives were sufficiently unpalatable that they had little choice but to hand the "pertinacious" Six Nations an embarrassing precedent.[71] However, the IAB's gambit did not prove successful, as later correspondence demonstrates that difficulties continued and that an estimated 1,000 people were still refusing to register in March 1943.[72]

The issue of Native military service and conscription demonstrated that both the attitudes of the Indian Affairs Branch and the image of the "Administrative Indian" employed by its personnel were less amenable to change than was the public view of the "Indian." The official image appears to have remained virtually identical from 1939 to 1945. The bureaucrats and field staff of the Indian Affairs Branch were able to accommodate the recruitment, resistance, and, less comfortably, the conscription of their charges within the framework of their existing corporate language. Military service and conscription did not develop any symbolic resonance among IAB personnel, who felt no need to construct a new icon to explain the novel issues raised by Native military service and conscription.

Viewed through the lens of the raison d'être of the IAB and cast in terms of its negative image of the "Indian," the meaning of Native military service was transformed into a means to an end and little more. The army was to be an assimilation machine, which officials hoped would create good citizens where only "Indians" had existed. However, a tension remained throughout the war between what the IAB wished the "Indian" to become and what its personnel believed the "Administrative Indian" to be. The negative and pejorative stereotypes, prejudices, and assumptions that the IAB had built over the years to help explain its failure to assimilate the First Nations raised doubts among its personnel about whether having "Indians" in military service was actually beneficial to the national war effort. This conflict explains the contradictions evident in IAB policies on First Nations enlistment, which at once encouraged it and at the same time aided Natives in legally deferring their service obligations. In part, this ambivalence reflected an underlying loss of purpose and a declining faith that the mission of assimilation could be attained.

The problems of conscription were not so easily accommodated and explained by the existing image of the "Administrative Indian." Conscription involved different philosophical and moral questions that were lacking in the debates over voluntary enlistment. For the branch, these questions often proved uncomfortable and awkward, putting pressure on the boundaries and imagery of the official "Indian." To have addressed the questions directly and accepted the positions of protesting First Nations communities would have necessitated a profound reevaluation of the IAB's conceptualizations of its charges, something it could not do since this might have undermined that which its personnel most needed to continue their work: an unquestioned belief in their own cultural, moral, and intellectual superiority. Instead, administrators confined their role to narrow legal concerns and declared themselves free from responsibility and jurisdiction. In this approach, and in the IAB's unwillingness to differentiate First Nations people from Canadians in general, there was an air of almost obsessive and reflexive denial. Incapable of meeting the accusations of the First Nations on the philosophical and moral high ground, the branch covered its eyes and talked loudly of its powerlessness.

However, the IAB took actions to defend against any challenges to its authority over its charges during the war. Even the custodial administration performed by the Indian Affairs Branch was deemed to be based on an unquestioned obedience by the "Administrative Indian." Thus the defiance of NRMA regulations demonstrated in many Native communities across Canada was routinely met with hostile and vigorous emotions and reactions by the officials involved. And any policies of the mobilization authorities that fostered or allowed such flagrant insubordination caused the IAB to enter the policy-making arena in order to safeguard its authority. In doing so, the personnel of the branch needed to explain the resistence of the First Nations and deprive it of legitimacy. For this purpose, the existing "Administrative Indian" was ideally suited. It had, in part, been developed to explain the historical First Nations resistance to the policies and goals of the Indian Act and to the government department charged with their implementation. As a result, they cast Native resistance as the product of ignorance, unintelligence, obstinacy, and the work of agitators and subversives. All these traditional tools of the IAB image were meant to disarm, trivialize, and delegitimize discontent among the First Nations. Able to accommodate both recruitment and resistance within its existing conceptual framework and having shielded itself on the more difficult issue of conscription through legal and jurisdictional machinations, the IAB had no need to alter its "Administrative Indian."

3
The "Public Indian" Goes to War, September 1939-December 1941

Less than two weeks after Hitler's legions marched into Poland on 1 September 1939, Canadians found themselves at war for the second time in a generation. The population exhibited little of the wild euphoria that had marked 1914. Nonetheless, thousands of young men presented themselves at recruiting offices, and the majority of Canadians dutifully steeled themselves for sacrifices and hardships to come. The various branches of the military girded for battle, and the economy began a measured shift into war production. After the lean and directionless years of the Depression, the country suddenly seemed to have a sense of mission again.

Following the initial burst of activity during the Battle of Poland, the war entered the static and calm period of the Phoney War. Little happened on the battle front between the Allied and German armies, and complacency dominated the home fronts. In Canada the government continued a relatively restrained rearmament program, while the economy slowly began churning out war materials. However, this stability was destroyed in the spring and summer of 1940 when the Wehrmacht smashed Denmark, Norway, Holland, Belgium, and France in quick succession. The fall of France in June shattered Canadians' peace of mind. In the summer of 1940 they were suddenly Britain's largest and most important ally, and the spectre of defeat hung over the population.

Beginning in May 1940, rising public pressure from the worsening situation in France forced the government to enact a series of measures that escalated the national commitment to the war. These included sending the 2nd Canadian Infantry Division to England ahead of schedule and mobilizing the 3rd Division, followed shortly by the 4th Armoured Division. In June the prime minister introduced the National Resources Mobilisation Act (NRMA) to allow for the efficient mobilization of the country's human resources for the defence of Canadian territory. The NRMA explicitly assured Canadians that the men conscripted under the plan would not be sent overseas, thereby meeting Prime Minister Mackenzie King's personal pledge not to enact conscription and assuaging the fears of French Canadians. It would take time before the country was fully geared to fight a total war, but in that frightening summer people came to grips with the idea.

Once the threat of a German invasion of the British Isles receded in the autumn of 1940, the situation did not noticeably improve despite the British victory over the Italians in North Africa. The new year brought the waning of Allied fortunes in a series of defeats that culminated in the fall of Yugoslavia, Greece, and Crete to the Axis in the spring. These disasters were followed by Operation Barbarossa and the stunning German advances deep into the Soviet Union. Each day Canadians read nervously about the latest reverses and wondered when the United States would join the cause. Throughout these dark days, the country was galvanized, transforming its war effort into a national crusade, with virtually every segment of the population pitching in to do its part. Not until the late stages of 1941 did the first glimmers of hope emerge for Canada and the Allies: The United States was brought into the war by the Japanese attack on Pearl Harbor, and the Soviet Union not only stopped the Germans short of Moscow, but also launched its own winter offensive, which drove the enemy back.

The first twenty-eight months of the Second World War were an emotional roller coaster for Canadians as they swung from overconfidence to profound anxiety and back to cautious optimism. Canadians were forced to clarify who they were as well as why they were fighting. Almost as important, in a threatening and highly charged environment, English Canadians needed to ascertain who was with them and who was against them. Consequently, it is a useful period in which to examine the image of the "Indian" in Canada's newspapers. Here we can see the transition from peace to war and its effect on the language and iconography used in the public discussion of the "Indian."

Within this context, the contradictory duality that had marked the peacetime "Public Indian" faced some significant challenges in the early stages of the Second World War. The nature of the pressures on the "Public Indian" and the ways in which English Canadians responded to those pressures suggest some intriguing questions. Most obviously, did the war force alterations in the way Canadians constructed the "Indian"? If so, what adaptations were evident and what were the mechanisms of change? Did a new image emerge? If so, what traits and characteristics endowed this new "Indian"? Did this new image supercede the old dichotomy, or were all the images able to coexist? The answers to these questions will help to clarify the Second World War's contribution to shaping the "Public Indian."

The outbreak of hostilities brought little change in the ways the public media represented the "Indian" and, surprisingly, even in the frequency of stories on indigenous subjects.[1] Only gradually did connections between the war and the "Indian" begin to be made in the papers, and these were constructed within the existing conceptual framework of the "Public Indian." By January 1940 the "Indian" was declining in salience in the face of more important war news, but there was little change in the frame of reference employed. Nevertheless, these early links between the "Public Indian" and the war betrayed a tension resulting from the poor fit of Native support for the war effort within the existing dualistic images. A number of stories hinted that this pressure was forcing changes in the way Canadians constructed the "Indian" and provided a glimpse at an emerging new archetype.

Through the early phase of the conflict, the "Public Indian" appeared in the media in all the guises that had been evident prior to the war. Crime stories in particular formed a significant proportion of the attention paid to the First Nations in all the papers. This attention was due, in part, to several sensational murders that occurred during the period under review.[2] In all of these stories, the offender was invariably identified in the headline as an "Indian." Such coverage, when combined with other stories about drunkenness, maintained the negative aspects of contemporary stereotypes. So casual and self-evident was the connection between the "Indian" and alcohol in Alberta that the list of persons who were legally deprived of access to liquor in the province for drunkenness was termed the "Indian List." As one article stated, "Your ancestors may have come over on the Mayflower, you may have hair as fine as cornsilk and eyes as blue as forget-me-nots, but to the government you may still be an Indian."[3] Interestingly, the *Cardston News*, after reporting on several such cases, felt it necessary to print a debatable disclaimer that "headlines in newspapers giving the race along with the name of the individual is more descriptive than distinctive."[4]

In addition to crime stories, a number of articles hinted at another long-standing myth within the public realm: that of the government's praiseworthy relations with, and benevolent treatment of, the indigenous population.[5] Some came in the form of reports about "Indian" crafts, art, and festivals, which were always glowing in tone. Usually, however, these pieces credited the work of the Indian Affairs Branch and the Indian schooling system for the quality and success of Native work and events.[6] However, the best coverage for the Indian Affairs Branch concerned the improvements in First Nations health and the fact that the population was again growing.[7] Such information assured English Canadians that their government was doing all it could or should for the "Indian." Then, as now, Canada's record of its relations with the First Nations was favourably compared to that of its southern neighbour, providing yet another means of differentiating Canadians from Americans.

Above all else, the "Indian" was still primarily represented as a colourful and exotic other during the early phase of the conflict. Such articles ran the gamut of the contradictory and ambivalent images and stereotypes that made up the "Public Indian."[8] The colourful character of "Indian" subjects extended beyond the factual human-interest story to lyrical and historical pieces in which journalists flexed their rhetorical and imaginative muscle. Few writers wrote more florid prose on the subject than Philip H. Godsell, who published occasional articles in the *Winnipeg Free Press*'s Saturday magazine section. In one essay about Indian Day on 30 September 1939, he informed his readers that "today, redmen of erstwhile warring tribes join in fraternal celebration to smoke the friendly calumet and engage in ancient sports that were old when the paleface first stepped on the rock-bound shores of the New World."[9] Godsell's writing, though sympathetic and informed, was couched in heroic and historical language that was sure to seize the imaginations of Canadians. Thus, in an article in which he argued for educating Canadian children about the "Indian" and lauded the contributions of the First Nations to Canadian history and society as well as their contemporary attempts to organize themselves politically, he also spoke of "dusky democrats," "tawny tribesmen," and "be-feathered sachems in all their barbaric glory." Canada's children can be forgiven if they were unclear as to the message Godsell was presenting.

Much less ambiguous was an utterly derogatory editorial in the *Vancouver Sun*. Entitled "Three Squaws," it described a number of folk and indigenous signs that forecast a severe winter for that year. However, the editor was unimpressed by the "Indian" claims. "I know the Indian who invents all the hard winters – my old friend Andy Ned, of the Three Horse Mountain Reservation. Why, Andy has been in the business of predicting snow three squaws deep for the last 20 years. It always makes all the other Indians get in plenty of firewood and then Andy can conveniently steal it at night. He has heated his cabin on these beaver stories and three squaw winters as long as anyone can remember."[10] The editorial presented a decidedly unflattering image of the "Public Indian." The war originally had little impact on these traditional representations, which survived in all their contradictory guises: historical and noble or contemporary and depraved.

Throughout the early phase of the Second World War, links began to be made between the current conflict and the "Public Indian" in a number of different ways. Infrequent and initially tentative, these stories tended to appear in the language and imagery that had marked "Indian" stories before the war. Thus the "Indian" appeared as a noble savage and social critic or as quaint and colourful. Even stories that talked about the enlistment of Native men in the armed forces or about First Nations support for the war effort tended to emphasize the "Indian's" colourful nature or historical context. However, in a number of these cases, a tension was evident in the language of the stories arising from the ill fit of such positive, contemporary events within the existing conceptual framework. Unable to fully accommodate the square peg within the round hole, the glimmerings can be seen of a new cultural construct that was both positive and contemporary.

A prime example of the colourful "Indian" in the context of the war was the attention generated by the comments of one Alberta chief about the loyalty of the First Nations and his predictions for the coming war. Chief Walking Eagle assured Canadians that young Native men would enlist because "every Indian in Canada will fight for King George."[11] His only fear was that they would not be able to get into the fight before the war ended because "Chamberlain is mad at Hitler now, and he'll soon fix him. Before they talked too much, but now the English heap angry and they'll sure get busy. Pretty soon Chamberlain blow Hitler to hot place." The quaint pigeon-English and claims of loyalty to the king harkened back to the historical "Indians" of stories and film, who always spoke in a broken idiom and were pathologically loyal to the British Crown. In this story, the "Indian" was delivering messages that Canadians wanted to hear. Indeed, when the story was picked up by the *Halifax Chronicle* from the *Stratford Beacon-Herald* in October 1939, it was edited down to its most colourful essentials: the claim that "every Indian would fight for the King" and the prediction, which the *Chronicle* termed a "delightful forecast," that Chamberlain would send Hitler to hell.[12] Chief Walking Eagle's sincerity and seriousness was lost in this pared-down and condescending presentation of his statements. Yet the pleased tone and wide distribution of this story demonstrated the genuine appreciation Canadians felt toward this display of loyalty by an "Indian." The war had done nothing to simplify the ambiguities that bedecked the "Public Indian."

Another Canadian Press story that received extensive attention similarly portrayed the "Indian" in a traditional light – in this case, as backward but still quaint and childlike. Residents of the Nelson House Reserve in northern Manitoba, who came to The Pas for supplies, only discovered that war had broken out on 14 September 1939. "Groups of Indians clustered around the traders radio ... would not at first even believe the broadcast stating Great Britain was at war with Germany."[13] The image of primitive people huddled around one of the wonders of modern technology, the radio, and their disbelief at what it had to say were striking representations of the "Indian's" backwardness. The *Calgary Herald* emphasized the lack of belief on the part of the Nelson House people in its headline, "Indians Did Not Believe War On." The *Halifax Chronicle* chose to highlight a different aspect of the story in its headline, "Indians Discover Conflict's Effect."[14] This headline referred to the "Indians'" dismay upon learning about the imposition of war taxes and to their fear of receiving less support from the government. Both papers accentuated aspects of the story that represented the First Nations from Nelson House in an unflattering light, one that fit within the existing dualistic image of the "Public Indian."

Nonetheless, both papers carried the story with a closing sentence in which the "Indian," using some primitive wisdom, played the role of social commentator. The articles closed quoting "one native" who said: "You white people have been talking of war for four years and it has never come." In saying this, the "Indian" is not saying something new but in a sense parroting for the readers the common sense spoken between Canadians themselves. Many Canadians had been stunned that after years of talking about war, it had suddenly become a reality again only a generation after the War to End All Wars.

The use of the "Indian" as a tool for this kind of social comment and criticism appeared more strongly in a peculiar editorial in the *Vancouver Sun* in October 1939.[15] The central character was Andy Ned, who had appeared in the "Three Squaws" editorial mentioned previously. Andy, who was guiding a friend of the editor on a duck hunt, asked the man how many people had been killed in the war. The fellow replied perhaps a hundred thousand. To this, in traditional "Indian" parlance, Andy replied, "Huh." The story went on:

> After an hour he asked again how many people had been killed. My friend said he thought about a hundred thousand. "Huh," Andy said. After a while he added: "If you was to pile all them dead people up, they'd reach higher than that tree." My friend said they would reach much higher than the tree, up to the top of the mountain yonder. Andy looked at the mountain for a long time and said "Huh" again. They got on their horses and rode towards camp. Ten miles along the trail, Andy stopped and, turning in his saddle, said: "That's too dam' many dead people."

Ambivalence permeates this odd parable. Here was the noble savage, although perhaps more dim-witted than noble, pointing out the folly of Western civilization with his simplistic, even childish, wisdom. Andy's conclusion was far from surprising and reflected prevailing sentiments about the horrors of war and the futility and waste of so many lost lives. However, it was significant that an "Indian" was the vehicle for this restatement of the obvious. The idyllic and pristine nature from which the "Indian" as noble savage had sprung had long been used in this fashion as a stick to beat the societies of Europe and their colonial offspring. Had any other icon but the "noble savage" been used to make such a truistic point, it would not have had the same resonance for the readers. Yet the editor defined the lead character in negative and age-old stereotypes, such as the grunted replies and the glacially slow mental processes.

Whereas using the "noble savage" or presenting the "Public Indian" as colourful could be accomplished within the confines of the existing image, accounts of young Native men enlisting or stories about their communities making patriotic gestures in support of the Red Cross and the war effort presented some difficulties. In this context, the historical and vanishing "noble savage" was of little use in making sense of "Indian" voluntarism and loyalty in the present conflict. Nor could the "drunken-criminal" image of the "Indian" explain the loyalty and enthusiasm of the First Nations' support for the national war effort. Occasionally, such references would be included without editorializing, as in a *Cardston News* story about local volunteers due to leave for army service.[16] It merely noted in passing that the first volunteer accepted locally was one of two Blood "Indian" enlistees from the nearby reserve. However, other papers took more notice of these incidents.

The *Saskatoon Star-Phoenix* printed a large and dramatic story of Cree enlistment in the Saskatchewan Light Infantry under the major headline on its secondary news page, "Eighteen Mistawasis Indians Join Infantry."[17] The story, which was positive and appreciative in tone, commented on the "good-looking group" of volunteers. However, the initial thrust of the story was the historical context of the Mistawasis Band and of its chief, Joe Dreaver, who had brought the recruits into Saskatoon.[18] The secondary headline read "Spirit of Chief Who Signed No. 6 Treaty Lives On," and the article referred to Mistawasis, the great-grandfather of Chief Dreaver, saying:

> Chief Mistawasis, one of the Indian leaders who signed Treaty No. 6 at Carleton in 1876, rests peacefully today in the Indians' happy hunting ground. As a young man a bitter enemy of the whites, Chief Mistawasis lived to be a friend of the British, and today he can sleep undisturbed, serene in the knowledge that his descendants not only adhere to the terms of the treaty which he signed with the Great White Queen but his sons and grandsons, living on the big reserve named after him, north of Leask, are still true Indians, true to their bargain and true to their beliefs.

Exactly what was believed to be a true "Indian" was clarified in the article's later description of the attitudes of the recruits: Evidently, "they did not look upon joining the army as anything unusual, the love of fighting still being strong in their veins." This simple phrase conjured up the image of the "Indian" as a natural and bloodthirsty warrior, one of the most compelling and long-standing historical manifestations of the "Public Indian." It also reflected the still-common belief that a warlike nature and other economic, political, social, and cultural characteristics ran in the blood and were immutable.[19] Despite the immediacy of the events described in the story, the journalist could not help but use the colourful terminology, imagery, and historical emphasis that had long characterized tales of the "Public Indian." However, this conceptual framework could not explain the whole story, and the latter stages of the article reveal an unabashedly positive and more respectful tone than was found prior to the war.

In the article's explanation of the keen spirit of the Mistawasis Crees, both Chief Dreaver and the high ratio of enlistment by the band received flattering portrayals. The story went on from its historical opening to say that Mistawasis would find few "braves in his wigwams," as almost every able-bodied man of military age on the reserve had already enlisted.[20] Chief Dreaver believed that "if people of all nationalities in Canada rallied to the colours as willingly as the Indians, the people who lost their country to the British, and who, by nature and instinct should be the last to offer their services, this Nation would be an example to the world." The journalist clearly endorsed Dreaver's views. To him it meant that the "Indians evidently appreciate their country and the Union Jack." Rarely did the media at the time report the words and opinions of First Nations people unless they were colourful. However, Chief Dreaver was quoted at length, without any colloquial "Indian" grunts or pigeon-English, and his articulate opinions were given respectful and positive consideration. In part, this novel treatment was probably due to the fact that his comments struck a chord with the patriotic sentiments of English Canadians. The point was made that he had served in the 3rd Canadian Engineers during the Great War and that he was both a leader of his people and a businessman. None of these roles fit the "Public Indian," but Dreaver was a man of the times despite his heritage, and both he and the actions of his band were inspiring. Their story, in the context of the war's early phase, required something more than the traditional images of the "Public Indian" and pushed the boundaries of the old dichotomy in new directions.

Another Native demonstration of support for the war effort drew media interest in January 1940. The Nelson House Band that had made the news across the country in September 1939 was again the centre of attention but this time in a very different article.[21] Following a council among the band members, described in the papers as a "war council," the chief and a councillor made the 200-mile trip in winter to The Pas, where they met with the Indian Agent.[22] They told the agent not to be "concerned about the problems of the Red Men" and that their band would make do without relief payments and government supplies so that the resources could be used for the war.[23] The Cree leaders went on to say that a Red Cross drive was under way on the reserve collecting "bundles of weasel skins, moccasins, and sometimes a little coin." In Winnipeg the editors of the *Free Press* deemed the incident of such importance that they made space on their busy editorial page for some commentary, rather than burying it in the minor news stories. The editorial emphasized that "it is a far out Reserve this of Nelson House and only the winds and the moccasin telegraph tell the news of the world in flames" and noted that the "Indians" had not come by air but by "dog and carriole." The imagery was romantic and historical, complementing the positive nature of the story. Had the editorial quit here, it would have been little different from other representations confined within the limits of the conventional "Public Indian." But it went on to cast the Nelson House Band in a positive and contemporary framework. The *Free Press* argued that "this [was a] tale of war effort, than which no proud city or settled county district can claim finer." Suddenly the "Indian," who Canadians had always believed ought to act more like themselves, was providing the example for the nation to follow.

The editorial closed with a curious comment on an incident that had received wide press coverage in Canada: the British press's fascination with the Native members of the first Canadian contingent to arrive in the United Kingdom, which had led to their being dubbed the "Maginot Mohicans."[24] While this literary license demonstrated that Canadians had no monopoly on fanciful and farcical ideas about indigenous people and their place in Canada, to the editors it had another meaning. They felt certain that "Canadians who know their history, realize that the suggestion is not without honor for them. The Red Man has written proud pages in Canada's story, and to these the Nelson House band has added a paragraph."[25] Once again, ambiguity infused the message even though the editorial was undoubtedly complimenting the Nelson House Cree. In having to "know their history," the editors referred to the positive historical image of the "Indian." However, the recent actions of the Nelson House people were not articulated as simply important for the contemporary national situation; instead, their significance lay in adding a "paragraph" to the "proud pages" that the "Indian" had already contributed to Canada's past. The event was sparked by the war situation, but much of its salience and meaning for the dominant society seemed to derive from the fact that the Nelson House Cree's selfless, noble, and patriotic gesture apparently encapsulated all that had been great about the historical "Indian."

Thus the early phase of the war did not significantly alter the peacetime "Public Indian" image. The traditional dichotomy between the positive-historical and negative-contemporary images continued to form the core of representations of Native people. Even stories that linked the ongoing conflict to the First Nations did not automatically discard this conceptual framework. Yet First Nations enlistment and support for the war effort did present ideas and emotions that were difficult to assimilate within the dominant society's existing conceptual structures. Repeatedly, these stories were cast in a historical context because that was the only manner in which positive stories about the "Indian" made sense to English Canadians. Nevertheless, the two stories about First Nations' support for the war effort revealed indications of a new "Indian" icon, not yet fully articulated, that could explain

Native people in a way that was both centred in the present as well as positive and sympathetic.

Beginning in May 1940, the bloated sense of security that had been prevalent in Canada throughout the first eight months of the war rapidly deflated. The German army had already crushed Denmark and Norway. However, the worst was yet to come, as Hitler launched the invasion of the Low Countries and France on 10 May. Within six weeks, the bulk of the British Expeditionary Force along with some French troops were forced to flee the continent at Dunkirk, and the French government sued for peace. The speed with which this occurred astonished the world. Only Britain and the Commonwealth remained to stand against the Axis, and complete defeat was no longer unimaginable. The results in Canada were dramatic, with massive expansions in the armed forces and concomitant acceleration of the transition to a war economy. Total war had arrived.

On the home front, press coverage of "Indian" stories remained relatively higher than during peacetime in most Canadian papers throughout the summer of 1940 but peaked during and after the French capitulation on 22 June. This is remarkable considering the extent and dire nature of the news from around the world that was competing for space with stories about the "Indian." Also noticeable was an increasing tendency to link the "Public Indian" to the war in a number of ways. These stories were all marked by a single defining characteristic: Each applauded and attested to Native support for the war effort. Almost every paper consulted carried at least one piece reassuring Canadians that "Indians" believed in the national crusade and were doing their bit for the cause. The summer of 1940 brought about the proliferation of a positive and contemporary image, that of the "Indian-at-war," ensconcing it alongside the other images of the "Public Indian" in the Canadian imagination.

By June 1940 the propagandists' most positive spin on the events taking place in France could not disguise a disaster in the offing. Newspapers stepped up publication of editorials and stories designed to encourage Canadians not to despair and to rally around the flag. Stories connecting the First Nations to the war formed a greater proportion of those about "Indians" than heretofore in most places in the country. In the *Winnipeg Free Press* and the *Brantford Expositor*, such stories became the norm, largely displacing other "Indian" stories throughout the summer. At the other extreme, the *Vancouver Sun* and *Kamloops Sentinel* restricted their always-minimal coverage of Native issues to the trivial and the traditional. Nevertheless, the overall impression was of a country taking a renewed interest in its indigenous population in light of radically altered circumstances.

The initial concern to Canadians was the loyalty of the First Nations. Could the "Indian" be trusted? Sensationalized reports of the activities of

Nazi agents, subversives, and saboteurs poured out of Europe in the wake of the German conquests. Some reports even claimed that the defeated had not been bested by military might but by the insidious work of fifth columnists, which had undermined their morale and fighting ability. An overwrought press and RCMP told Canadians that even their own country had been infiltrated by potentially thousands of these "dangerous agents in the guise of German immigrants, refugees, German Canadian citizens, even discontented Eskimos or Indians, and who knew what else."[26] The result was a highly charged environment in which every segment of Canada's polyglot society was suspect, including "discontented Indians." The Canadian Press (CP) wire service first raised the alarm with a story about concerns in the United States that "foreign-fostered groups and domestic anti-Semitic organisations were trying to stir up dissention [sic] among the Indians by stressing grievances against the government."[27] There was in fact a concerted, if ill-informed and poorly executed, German propaganda campaign aimed at Native Americans during the late 1930s and into 1940. American-based pro-Nazi and anti-Semitic groups also worked diligently to woo Natives to their cause from the mid-1930s onward with slightly more success. Such efforts had largely fizzled out by the fall of 1940 under concerted pressure from the Indian Affairs Bureau and the Federal Bureau of Investigation.[28] The CP wire story also carried Canadian reaction to the news, which amounted to Indian Affairs officials assuring journalists that "there is no reason to believe that any Indians in Canada have Nazi inclinations." However, the loyalty issue did not simply disappear with this casual official dismissal.

A more articulate and substantiated appraisal of First Nations loyalty appeared a month later in the *Calgary Herald*, which carried a full-column editorial under the simple title, "Indians Are Loyal."[29] The editor went so far as to claim that there was "no more loyal element in Canada's mixed population than the Indians." The editor referred to historical alliances among the Six Nations and to the mystic loyalty to the British Crown among "Indians" in remote regions. However, the most convincing demonstration was that their men had served in the Great War: "over four thousand" according to government sources, and "it is expected that the Indian contingent this time will be at least as large." This was lent greater significance because the point was made that "all Indian participation in the war must be voluntary," as it had been in the last war. This assumption turned out to be unfounded. Not only had Status Indian men been liable to conscription for noncombatant duties during the Great War, but they would be conscripted for both home defence and even overseas active service during the Second World War.[30] Nevertheless, this belief tapped into the symbolic nature of voluntary military service and sacrifice that underscored these positive and contemporary manifestations of the "Public Indian."

The editorial concluded with glowing praise for an award-winning essay by a local Native student about the current war, the Nazi menace, and Britain's fight "for liberty and free institutions ... [and] maintaining the force of decency against barbaric peoples."[31] The student's essay ended on a fervent and patriotic note: "So in the meantime let us pray, pray, pray, and at the last may God save the King." This seems to have encapsulated the feeling of the moment for the *Herald* editors, who gushed that "few white children in the Dominion could improve on this statement of a young Indian inhabitant of the Blood Reserve in Southern Alberta." Conspicuously, there was no mention of the "Indian" child's name; the significance of the essay's message came not from the youth's identity as a person but from the racial group that he or she represented. Nonetheless, it was high praise. Calgarians could take comfort from the positive news that the "Indian" was emphatically onside. Given such passionate comment and glowing editorialization, who could doubt that the "Public Indian" was loyal?

More than the assurances of Indian Affairs bureaucrats or self-styled specialists, it was news of the actions and sacrifices of indigenous people themselves that laid to rest English Canadian anxieties about their loyalty.[32] On the same day that news of France's imminent collapse broke in the papers, the *Saskatoon Star-Phoenix* carried a prominent story under the headline "Indians Display Loyalty in Gift Of Treaty Money."[33] It referred to a number of bands from the Battleford Agency that had refused to request government assistance or accept their treaty payments for that year so that the money might go to aid their "Glorious King and Queen" in the war. Even more impressive, the First Nations of northern Saskatchewan found what other money they could offer in support of the war effort. In light of such gestures, questioning the loyalty of the First Nations must have appeared almost absurd, and the concerns seem to have been allayed.

Whereas the papers had been both feeding and assuaging the fears of Canadians following the initial shock of the fall of France, the news began increasingly to reflect the need for shoring-up civilians' morale, preparing them for the sacrifices ahead, and encouraging support for a total war effort. In this changing context, the "Public Indian" also went through a transition. The positive, present-day "Indian" filled several new roles to meet the differing needs of English Canada as it adjusted to total war. The tone of media stories no longer suggested a need to mollify Canadians' worries about First Nations' loyalty. Instead, the interest in the "Indian" focused on their positive demonstrations of patriotism and sacrifice. These reports proved beneficial in reassuring Canadians, in encouraging their own patriotism, and even in shaming them into greater exertions for the war effort.

The humanitarian spirit and compassion of the First Nations received notice in stories about their generous support of the Red Cross. Even the *Vancouver Sun*, which seemed scrupulously to avoid printing material imparting the new positive "Indian" image or stories linking Native people to the war, published a heart-warming story about the marvellous work done by Stó:lô children for the Red Cross.[34] Interestingly, although the majority of the story concerned the other projects and achievements of the the Red Cross's Chilliwack branch, the headline spoke only about the case of the "Indian children."[35] The story noted that the pupils of the Coqualeetza Residential School, ranging from seven to eighteen years of age, had "expressed a wish to do war work some time ago, and said that they could knit and sew." Here is another element of the new positive contemporary "Indian": a sense of agency.[36] Whereas both the "noble savage" and the negative contemporary "Indian" so often appeared to be passive, in this case the journalist was careful to say that the children had been the instigators.

In the context of the war and this ongoing reassessment of First Nations people in the public forum, even undertakings that would have been viewed as traditional and colourful "Indian" activities prior to the war took on a more nuanced meaning and gained respectful consideration. An excellent example of this was the *Calgary Herald*'s coverage of a Sun Dance in late June 1940.[37] The paper ran two major stories about the event, both by the same journalist. Interestingly, no mention was made of the fact that the Sun Dance, the potlatch, and other indigenous spiritual ceremonies were still officially outlawed by the federal government. The first article opened with the colourful phrasing so long typical of "Indian" tales: "Indian drums throbbed along the banks of the Bow in the heart of the legendary Sun Dance Valley."[38] The second began with a long evocative introduction:

> "Heh-h-h, heh-h-h, heh, hei, ho, hei-h-h." It is night on the prairie and from the dimly lit Sun Lodge in the middle of the Indian camp comes the plaintive wail of the Sun Dance song, clear and high above the steady beat of the drums. Outside in the big circle of the main camp, fires gleam dully, throwing fanciful shadows on the bushes and the trees. Here and there a hobbled pony crops at the short grass. The camp is silent except for the continuing singing and drum beating in the Sun Lodge. The interior of the lodge presents a weird and colorful sight. In the main circle to the left a group of old men sit and grunt approval as the younger braves pound their tom-toms and chant the Sun dance song.[39]

Had the tenor and emphasis of the articles not changed dramatically, they could have been dismissed as another example of the "Public Indian" as colourful and exotic.

However, the first story went on to give a detailed and sympathetic explanation of the Sun Dance and its spiritual meaning for the Stony (Nakoda) people, mixed with their patriotic concerns: "It was not the barbaric Sun Dance of the early '70s where Indian braves were forced to dance until the buckskin thongs affixed to the muscles of their chests were torn loose from their fastenings, but a colourful ritual which culminated with the Indians, young and old, joining in a prayer for victory for their King across the water and the armies under his command."[40] In great detail, the journalist described the decision to hold the ceremony as well as the complicated process of setting up and conducting the Sun Dance. He recognized the fusion of Christian beliefs and traditional spiritualism, informing the reader that, far from participating in an un-Christian or heathen ritual, "the Indians, through the medium of the dance, are merely praying to Almighty God for help and guidance in the age-old native fashion, rather than through the medium of the Christian church." The second article went on to describe the prayers in support of the war and Britain, noting the people's hope that they would not be called upon to kill as well as their willingness to do whatever was needed to further aid in the successful prosecution of the war. It is difficult to imagine, even with its traditional imagery, such a balanced and insightful representation of an indigenous event in the years prior to the war.

Even more noteworthy than Native compassion and spirituality were the First Nations' frequent demonstrations of enthusiasm for the war effort, which the press appeared eager to report whether they involved cases of enlistment or other topics.[41] A series of stories kept the "Indian" in the public eye in Saskatchewan throughout the traumatic the summer of 1940, beginning with the northern bands' decision to refuse their relief and contribute their treaty money to the war effort, reported on 17 June. Two days later, the *Star-Phoenix* printed another dramatic announcement, declaring that "the Indians of the Mistawasis Reserve are patriotic to say the least" because they had made a donation of more than $2,000 for the purchase of an ambulance for work overseas.[42] This was followed on 2 July by a story about a Métis declaration of support, on 5 July by a story about Chief Dreaver's call for an "all-Indian" battalion, and on 25 July by another story about the donation of $1,000 by the Fishing Lake Band.[43] In all these cases, the actions were interpreted as patriotism of a highly developed sort and as a great example for Canadians to follow. In this sense, the example of the "Indian-at-war" image helped to inspire Canadians to do their utmost for the war effort by providing a benchmark of what could be done. But the stories also presented an exaggerated sense of the zeal behind these actions and ascribed meaning and motives that perhaps reflected Canadian desires more than the real attitudes of the First Nations themselves.

This is not to say that Canada's indigenous people did not believe in the fight against Hitler or that they did not demonstrate genuine loyalty to the Crown and patriotism in supporting the national crusade.[44] A desire to end the tyranny of Hitler's Nazi regime certainly spurred many First Nations men to enlist and many bands and communities to contribute in any way possible to the war effort. However, their young men's reasons for enlisting were as numerous as those of any other young man in Canada: for some it was patriotism; for others it was the prospect of a steady pay cheque and three square meals a day; some wished to escape an unhappy home or reserve life; others craved the adventure of travelling overseas; but as often as not, young men enlisted because their buddies did and it was the thing to do. Added to these rationales – in those few First Nations communities that still had warrior societies and that continued to value the attributes and status of the warrior – was the desire that young men attain their rights of manhood. At present, this remains a supposition, as there has yet to be any research published on the Second World War showing that young Native men were avowedly following in the steps of fathers and uncles who had fought during the Great War and of ancestors further back who had fought other indigenous nations and the advancing Europeans in previous centuries.[45] Some First Nations leaders consciously hoped or believed that the sacrifices of their young men and women would lead to improved status, greater autonomy, or the right to vote. Clearly First Nations people supported the war, but their reasons for doing so were more complex than the dominant society's discussions acknowledged.

The examples of the "Indians" aiding the nation not only encouraged Canadians to make greater sacrifices, but, due to the underlying perception of the "Indian's" inferiority, also served to push them to compete with the "Indian" to assert their patriotic superiority. This dual purpose can be seen in stories about the gestures made in support of the war effort. For instance, poverty was emphasized in stories about the refusal of government assistance by northern Saskatchewan First Nations and their subsequent contributions to the war effort.[46] One story made careful note that $101 had come from the Thunderchild Reserve alone even though the "Thunderchild band has known every vicissitude of recent drought years." Similarly, the *Halifax Chronicle* noted that these peoples were "never in the best of circumstances financially."[47] The consistent emphasis on the difficult straits of the First Nations during this period of the war is noteworthy in that it amplified the depth of the sacrifices made. Doing so set the bar that much higher for the rest of the population and perhaps served to quiet any grumbling by those Canadians who felt that they had yet to shake off the hard times of the Depression. How could those supposedly superior Canadians not do as much as the lowly "Indian"? During the Great War, efforts to encourage contributions to patriotic funds had quite explicitly set out to shame Canadians in this way; for example, the caption of a famous poster of the Cree chief Mooche-we-in-es read, "Pale Face, My skin is dark, but my heart is white" (see Figure 3.1).[48] During the Second World War, media emphasis on Native poverty harkened back to this poster, although this fact may not have been overtly recognized by those who either produced or consumed such materials.[49] In

3.1 "Moo-che-we-in-es. Pale Face, My skin is dark but my heart is white. For I also give to Canadian Patriotic Fund." Poster, c. 1912-16. *National Archives of Canada C-121137*

a sense, this was the "noble savage" reborn in a very different and modern guise that nevertheless retained its age-old role as an instrument of social criticism.

While the preceding analysis might suggest that the positive contemporary "Indian-at-war" image completely displaced other representations of indigenous people in the public realm during the summer of 1940, such was not in fact the case. The traditional dichotomy also thrived throughout June, July, and August of 1940, although to varying degrees depending on the paper. For instance, in the *Vancouver Sun* these older images continued to dominate stories about the "Indian," whereas the *Prince Albert Daily Herald* and the *Globe and Mail* maintained a more even balance.[50] On the other end of the spectrum, the *Winnipeg Free Press, Brantford Expositor,* and *Saskatoon Star-Phoenix* circulated the "Indian-at-war" image to the exclusion of any other. Yet, overall, representations of the "Public Indian" remained as complex and contradictory as ever, with gratuitously headlined crime stories running alongside the colourful and quaint, and the historical juxtaposed with the contemporary. The continuity in the imagery and rhetoric of these stories is remarkable in the wake of the changes brought about by the war's first year.

Nonetheless, in some of the stories about subjects other than the war, a sympathetic and less fanciful tone can be detected. A prime example is a story about the First Nations' celebrations following their receipt of annual treaty money.[51] After receiving their yearly payment from government officials, the families spent the day buying supplies from a host of vendors and enjoying some entertainments. In the past, such an event, if it received any attention at all, might have provided an opportunity for many of the negative "Indian" stereotypes to emerge. The story might have spoken angrily of the indolence of a people dependent on government handouts or demeaningly of the "Indian's" profligate and impulsive spending or have included innuendo implying the illicit consumption of liquor. Instead, the author noted how meagre was the treaty money allotted to each person, the cautious purchases made, and that the families made the money last all day. In a similar vein, the *Herald's* coverage of the Calgary Stampede in July 1940 gave extensive treatment to Native competitions, parades, and events.[52] Always, the "Indian" appeared as a respectful and full participant in the larger Stampede, and stories that might have reduced the First Nations to the colourful and exotic subject of a human-interest piece refrained from doing so. However, these were still the exception to the majority of "Indian" stories, which continued to be constructed within the parameters of the traditional dualistic image.

The summer of 1940, with all its trials and strains, drew indigenous people to the attention of Canadians in a fashion that forced a reevaluation of long-standing notions about the "Indian." The dominant society could not explain the First Nations' contributions to the war effort using the images available; thus a new image of the "Indian" developed to fill the need. This new icon, the "Indian-at-war," was a sympathetic and flattering figure who existed in the present. Infused with an enviable spirit of sacrifice, unswerving loyalty, fervent patriotism, and dynamic initiative, this super "Indian" image was as distorted as other popular conceptualizations of the First Nations. However, despite the utter dissimilarity between this new image and the existing versions of the "Public Indian" – indeed, despite the outright conflict between the various images – all continued to coexist in seeming harmony in the public forum. While the "Indian-at-war" took its place alongside the contemporary "drunken criminal" and the historical, vanishing "noble savage," it did not displace them.

Heartened by the spectacular British victories over the Italians in North Africa in the winter of 1941, Canadians regained some of their equilibrium and threw themselves into assembling the armed forces and material needed for the coming year. However, the worst was yet to come as Allied fortunes reached their nadir. Canadians were not as shocked by the continuing reverses as they had been by the defeat of France the year before, but gloomy concern persisted. The media, either censored or self-censored, amplified the minor victories and played down the losses and setbacks, doing what they could to foster civilian morale. Even the fact that the Soviet Union and the United States had joined the cause by year's end could not fully dispel the apprehension. Germany remained at the height of its power, and December 1941 provided a long litany of what Japan was capable of accomplishing in the Pacific. Canadians held no illusions about the job ahead, but they hoped that they had weathered the worst of the Axis storm.

In the face of such important international events, stories about the "Indian," regardless of which incarnation, continued to hold their ground.[53] While there was a noticeable drop from the crescendo of interest during the summer of 1940, the "Indian" appeared in the media at least as frequently as in peace time in most publications.[54] Given the ongoing and relatively high profile of the "Indian" in the public forum, it is worth exploring whether the image changed further in 1941.

Stories linking the "Public Indian" with the war continued to form a significant proportion of the representations of Native people in most publications and remained dominant in the *Expositor*, *Free Press,* and *Star-Phoenix*. Stories largely focused on Native enlistment and soldiers, such as a photo essay about Six Nations Indians in the Dufferin and Haldimand Rifles.[55] The photos were taken during the visit of two chiefs to the Six Nations soldiers who were training with the unit at Niagara-on-the-Lake. Their traditional dress and feathered bonnets figured prominently in all the pictures alongside the grinning faces of the uniformed young men. But the tone was upbeat and cheerful, as evidenced by one picture with the caption "Lesson in

Scalping – Chief Blueyes shows how the process might work on one Adolf Hitler." The other principal manifestation of the "Indian-at-war" was conveyed in stories about donations by bands to the Red Cross or to patriotic funds for the furtherance of the war effort.[56] In Cardston, the residents of the Blood Reserve contributed about 10 percent of the district amount to a Victory Bond drive.[57] A grateful gathering of local dignitaries held a banquet in honour of the Blood's $200 contribution from their band funds, which was presented in a "colourful and almost dramatic manner" by Chief Shot Both Sides. The speeches of the many Blood and civic leaders at the event were fully recorded in a lengthy story run by the local weekly, which made repeated note of the fact that the Blood Nation was loath to sell its land and thus had rather "meagre tribal funds." There is no mistaking the sincere appreciation in the speeches by members of the Cardston Canadian War Services Committee nor the genuine feeling that disparate elements had pulled together as a community for a common cause. This story was remarking on the event not because an exotic other had performed something unusual and bizarre but because a prominent segment of the regional population had made a patriotic and heartfelt gesture.

While tales of First Nations generosity and patriotism must have pleased Canadians, this in and of itself does not explain the high salience that the information continued to hold in the public forum throughout 1941. An editorial in the *Winnipeg Free Press* provides a hint as to the meaning of the "Indian-at-war" and why it remained a steady presence in the public realm.[58] The piece addressed reports that "Indians" were not being accepted as recruits, declaring them untrue, "as an inspection of almost any battalion now training in the country would show." Evidently, officials in Ottawa had declared that there were no official impediments to indigenous enlistment.[59] Reassured that the allegations were not official policy, the editor nevertheless had no trouble conceiving of how such an incident might occur:

> Every now and then some stupid local official undertakes to lay down some rules for himself on the subject of who should or should not be admitted to our armed forces, and sooner or later such persons develop a form of racialism as objectionable in its way as the racialism of the Nazis themselves ... This they do without knowing, or without understanding, that racial prejudice, be it against Indians, Jews or Scotsmen, is one of the evils in the world that this war is being fought to eradicate. Perhaps we have come now to a time when such statements about the loyal Indians of Canada can be stopped once and for all.

In this sense, the "Indian-at-war" served as an allegory for why Canada was fighting against the Axis, for what made Canada different and morally superior to fascist Germany, and for the type of country Canadians hoped to build once peace returned. Thus, hindering the ability of Native men to enlist struck at the very heart of the symbolic importance of voluntary military service in a democracy, and at the legitimacy of Canada's just war.

Given the profound nature of the "Indian-at-war," it seems remarkable that there were still numerous examples of the "Public Indian" in its traditional guises. Contemporary stories about the Native war effort continued to reflect the historical "noble savage" in some cases. The quintessential example of this appeared in the dramatic article quoted at the beginning of this book, "Red Men Dig Up the Hatchet."[60] More clearly than any other article, this colourful piece, in stating the litany of Native contributions to the war effort, evoked the image of the great "Indian" warrior:

> Now the red men are on the war-path once again. But Fennimore Cooper would rub his eyes if he could see the khaki-clad warriors of the Mingo, Mohawk, Seneca and Shawnee tribes advancing in single-file through the hedge-covered byways of the English countryside. Still more would he wonder to see sons of buffalo-hunting Crees and Blackfeet mounted on snorting motorcycles instead of galloping pintos ... armed with Bren guns in place of tomahawks and bows and arrows ... and wearing the tin hat and tunic of the modern soldier in place of the war paint and dancing eagle feathers of former days.

While the "noble savage" remained, the negative contemporary image of the "Indian" appeared to wane during 1941, although it did not disappear completely.[61] While most newspapers continued to identify Native people in the headlines of crime stories, the tone tended toward that of a balanced hard-news story; gone were the colourful and gory details, coupled with innuendo about alcohol, that had so often marked these reports in the past.[62] It is unclear whether Canadians no longer deemed it proper or seemly to discuss the First Nations in this fashion in the public domain. Perhaps they had simply grown uncomfortable with the contradictions inherent in their images of the "Indian." In any case, the change was noticeable.

The "Indian-at-war" had made it possible for the present-day "Indian" to be a positive and respectable figure. Though still limited, this image increasingly spilled over from stories about support for the war effort into other subjects concerning the First Nations during 1941.[63] The *Calgary Herald* printed an unusual "Indian" story in July about a man proud of the accomplishments of his daughter.[64] She had organized a patriotic pageant with her schoolmates that had been performed both at her school and in Banff, launching the girl into the public eye. The same story might have appeared about any father and daughter, but it just so happened that the man in this story was Chief Walking Eagle and that his daughter was Annie Beaver of the Stony (Nakoda) First Nation. The story went on to mention the history of the Stony people, the Morley Residential School, which Annie attended, and Walking Eagle's other children. The tone was respectful, and the First Nations characters were neither demeaned, nor reduced to being colourful, nor even relegated to a historical context. What is stunning is that Chief Walking Eagle was the same man who had appeared in the press in September 1939 for his comments about the British being "heap angry" and Chamberlain "blow[ing] Hitler to the hot place."[65] A greater juxtaposition of the changes in the "Public Indian" is hard to imagine. This shift reveals that the sharp duality in the "Public Indian," evident prior to the war, was beginning to break down under the pressures of the war and the "Indian-at-war" image. It also suggests an increasing willingness among Canadians to construct First Nations people inclusively as human beings, rather than solely as an external and alien other.

The answer to the initial question guiding this chapter – "did the war force alterations in the way Canadians constructed the 'Indian'?" – is clearly "yes." The dualistic peacetime images of Native people found in the public discussions were simply not designed to accommodate and make comprehensible the "Indian" response to the war. The result was an expansion of the parameters of the public image to include a positive, present-day manifestation. The beginnings of this new "Indian-at-war" icon were evident almost immediately after war was declared but did not gain widespread currency and usage until the summer of 1940. The ascendancy of the "Indian-at-war" image throughout 1941 created a distinctly different "Public Indian" than that with which Canadians had entered the war.

More important than the advent of a new "Public Indian" image were the reasons for its emergence and the mechanisms that fostered or forced change in how the dominant society constructed its notions of Native people. Clearly, the reporting of statements made by First Nations people and their demonstrations of loyalty and support for the war effort had an effect on the way Canadians perceived and spoke of them. Such activities were far outside the collective assumptions and stereotypes that composed the "Public Indian," and in this sense, the First Nations were able to force the dominant society to take note of them and to acknowledge their contributions and loyalty. The static nature of the "Indian" during the 1930s certainly gave no indication that Canadians could be so receptive to influences, actions, and attitudes of Native people themselves. To a certain degree, therefore, part of the mechanism transforming the "Public Indian" was the very fact that the First Nations believed in the fight against Hitler and lent their support, money, and young people to the national war effort.

On their own, however, such actions probably could not have forced the creation of a new image, because Canadians had long enjoyed the luxury of thinking about and discussing the "Indian" as they wished. The First

Nations performed patriotic deeds, but the dominant society assigned these deeds meaning and significance for their own purposes. That these stories could not be easily articulated within the existing commonsense knowledge about "Indians" need not have been a problem, as they could have been ignored. Instead, these stories proliferated. That they were not ignored – indeed, quite the opposite – demonstrates that the actions of the First Nations mattered to Canadians, that they fulfilled some emotional or intellectual need within the dominant society. The dramatic changes in the international situation played havoc with the emotions and morale of the population throughout the first twenty-eight months of the war. A definite correlation appeared between events affecting the dominant society and the transformations of the "Public Indian." This was the primary element of the mechanism driving change in the image of First Nations people. Their actions were circulated and publicized because Canadians wanted, even needed, to know and because these actions provided some comfort in anxious times.

The attention that the media lavished on the First Nations and the creation of the "Indian-at-war" served the emotional needs of Canadians in four principal ways. First, the public appreciated information about the "Indian's" support for the war effort because it meant that they were not alone in the fight. English Canadians were concerned not only about the First Nations in this regard: News that French Canadians were not shirking their duty, that the various ethnic minorities were behind the war effort, and that other nations and peoples around the world stood with them also mattered greatly. Indeed, here we see revealed a deep-seated anxiety within English Canadians' psyche about the unity and potential weakness of their multi-ethnic country. When thrust into the front rank as Britain's major ally after France's defeat, it was natural that English Canadians should look behind them to ensure that they were not stepping forward alone.

Second, the "Indian" gained prominence during the summer of 1940 because of the paranoia about fifth columnists that swept through Canada following the shock of Germany's victories throughout the spring and summer. News of the demonstrations of loyalty made by indigenous groups in various parts of the country quickly quelled any such anxieties. Third, the "Indian-at-war" helped Canadians to feel better about themselves, their society, and their government. Canadians viewed the First Nations' enthusiastic support for the war effort as a product of the benevolent administration provided by their government over the years. Confirmation of this benevolence may have expiated some of the collective guilt Canadians felt about the Euro-Canadian displacement and domination of the First Nations – guilt that seemed to underscore the conventional "Public Indian" image. At the least, First Nations support was interpreted as validating and confirming that Canada was a kind and just society. The "Indian-at-war" in some ways symbolized the difference between Canada and the Nazi regime, and fit with the nation's moral crusade.

Finally, the "Indian" served as a useful incentive in the efforts to foster national morale and encourage full participation in a total war effort. This role for the "Indian-at-war" was increasingly evident as 1940 turned into 1941. In this capacity, the "Public Indian" proved remarkably flexible, providing both an example to inspire and encourage as well as a whip to shame and pressure. The distorted superpatriot that the "Indian-at-war" became provided an ideal of loyalty and self-sacrifice for the rest of Canada to try and match. However, beneath the surface of the positive characteristics of the "Indian-at-war" were the negative stereotypes that pressured Canadians to equal such efforts or be humiliated at being bested by the "lowly Indian." This utility should not be overlooked as a reason for the proliferation and salience of "Indian" stories even as the world seemed to be falling apart. Thus the activities of the First Nations not only made Canadians feel good about themselves, but also became part of the forces that galvanized and prepared the country for the long and difficult road ahead.

4
Winning the War Only to Lose the Peace? Reconstructing the "Public Indian," 1943-45

With the dawn of 1943, the fortunes of war had begun to turn against the Axis. The Soviet winter counteroffensive had led to the defeat of the Germans at Stalingrad, the Americans had seized the initiative from the Japanese in the Pacific, and by spring the Allies had defeated the German and Italian forces in North Africa. Although no one saw final victory on the horizon, the possibility of imminent defeat had at last been banished. This confidence that the war would eventually be won grew steadily through 1943 and into 1944, as Allied armies, navies, and air forces drove back Axis forces in every theatre. With the immediate task of winning the war seemingly well in hand, the world at long last began to turn its attention to the future and the shape of the postwar world.

These developments were mirrored in Canada, which was booming by 1943. Wartime production was increasing exponentially to peak in 1944, full employment had been reached, and most of the population looked with pride at the nation's war effort and the accomplishments of its military forces. All across the country, people, the media, and governments began to plan for the great new order they hoped to build out of the ashes of the present conflict. Driving the agenda was a deep anxiety that Canada, having won the war, might lose the peace. In large part this was a legacy of the Great War experience and the lingering sense of dissatisfaction with its aftermath. For a cautionary tale, Canadians had only to look back at the social unrest of 1919-20, the inadequate provisions made for the veterans who had sacrificed so much, the crushing worldwide depression of the 1930s, and the rise of totalitarian, fascist, and communist regimes in various parts of the globe.

This chapter explores the impact of the changing world and national situation on the public discussions of the First Nations from 1943 to the end of the war in Europe in early May 1945.[1] Of concern is whether the confidence in victory and the anxiety for the future, so prevalent in Canada during the latter years of the war, left their mark on the "Public Indian." What kind of country did Canadians hope to build in the postwar years? Was there a place for First Nations people in the new order? If so, why and on what basis?

In late September 1943, the National Liberal Federation held a convention of the party faithful. The delegates expressed their concern that the government ministers, "in directing all their energies to the war, have failed to meet a real interest on the part of the public in post-war policy."[2] Until this time the Cabinet had been loath to engage in public debates about reconstruction for fear "that the fighting morale of the nation might be affected adversely by over-much talk of post-war planning."[3] The stodgy Tories had already jumped on the social-security bandwagon at their national party convention in December 1942, but those attending the Liberal convention needed little reminder of the importance of the issue for Canadians: They had seen the stunning rise in the fortunes of the Co-operative Commonwealth Federation (CCF). In the two months prior to the Liberal convention, the CCF had won two federal by-elections, become the official opposition of Ontario with thirty-four seats, and received the support of 29 percent of decided voters in one of the early public opinion polls, which placed them ahead of both the Liberals and the Conservatives in popularity.[4] While its social-democratic message had not won the party widespread support or electoral success during the Depression or the war's early years, by 1943 it had begun to resonate with voters hungry for social security and a clear vision of the postwar era. Liberal delegates saw "no reason why the government should give the C.C.F. a clear field on post-war policy."[5] The convention passed resolutions promising a substantial and generous benefits package for returning veterans and calling for "the Liberal party to occupy the broad field of social policy, including family allowances, higher and contributory old age pensions, health insurance, housing, rural electrification, etc."[6]

Editorials and letters to editors in 1943 suggest that public interest in reconstruction and the postwar period was coming to dominate the national agenda and that not all Canadians were confident that the government's promises would amount to much. As one veteran queried in a letter prominently featured in several major papers: "I have been wondering what other men discharged from the army, particularly those who were overseas, think of the prospects for a new order in Canada. From many discussions in camps they will have formed ideas, visions, expectations, of what the new Canada should be like. Does what they now see promise fulfilment of those hopes? Do they see the dawning light of the new day?"[7] The writer noted with skepticism the plans drawn up by the authorities, claiming "promises just as glowing were made for the future during the last war, with results we know all too well." Those soldiers who had been fighting and those who had played their part on the home front were "entitled to some guarantees of the new order. After all they have endured, are they going to leave the future to chance and the politicians again?" While such cynicism was not uniformly present, it was indicative of how strongly Canadians, particularly veterans, felt about these issues. Reconstruction and social security mattered, a point driven home unequivocally in the closing sentence of this letter: "Next to winning the war, there is nothing of more urgent importance than that we, on the home front, shall have taken some definite steps toward winning the peace before the boys return."

In fairness to the Liberal government, preparations for the eventual peace had begun almost as soon as the hostilities commenced. Indeed, the first such measure was passed through Cabinet on 8 December 1939: an order-in-council creating a Cabinet committee to study problems of demobilization.[8] In 1943 the Advisory Committee on Reconstruction submitted its report, titled "Report on Social Security for Canada," commonly called the Marsh Report after the research director of the committee, Leonard C. Marsh.[9] Though controversial and initially downplayed by the King government, this remarkable document, with its provisions for family allowance and health insurance, would provide the blueprint for Canada's social-security system.[10] By 1943 an extraordinary and complex system of committees and subcommittees had been erected to explore, examine, and make policy on every imaginable aspect of the problems associated with reconstruction and the development of social security.[11] Nonetheless, the public forum was clearly dominated by these concerns after 1943. The Throne Speech in January 1944 included almost no mention of the war per se. Instead, the speech focused on the government's reconstruction agenda, which was composed of three main components: the rehabilitation and reestablishment of returned veterans; the smooth shift to a peacetime economy; and the construction of a social-security safety net.[12] While this extended discussion of domestic political and social concerns about reconstruction and the new order may seem tangential to First Nations people and issues, it formed an essential context of which the "Indian" image formed one distinct thread.

Equally important were Canadians' visions of what the new order ought to look like, of what kind of country they believed Canada should become. Undoubtedly, there were as many versions of the future as there were Canadians, and not all would have agreed on many key points, but most agreed that something needed to be done. In a poll taken on 1 October 1943, 71 percent expressed a preference for postwar reforms rather than a return to the way things had been before the war.[13] It is not certain, however, that a clear sense of what the new order should consist of had been fully articulated by this time. Judging from opinion polls, editorials, and news stories of the period, several major elements seem to have been popular and widely held. Essentially, Canadians wanted a country protected from the excesses of war and depression that had wracked their society for much of the previous

generation. As one commentator put it in a speech before the Cardston
Rotary Club, what Canadians wanted was "freedom – economically, reli-
giously, and physically, and the latter freedom especially from war ... [and]
any government that will eliminate want and unemployment, is the one
that we would ordinarily, and in wisdom, support."[14] In addition, tolerance
of difference – be it racial, linguistic, or religious – was touted as desirable.
George Drew, Premier of Ontario, argued at a banquet in Guelph on 14
October 1943 that one of the outstanding lessons of the war was "the danger of any new order based upon appeals to prejudice."[15] A third noticeable
trend was the increasing number of Canadians willing to accept an active
and leading role for government in the economic and social life of the country.[16] These three elements of the new order were not the sum total, but
they did form the commonly accepted core of the concept.

So how did the "Public Indian" fare in this climate? The short answer is
that the "Indian" images had lost a good deal of their relatively high profile
across the country so evident in 1940-41. The pervasive anxiety of that
period had been banished by the Allied military successes of 1942 and 1943,
and the "Indian-at-war" was no longer required to bolster shaky morale,
although it could and did still draw admiration. The "Indian-at-war" continued to appear, but it was no longer weighed down with the moral responsibility of being a tool for social criticism.[17] Instead, "Indians" were
returned to their traditional place in human-interest stories, where they
were depicted as heart-warming, positive, and sometimes colourful, although
now without the bemused and farcical tone that had characterized the "Public Indian" of the pre-war era.[18] In the wake of the wartime experience, Canadians' public discussions of indigenous people reflected more respect and
sympathy even in the human-interest story.

This change was nowhere better demonstrated than in a major story and
photo collection in the *Globe and Mail*, a paper that had been more inclined
than most to portray the "Indian" in a comical and trivializing fashion.[19]
The article opened claiming, "Cape Croker's Chippewa Indians have gone
to war. Without fanfare or trumpets or even a mild sort of war-dance, practically every able-bodied Indian man – and nine of the women – are in the
uniform of one of the armed forces. And those that are staying behind are
doing their bit toward making their little world a better place in which to
live." In this case, it was not just the chief who encouraged his band to
donate money or to buy bonds and not just enlisted individuals who earned
the positive accolades of the "Indian-at-war" image, but the whole community. The story did not end with the usual details of high enlistments – in
this case, over 10 percent of the population – or of the band contributions
to local Victory Bond drives but went on to give a detailed description of the
activities of the women and children who remained on the reserve. Of note
is the fact that they were credited with traits and activities not commonly

associated with the "Public Indian" before the war. The author mentioned cases of women repairing their homes, planting gardens, taking over the lake-trout fishery on Georgian Bay left vacant by the men serving in the armed forces, and exercising care and caution in their spending. The moral of the story was best summed up by Chief Thomas Jones: "'We appreciate the seriousness and horror of the war,' Chief Jones said. 'We want to get it over as soon as possible, and anything we can do will be done. But one thing is certain – Cape Croker's women and children will have better homes, better economic conditions, and better health because of their own efforts when their men do come back.'" Canadians, given a choice, had typically exercised the luxury of thinking of the First Nations in the least painful way possible. By 1943 this respectable, intelligent, and thoroughly modern "Indian-at-war" was by far the most appealing image available in their cultural tool box and it remained dominant.

The major indigenous story in October of that year concerned the large conference of First Nations leaders in Ottawa, mentioned in Chapter 2. It was organized by Jules Sioui, John Tootoosis, and Andrew Paull, and attempted to air First Nations grievances with government officials as well as to establish a national Native political organization. The First Nations' politicization was sparked by issues of conscription and taxation resulting from the war, but the overall grievances bespoke long-standing concerns about their relationship to Canada.[20] The next several years would see a proliferation of new organizations.[21] This particular convention gained significant national attention as the Canadian Press wire service turned to the subject with a series of stories between 20 and 23 October.[22] Many English language dailies carried these stories of the conference on at least one day, while both the *Vancouver Sun* and *Globe and Mail* ran their own independent analysis of the events.[23] An "Indian" delegation of between forty and fifty-five, in Ottawa for the conference, spent several days trying to gain an audience with the prime minister or some responsible minister in order to press their claims for exemption from the provisions of compulsory service and income tax. Reporters noted that the representatives were kept waiting for two days as the Indian Affairs Branch refused to see them because the delegates were "unauthorised" and administrators were uncertain whether they had "a bona fide right to speak for their people."[24] In the end, the petitions were presented to various officials, and the First Nations leaders returned home having generated national exposure for their concerns.

What stands out in all the coverage is the utter lack of any recrimination directed at the First Nations for their desire to be exempt from compulsory service and income tax. At an earlier stage of the war, such a stand might have drawn a backlash from highly jingoistic Canadian journalists and been regarded as a cowardly shirking of responsibility, likely to undermine the war effort. Nothing of the sort appeared. The issues were presented in a detached fashion, with little attention to the pageantry of "Indians" in traditional costume. Native grievances appeared reasonable, and their assertions of full support for the war effort were accepted without commentary.[25] Lack of media reproach suggests that with the war going well and the highly documented efforts of the "Indian-at-war," it was possible for Canadians to accept the legitimacy of First Nations protests.

In 1941 the contemporary and positive characteristics of the "Indian-at-war" had spilled over into sensitive treatment of other First Nations subjects not linked to the war. This trend was obvious by 1943. Such stories appeared in two distinct types. The first examined "Indian" issues or events in a complimentary and approving manner, such as that exhibited in a story in the *Saskatoon Star-Phoenix*.[26] The reporter spoke of the agricultural success that the "Indians" of the Battleford Agency had met with that year despite having to overcome the hardship of a late planting. The reason for their success was the simple fact that "the Indians had worked hard this year." This article was based on information from the Indian Agent J.P. Ostrander, who undoubtedly had his own reasons for emphasizing the positive results obtained by his charges. Nonetheless, the manner in which the material was reported was straightforward and did not ascribe the achievements of the various reserves to anything other than the initiative and efforts of their inhabitants. Prior to the war, such a story would likely have included a sermon on how this result was the crowning feat of Indian Affairs' benevolent and wise management. No such slant was visible. The "Indian-at-war" had made it possible to recognize Native accomplishments for their own sake.

The other manifestation of this sympathetic construction of indigenous people was the inclination to portray the "Indian" as the victim. In a *Vancouver Sun* article about the First Nations delegation in Ottawa in October 1943, the focus was on a hero of the First World War.[27] Francis Pegahmagabow, a chief of the Parry Island Ojibwa, who had "service medals of the last war and the military medal with two bars," was among the "Indian" representatives. He was credited with killing as many as 378 Germans when he served as a sniper in the Canadian Expeditionary Force in France during the First World War.[28] Having noted his extraordinary record and that of his band in the previous conflict, the story closed with a stunning revelation: "Friday he dropped in on the Canadian Legion and bought the first poppy of this year's campaign. Then the Legion discovered that it was his last 50 cents." That such an obviously capable man with strong claims on the society's generosity, as both a war hero and a legal ward of the state, could be brought so low revealed something profoundly wrong with the country. Though undoubtedly trying to make a poignant comment, it is not clear whether the journalist recognized what a devastating indictment this story was of Canada's handling of its First World War veterans and more particularly of its treatment of the First Nations. Certainly many readers may have interpreted the story in such a way. However, the journalist did not go beyond the veiled criticism to clarify precisely what this anecdote symbolized.

Other writers, keen to avoid blaming the victim, were more willing than heretofore to specify failings in the system and in Canadian society that prevented a solution to the "Indian problem." At a ceremony making Conservative MP J.D. MacNicol an honorary chief of the Delaware First Nation in Moraviantown, the newly named "Chief Wassaingua" advocated the "appointment of a Royal Commission to find why the education of Canadian Indians has not been stressed."[29] The politician went on to claim that "the Indian population has not been given the opportunity to which it is entitled ... Indians should be teachers and doctors." This story provided one of the early measures of criticism levelled at Canadian Indian policy in what would become a torrent during the debates about reconstruction. Public censure of the country's Indian administration was not unheard of, but previously such commentators had been lone voices in the wilderness.

In another article reporting a postwar plan of action developed by Major D.M. MacKay, the Indian Commissioner for British Columbia, to solve the Indian problem, the blame was thrown wider.[30] The writer of the story editorialized that "at present there is an unfortunate lack of interest in the Indians of B.C. and their care is the responsibility of the Canadian people." While both of these articles reveal critiques of the system or society rather than of the victims, neither goes very far beyond vague recognition that the continuing existence of the Indian problem should no longer be blamed on First Nations people themselves. These stories mark the beginnings of Canadians' willingness to examine themselves and the Indian administration to which they had acquiesced for so many years.

The sixteen months between January 1944 and May 1945 witnessed the dramatic march of Allied armies to victory in Europe. In Canada the focus of the national crusade had always been on defeating Nazi Germany, and in terms of their own forces, what mattered was the fighting in Italy and then in Northwest Europe, after 6 June 1944. Between late July, with the American break-out from the Normandy bridgehead, and early September, as the First Canadian Army drove south to close the Falaise Pocket, the Allies shattered the beleaguered German army in France. By September all Allied forces were racing eastwards, liberating France and Belgium before reaching the Netherlands. When Operation Market-Garden, the Allied airborne gamble to get across the Rhine River that autumn, ground to a close having failed to gain the last bridge at Arnhem, the euphoria of the previous weeks died. More hard fighting lay ahead, particularly for the Canadian forces in the flooded polder countries of Belgium and Holland. However, the overwhelming strength of Allied arms could not be withheld for long, and the papers of April and early May 1945 were filled with the exploits on the front and anticipation of the joys to come on V-E Day.

On the home front, the excitement about the victories overseas was tempered by increasing concern about the postwar period. In August 1944, 61 percent of the country's population believed that the end of hostilities would be followed by a period of significant unemployment, and only one in four Canadians believed that such a period could be avoided.[31] The depth of concern was evident in the willingness of a majority of the population to accept a thirty-hour work week in order to spread the work among more people.[32] However, the first concrete steps had been taken in the realms of social security, with the introduction of unemployment insurance in 1940 and the institution of family allowances just prior to the federal election in 1945. Other prominent elements of the social-security net promised by the Liberals, most notably contributory old-age pensions and national health insurance, were put on hold because of jurisdictional battles with the provinces. Within this environment of unease, public debate about the plight of the "Red man" accelerated and diversified.

Perhaps nothing better demonstrated the new level to which the Indian problem was being taken in debates about the postwar period than the several sessions that the House Committee on Reconstruction and Re-establishment dedicated to the issue in May 1944.[33] This was the primary Parliamentary body dealing with a broad range of postwar reconstruction matters. That it took two days from its busy schedule to enquire into plans for Canada's indigenous population after the war is indicative of both the connection between the "Indian" and the war and the increasing salience of the Indian problem in the minds of Canadians. The committee members became interested in the issue of Indian administration in response to petitions forwarded to Ottawa by both Native and non-Native organizations and individuals as well as several well-publicized visits to the capital by First Nations delegates trying to raise awareness of their grievances. Branch officials were called before the committee in May 1944 to present the IAB's plans for the postwar improvement of reserves. Controversy, outrage from First Nations people, and substantial media coverage was sparked by T.R.L. MacInnes, the secretary of the IAB, who expressed his personal opinion to the committee that some "Indians" "should be divorced from the reserve system entirely and put out on their own."[34] After two days the obvious problems and the lack of departmental vision revealed by the MPs' questions produced the general conclusion that a special committee was needed to investigate fully the entire Indian problem and Canada's Indian administration.

In the media during these final sixteen months of the war, the "Indian" again made a resurgence in most parts of the country. In the *Cardston News*, the *Globe and Mail*, and the British Columbia and Saskatchewan papers canvassed, the "Indian" returned to, or exceeded, its relatively high salience of the summer of 1940. Conversely, it continued to be virtually absent from the *Halifax Chronicle* and much diminished in the *Winnipeg Free Press*. Throughout the period under consideration, the "Indian-at-war" image remained prominent, but only in the *Cardston News* was it still the dominant public representation of the "Indian." The historical and colourful "noble savage" remained scarce, but demeaning stereotypes of contemporary First Nations people still occasionally appeared. The *Prince Albert Daily Herald* carried a trite American cartoon that portrayed an "Indian" character as both foolish and lacking understanding of civilization (see Figure 4.1). While such stereotypes had almost vanished from the public forum during the war years, they had long been deeply entrenched elements of the "Public Indian" and were never far beneath the surface.

Despite the continuing existence of such divergent images of the "Indian" in Canada, what marked the latter stages of the war was the rise of a clear and articulate call for reform in Canadian Indian policy and administration. The first such call appeared in the spring of 1944, but more such articles were published after the Normandy invasion, reaching a crescendo throughout the fall of 1944 and into the spring of 1945. The trend was perhaps nowhere more evident than in the *Kamloops Sentinel*. This weekly paper had traditionally been disinclined to print "Indian" stories, and those that had appeared usually adhered to the contemporary "drunken-criminal" image. However, for unknown reasons, the paper made a complete about-face in its representation of indigenous people during 1944 and early 1945. The "Indian-at-war" appeared repeatedly in a highly positive light.[35] Beyond this change, a number of stories were published about provincial measures in favour of Indian-policy reform, the good work of the Kamloops Residential School and its pupils' diligence, and efforts of First Nations agricultural labourers.[36] In addition, several public lectures on First Nations peoples, cultures, and crafts as well as on Canadian Indian policy received extensive coverage.[37] Finally, one issue of the *Sentinel* provided an in-depth presentation of the debate over the "Indian" land question in British Columbia, complete with the *Vancouver Sun* story that had sparked the controversy, as well as the editorial opinion of the *Vernon News*, *Penticton Herald*, and its own staff.[38] It is hard to imagine a more complete transformation in how a newspaper constructed the "Indian" than that demonstrated by the *Sentinel*. Viewed as a whole, the paper's "Indian" stories of this period suggest a concerted attempt to educate and influence the readership about the need for reform in Indian policy and the worthiness of Native people for such consideration. Whether this was a conscious editorial policy, the paper was not alone in its growing attention to the need for reform.

The desire to change the circumstances of First Nations people and the nature of their relationship to the state had its roots in the unavoidable

4.1   "Cuties." Prince Albert Daily Herald, 30 September 1944, p. 9.

reality of Native military service. The *Saskatoon Star-Phoenix* noted that "some 3000 Canadian Indians were serving in the armed forces, a fact that has injected the problem of Indian policy directly into the field of post-war plans."[39] Indeed, the inequity and bitter irony of accepting and even compelling the military service of those denied the franchise and the rights of full citizenship was not lost on Canadians. As one woman from Espanola, Ontario, wrote in a letter to the Committee on Reconstruction and Re-establishment: "There are Indian men and boys in the Services who will not want to come home to Reserves. They are making sacrifices on a par with the 'Whites' for Freedom, they are fighting for a freedom they never had. One of the first places where we could well begin to dispense the 'Four Freedoms' is right in our midst: to the Indians."[40] Nor was this anomaly recognized in reference to indigenous people alone. An editorial in the *Kamloops Sentinel* referred to a petition circulated by the Indo-Canadian community of British Columbia, which claimed that extending the franchise to them would, among other things, "remove the inconsistency of receiving East Indians into the Canadian Army to shed their blood for Canada, while denying them the symbol of citizenship."[41] Both Japanese and Chinese Canadians eagerly attempted to enlist in the armed forces for precisely this reason and met significant resistance from BC political authorities, who urged the military to refuse their enlistment because they feared that "military service was the 'thin edge of the wedge' leading to enfranchisement."[42] By 1944-45 war service by First Nations men and women had clearly pried open the minds of Canadians and made it uncomfortable to ignore the status quo any longer.

For the first time, intellectual elites entered the fray, driving the public discussions in new directions. A *Canadian Forum* article appearing in July 1944 marked the beginning of this trend.[43] The author asked the question, "What are the responsibilities of a democratic society towards Canada's Indian population of 118,000 human beings?" He went on to explore the nature of the "Indian problem" in socio-psychological terms: "Human beings are better adjusted in a predictable, thoroughly comprehended cultural environment than in one that is new and foreign and which has been forced upon them ... Where the old culture produced balanced human beings living harmoniously within a pattern of well-understood relationships, the new conditions produce confusion, disorganization and strong anxiety that often shows itself in a complete inability to do anything – what psychologists call regression or flight." Such an argument carried a great deal of weight, backed as it was by the increasing legitimacy and influence of science. By the end of the Second World War, the scientific study of human beings and their social relationships was gaining influence, with the disciplines of sociology, anthropology, psychiatry, and psychology carving prominent places within national life.[44] Seemingly, two decades after a similar movement in the United States, an educated and liberal, or social-democratic, elite at last expressed an interest in Canada's First Nations and Indian-policy reform.

However, budding concern for the plight of the "Red man" should not be dismissed as merely a narrowly based movement of intellectuals and academics. There were indications that the foundations of support for rehabilitating the "Indian" in the postwar period were much broader. For instance, in March 1944 the British Columbia Legislature unanimously passed an unusual motion proposed by the CCF members from North Vancouver and Similkameen. The motion stated that "under the Atlantic Charter no minority section of Canadians should be debarred from the enjoyment of the rights and privileges of full citizenship" and that the federal government therefore ought to do more to help the First Nations prepare "to participate in all the rights and privileges of Canadian citizenship."[45] Another good example was an articulate brief submitted to the Committee on Reconstruction and Re-establishment by the Okanagan Society for the Revival of Indian Arts and Crafts from the small British Columbian town of Oliver.[46] In a review of this document that appeared in *Saturday Night*, one author thought "it seem[ed] odd that the most intelligent and understanding suggestion for the modernisation of Canada's policy towards the Indians of the Dominion should come from a little community in British Columbia ... None of those signing the brief is, so far as we know, well-known outside their own province; none is an official. They are simply good citizens, exercising their right to be heard, and feeling, as Quaker elders used to say, a 'concern' about an important matter."[47] This brief was founded on the "desire to see a Canada made up of many racial origins, and we want no theories of holding aboriginal inhabitants down to the quaintness of the past, isolating them in picturesqueness for the tourist trade."[48] This *Saturday Night* article prompted a letter to the editor from an individual in Prince Edward Island two weeks later. The writer stated that the "condition of the Indians ... [was] receiving consideration here [in PEI] also," noting a report presented to the Diocesan Church Society of PEI the previous spring that had called on the government to do something to raise the "low estate" of "Indians" in the province.[49] Thus there were suggestions that many Canadians were moved by the challenge that the plight of the First Nations presented to their views of what their country ought to look like.

Inherent in these calls for changes to Canada's Indian policy was a painful self-examination of the social and systemic causes of the Indian problem. The crux of the Indian problem, as it emerged in the public discussions of 1944-45, was that "in Canada, the Red Indian, the noble red man of the romantic novel of Canadian history and the Hollywood screen has been bound by a policy of perpetual wardship and denied the status of citizenship and the ordinary opportunity of economic advancement."[50] In essence, the "Indian" had not been integrated into the physical, constitutional, and economic mainstream of Canadian society. For most Canadians this meant that assimilation had not occurred.

Failure was universally blamed on two factors, as articulated by the president of the Okanagan Society for the Revival of Indian Arts and Crafts: "The truly sad picture these Indians present today is a direct reflection of our unjust administration. They are wards of the government in the fullest sense of the word, and we, the citizens are responsible for the actions of our government. What the Indian is today we have made him through neglect ... [and] in criticizing the Indians, we are but criticizing ourselves."[51] First and foremost, Canadian Indian policy and its administration bore the brunt of the blame: "The effect of Canadian policies of paternalism and wardship have left the Indian dependent upon a primitive order of things that has vanished in Canada while they have not been able to adapt themselves to the full opportunities of Canadian life."[52] According to one report on the Northwest Territories, "centuries of tutelage have robbed the Indian of his independent spirit and self-reliance ... a heavy indictment against us in our treatment of a once proud people ... and we have meant so well."[53] Not all commentators were so self-aware. In contrast, the *Penticton Herald* claimed that all that was necessary was "to bring a sleep-walking department into awareness at the present hour."[54] However, this simplistic solution failed to recognize what most other commentators were quick to concede: that in a democratic society the Indian problem could not be blamed solely on "the deplorable neglect of the Indians by the responsible dominion government authorities."[55]

The second major impediment to improving the lives of First Nations people and welcoming them into national life was a more general ignorance, apathy, and even racism among the population. One article argued that "to modernize Canada's Indian policy, a thorough transformation of public opinion will be required ... so long has the public neglected the Indian and so fixed has become the idea that he is an inferior person."[56] A writer in the *Canadian Forum* went further, making direct reference to the current conflict and decrying the existence of "that complacent racial superiority that we dislike so much in other people that we're willing to fight a war with them about it."[57] These were strong words, and a remarkable change from the pre-war discussions that had found little fault with either the Indian administration or the attitudes of the dominant society.

Such a transformation in the debates led to a further evolution of the "Public Indian." What became most noticeable was that, as a rule, the public discussion of the "Indian" increasingly began to emphasize the problems and poverty that were the norm for many Native people. For instance, when staffing shortages at Indian hospitals across the country reached an acute stage in early September 1944, the media took note. The *Globe and Mail* picked up a Canadian Press article about Indian Affairs announcements that wartime demands were making it impossible to maintain several reserve hospitals in the West.[58] The story warned that the closures would leave almost 1,500 Stonies and Peigans and over 4,000 Cree in Norway House, Manitoba, without any medical care. The *Free Press* also ran a story about the dire situation in Norway House, and it pulled no punches, quoting the words of Dr. Percy Moore, superintendent of Indian medical services for the

IAB, who warned that "unless the plight of these hospitals is relieved it will mean suffering and death for many of our Indians."[59] A more sensational-ized story reported that "inadequate medical care is given to several thou-sand Indians around James Bay district, where there is wide spread suffering."[60] The claims were made by a magistrate and chairman of the Cochrane District Red Cross Society, who asserted that thousands were "en-during untold suffering and death because of a lack of adequate care and medical attention ... They are at the mercy of a civil service so far removed from their daily lives as to be beyond reach."[61] The story carried a brief official reply to these graphic declarations, which denied that the situation was as grim as described, but after such lurid and shocking details, the gov-ernmental viewpoint came across as flat and unconvincing. Canadians could hardly have heard such horror stories without being moved.

In the writings advocating reform, the indictments were as blunt and even more pointed. The Okanagan brief to the Committee on Reconstruc-tion and Re-establishment claimed that "Indians whose crops failed get only $4 a month for groceries, when they are too sick and old to work slow starvation. Those needing clothing are fitted out with discarded military garments. Per capita income in 1943 was $105 a year, and out of that the men of Caughnawaga employed as steel-workers lift the average, so that most Indians get far less."[62] Even before the pressures of war began to drive up salaries, the average Canadian blue-collar worker was earning almost a thousand dollars a year. This juxtaposition drove home the disparity be-tween the standard of living on many reserves and that of the Canadian mainstream. Nor was this focus on the hardships confronting First Nations people confined to such articles alone.

Even in other "Indian" stories the emphasis on the hardships faced by Native communities continued to be a theme. In a classic "Indian-at-war" story published in *Saturday Night*, the author went beyond the colourful contributions of the Blackfoot to the war effort, which included digging up the buffalo bones from *"Piskuns,"* ancient buffalo-jumps, to mention re-peatedly the difficult circumstances of reserve life.[63] In the article, the au-thor commented on the $2.5-million community fund, established by the sale of reserve lands and railway rights-of-way, which was touted as a wise measure because the accruing interest would go "toward an existence free from the extreme poverty and hardship that may be seen on many other reserves." The author's old friend Many Guns could recall "the days when the Blackfeet still hunted the buffalo – the days before they became so poor that they had to snare gophers." The story, although a colourful and posi-tive tribute to the efforts of the Blackfoot people to do their bit by meshing their past with the present need, actually highlighted the poverty and plight of these people. In this way, the new image of the "Public Indian" came to inspire pity.

Remarkably, throughout these stories Canadians consistently emphasized that the blame for the often wretched living conditions on reserves did not lie with the "Indian." Even though some did acknowledge "backwardness and shortcomings" in the "Indian's" character, "his lack of interest in work, and fondness for holidays and drink, his bad inferiority complex," these failings were assigned to systemic factors that had retarded the First Nations' ability to adjust to the social and economic circumstances of contemporary Canada.[64] The culpability for the creation of the situation and for the continued failure to solve the Indian problem was ascribed to an initiative-killing system of administration and an indifferent and even racist society. Indigenous communities were construed as "unfortunate and helpless" before this smothering combination.[65] The dynamism and agency that had been a hallmark of the "Indian-at-war" was stripped away, and in its place appeared a figure both pitiable and tragically powerless. The "Public Indian" appeared predominantly in this guise of the "Indian victim" as the war drew to a close in Europe.

The philosophical foundations of support for Indian-policy reform were broadly accepted in Canada. Essentially, the war proved central to constructing a place for First Nations people in the country's future. In the first instance, people realized that as "a result of the war, the Indian population has become more fully drawn into Canadian life than at any previous time" and that the time was thus propitious for reform.[66] But more important, if the country was fighting racism and totalitarian-state oppression in the world, then it had better ensure that such conditions did not exist in its own backyard; and if Canadians were fighting for democracy, freedom, equality, and the Atlantic Charter, then these principles should be embodied by the conduct in their own country. These sentiments were expressed in the House of Commons in July 1944, when one member rose and stated that "we are not fighting to-day merely to defeat Germany and Japan; we are fighting in defence of definite principles. We are fighting for a peace based on justice, and justice must be granted to minorities as well as majorities."[67] The same notions were produced for a mass audience through the words of an advertisement for Victory Bonds: "Out where the bullets are flying, our boys – our *Canadian* boys – do not care if a wounded buddy is Catholic, Protestant or Jew. All, all are *Canadians*, regardless of religion, race or colour ... These boys – YOUR BOYS – on the world's far flung fighting lines – have risen above the spectre of religious or racial discrimination. TAKE HEED, lest you weaken their faith in the principles for which they are fighting."[68] The difficult realities of reserve life fell far short of such lofty rhetoric. These feelings were translated into concern for the Indian problem: "We who have our sons and daughters in the fight and who pray and work from dawn till dusk, that honor and right shall prevail in this struggle are not going to permit our own officials to act like Huns towards the Indians right under our noses."[69] To do otherwise would have diminished the sacrifice of those who served, devalued the national crusade, and threatened to undermine the vaunted new order Canadians hoped to erect. While such high-minded idealism might normally sound trite and somewhat removed from everyday matters, the immediacy of total war lent these claims relevance and palpable sincerity.

Most English Canadians were in agreement with a number of short-term actions designed to alleviate the immediate hardships of First Nations people. Most urgent, particularly in light of the attention given to the poor health of Native people in the media, was an improved system of medical care.[70] No objections to this idea were voiced, and most people recognized that it was "chiefly a matter of money," of injecting the resources necessary to expand existing facilities and perhaps even "providing additional hospitals specially for Indians."[71] A second component of the short-term solutions proposed was to provide more and better housing on reserves. The British Columbia Legislature envisioned a system whereby "the Indians, on leaving school, should be encouraged by financial assistance and advice to build modern homes."[72] In part, this system was linked to the health benefits of hygienic living conditions, but underneath the altruism perhaps Canadians preferred not to see tangible signs of the "Indians'" marginalization, such as Native homes "in the category of slums."[73] Also acknowledged was the need for the immediate economic betterment of the First Nations, with an emphasis on equal treatment for their veterans in the government rehabilitation program and "Indian relief and old age pensions on the same basis as white."[74] Finally, the government had to conserve fur resources and protect game preserves from white trappers so that the Native trapper could continue to make a living.[75] However, these were viewed only as stop-gap measures rather than as long-term solutions to the Indian problem.

What was really needed was a complete overhaul of the administration system and Indian policy in Canada and, some argued, of the entire philosophical underpinnings on which the existing system had been based. The first calls for an in-depth review of the issue were heard, such as that of one author who believed that "there ought in the first place to be an investigation and appraisal of our Indian policy by a group of experts in various fields, sociologists, economists, anthropologists, educationists, and others, working with Indians and men in the field. It should receive the co-operation but not the direction of the Department of Mines and Resources which, ironically enough, now administers Indian affairs."[76] Such a call was likely to be met with acceptance by a public that had witnessed the benefits of an interventionist government pursuing economic and social-engineering policies generated by academic experts drawn into many government departments over the previous two decades. As yet, the almost anti-intellectual Indian Affairs Branch had demonstrated little comparable willingness to consult academe.[77] However, the experts of the ivory tower were gaining greater esteem within the public domain, and their active participation in the day-to-day running of the country was not only legitimate, but increasingly expected.

To most Canadians, revamping the Indian Act meant developing better means to achieve what had been intended with the original act: "Up to now Canadian Indian policy has done little beyond save the Indian from extinction. It has done little to open up the way for his assimilation into Canadian society."[78] A *Vancouver Sun* editorial, prompted by T.R.L. MacInnes's comments before the Committee on Reconstruction and Re-establishment, was not so hard on Canadian Indian policy, arguing that the "system worked well on the whole from its inception early in the 17th century til the present day, but Mr MacInnes may be right in thinking that it is now outworn, and that all Indians should now assume the status of regular Canadian citizens, with no special privilege or obligations."[79] This last point is significant, as English Canadians, for the most part, were unwilling to grant "Indians" full citizenship unless they surrendered all special rights. To do so clashed with their sense of democratic fairness as much as did Native peoples' present lack of citizenship and wardship status. However, while assimilation continued to form the commonsense solution for most Canadians, there was a countercurrent within the debate.

A new thread within the public discussion articulated an alternative vision of the appropriate end goal: the continuing existence of the "Indian" as an "Indian" and the integration of First Nations into the body politic as culturally distinct collectivities. This agenda was largely influenced by cultural relativism in the social sciences and by the ideals and policies of the Indian New Deal in the United States, which had fostered some cultural resurgence among Native Americans. To a degree, intellectual elites pressed this course, arguing that "the Indian can be truly free only when he has defined his freedom in a cultural frame of reference for which he alone is responsible and which he understands."[80] However, the proponents of a New Deal-style solution to Canada's "Indian problem" were not uniformly academic in origin, as the Okanagan Society for the Revival of Indian Arts and Crafts articulated a similar philosophy.[81] In this realm of thought, any new Indian Act had to assure "cultural entity and independence," preferably after a study of the US's Indian Reorganization Act (1934), the legislative cornerstone of the American Indian New Deal.[82] The willingness not only to allow, but to encourage, indigenous communities to maintain their cultural identity went against centuries of Indian policy, practice, and popular belief in Canada.

The result of these differing visions was diverging opinion on specific policies for the future progress of First Nations people. For instance, most commentators articulated a common end goal of full citizenship, complete with the franchise for the First Nations. The advocates of a New Deal envisioned immediate "full citizenship" or at least "an educational program for Indian men, women, and children, directed towards complete and responsible citizenship for them."[83] But this status was expected to be granted without demanding that First Nations people renounce their indigenous identity and treaty rights. Assimilationists, on the other hand, would have agreed more with Winifred Paris, who wrote that "the ultimate aim for the Indian should be citizenship, equality of rights and privileges with every other Canadian. With the privileges of Citizenship would naturally come the responsibilities of Citizenship. With equal educational advantages and opportunities they would not only be self-supporting, but would pay taxes, computed on the same standards."[84] This school of thought expected citizenship to occur when the "Indians" became "doctors, nurses and teachers" and "fill[ed] their places in labour, and the professions."[85] In other words, full citizenship would be achieved when First Nations people ceased looking and behaving like "Indians."

Education was widely acclaimed as critical to solving the Indian problem, and for some it was viewed as a panacea. Yet the two camps had much in common on this issue, as identical policies could be defended from both perspectives. The educational system for Native people was the one factor universally considered problematic, if not "a national disgrace," and in need of change.[86] Essentially, English Canadians thought that a larger number of better-qualified teachers was needed to staff more schools teaching a more useful and relevant curriculum. For instance, the Young People's Organisation of the First United Community Church in Arvida, Quebec, submitted a resolution to the IAB, which stated, among other things, that "the present curriculum of education for Indians does not appear to fit them for their particular needs" and called on the director to "seek methods as may be in his power to improve the citizenship status of the Canadian Indian, and provide the type of education that will fit him to discharge his functions as a Canadian citizen."[87] A motion by the British Columbia Legislature urged Ottawa to expand "their [the First Nations'] existing facilities and opportunities for higher education, including vocational training, to the native Indian population of this dominion: that guidance officers be appointed and provided for the purpose of assisting and encouraging Indians to take advantage of all available educational facilities."[88] The underlying assumption was that if "Indians" had really been encouraged and educated properly, they would have chosen to become assimilated. The confidence that assimilation could be achieved "in a generation or so" had always proven remarkably resilient in Canada, seeming to wax each time a new swelling of interest in the "Indian" and Indian policy occurred.

The New Deal-style reformers could envision a similar emphasis on vocational training that would have some bearing on reserve life: "They have been deprived of their old tribal education and ... nothing comparable as a means of fitting them for the life they have to live has been provided ... If someone would just teach his lads carpentry and boatmaking now, or machine mechanics, that would be something. And if reading and arithmetic were pointed in these directions – well, they would have a point."[89] Still others argued that Native children should be integrated into the public school system either because it was believed they could hold their own or because it would facilitate assimilation.[90] Whether Canadians wished "Indians" to excel in their own right or in order to raise them up to a level where they might be absorbed into the mainstream of society, education was the essential vehicle.

A final point appeared in the public discussions of the future of the "Indian": Should they continue to be segregated on reserve lands?[91] Reserves generated mixed emotions from Canadians, who even disagreed as to the quality of the land. One story argued that "the reservations do not, indeed, support the Indian population ... Reservation areas are generally poor land, without mineral or other resources," while another complained that "this land, more often than not, is in the choicest locations."[92] The issue was perhaps nowhere more hotly contested than in British Columbia.

The *Kamloops Sentinel* carried a fascinating pair of stories revealing the debate on this question in April 1945. The first reprinted an editorial from the *Vancouver Sun* and the responses from the *Penticton Herald* and the *Vernon News*, and the second was the passionate reaction of Albert Millar, the president of the Okanagan Society for the Revival of Indian Arts and Crafts.[93] The *Vancouver Sun* editorial that precipitated the debate, entitled "Blocking Progress in the Okanagan," opened saying that "the most striking fact observed by the visitor to the expanding landscape of Canada's greatest fruit area is that so much of the best land is wasted in Indian reserves."[94] These reserves were deemed "both archaic and objectionable in operation," and while they had been an appropriate provision for the indigenous population of the valley "six or eight decades ago, [they] remain today to interfere with progress and orderly development." The editorial did not go beyond damning the reserve system and the "Indians" who were seen as not making any use of the land to suggest what ought to be done, but the implication was that the land should be taken away from the "Indians" so that it could be properly utilized to "provide food for thousands of people." The *Penticton Herald* fully agreed, insisting that the reserves "offered a barrier [to the path of progress] that must go, and there need be no inequitable treatment of the Indians in the process."[95] Exactly how such a little miracle of administration was to be achieved, the *Herald* editorial neglected to clarify.

The *Vernon News*, on the other hand, took the *Sun* to task, not so much for its assessment of the backwardness of the reserve system, but for its blaming the "Indian" for the shortcomings in cultivation of Okanagan reserve lands. Instead, they laid the blame squarely at the door of the Indian Affairs Branch and its "lack of education and supervision of the Indians in the Okanagan," and chided "a powerful medium" like the *Vancouver Sun* for neglecting these glaring deficiencies.[96] Millar praised the *Vernon News* editorial, which, in his words, "evoked [interest and pleasure] in those of us who regard the Indians as human beings having the same rights as other human beings and in those of us who really believe we should practice what we preach, viz. the democratic way of life."[97] He went further, castigating the *Sun* for its "unfair and almost prejudiced criticism of the Okanagan Indians" and providing a long litany of reasons why the circumstances on Okanagan reserves were the fault of Canadian society and the federal government. His organization was a firm follower of the principles in the American Indian New Deal and had argued that the First Nations ought to be granted "full citizenship without loss of land."[98] However, the opinions of the *Vancouver Sun* and the Okanagan Society for the Revival of Indian Arts and Crafts were two extremes between which existed an ambivalent grey area where the mainstream of the public milled about on the Indian land question.

One unavoidable aspect of this public discussion about the future of the "Indian" in Canada was that in almost every case, this was a debate involving English Canadians talking to other English Canadians about what English Canadians ought to do. Very few commentators even mentioned the concerns of First Nations people, and one who did "couldn't advocate the granting of all their wishful thinking as a solution for the Indians or for Canada."[99] Though they wished to help them, in most cases it simply did not occur to private citizens, authors, journalists, and editors to consult the First Nations. Even those with the best of intentions fell into this practice, as did Albert Millar's organization, which pressed the government for a new Indian Act "assuring cultural entity and independence, to be extended to all with one-quarter Indian blood."[100] Quite apart from the slippery slope of hereditary fractions, they were determining who would be considered an "Indian" and who would not based upon criteria of their choosing.

Canadians assumed either that they knew what was best for the "Indian" or in some cases that they knew what the "Indian" wanted. One article closed stating "that the young and intelligent Indian objects that he is being forced to remain in an old and obsolete mode of living."[101] Though there was some limited support for, or fatalistic acceptance of, assimilation among First Nations people, this exercise in wishful thinking had more to do with projecting Canadians' desires for assimilation onto the "Indian." The Indian problem was no longer just the "Indian's," but even as Canadians assumed responsibility and proprietorship, they also assumed the onus of fixing the problem. In a sense this was fitting because it was the dominant society that had problematized the existence of the First Nations in their midst. However, although well meaning and altruistic, their presumptuousness was also both patronizing to Native people and laced with paternalism. In effect, what these public discussions in the war's last years demonstrated was a society preparing once more to take up, in earnest, the white man's burden.

Whereas during the war's early years, when Canadians had closely reexamined their notions of First Nations people in light of the indigenous support for the national crusade, in the latter years of the war the dominant society revealed a willingness to turn the scrutiny inward. This readiness to look within developed out of the nation's desire to create a new order, a better Canada in the wake of the Great Depression and the Second World War. Most people believed that changes were needed and that it was not enough to return to the pre-war status quo. In envisioning the new order, Canadians were forced to think hard about the kind of country they desired and to clarify the principles upon which it should be based. Such debate was the more visceral and sincere because these were the same principles for which the country was fighting a total war and for which its sons and daughters were dying.

Within such a context, Canadians turned their gaze upon the "Indian," the conditions in which First Nations people lived, and the nature of the country's treatment of them. What they saw failed to measure up to the passionate rhetoric of the war and clashed with the ideals of the new order. The structures and measures of the government's Indian administration came under attack, but most people recognized that the problems went deeper than bureaucracy or even underfunding. Canadian society also had to bear its share of the blame for the continuing marginalization of the First Nations, for racism, indifference, and an unwillingness to accept the "Indian" as a full member in its midst. The collective guilt always latent in the "Public Indian" image was finally acknowledged and even embraced in these discussions. It was a remarkable change from the 1930s, when the image had served to suppress, divert, and defuse Canada's culpability for the plight of the First Nations.

A new image of the "Public Indian" developed during this period, arising largely from the discussion about the plight of the First Nations, the shortcomings of Canada's Indian policy, and where the "Indian" ought to fit in the future. This new image, the "Indian victim," resembled all its predecessors in some way, but the combination of characteristics was unique. In line with the "noble savage," it was cast in a tragic light and exhibited the same stoicism in suffering adversity; however, it was neither vanishing nor banished to the distant past. Like the "drunken criminal," the "Indian victim" also existed in deplorable conditions of poverty, social dysfunction, substance abuse, and ill health, but the victim no longer bore the blame. In common with the "Indian-at-war," the new "Indian" was both contemporary and sympathetic, but it was bereft of the dynamism and sense of agency that had animated the former. What emerged were positive yet tragic present-day figures who, through no fault of their own, lived in wretched conditions they were powerless to change. Such a construction fostered pity and anger in Canadians and left the sensation that, having suddenly accepted responsibility, they were wallowing in their rediscovered collective sense of shame. For those advocating reform, the "Indian victim" was the principal rhetorical weapon for mobilizing national attention and generating public pressure for change.

The "Indian victim" and the reformers appear to have been successful in generating a consensus that something needed to be done. There even appeared to be unanimity about specific short-term policies to correct immediate and urgent health and economic concerns. However, long-range issues and policies turned on the essence of what Canadians wished the "Indian" to become and where they wished the First Nations to fit in society. Even if they agreed on the means, there was a split over the ends. The majority honestly believed that assimilation was the best and only solution, both for the dominant society and for the happiness, health, and prosperity of the First Nations. A vocal minority advocated allowing and encouraging the "Indian" to remain as culturally distinct and independent entities within the national multicultural milieu. At its essence, this divide reflected the age-old conflict between the principles of individualism and collectivism: between the belief that true democracy rested in the individual and the belief that democratic states ought to recognize the rights of people to develop their own sense of collective identity.

The last significant commonality in the public discussions surrounding the "Indian" during the later years of the Second World War was that the debate occurred among Canadians arguing about what they believed the problem to be and about the kind of solutions they needed to pursue in order to correct it. Very little attention was paid to what Native people desired or to the reforms they believed necessary. This omission clearly demonstrates that while the content of the "Public Indian" image had evolved significantly since the 1930s, the power relations upon which it was founded had not. The dominant society could still define its ideas about the First Nations as it saw fit, to meet its own needs. Underpinning this power disparity was English Canada's continuing confidence in its cultural and social superiority over its "Indian." The white man's burden was dusted off and reinstated by Canadians as they once again renewed their commitment to raising the "Indian" up to the point where he disappeared within the body politic. Symptomatic of this revival was the very process of conceptualizing the issue under the complex rubric of the Indian problem, as though it belonged to the First Nations. At its base, however, the Indian problem was not the "Indians'" problem although it certainly had far-reaching consequences in their daily lives; it was the dominant society's quandary. Canada's problem with First Nations people was that they continued to exist as "Indians"; as such, they remained a constant reminder to the country of their displacement and subjugation. Only with their disappearance as a distinct people would the dominant society be able to lay its guilt to rest. The war and the desire to win the peace had therefore had a deep impact on the "Public Indian" image in Canada, but it had not fundamentally altered the nature of the relationship between the dominant society and its original inhabitants.

5
The "Administrative Indian" at the Threshold of Peace, January-March 1946

Following the defeat of Japan in August 1945, Canadians could finally put into practice the rhetoric and theory of reconstruction and begin building their better Canada. Partly this meant participating in a meaningful way in the international community either by taking an active role in the formation of the United Nations or by helping to rebuild the shattered economies of Europe. Canadians generously accepted the continuation of stringent rationing, although not without some grumbling, so that the starving Dutch population could eat and British families might have a spot of meat for their tables. At home the machinery of war, particularly wage and price controls, was still in place, while that of reconstruction was in full swing even before the end of hostilities. Almost a million military personnel were being demobilized as quickly as shipping could be found to bring back those who were overseas and the bureaucratic machinery would allow: 395,013 returned to civilian life in 1945 and a further 381,031 in 1946.[1] Two essential elements of a social safety net were in place: family allowances and unemployment insurance. The generous benefits of the Veterans Charter awaited returning servicemen and women to help smooth the difficult transition ahead. In this complex, dynamic, and hopeful environment, Canadians sought a return to an idealized normal life free from war, depression, and insecurity.

The transition to peace was an even less certain time, riddled with mixed emotions for First Nations families and communities. On the one hand, the return of veterans was a matter for great joy and celebration. Also significant were the inroads made by First Nations men and women into jobs that they had never occupied prior to the conflict, the increased interaction with the society in which they lived, and the technical, linguistic, and leadership skills that many brought back to their communities. On the other hand, the unprecedented employment opportunities opened up to First Nations people by the war were bound to dry up in peacetime as war industries closed down and veterans returned to their old jobs. Fortunately, the family-allowance program went a long way toward assuring a basic standard of living and easing the sudden drop in income. But perhaps most important for the future of the First Nations population, the war had helped to create the conditions for reform of the legislation and administration that ruled so many aspects of their lives: There had been a growth in public and government interest in their plight as well as a remarkable proliferation of indigenous political organizations on reserves across the country.

In the halls of the Indian Affairs Branch, peace brought the prospect of relieving the chronic shortages of personnel left over from the war's labour crunch both among field staff and in educational institutions. Two important personnel changes in senior posts ushered in a new era in the branch. Dr. Harold McGill, who had replaced Duncan Campbell Scott as director, retired and R.A. Hoey, the superintendent of education and training since 1936, assumed his position in an acting capacity in early 1945. Also significant was a Cabinet shuffle that brought in the vibrant J. Allison Glen to replace the long-serving and indifferent T.A. Crerar, who retired to the Senate in April 1945.[2] Although the combination of these new appointments helped to rejuvenate a demoralized corporate structure, it would take more than a new minister and director to truly change the course of Canada's Indian policy; it would require Parliamentary involvement and public pressure.

This chapter will explore the "Administrative Indian" on the cusp of war and peace. On 14 December 1945, the new minister of mines and resources informed the House of Commons that he would begin an investigation into reform of the Indian Act and administration once an appropriate mechanism had been determined. Several weeks later, he wrote a circular letter to all Indian Agents and Inspectors in an attempt to "establish a personal and intimate relationship" during his tenure.[3] In the letter, Glen outlined some of the plans for Indian Affairs in the postwar era, and solicited the confidential advice of his field staff on several problems he viewed as impediments to the "care and advancement of the Indian population in this country."[4] He was concerned in particular with how best to overcome a perceived lack of trust in the government among First Nations people and with ways to encourage the "gospel of self-help" among them. Over the next several months, thirty-nine of the country's ninety-four Indian Agents, or 40 percent, and the provincial inspector of Indian Agencies for Saskatchewan replied to the minister's letter.[5] Most were pleased with the minister's gesture and used the opportunity to provide considered responses to the questions asked, each writing on average two legal-sized pages of single-spaced text.[6] This body of correspondence, then, provides a unique opportunity to examine the "Administrative Indian" at war's end as the IAB collected itself for a policy and legislative reassessment and a renewal of purpose.[7]

Interestingly, this was not the first time that the field personnel had been asked for their advice on policy and administrative matters. In November 1938 Dr. Harold McGill had sent out a circular to all Indian Agents requesting their views on potential revisions to the Indian Act. He received fewer replies than did Glen, mostly from the western provinces. Interestingly, almost every one of the agents who replied to this circular also replied to the minister's letter in 1946. Two inferences might be drawn from this. First, these were long-serving personnel with extensive experience working for the branch; indeed, some commented on their lengthy service. Second, these gentlemen were inclined toward thoughtful reflection on their work and the Indian problem and probably were among the IAB's more conscientious field personnel.

The questions asked by Glen in his letter cut to the core of the Indian Agent's conception of the "Administrative Indian," the Indian problem, and its solutions. For this reason, they provide an ideal entry into the minds of IAB officials at the end of the war and before the legislative and administrative upheavals of the subsequent five years. However, this body of documents is not methodologically unproblematic. The agents were replying to their superior in a highly hierarchical bureaucratic structure with autocratic tendencies. This undoubtedly encouraged them to underplay the difficulties in their own jurisdictions. A number of them used the opportunity to sing their own praises, appeal for higher wages, and, in one case, to shamelessly press for an improved posting. In addition, it is not evident why 60 percent of the agents refrained from replying, nor is it clear how they might have answered the questions of the minister had they done so. Nonetheless, as stated above, most of the field staff who did provide Glen with advice appear to have taken the request seriously and spoken candidly, providing a wide range of explanations and suggestions for the future.

Freezing the official image in the early months of 1946 allows the researcher to explore a number of questions relevant to this study. How did the field staff of the IAB construct the "Indian" in the immediate postwar period? How, if at all, did the postwar "Administrative Indian" differ from the pre-war version? Where did Indian Agents and Inspectors see the place of the "Indian" in Canada's future? Did the swelling public interest and dissatisfaction with the country's Indian administration and the quality of life on reserves have any influence on administrators' views or language? The answers to these questions allow for the construction of a distinct impression of the "Administrative Indian" in the first year of the postwar period.

The minister's letter was clearly designed to do more than merely introduce the new minister to his employees or acquaint them with the government's postwar program for "the advancement of the Indian population."[8] Glen went out of his way to praise the agents and inspectors and thank them for "the services rendered the department – services rendered

by many of you faithfully and conscientiously over a long period of years."
He flattered them, asserting that the success of the postwar program would
"depend to a very large extent upon the ability and the efficiency of our
field officers. There is a sense in which it can be said that you occupy the
front line trenches and are subject to criticisms and annoyances that many
of us less intimately associated with life on the reserves escape." More important, he pledged that in the future the direction from Ottawa would be
better and more understanding of conditions on the reserves. He concluded
by assuring his staff of his interest and willingness to help and solicited
their views on several policy issues. The impression created by Glen's letter
was that of a general rallying his beleaguered and demoralized troops, a
notion further emphasized by his military allusion to Indian Agents occu-
pying the frontline trenches.[9] Judging from the genuine pleasure and surprise expressed by most of the agents who replied, his efforts were much
needed to reverse the intense alienation felt by field personnel across the
country.

Significantly, the minister informed them that the branch would no longer
actively oppose Native political organization. This reversed decades of law,
policy, and practice under Scott and McGill. Glen perceived First Nations
activism and political organization, which had accelerated noticeably during the war years, as a sign that the "Indians" were "becoming steadily
more conscious of their responsibility for conditions on their reserves ...
[and] evidence of the interest of Indians in their own advancement."[10] From
his perspective, "it is unthinkable to me in an age of organized effort and
collective action that the Indian would seek to remedy his ills by individual
action." However, this acceptance was not unconditional or unequivocal.
Glen believed that this activism "should be guided by our officers as far as it
is possible to guide it into sane and constructive channels." More important, "Indians should be encouraged to exercise the greatest possible care in
the selection and election of their officers ... [and] also to exercise moderation in their claims for public support." Assuming these two things occurred,
Glen foresaw a constructive role for Native organizations within Canadian
Indian administration.

The minister specifically sought advice on three matters that were of paramount importance to him. First, he desired "the establishment of a greater
measure of confidence on the part of the Indians in the department and in
the good intentions of its officials."[11] In particular, he hoped that the IAB
would take the "Indian" into its confidence to a greater extent than previously and even employ indigenous people in its operations in the near future. Second, he wished "to see a sincere attempt made to encourage the
gospel of self-help amongst Indians." Glen hoped that instituting advisory
boards on reserves to care for and organize activities in reserve buildings
and specifically community halls would aid in this direction, assuming these

endeavours had "proper supervision." Finally, the minister wondered whether there might be great benefit in taking advantage of more provincial services, such as educational courses in health, sanitation, and agricultural activities or the restocking of fish in lakes and the conservation of fur and game animals. He then closed by acknowledging that, "while the results at times appear disappointing, nevertheless we can proceed – extracting a measure of satisfaction from the consciousness that we are assisting a group of people to adapt themselves to modern conditions and in so doing, encourage them to assume a greater share of the rights, duties and responsibilities ... In this task, the thought of failure should have no place in our minds." This optimism, combined with the sympathy and deference with which Glen treated the field personnel in this letter, aside from marking a profound change from the aloof and autocratic Crerar, appears to have won the confidence of many of the agents and inspectors.

One of the hallmarks of the official image of the First Nations prior to the war had been its cohesion. Some representations of the "Indian" did not fit with the dominant administrative image, but these arose from the idiosyncrasies of a few members within a large corporate entity, with no agreement among the dissenting views. During the war, this cohesion held together to a large degree despite the pressures of First Nations enlistment and conscription. A perusal of the Glen correspondence reveals that, although old stereotypes of the "Administrative Indian" were still prevalent, the disciplined adhesion to the norms of branch culture, so striking before and even during the war, had loosened slightly. This emerged most clearly in the Indian Agents' answers to Glen's concern about the "Indians'" lack of confidence in the IAB and their perceived lack of ambition. Many still articulated negative characteristics and demeaning stereotypes that enabled them to blame the victim for the failures of the assimilation project. However, to a degree unseen before in official correspondence, many also accepted that the hostility of their charges might be justified by legislative or administrative inadequacies, past errors, and the degree to which Canadian society marginalized them.

In explaining the lack of trust in the IAB among the First Nations, the agents commonly blamed character or racial flaws of the "Administrative Indian," all of which had long been core elements of the official image. In line with the commonsense knowledge about racial traits of the era, several agents assumed that the mistrust was "inbred," "inherent," and "handed down from generation to generation."[12] One agent veiled the same sentiments in the more modern accoutrements of social psychology, claiming that "the Indian problem is basically psychological and the removal by uplift of a racial inferiority complex must be paramount in any approach to Indian rehabilitation."[13] Other agents simply wrote off the suspicion of their charges to a "backward" nature or to the fact that they were "more or less the primitive types."[14] As the agent from Charlottetown explained, the "Indian" had "to rise above the stage of illiteracy and ignorance" before there was any chance of advancing.[15] The social-Darwinian assumption of the "Indian's" intellectual and eugenic inferiority still formed an important element of the official image in 1946.

The First Nations' wariness of government was also blamed on the traditional scapegoats of the IAB: the white agitators and Native troublemakers who stoked the fires of suspicion in the impressionable minds of the gullible "Administrative Indian." Indian Agents had traditionally undermined resistance to their efforts by branding the leaders malcontents or self-interested rabble-rousers in their correspondence with Ottawa, and the responses to Glen reflected this behaviour.[16] The agent from the Caradoc Agency in Muncey, Ontario, acknowledged that "there is ... a spirit of suspicion and distrust. This condition to a large extent emanates from minority groups whose only policy is and always has been to oppose local administration, destroy and oppose government assistance and council, and generally, unduly, criticise their Indian Councils."[17] Unfortunately, from the agents' perspective, the only Native people willing to take an active role on the reserve had, "in most cases, very little to recommend them other than the ability to talk fast."[18] However, the difficulty with troublemakers among their charges was less of a concern in 1946 than was the agents' frustration with meddlesome outsiders and the "readiness of so many Indians to give credence to the statements of ill-informed and irresponsible whites, who confuse the Indian with a hodge-podge of radical ideas and malicious information."[19] One Manitoba agent felt that it was easier to deal with the outlying reserves than with those "near a white settlement [where] the Indians are often more dissatisfied owing to persons outside the reserve agitating that the Indians in the reserve are not getting the help they should."[20] The agent in Parry Sound, Ontario, was clearly angry when he claimed that the obvious suspicion of the First Nations population, whose "minds are clogged with very hazy notions as to the rights which they are entitled to enjoy under various treaties," was "not at all helped by irresponsible white people, many of whom should know better but apparently do not know any more than the Indian himself just what his standing is with regard to the Dominion Government and the other citizens of Canada."[21] Such willingness to be led astray by unwise council marked the "Administrative Indian" as impressionable and childlike, confirming that the First Nations still required the benevolent guidance of the IAB.

Glen's concern about ways to encourage the "gospel of self-help" among Native people tapped into one of the eternal complaints of IAB personnel about their charges: They had no sense of responsibility and less ambition.[22] One agent stated that "an Indian lives for today and hopes for tomorrow," this being "a problem which has been upper most on all reserves."[23] However, worse than irresponsibility was the laziness and indifference that the field staff found blocking their endeavours: "If they just had a little ambition we would have no problems on their behalf at all."[24] Many agents agreed that "the Indians generally speaking are a shiftless lot (with some exceptions) and wont [sic] help themselves if they can get help elsewhere."[25] The agent in Griswold, Manitoba, was certain that "if they are not in need of food they prefer to 'sit and sun themselves.'"[26] Another field officer thought that the problem was due to "Indians'" belief in their divine right as the initial occupants of the continent: "It seems to be the general opinion of an increasingly large number of Indians at present to endeavour to get something for nothing or at least at the expense of the other fellow, so long as they are not called upon to foot the bill. They seem to consider they are entitled to this as a Divine Right, having been the original inhabitants of this Country, which they claim was taken from them by force."[27] The level of frustration is evident in the tone and derision of the language in these letters, as is the less than flattering impression many IAB personnel still had of their charges. Whatever the changes that the war and the coming of peace had brought to their relationship with the "Indian," it remained adversarial.

Importantly, however, the field personnel did more than just blame the "Indians" for their mistrust and perceived lack of ambition; they also turned their critical gaze inward upon their own administration and outward upon the society they served. The first thing that came under attack was Ottawa's distant manner and indifferent direction in its relations both with the field staff and more significantly with the Status Indian population of the country.[28] The agent in Bella Coola, British Columbia, summed up the essence of the issue, arguing that "the attitude of the Government towards the Indian has been in large measure, a reflection of the position occupied in Indian custom by the Chief; supreme, benign and largely unapproachable."[29] Many of the responses stated, or inferred, that one of the main reasons for First Nations' suspicion was that "in the past there was a tendency to keep the Indians uninformed in regard to the workings of the Department."[30] Another agent criticized "the superimposing of a strictly cold legalistic implacable attitude on all Reserve matters," making the point that "a cold, aloof administration, however efficient, will not win the support of these people."[31] Most of these critiques of the imperious bearing of the Ottawa bureaucracy were measured and restrained. However, one Indian Agent from Saskatchewan apparently took advantage of the confidentiality promised by the minister to offer this biting indictment: "There was a time when I was under the impression that the Officials at Ottawa felt that the Indians were a problem that we would always have on our hands and there was not very much that could be done about it other than seeing that the old and destitute were given sufficient food and clothing for a bare existence, and the sick were provided with some medical and hospital care sufficient to more or less satisfy the general public."[32] Such a scathing condemnation sent to the senior bureaucrats in Ottawa would probably have gotten this individual fired, but it demonstrates that the minister's letter had won the field staff's confidence and had elicited some very candid responses.

Beyond the general tenor of IAB administration, the Indian Agents also felt that the First Nations' anger and distrust of the government and lack of advancement were a product of a substandard education system and the inadequate provision of health and welfare services.[33] The Indian Agent from Punnichy, Saskatchewan, surmised that "if we had better schools, with competent teachers and up to date teaching methods including manual training, etc, the Indians would feel the Department is taking a real interest in them, and consequently we would gain their confidence."[34] The sentiments were similar with regards to the other services provided by the IAB, particularly for health care. The agent at the Sioux Lookout Agency in northwestern Ontario informed the minister that "many of our Indians feel that the Government has not provided adequate Medical services ... if remedial measures could be provided in this field alone, it would go a long way toward eliminating the feeling of distrust. In fact at present I believe this to be the crux of the whole situation insofar as the establishment of friendly relations and confidence is concerned."[35] Just down the road in Kenora, Ontario, the Indian Agent assured the minister that there was much room for a greater measure of help for the sick, aged, and destitute, "such as a more balanced and increased monthly relief ration, and more and better clothing. This extra help, I believe, would break down a good deal of the hard feelings towards the Department's policy."[36] These concerns would not have come as a surprise to the minister, particularly given the widespread public discussion of these specific points.

Another common point of concern highlighted by the field personnel was past mistakes in administration and policy, which had alienated the "Indians" and soured relations with the branch. First and foremost among these were past injustices but especially the breaking of promises made to indigenous people and communities. In most cases, this meant promises made during treaty negotiations. One Saskatchewan agent proposed supplying a copy of the relevant treaty to each agent or a list of treaty rights because "the number of Indians who complain that the Government has not carried out its treaty promises with them is surprisingly large."[37] In Chapleau, Ontario, the agent had found "during this last five years that the greatest handicap in my dealings with the Indians has been the lack of confidence they feel due to promises being made without due consideration and which were ultimately found to be impracticable."[38] However, he hastened to add that this dated back ten to twenty-five years and did not apply to the present administration. The potential difficulties led some field staff to take rather extreme measures to protect themselves from this contingency, such as the agent from the Fisher River Agency in Manitoba who made it one of his personal rules to "never make a definite promise to any Indian about anything whatever. I learned the folly of doing this very early in my experience. If one makes a 'promise' to an Indian, and then for some quite unforseen reason is unable to fulfil it, then no amount of explanation, however logical it may be, will satisfy him. You 'promised' and did not keep your promise, so lose the confidence of that particular Indian, and he tells others about it."[39] This remark is a good example of a consistent pattern in the Glen correspondence. Even when expressing an understanding and sympathetic idea about IAB policy or their own dealings with the "Administrative Indian," Indian Agents frequently entwined it with unflattering inferences – in this case, that Native people would not accept logical explanations.

Beyond broken promises, a number of the responses to Glen's letter expressed dissatisfaction with the IAB's lack of consideration for the viewpoints and culture of First Nations people. The agent in Kamloops, British Columbia, partially blamed the distrust of the "Indian" on the "failure of many of us, in the Department, to understand the Indian's viewpoint and mentality."[40] His sentiments were echoed by the agent in Moose Factory, Ontario, who approved of hiring "educated and well trained" First Nations people in responsible field positions so that "we could more readily come to a better understanding of basic needs and mental processes of their own people."[41] A remarkable letter from Indian Agent F.J.C. Ball, in Vancouver, who had held his post since 1919 and was due to retire, was also critical of branch behaviour. He castigated senior officials who had recently been "treating the Indians as if they [were] employees of the Department."[42] He also criticized an earlier decision to number all Status Indians for efficiency, which had hurt their pride, arguing that "we are not here to be efficient office people only." In recognizing that IAB policies and administration were demeaning and made ill use of the very people they were designed to help, these field personnel accepted First Nations people at a more human level than had previously been voiced in the official image.

Looking beyond their own activities, two field officers found part of the cause of the Indian problem in general societal attitudes and prejudice toward the First Nations. The lack of confidence among their wards was attributed by one agent to "the quite natural reaction of the Indian to this exploitation through past years, and the arrogant superiority shown towards him by so many Whites."[43] In Port Arthur, Ontario, the official linked the Indian problem to discrimination by provincial laws and regulations in commercial fishing, forestry, and mining: "The Indians cannot understand why the white man should be given much greater privileges than he ... In many cases, the Indian has been treated unfairly, and it is very difficult to keep him from being suspicious of, and distrusting, the white man."[44] There was little the agents could do about such problems, except hope that the level of racism and indifference in Canadian society would diminish in the future.

Most of the field staff's explanations, thus far, had blamed the shortcomings of the "Indian," society, and, to a considerable degree, their own organizations' policies and activities. However, a small minority of the responses also raised systemic issues that challenged the underlying raison d'être of the IAB and the essence of its program. For instance, two Ontario Indian Agents expressed doubts about isolating the First Nations on reserves. The official from Desoronto said: "I do consider that too much segregation on Reserves under the provisions of the Indian Act, as now constituted, too much inter-marriage, lack of contact with other citizens of the country, to be harmful rather than beneficial to Indians and is retarding their advance to obtain qualifications that will eventually fit them for enfranchisement to accept full Canadian citizenship."[45] J.A. Marleau, from Sturgeon Falls, believed that "Indian" students should go to school with their Euro-Canadian counterparts, as "these children get much more out of mixing with whites than they do segregated on the reserve."[46] Success with shaping the "Indian" child was a matter of extreme importance. Most agents would have agreed with Marleau that "for the average Indian of fifty years of age or more the case is hopeless, but the younger generation, through mixing with whites at school, work, sports, also reading and listening to the radio, are much more amenable to advancement." Originally, the reserve had been intended as a protective measure so that the "Indian" could be tutored in civilized behaviour, safe from manipulation and exploitation by unscrupulous whites. However, these letters mark some of the first indications that branch personnel were considering a termination of the First Nations' relationship with the government, such as was pursued in the United States after 1953.[47]

Others believed that their wards' problems sprang from a lack of consideration for their cultures and ways of doing things; in the words of the Indian Agent from Portage la Prairie, Manitoba, "pride of race and tradition has never been instilled in the Indian."[48] Another individual went further, expressing his belief that the branch should reconsider the "ignoring of Indian customs and traditions ... The Indians, as all native races, have certain ways of doing things which appear haphazard to us, especially in dealings among themselves regarding property, land, etc., but it is surprising how well their unbusinesslike [sic] methods work, where strictly legal methods cause confusion, resentment and unrest."[49] Such suggestions flew in the face of the whole purpose of the Indian Affairs Branch and much of

Canadian Indian policy, which had sought to stamp out the First Nations' culture and "haphazard" ways and to replace them with an idealized version of Euro-Canadian values and practices.

Finally, a number of responses suggested that the government had created the very dependency it hoped to correct; as one agent politely stated, "the Indians have been relieved of many responsibilities, which perhaps has not been a kindness to him."[50] The IAB had gradually assumed greater and greater control over the day-to-day lives of the First Nations: their business practices, their spending habits, their political lives, their social activities, their movements, and even their morality. In so doing, some field personnel argued that the branch had become too invasive and autocratic in exercising its power, thus stifling Native people's scope for independent action and thought. One West Coast agent argued that "too much has been done *for* the Indian; not enough *with* him."[51] This was a repudiation of the coercive elements of the directed-civilization program. However, as will be seen later, this did not mean that they were prepared to limit their supervision and control of First Nations activities; indeed, dichotomously, most wished to reaffirm or even expand their capacities. In the context of government-fostered dependency, the field staff praised the initiatives promised by the minister and suggested some of their own that might help to foster the gospel of self-help.

The diverse nature of many of the explanations for the "Administrative Indians'" suspicion of government and lack of ambition might create a misleading impression that the departmental image had suddenly fragmented. However, this was not necessarily the case. The large majority of letters from Indian Agents and Inspectors articulated an image of their charges conforming fairly closely to the "Administrative Indian" of the prewar and war years. Moreover, all but a few of the explanations critical of the branch and past policy were precursors to technocratic solutions that sought to improve upon how they did their jobs. Only a tiny fraction raised the spectre that something might be wrong with the very nature of Canada's Indian policy or with the IAB's daily practice. Arguably, this variety of responses indicated a loss of the discipline that had marked the official representations of the First Nations previously. Like the "Public Indian," which was riddled with ambiguities and inconsistencies, the cohesive "Administrative Indian" now exhibited its own quirks and contradictions. It seems likely that this change appeared partly in response to the changes in the senior personnel. The confidence that many field personnel expressed in the new director, R.A. Hoey, and particularly the open and frank nature of the minister's circular letter, created a novel environment of candour. Whether this degree of dissent had existed previously is not clear, but if it had, it was largely muzzled by the strongly centralized and rigidly hierarchical structure of the bureaucracy as well as by the culture of conformity within the organization.

The nature of Glen's requests provoked responses that reveal the field personnel's vision for the future direction of Canadian Indian policy. The majority of letters agreed that "the Indian is capable of great and lasting improvement," but beyond this basic affirmation of their mission, the field staff differed over the prospects of success and the goals attainable.[52] For a quarter of respondents, the war had made an appreciable impact on their wards' progress.[53] Some remained wedded to the conviction that assimilation could and should happen. Others would only venture that advancement, improvement, or progress might be achieved through better funding and administrative reform. Overall, there was a notable slackening of the missionary zeal that had previously motivated the IAB in its quest to assimilate the "Administrative Indian."

Only a few agents actually stated what they perceived the final goal of their mission ought to be, and all who did were essentially in agreement. The goal was articulated as full citizenship by some and as assimilation by others but was predicated on fostering self-reliance and eliminating indigenous dependence on the government.[54] The agent from Charlottetown conveyed the basic message, with its overtones of paternalism, claiming that "the Indian in order to survive must become a self-supporting reliable Canadian citizen."[55] The wording used by a Saskatchewan agent was almost identical: He argued that the branch needed to assist "these people to become decent self-supporting citizens."[56] The use of the words "reliable" and "decent" is noteworthy because their presence implied the lack of these qualities in the contemporary "Indian," betraying a strong degree of continuity in the "Administrative Indian" despite its new variability. Other agents constructed the end goal as assimilation, as "the absorption of [a] minority group into the body politic."[57] A.D. Moore, from Desoronto, seemed confident about the outcome: "Considering that the Indian population is 125,000 in a Canadian population of approximately 12,000,000, it would not appear too big a task for this country to absorb the entire Indian population within the space of four or five generations, in the same manner as it absorbs European races."[58] Thus, when they addressed the issue, the field personnel remained consistent in their belief that assimilation remained the logical goal to end the Indian problem and the best option for all concerned.

Moore was not alone is his faith that the IAB could achieve its purpose. Two agents assured the minister that they made it a practice to "try to impress upon the Indian that the officials are endeavouring to help them conduct their affairs only until such time as they are in a position where help is no longer needed" and that the temporary nature of the assistance provided did not "imply on the part of the government a responsibility for [the

"Indians'"] upkeep."[59] Some assumed that assimilation was in a sense natural and inevitable. One agent stated, "let us try and educate our Indians and the rest, by proper guidance from the Department, will come by itself."[60] It was difficult for IAB personnel to understand that First Nations people might not actually want to assimilate, and they felt sure that if the impediments could just be removed, the process would resume its logical course. However, these were merely a tiny minority; the majority of responses were not quite so sanguine.

No other letter offered the same degree of certainty about assimilation or optimism about the readiness of some indigenous communities to graduate from their status as wards as did that of A.D. Moore, mentioned above. He alone, among all the field personnel who responded, suggested that "in the not too distant future, all Indians will obtain full citizenship, and segregating Indians on Reserves will be abolished entirely."[61] From his perspective, "many of the Indians, including all Service men, of our Southern Reserves are, at the present time, better qualified for full Canadian citizenship than are a good many of the foreign peoples that enjoy the privilege." Moore argued that once the improvements proposed in the minister's letter were instituted and "the Reserves brought on a parity to adjoining municipalities, possibly within 10 to 20 years or so, that a Board of Inquiry be instituted to investigate and report to the Government on the advisibility [sic] of enfranchising, or giving full Canadian citizenship, to all Indians in Ontario south of the 45th Parallel." This policy was then to be extended to "the Indians of the more remote sections of the country ... when their state of advancement warrants such action." Moore's opinions diverged sharply from those of his colleagues in the field although they matched quite closely those of the branch secretary, T.R.L. MacInnes. Speaking before the House Committee on Reconstruction and Re-establishment on 18 May 1944, MacInnes created a bit of a furor among First Nations people across the country and earned reproach from his superiors for suggesting that Status Indians in organized districts ought to be "divorced from the reserve system entirely – put on their own."[62] Such sentiments were radical by the standards of the IAB in 1946. Most still held strongly to an image of the "Indian" as too backward, lazy, stubborn, and childlike to accept such an acceleration of the assimilation agenda.

More common by far was a tendency to formulate vague, limited, or short-term goals. Generally, this was in reference to a specific policy that would "further the education and welfare of our Indian population," "improve his lot," and lead to "advancement" or "progress."[63] For instance, in advocating a policy of increased interaction between First Nations and white children in schools, R. Howe, from Vanderhoof, British Columbia, argued that "contact with whites hastens progress and greatly improves their mode of living."[64] Another official wrote that "with hard work, sufficient help, careful planning and practical consideration of our many and peculiar problems that will arise from time to time, I am sure the coming year will see further advancement in the betterment of the people with whom we are work-ing."[65] The majority of field personnel seemed unwilling or unable to con-ceive of a goal beyond the immediate and open-ended improvement of their charges, although most refrained from explicitly declaring that they were skeptical of achieving the IAB's stated aim.

Two of the Indian Agents, however, indicated their satisfaction with the current rate of progress exhibited by the "Indian" population and warned that to accelerate the process might prove counterproductive.[66] The agent in Duck Lake, Saskatchewan, opined:

> We must bear in mind that our Indians are still in a transitory stage in comparison with present modern civilization and it can be said that the Indian has improved his living condition and adapted himself to our way of life in a shorter space of time than in comparison with our ancestors, especially in view of the fact Western Indians have only in a short space of time (Approximately 150 years) adopted our way of life and are finding some difficulty adapting themselves at this time. It is impossible to expect, overnight as it were, changes in their way of life and it would also prove disastrous to the Indian Race were they to change their way of life as quickly as a few men, especially in this province, believe it can be done.[67]

However, most others did not show such contentment with the status quo.

Even such muted aspirations as they expressed were not expected to be easily achieved. Letter after letter in the Glen correspondence complained that the results of their efforts were "at times very discouraging" and ac-knowledged that the task of bettering the "Indian" would be a long one requiring hard work, perseverance, and patience.[68] Simply renewing the First Nations' trust in the branch, in the words of one agent, would "not be accomplished immediately," as it was something that would "have to be sown, nurtured and grown over a period of time."[69] Similarly, increasing the economic wellbeing on reserves was also expected to be difficult: "I have no Illusion [sic] that this raising of the standard of living etc. is going to be either easy or of short duration; but feel sure that after two or three generations have had the benefit of education and improved medical care, we will then be able to see some worth while results for the work that has been expended."[70] The agent from the Griswold Agency in Manitoba pre-cisely summed up the common sense of most field personnel when he wrote: "Our hope undoubtedly lies with the boys and girls. We may by intensive thorough training give them a different outlook on life and a different sense of values, but I am convinced the change will be slow and will re-quire patience and perseverance. Leadership in thought, in work, and in amusement is necessary, but to overcome indifference, indolence, distrust and natural inbred desires is a real task, and one that only years of relentless work will change."[71] Few of the IAB personnel who responded to the minister's letter seemed to envision a place for the "Indian" in postwar Canada significantly different from the place the First Nations already occupied. Instead, they could articulate only incremental improvements in the "Indian's" condition and vague progress with no end in sight.

In the Glen correspondence, field personnel suggested a wide range of possible solutions to the First Nations' problems, but running throughout the responses was a concern with the power relations between themselves and their charges. For instance, the primary rationale for expanding the staff in the agencies was to insure that adequate supervision of reserve activities could be maintained. The IAB's fixation with its authority was so inextricably interwoven into the IAB structure and purpose that it coloured almost every solution proposed.

The wartime constraints on labour had left the branch lacking agents, farm instructors, teachers, medical personnel, and other support staff, which, when combined with the rapidly increasing indigenous population, left the IAB bureaucracy stretched to the limit of its capacities. "We in the Field service feel our offices are understaffed and the reserves under our supervision are in some instances (due to increasing Indian population) without proper supervision and proper attention cannot be given to individual Indian problems arising from time to time due to overworked field staff with the results that plans and organization work amongst the Indians is not being followed up in the proper manner to produce results."[72] A number of the responses to Glen's letter advised that the future plans of the branch ought to include significant hiring. However, it was the agents' justification that was enlightening. Whether they were talking about schools, commercial fishing, or agriculture, more help was desired because "such work requiring as it does, daily encouragement and constant supervision, can only be attempted on widely scattered reserves, with adequate help."[73] The assimilation mission required the continuous surveillance and direction of all reserve activities. The consequences of this lack of control through inadequate staffing were serious, as one agent with thirty-two years' experience made clear in his letter's closing sentence: "I know from practical experience what can be accomplished by Indians under suitable guidance and I have seen failure through lack of supervision and encouragement."[74]

The paternalistic theme of supervision and guidance was a constant in the field staffs' reaction to three of Glen's suggestions for transferring more responsibilities to their charges: first, allowing the political organization of the First Nations to proceed; second, instituting reserve advisory boards to care for and operate community buildings; and third, hiring Native people to work in the IAB bureaucracy. All these proposals required IAB personnel to surrender a measure of their control over their wards. Only a single agent openly disagreed with one of Glen's ideas, and even he did not dismiss it out of hand, accepting that "Indians" should be employed in the future. But in his estimation, "the time has not yet arrived when employment of Indians in administration of their own affairs will meet with the approval of the Indians and will cause jealousy and incompetance [sic] in the administration of their affairs."[75] Aside from this bold individual, no one spoke directly against the minister's proposals, but only a very few were willing to support them unequivocally.[76]

More commonly, the field personnel acknowledged the benefits of the three ideas, while advising caution and providing caveats. For instance, many agents were willing to accept the setting up of advisory councils to run community halls for public functions; indeed, many reserves already had such structures. As one individual noted, "all the villages in this Agency have pretentious halls for public use, but in every case lack proper supervision and organizational guidance."[77] Another Indian Agent would agree to this suggestion on the condition that "the hall should be supervised and it should be given for socials or meetings only on the condition that it will afterwards be scrubbed and made clean."[78] The response to the idea of permitting Native political organization was similar. The senior field officer from the Fisher River Agency in Manitoba was "of the opinion that such organizations, if competently guided in the right channels, could accomplish much for the general advancement of the Indian peoples."[79] Another respondent agreed that "a good organisation can be useful to the Indians" but warned that "a badly officered one could be an embarrassment to the Department."[80] In all cases, the field personnel expressed reservations and argued that such policies would be successful only if they could provide the leadership and organizational ability that they found lacking in the "Administrative Indian."

At the heart of the field staffs' hesitancy about allowing these activities, even if supervised, was an apprehension about, and distrust of, the type of "Indian" that would be selected to lead these endeavours. J.L. Bryant, from Kamsack, Saskatchewan, counselled against too hastily hiring First Nations people to work in the branch, insisting that the process "should be very gradual" and that due care be "exercised to get the right men."[81] The concern was even more acute in the case of encouraging their charges to organize. One field officer argued that "much care would have to be taken in choice of the right type of men to represent the reserves" because "it has been my experience and I think that of other Agents that the men most willing to accept such positions are not the most suitable for such appointments."[82] One agent admitted that the branch had "in the past, looked with suspicion upon Indian organisations, probably because we felt that the key men were self-seekers, who were doing more harm than good."[83] But having followed a policy of opposing and stigmatizing First Nations leaders and organizations for so long, most agents were clearly uneasy about encouraging such efforts, fearing that "in the wrong hands they could become a menace."[84]

Somewhat surprisingly, many responses to Glen's letter demonstrated a similar dubious reaction to the rather innocuous measure of advisory boards. The agent in Birtle, Manitoba, claimed that they would only work well "if we had the right Indians on them, but likely they would elect some agitators to the said boards, and if so we would get nowhere."[85] The field officer in Portage la Prairie provided his assessment and a potential solution to the problem.

> Advisory Boards are workable. The Indians on the board would have to be carefully chosen; and I would suggest that the choice be made by the Indian Agent. The Indians chosen would also have to have the confidence of the Indians also. If the members of the board were chosen by the Indians, the non-progressive Indian, who is not afraid to ask for "hand-outs" would be chosen. However, if the board was chosen by the agent, the Indians would soon fall in line behind a board that had their confidence.[86]

IAB personnel rejected and feared indigenous leaders who they could not adequately control, who might not agree with the assimilation project, and who could embarrass the branch. What they wanted was to ensure that "the better class of Indian," those more inclined to assimilation and more amenable to their direction, attained the positions of leadership in these organizations and on advisory boards.[87] The answer was to increase the Indian Agent's power to regulate the political and social activities of First Nations communities.

This preoccupation with control in the Glen correspondence was evident across a broad range of issues beyond those already discussed. On a macro level, several agents suggested that the IAB ought to seize more complete control of Indian education and health services. One officer went so far as to argue that "all matters, health, etc., more so in the field should be 100 percent a matter for this 'Branch,' "because provincial administrators did not have the requisite knowledge and experience of Native people.[88] At a more finite level, field personnel wanted the ability to manage their charges' monetary habits and business transactions: In the words of a Manitoban official, "some control of their earnings would be beneficial."[89] This was not new: During the war, the IAB had managed to get the Department of National Defence to send First Nations soldiers' Dependants' Allowance cheques to the respective Indian Agents, who could then manage them for their spendthrift charges.[90] The establishment of family-allowance payments to indigenous people provided much the same opportunity to the field personnel.[91] One agent wished that a full-time social worker could be employed on each reserve "to supervise the expenditure of the monies."[92] A relocation policy was proposed by the official on Prince Edward Island that would concentrate all First Nations people in a central location because, in their scattered communities, it was "difficult at times to exercise control over them."[93] A final example was the rationale used by the agent from the Peigan Agency to support his case for higher wages: "When an Indian Agent has to handle Indians who are making from 4 to 5 times as much money as the Agent does, it looks very ridiculous for us not to meet them on a level of one business man with another."[94] The loss of face from the disparity in income undermined the authority of the agent among his charges; from the administrators' viewpoint, this was just one step shy of chaos. These responses highlight the degree to which the maintenance of authority permeated the official language at war's end.

Many of the administrators who advocated that they be given more control, or at least that there be restraints on the power being transferred to the "Indians," were the same individuals who had acknowledged that too much responsibility had been taken from the First Nations in the past and that encouraging the "gospel of self-help" was their primary goal. Even though the diagnoses of the Indian problem contained in the responses to Glen's communiqué recognized faults in the way the Indian administration had been conducted, the field personnel could prescribe only more supervision, more control, and tighter constraints on the scope for independent thought and action among indigenous people. One agent went further than any other, arguing that "since the Indian is considered a minor, he is incapable of spending money for the betterment and advancement of the band ... Officials of the Department should decide what is good and worthwhile if we are to better their condition."[95] Missed, as it always had been in these official discussions, was the irony that the sole means to make the First Nations like everyone else was to differentiate them legislatively, constitutionally, administratively, spatially, and socially – in effect, to make them "Administrative Indians."

What then can be inferred from the Glen correspondence about the state of the "Administrative Indian" at the transition from six years of war to a much anticipated peace? As with much else discussed in this book, the answer to that question is neither simple nor unambiguous. At war's end, there was some discontinuity, which was manifested in the emergence of contradiction and a disappearance of the discipline that had previously marked the official construction of the "Indian." However, these letters also revealed a remarkable continuity in comparison with the transformations in the public image during the same period.

The official image of the "Indian" in 1946 differed from that in evidence during the war years or the pre-war period in two key ways. First, the field personnel of the IAB demonstrated a newfound willingness to look outside the traditional avenues of the "Administrative Indian" in order to explain their failure to achieve the organization's purpose of assimilating the First Nations. In so doing, they exhibited a greater appreciation for the intelligence of Native people and, in some cases, a more respectful assessment of the First Nations' cultural, social, and moral norms and capabilities. Constructing their charges in this way did not fit within the more pejorative framework of the "Administrative Indian"; however, there were limits to these shifting perspectives. None of the agents was entirely consistent in constructing the "Indian" in this new fashion, usually mixing demeaning or paternalistic elements with those that did not fit the official construct. Nor was there a sufficient degree of agreement to constitute the formation of a distinct new image of the "Administrative Indian." Thus what resulted was a complex and contradictory collection of conceptualizations of the "Indian," not unlike the range of inconsistencies always evident in the less cohesive "Public Indian."

The second factor that distinguished the postwar discussions was the clear loss of vigour and optimism for their raison d'être among IAB personnel. Arguably, one of the reasons why more than half the Indian Agents and Inspectors did not answer the minister's circular letter was apathy or cynicism. For the most part, those officials who replied continued to accept that assimilation remained the logical goal for Canadian Indian policy, but there was a noticeable decline in the certainty about the prospects of success. This defeatism emerged clearly in the small number of responses that bothered to mention a final objective. But more striking was the large number who could at most articulate finite and open-ended aspirations to achieve some form of limited progress or improvement. Here, surely, is evidence of the IAB's descent into custodial administration during the middle part of the century, bereft of purpose or hope, mentioned by other commentators on Canadian Indian administration.[96]

Despite the discontinuities, the postwar official "Indian," as revealed by the Glen correspondence, remained intact. Somewhat surprisingly, there was very little evidence of influence from the growing public debate about the Indian problem nor pressure for reform in the field staff's responses. Several agents remarked on the phenomenon of public interest, usually positively, because the minister had mentioned it, but some also expressed their frustrations at public criticisms of their efforts. It was no coincidence that the branch would make its first attempts to formulate a coherent, proactive, and modern public-relations policy over the next few years.[97] While there was some overlap between solutions discussed in the public domain and those presented by Indian Agents, the field personnel represented their own reflections on the impediments to their work and an internal desire for technocratic reform without any direct references to public demands. There was none of the philosophical discussion evident in the public forum; instead, the agents appeared to greet the advent of reconstruction with the hope that it would mean more funds to ease their own administrative concerns. The IAB remained somewhat insulated from the broader trends and pressures of Canadian society, separated by its purpose and intimate contact with First Nations people.

Perhaps most important, the official image was still founded on the continuity of the "Administrative Indian" and the paternalism and power inherent in its construction. All the essential elements of the "Administrative Indian" remained dominant in the language and imagery used by IAB personnel to explain the causes of the Indian problem and permeated their proposed solutions. In the estimation of most of the field personnel, the assimilation program of the branch had stalled at least partly because of flaws in the character, intellect, morals, and culture of the wards under their jurisdiction. Moreover, despite their cautious willingness to transfer more responsibilities to First Nations communities, the field staff's obsession with their own authority remained and, in the minds of some, needed reinforcing. It was the ongoing pervasiveness of the language of control and paternalism that formed the most significant continuity in the Glen correspondence. While the international and national context of Indian Affairs had changed significantly with the end of total war, the dialectical link between the working image of the "Indian" and the branch's relationship with Native people remained much as it had been. Whether the resilience of the "Administrative Indian" could survive the review process of the subsequent years remained to be seen.

6
Into the Arena: Marshalling the Competing Indian Images in Postwar Canada, 1945-48

Following the final defeat of the Axis powers, Canadians did not pause long to celebrate their victory. Though there was an undeniable sense of pride and accomplishment in what the country had done, there was too much to do if they were to win the peace and justify the sacrifice of the war years. Close to a million young men and women, many of whom were still overseas, still wore the uniforms of the armed forces. The country's war industries, which had been churning out bombers, machine guns, and destroyers, had to be transformed and retooled quickly to produce goods suitable for civilian purposes. Housing, which was strictly controlled in major urban centres during the war, was still in critically short supply, and the labour and materials required to correct the problem were themselves largely unavailable. Other painful reminders of wartime's pinch were still evident in the maintenance of rationing and wage and price ceilings. However, the Canadian government was prepared for most of the hurdles ahead, with the massive machinery of reconstruction and rehabilitation already coming up to speed. Despite these other concerns, the issue of the "Indian problem" continued to maintain the high profile it had held in the late stages of the war. The calls for reform, in the House of Commons and in the media, only increased as 1945 turned into 1946.

By the spring of 1946, with a goodly portion of Canadian troops already returned home and the most immediately pressing matters of the transition to peace seemingly well in hand, the issue of what to do about the Indian problem came to the fore of the national agenda. In mid-May, the government created a special joint committee of both the Senate and the House of Commons to hear evidence and make recommendations for the revision of the Indian Act. Some Native organizations and English Canadian social and religious groups had called for a full Royal Commission to investigate the issue and were upset that a mere Parliamentary committee would perform the important task. However, the Special Joint Committee of the Senate and the House of Commons appointed to examine and consider the Indian

Act (hereinafter the SJC) was awarded a broad mandate to hear witnesses and gather evidence. The government motion that created the SJC charged it with examining Indian administration generally and with reporting on the following specifically:

1) Treaty rights and obligations.
2) Band membership.
3) Liability of Indians to pay taxes.
4) Enfranchisement of Indians, both voluntary and involuntary.
5) Eligibility of Indians to vote at dominion elections.
6) The encroachment of white persons on Indian reserves.
7) The operation of Indian day and residential schools.
8) And any other matter or thing pertaining to the social and economic status of Indians and their advancement, which, in the opinion of such a committee should be incorporated in the revised act.[1]

The last point, in particular, gave the committee carte blanche to evaluate the nature and extent of the Indian problem – a process that would take more than two years.

For the purposes of this study, these hearings will be treated as an arena. Into this arena, various groups brought their own images of what the "Indian" was and articulated what they believed the "Indian" ought to become. Like gladiators, these images strove for ascendancy on the floor of the SJC to see which would shape the future of Canada's relationship with the First Nations and be enshrined in legislation. The preceding chapter revealed the postwar "Administrative Indian" that the Indian Affairs Branch would present to the SJC. This chapter will examine the two remaining images of the "Indian" that were brought to the table to contend for the future of Canadian Indian policy.

The two groups that presented their versions of the "Indian" before the SJC were the Canadian public and First Nations people. Various elements of the "Public Indian" entered the fray and are reconstituted here from two main sources: first, from the dozens of briefs and resolutions from various interested groups received by the Indian Affairs Branch or printed in the appendices of the "Minutes of Evidence and Proceedings"; and, second, from the extensive and continuous newspaper coverage of the SJC activities and hearings. One of the truly fascinating aspects of the SJC is that it provides a unique opportunity to explore the First Nations' sense of themselves in the immediate postwar period. This consultation process was the first time that they had been given the chance to present their views before the dominant society in such a public and meaningful fashion. A large number of written briefs were submitted to the committee by Indian bands, tribal councils, chiefs, and Native-rights organizations, revealing both the diversity and the distinctiveness of their ideas about Canadian Indian policy and their own identity.[2]

The following exploration is guided by a series of questions. Did the "Public Indian" still command strong interest and sympathy once the war was over and its immediacy had receded? How did Canadians foresee Native people fitting into Canada's society and state in the years to come? How widespread was the public interest in and sympathy for the "Indian's" plight? To what extent were Canadians listening to the grievances and aspirations of the First Nations? How much unity appeared in the opinions and hopes expressed by First Nations groups? To what extent were Native views formulated using the language and conceptual framework of the dominant society? Were these visions of the future fundamentally in line with, or opposed to, those articulated by Canadians? Was there any evidence of a pan-Indian consciousness forming throughout this period? The answers to these questions will provide a foundation from which to better comprehend the hearings and the process of Canada's collective reassessment of the nation's relationship with its indigenous population.

The Special Joint Committee was called and sat during a period of unprecedented public concern about and involvement in the state of the country's relationship with the First Nations and their standard of living. During the year between V-E Day and J. Allison Glen's resolution in the House of Commons to establish a Parliamentary investigation of the Indian Act, Canadians were confronted regularly with debate on the issue in the media. In addition, the number of letters, briefs, resolutions, and recommendations received by the Indian Affairs Branch suggests that Canadians were discussing the Indian problem privately. Nor did the intensity of public scrutiny of the process and the problem diminish once the government met the demands for a review of Canada's Indian policy and established the SJC. The hearings were attended by Canadian Press reporters as well as by many of the major newspapers' staff reporters in the capital. The result was detailed coverage in all the country's major dailies of virtually every report presented and delegation that attended, with the smaller community papers supplied by wire-service reports. In this diverse and massive amount of material, the "Public Indian" emerges clearly in all its various forms, but the "Indian victim" and the "Indian-at-war" dominate these representations.

The material for the subsequent analysis is drawn from two major sources. The first, the extensive and continuous coverage of the SJC activities available in the nation's print media, was partly collected through the same sampling of papers used in previous chapters but was augmented by two IAB files of clippings collected from across the country by various field personnel. These files are large, containing stories and editorials pertaining to "Indian," IAB, or SJC activities, with coverage of the latter being dominant. The clippings were taken from papers in all provinces, most of which are not included in my own sampling, thus serving to broaden the spectrum of data. Generally speaking, any bias in selection of the stories forwarded to Ottawa by field personnel should be balanced by a tendency to send published material that was either especially complimentary or deemed overly critical of the branch and its work. Beyond the media material, the "Public Indian" can be gleaned from letters and briefs sent by interested Canadians to either the Indian Affairs Branch or the chairman of the SJC. The former are available in IAB correspondence files pertaining to the committee, and the latter appear in the appendices of the "Minutes of Evidence and Proceedings" of the SJC itself. The combination of these sources provides a broad and extensive foundation from which to reconstruct the dominant society's image of the "Indian" and its thoughts on the Indian problem during the country's collective reexamination of the matter.

The most striking feature of the communications received by the SJC and the IAB was the varied nature of the people and groups interested in the Indian problem. Even prior to the establishment of the committee by the government, the IAB was receiving numerous letters from organizations demanding that a Royal Commission review the Indian Act in order to improve the lot of the First Nations. For instance, the Dock and Shipyard Workers Union of Vancouver and District sent a letter to the prime minister fully endorsing the "legitimate demands" of the Native Brotherhood of British Columbia for "a complete revision of the Indian Act."[3] Further, they argued, "in light of the declarations of the Atlantic Charter that it would now be timely to accord our Native Indians equal status with other citizens of Canada." Similar calls were received from pro-Native groups such as the Alberta-based Committee of Friends of the Indians. However, the same sentiments were expressed by a wide range of organizations: by veterans' organizations in Vancouver and Duncan, British Columbia; by the municipal councils in Sudbury and Sault Ste. Marie, Ontario; and by civic-minded associations, such as the Canadian Federation of Home and School and the Social Security Council of Canada.[4] By far the most detailed such communiqué received was from "a small group of interested representative Canadian citizens." These included academics C.W.M. Hart and T.F. MacIlwraith as well as Brig. Oliver M. Martin, an enfranchised Six Nations Indian and magistrate in Toronto, and Mrs. John F. McCay, who had founded the Vancouver Folk Festival.[5]

Once the committee was in session, the already heterogeneous nature of these correspondents was further accentuated by the addition of submissions from the municipal council in Fredericton, New Brunswick, and the Board of Trade in Gogama, Ontario.[6] Beyond these examples, letters and briefs arrived from religious groups of numerous denominations, political associations of various affiliations, veterans' organizations, professional societies, youth groups, and social clubs such as the Calgary branch of the

Canadian Authors' Association.[7] The sheer diversity of agencies demonstrated that the plight of the "Indian" resonated with a multiplicity of Canadians. The content of these submissions ranged from elaborate manifestos to simple statements of support for the SJC's work, from resolutions on specific subjects to more comprehensive schemes for the solution of the Indian problem. Nor were all such submissions written with the sole intent of supporting a new deal for the "Indian."[8] One example was a letter from the secretary of the British Columbia Beef Cattle Growers' Association complaining of the lack of fencing around Indian reserves that allowed non-Native's cattle, grazing on surrounding Crown land, to accidentally trespass on reserve land. This situation put the associations' members at risk of prosecution.[9] Taken as a whole, however, the material submitted to the SJC or sent to the IAB suggests that a large number of Canadians were actively engaged by the Indian problem in the years immediately following the Second World War.

As in the past, the public discussions revealed the usual complex mix of "Indian" images, but the extent of passionate rhetoric being bandied about in relation to the Indian problem tended, if anything, to sharpen the distinctions of the various images. This process was clearly seen in the case of the two most common manifestations: the "Indian victim" and the "Indian-at-war." The former had been steadily gaining ascendancy in the public realm since the final stages of the war, while the latter had briefly disappeared after V-E Day, only to reemerge again by the spring of 1946. The dominance of these two images should not be interpreted as meaning that other Canadian constructions of indigenous people had disappeared. Crime and alcohol stories still appeared regularly in many papers, and the negative contemporary interpretation of the "Indian" was evident, although slight, in briefs received by the SJC.[10] Moreover, the fanciful and trivialized "noble savage" made a comeback in the media coverage of the "Ottawa pow-wow," where "Indian Braves" went on the "warpath," "stalk[ing] MP's in their lair," and aimed "verbal tomahawks" at the government.[11] Such representations suggest that perhaps not all Canadians were comfortable directly confronting the Indian problem even after the war. Nonetheless, the essence of the public discussion of the policy review was dominated by portrayals that emphasized either the wartime contributions of the First Nations or their plight and powerlessness.

Of the two, the "Indian-at-war" was the more prevalent. Editorials, news stories, and briefs addressing the plight of the "Indian" consistently made reference to the wartime efforts of the First Nations and always highlighted Native veterans. For those commentators advocating changes in the country's Indian administration, the memory of First Nations military service formed a central component of their appeal. The British Columbia Indian Art and Welfare Society, in its submission to the SJC, challenged Canadians with the question: "How many ... have realized the quite recent shock experienced by young Indian soldiers on their return to civilian life, to find themselves relegated to the restricted status under which they lived before enlisting to fight overseas shoulder to shoulder with fellow Canadians, in the cause of freedom and equality for all nationalities, for which many gave their lives."[12] The "Indian-at-war" was not always spoken of in as generalized a way. Often it became personalized in the stories of individual veterans, such as the treatment accorded by the *Winnipeg Tribune* to Manitoba First Nations' efforts to organize themselves for their appearance before the SJC in 1947. In two extensive stories run on 4 and 7 December 1946, the paper highlighted the experiences of the spokesperson for the Manitoba Indian Association and the most highly decorated Native soldier of the war, Sgt. Thomas Prince.[13] "Sgt. Tommy Prince, the Scantebury Indian, who spread terror through German and Italian troops in the recent war with his savage attacks and deadly sniping, is now leading fellow treaty Indians down another warpath. They are fighting for many reforms for the Canadian Indian."[14] It was unsurprising that journalists would key in on a high-profile case such as Prince's, but this pattern did not require a famous war hero. Moreover, references to specific soldiers or general military service were included even when they had little to do with the main thrust of the story. For instance, in an article on a First Nations council in Duncan, British Columbia, the last paragraph of a long story noted in passing that the "records of the meeting were taken down by Pte. Elliott, of the Canadian Army, a member of the Somenos band who served with distinction overseas, and fought throughout the entire Italian campaign."[15] Little else needed to be said to touch Canadians' sense of obligation and appreciation for the Native war effort.

Not to be left out of the public debates, the picture of the powerless "Indian" living in abysmal conditions and crushed under the weight of an indifferent society, a parsimonious government, and an oppressive, incompetent administration was frequently conjured up by commentators. Few put the case as strongly as did the Vancouver branch of the Canadian Civil Liberties Union in its brief to the SJC: "The Canadian Indians are a backward and a depressed race whose morale is shattered and whose self-confidence is lost. Educationally they are either illiterate or little better, and economically they are incompetent and dependent. For this condition the Indians are not to blame. Whenever and wherever they were first encountered by white men no one of these descriptions applied."[16] The key elements of the "Indian victim" remained. The fault for their condition lay not with themselves but instead at the feet of the dominant society and its government. Guilt over this circumstance wracked many Canadians, undercutting what they believed themselves and their society to represent. One letter to the editor that appeared in the *Winnipeg Free Press* struck a righteous note: "To have taken the Indian lands is bad enough, then to put the Indians back on reservations and segregate them is worse. But to crown it all; to call ourselves a Christian nation and send them missionaries is the height of hypocrisy. Truly we need to set our own house in order, if we are true Christians in Canada, and not only repent our sins, but rectify them."[17] The "Indian victim" was perhaps the best tool to mobilize public support for Indian-policy reform because it tapped into the latent collective sense of guilt in Canada over the displacement of the "Indian."

Significantly, these two images of the "Public Indian" were frequently paired together, particularly by proponents of Indian-policy reform. An editorial that appeared in the *Saint John Telegraph Journal* in July 1946 demonstrates this phenomenon:

> If anything further were needed, the war effort made by the original Canadians should have earned them a right to a hearing. They served well both in the armed services and as part of Canada's labour force. But even without this war service, Indian grievances alone should have been sufficient to arouse public attention ... They are not given the franchise, however, but they are required to accept military service and pay income tax ... Those remaining on reservations, "the treaty Indians," complain of inadequate medical care, improper food, lack of housing and violations of their fishing and hunting rights. That these complaints have foundation in fact may be gathered from statistics like the following: infant mortality rate of 400 per thousand compared with fifty-two per thousand among the white population; 732 deaths per thousand from T.B. compared with fifty one [sic] among whites.[18]

Similarly, the joint submission of the Canadian Welfare Council and the Canadian Association of Social Workers to the SJC combined the two images in a succinct manner: "The Indian population, by virtue of its special status, has been precluded from benefit under all types of social legislation with the exception of family allowances. The Indians have assumed responsibility as citizens both in World War I and World War II and have made a valuable contribution to national defence."[19] Juxtaposing the "Indian victim" with the "Indian-at-war" so sharply was designed to shock readers and make plain what Native sympathizers saw as the essence of the injustice of the First Nations' plight: denying them the rights and privileges of citizenship while at the same time forcing them to accept the most onerous duties citizenship entailed in military service and taxation.

In underpinning the call for reform, both "Indian" images played a dual role. The "Indian victim" served to tap into the collective guilt about the historically poor treatment accorded the First Nations by forcing Canadians to face the racism, intolerance, and indifference in their own society and administration. Equally important, it exonerated the "Indian" for those same conditions, allowing the First Nations to be classed, in a sense, as deserving poor who were worthy of pity and help. The "Indian-at-war" most obviously associated the reform of Canada's Indian policy with the potent emotion of the debt owed to First Nations people for their sacrifices for the collective good in wartime. Beyond this well-established role, the "Indian-at-war" also served a new purpose: It conveyed a sense of promise for the future, of what the "Indian" was capable of achieving when given the opportunity.[20] Surely, if they could demonstrate civic virtues through giving to the Red Cross, buying Victory Bonds, and excelling in military service, then they could become productive, full-fledged citizens in Canada's new order. Previously, the "Public Indian" had always been constructed as either a historical or a contemporary creature. However, these manifestations had said little about the future, either because Canadians believed that the "Indian" was a vanishing race and the Indian problem would die with them or because the immediacy of the war prohibited much attention to the future. Nevertheless, at the peculiar moment when the SJC sat in session, Canada was not only coming to the realization that the indigenous population was growing strongly, but was also prepared to look forward and come to grips with the difficult issues involved.[21]

Canadians for the most part held similar views about the appropriate solutions to the Indian problem, although not necessarily about the final goal. The principles for which the nation had fought formed the foundation for the proposals that the dominant society produced. This foundation was essential because the status and marginalization of First Nations people were arguably the clearest contradictions of the freedom, equality, and democracy that English Canadians believed their country ought to embody. These sentiments appeared in an introspective *Globe and Mail* editorial that was picked up and reprinted in Saint John, New Brunswick. Expressing some encouragement at the appointment of the SJC, the writer was nonetheless appalled that the evidence already presented

> describ[ed] restraint of freedom and maladministration in the Indian Affairs Branch, [which] is a poor commentary upon our appreciation of democracy. The people of this country are quick to rally against injustice to their Japanese, Italian or German minorities and to ill-treatment of similar groups in other lands. We are inclined to deplore the treatment of coloured people in the Southern United States; we are eager to spring to the defence of the Jews in Europe. But we are strangely reluctant to gaze inward for even a momentary consideration of our obligation to the race to which we owe the most.[22]

All critics agreed with the need for improvements to health care, education, social security, and economic opportunity for Native people, but beyond that, "few [would] deny that the time ha[d] come for a greater equality of rights for Canadian Indians."[23] The Vancouver branch of the

Civil Liberties Union went further, setting forth the principle that "all members of our democratic society are entitled to, and should be granted, the same rights and liberties."[24] A new tendency to refer to First Nations people as the "Original Canadians," as "Canada's First Citizens," or as the "original owners of the country" all served to legitimize this desire to extend citizenship to the "Indian."[25]

Most Canadians seemed ready to accept that the time had come to grant the "Indian" citizenship and equality. Such was the demand of the Co-operative Commonwealth Youth Movement, the National Council of the Young Women's Christian Association, the Oak Bay Liberal Association, and the Convention of Baptist Churches of British Columbia.[26] One veterans' group phrased its views in a resolution that called on the government "to amend the Indian Act to bring all North American Indians who have served their country Overseas, outside the scope and provisions of the Indian Act, thereby placing them in the position of free men."[27] Many were unaware of the complexities involved in making Status Indians into citizens or even whether they desired such status. Certainly, few demonstrated the perception of one writer who recognized that to "remedy such contradiction of modern concepts of human rights, while yet preserving the essence of guarantees embedded in Indian treaties, presents a real challenge to both the Parliamentary committee and the people of Canada."[28] Nor, indeed, was everyone confident that granting citizenship would solve the Indian problem because "our Red people are in a sense *children* and need guidance, instruction on how to live and work. The giving of votes will be of little benefit."[29] Despite this skepticism, the vast majority of public discussion during this period appeared to accept that removing the anomaly of the "Indian's" ward status should be the first and most important step.

More significant divisions appeared in the public debate over the question of the final goal: where the "Indian" should fit into Canadian society. The majority, if they even bothered to articulate the prevailing common sense of the day, assumed that the "Indian" ought to be assimilated into the mainstream of Canadian society. In the opinion of the Canadian Welfare Council and the Canadian Association of Social Workers, "the only defensible goal for a national program must be the full assimilation of Indians into Canadian life."[30] Underlying the certainty in assimilation was a faith that the process was somehow inherently natural, that if only the proper policies and education were provided, the "Indian" would progress up to the necessary standard of civilization. Hand in hand with this conviction went a remarkable sense of optimism that a final solution to the Indian problem was obtainable within a generation or two: "The officially declared objective of the Government of Canada should be the equalization of status between Canadians of whatever ancestry as will entail the disappearance of any specific Indian problem probably within a generation and certainly within half a century."[31] The Indian problem was solvable; it simply required the removal of administrative and financial barriers so that assimilation could resume its inevitable course to the logical destination.

There was a vocal and articulate minority who continued to advocate a process of integration rather than assimilation, although in practice the terminology was loosely applied. The best example of this view is seen in the brief of the Vancouver branch of the Canadian Civil Liberties Union, which argued that there was only one way in which the SJC could produce a "Magna Carta of the Indians": "It must propose a policy and program for the Indian Branch that are directed in a very positive way toward bringing out in the Indians the qualities of independence, initiative, self-respect, responsibility, self-reliance, and, in general, the heightened morale, to the end that, culturally and economically, they shall soon become capable of sustaining themselves in Canadian society, and of being assimilated to it."[32] The brief acknowledged that "to many Indians the word 'assimilation' is repugnant because to them it implies the loss of their identity as Indians. As we use it, no such meaning is intended."[33] It then went on to say that,

> in becoming assimilated, the Indians need only to add to the background they already possess, the abilities, outlook and knowledge that are necessary if they are to participate independently and responsibly in Canadian life. But we are convinced that in the final analysis, the Indians really have no choice. They must become assimilated (in the sense that we use the word) if they are to survive. History shows what will be their own historical fate. Unless, individually, they are able to adapt themselves to the society in which they exist, they are doomed to racial submergence.

Some advocates of integration were willing to accept that the "Indian" could continue to hold the benefits and protections of the Indian Act and their treaties as well as be granted all the rights of citizenship. However, others assumed that Native people might maintain some benign cultural traits and communal connections, as did Highland Scots for instance, but only after surrendering their special constitutional status. During this period, Canadians were more dedicated to equality and the notion of universality, as enshrined in the development of social-security measures such as family allowances, than at any other period in the country's history. In such a cultural environment, the idea of differentiated citizenship was not a concept likely to be greeted with widespread acceptance. In April 1947, the *Calgary Albertan* printed the following anecdote:

> "Rodeo somewhere?" the black-faced porter asked as nine Indians clambered aboard an eastbound C.P.R. train Friday night. But the Indians were not on their way to a rodeo. They took with them no feathered headdresses,

buckskin jackets or sham war paint. For the first time in 70 years the Indians were on their way to Ottawa – to make history.[34]

Much could be drawn from this quotation, but it is the final three words that are especially striking. Thus far this study has been about English Canadians making the "Indian," and in a sense making history, largely insulated from input from Native people. For the most part, the dominant society had not been especially interested in what the First Nations thought themselves to be or what they aspired to become. English Canada wielded sufficient power in the relationship to ignore that which did not fit their conceptualizations of the "Indian" of fulfil their own needs. However, the peculiar context of the late 1940s would make this wilful ignorance increasingly untenable. Following the war, several factors converged that made it impossible for Canadian society to disregard the "Indian" any longer: a growing awareness of the neglect that had characterized the country's treatment of the First Nations, the memory of their contributions to the war effort, and the profound desire to win the peace. In no small measure this recognition was the product of the publicity accorded to an increasingly active and vocal First Nations political movement.

Native people, in the war's wake, were themselves unwilling to have their fate dictated. There seems to have been some unrest and an increasing degree of excitement on a number of Indian reserves across the country, spurred on by the promise of reform and improved conditions. Nor were IAB personnel happy with what they viewed as agitation and the change in attitude among their charges.[35] The agent on Walpole Island, Ontario, noted that the "unrest of the Reserve at the present time is without a doubt the greatest it has been during the past 16 years," while his counterpart in Fort Frances, Ontario, complained that "the Indians [sic] manner is changing in demanding certain concessions since they have been receiving so much publicity through the press."[36] On one reserve in Ontario, the agent's quarterly report at the end of 1945 complained that "there is also a noticeable change in the attitude of the Indians towards Departmental Officials and the Indians quite often express the opinion that they are dominated by rules, regulations and decisions that have not been fair to the Indians and made without being given any voice to express approval or disapproval, who maintain they are being treated more like a conquered minority." This agent also noted the "marked feeling of unrest among the Indians of Tyendinaga Reserve, which, in part, can be attributed to a participation in the activities of the North American Indian Brotherhood and other Indian organizations."[37] These communiqués suggest that IAB personnel were still not at ease with the idea of allowing their charges to organize, but more important they reveal how intensely engaged indigenous people were in the reform proceedings and in preparing for their part in them.

Central in articulating and publicizing the First Nations' grievances and convictions were the numerous political associations that had formed in recent years. During the war years, sparked by outrage at being deemed liable to national registration, conscription, and unprecedented taxation, they had begun to organize themselves in earnest in many parts of the country despite administrative opposition. This process accelerated once the government's intention to form the SJC was announced in December 1945.[38] Generally speaking, these organizations reflected the typical pattern of early First Nations political organizations.[39] They tended to spring up in reaction to a perceived threat or crisis, such as conscription, or in response to an opportunity like the SJC and often disbanded or lost momentum once the event had passed. In addition, these associations tended to be local or regional in character, as tribal and religious factionalism combined with difficulties in communication and lack of financial resources to inhibit more widespread activities. In some cases, the aid and support of sympathetic non-Natives was essential to these formations, as it was to forming the provincial organizations in Alberta and Saskatchewan.[40] Finally, the majority were reformist rather than revolutionary in intent; they sought to alter the existing administrative, legislative, and constitutional structures and to increase the services and benefits provided them by the government.[41] These organizations and their leaders would be critically important in articulating the First Nations' views of Canada's Indian policy and administration and in conveying these views to the dominant society.

The wave of organizing was noticeable during the war, when already existing organizations, like the Native Brotherhood of British Columbia and the Indian Association of Alberta, accelerated their activities.[42] In addition, a number of new organizations sprang up in Saskatchewan, Quebec, and Nova Scotia.[43] Perhaps the most significant of the new collectivities to emerge during the war, and the only one with national aspirations, was the North American Indian Brotherhood (NAIB), which was formed in 1943. This organization was led by the flamboyant, well-educated, and eloquent Andrew Paull, a staunch opponent of anything resembling assimilation. Paull had a long track record as an advocate for First Nations rights as well as much experience dealing with the media.[44] Ironically, the SJC's policy of soliciting Native representatives by province served to foster the creation of several additional important provincial organizations in Ontario, Manitoba, Saskatchewan, and British Columbia.[45] Whether the dominant society was prepared or not, the war and the postwar reform process had provided the First Nations with the catalyst to organize, the confidence to assert their right to a new deal, and the moral currency to gain a sympathetic hearing.

In all, the SJC received 150 submissions from Native sources in response to a letter soliciting their views circulated by Norman Lickers, the SJC's legal counsel.[46] The submissions originated from Native-rights associations, tribal leaders, band councils, and social organizations from the Pacific Coast to Quebec and from the Mackenzie River Valley to the Grand River Valley. Some were no more elaborate than the pointed and succinct letter from James Mitchall, acting chief of the Siccameen Band in Hammond, British Columbia, who stated:

I want to remain an Indian.
I do not want to pay taxes.
I want to remain on the old Indian Act.
I have nothing against any school.
I do not want white people on our reserve.[47]

Others, such as the Indian Association of Alberta and the Mississauga of the Credit River, submitted much longer and more technical and legalistic written briefs that suggested a sophisticated blueprint for the renewal of Canada's Indian administration and relationship with the First Nations or that critiqued shortcomings in the existing Act on a section-by-section basis.[48]

Unfortunately, there is a problem with a significant minority of these submissions. Letters from Indian band councils and chiefs in widely scattered parts of Canada bore identical wording in some of their answers. These were uniformly from predominately Roman Catholic First Nations communities, to whom "form letters" were apparently provided to be signed by the chiefs and councillors and forwarded to Ottawa.[49] It is uncertain how much weight to lend to these submissions. The wording does vary somewhat; there seems to have been several forms to each answer, and each contained some local issues of concern. But it is not clear whether the variations in wording accurately reflect the opinion of the bands. Nevertheless, even if these are disregarded, there is more than enough evidence to reconstruct the distinct and complex sense of self articulated by First Nations people.

It was the very complexity and diversity of First Nations peoples, cultures, and aspirations that proved surprising and, at times, baffling to the dominant society. The contentious issues being addressed by the SJC revealed strong opinions and deep divisions among, as well as within, Native communities. Perhaps most controversial and divisive were the issues of liquor regulations and education. Access to alcohol was all the more evocative in light of the experiences of Native veterans, who had enjoyed the same privileges as their non-Native comrades in the military during the war but who risked arrest upon their return. Many briefs expressed a desire to see the special regulations regarding Indians removed from the Act and asked that "the Indians be granted the privileges and be governed by the same laws and regulations as the Whites."[50] However, the emotions and sordid history that cloaked the "liquor question" drew strong opposition from other bands, such as those living in the Duck Lake Agency in

Saskatchewan, who "view[ed] with alarm attempts made by whites to induce our people or condone Indians who are addicted to the consumption of intoxicants. Our treaties contained a promise that no intoxicants would be permitted on our reservations and we wish to adhere to the regulations."[51]

The split was even sharper in the discussions about education because all parties recognized its centrality in any program to improve the First Nations' living conditions and economic prospects. In particular, this division can be seen in the debate over whether to have the churches continue their prominent role in providing education to the First Nations or to replace the existing program with a nondenominational one along the lines of the standard provincial systems.[52] Almost half of the First Nations briefs were "very much opposed to the public school systems of education being foisted upon us."[53] A majority agreed with the brief from the Union of Saskatchewan Indians, who argued that, "though parochial schools have contributed much to the education of the Indians, the time has now come when it is necessary to separate education from religion."[54] While there was greater agreement on many other issues among the First Nations, the range of opinions was wide, and there were always exceptions to the rule.

At times, Native people articulated their views using language and concepts similar to those of the dominant society. In part, the First Nations had to couch their cases in terms that the dominant society could understand. A good example was the submission from the Big Trout Lake Band, administered by the Sioux Lookout Agency, Ontario, which concluded that "the above would be our idea of helping the Indians help themselves with what they have."[55] The phrase "help the Indians to help themselves" was adopted as a slogan by the SJC and summed up much of the dominant society's hopes for the reform process.[56] However, even though First Nations' briefs revealed similar terminology, the meaning could and did differ from that understood by the dominant society. Terms like democracy, freedom, progress, citizenship, and equality were broad enough to accommodate a multiplicity of meanings, and indigenous leaders and spokespersons used such language almost as liberally as their Canadian counterparts. The brief from the Aboriginal Natives of the Fraser Valley and Interior Tribes of British Columbia argued that "the time has come for the recognition of us Natives as people with equal intelligence and integrity, eligible to exercise equal status of full citizenship privileges." But, whereas these words for Canadians presupposed assimilation and the disappearance of special "Indian" rights and status, in this brief there was no incompatibility between exercising citizenship privileges and "maintaining all our traditions, aboriginal rights, interests and benefits."[57]

Moreover, the First Nations' briefs presented claims in terms that would resonate in English Canada's collective psyche in order to win sympathy and support for their cause. This does not imply that First Nations people were cynical or insincere in the beliefs they expressed, but they certainly recognized that the environment was ripe for Indian-policy reform and developed the most effective lines of argument to sway their non-Aboriginal neighbours. Thus protests against having to pay taxes were sometimes framed in reference to that classic tenet of British justice: "no taxation without representation."[58] Or, more commonly, First Nations groups harnessed their general appeal for a new deal to the emotion of reconstruction through references to their loyalty and their military service during the wars. In their demand for recognition of their status as sovereign allies of the British Crown, the Hereditary Chiefs of the Iroquois on the Oka Reserve near Montreal pulled at the heartstrings of Canadians in this manner:

> Lest we forget now and forever that in Europe and Pacific battlefields the flowers bloom between the crosses, row on row, and in other places, lie many of our Indian braves. They went through the stench of hell fire, met the onslaught of ingenious instruments of modern warfare, the insidiousness of poison gas and other diabolical weapons of death. They lie in honoured death that the British flag may never fall, the sun never set on the British Empire, so that Britannia rules the waves and that the escutcheon of the House of Windsor be not desecrated ... Also that some day their laws and rights and sovereignty of their own people might be honoured and respected.[59]

Conjuring the haunting and familiar cadence of John McCrae's poem "In Flanders Fields" alongside the stark imagery of death and fervent loyalty produced a potent combination of imagery not easily shrugged off by English Canadians in the immediate aftermath of the Second World War.

Despite the heterogeneous nature of the First Nations and their views expressed before the SJC, a clear sense of themselves as distinct and separate cultural entities emerges. Two briefs even went so far as to request abolishing the term "Indian" and renaming the legislation the Native Canadian Act. "Why should we (Natives) be called Indians. There is no valid reason for calling us (Natives) Indians simply because one white man made a mistake. We (Natives) are not living in India, we (Natives) are living in Canada."[60] Native responses to two key issues in the SJC's terms of reference set their sense of identity apart from the prevailing "Public" and "Administrative Indians." Specifically, it was their views on treaty rights and obligations and on enfranchisement, both of which were integral to the future of First Nations people, that best exemplified the strength of their conviction and their determination to maintain their separate cultural existence.

For most of the First Nations' communities, the treaties negotiated by their ancestors and representatives of the British Crown or Canadian government were the bedrock upon which rested their relationship with the society in which they lived. Almost without exception, the submissions to the SJC expressed a reverent faith in, and adamant adherence to, the terms of their treaties, and they expected and demanded that the government treat the agreements with equal respect. Numerous groups even argued that they would prefer to be rid of the Indian Act and to reestablish their association with Canada on the basis of the treaties alone.[61] The depth of feeling and all its ramifications were best expressed in one of the eloquent briefs from the North American Indian Brotherhood, in which Andrew Paull, president of the organization, decried the fact that

> the average layman has a very vague notion of the position and status of the Indian in Canada. To him an Indian is very much as any other Canadian subject, except that he suffers certain restrictions ... This attitude would not matter very much if it were confined to the ordinary layman. Unfortunately it frequently extends to persons of prominence, persons who have some say in the promulgation of our laws ... They often insist that such legislation should apply to the Indians and completely disregard the ancient treaties entered into with the Indians ... Indeed, at times they find it irksome that any ethnic group or race should live within the confines of Canada and not be subject to all the laws and obligations of regular citizens.[62]

Paull argued that this attitude

> fails to take into account the whole history of Canada, the treaties made with the Indians and the solemn obligations created thereunder; it fails to take into account that most of this country was ceded to the Crown by the Indians in virtue of such treaties and the solemn obligations to protect the Indians in their rights and the comparatively small areas reserved for them, and them alone. It ignores the protective laws created for the Indians by the Imperial Government and the spirit and notives [sic] that actuated them, perpetuated in the British North America Act and the Indian Act. It loses sight of the fact that this whole beautiful country belonged to the Indians and that it was ceded, not as a result of conquest, but as a result of honourable treaties between honourable and independent nations.[63]

The last point is a crucial one. The relevance of treaties to Native people arose in part because these agreements confirmed their legitimate right to be separate peoples. The validity and respect accorded their treaties were synonymous with the First Nations' continuing existence: The ongoing and steady whittling away of the rights guaranteed in treaties spelled their demise, while a reaffirmation of the terms of the treaties augured well.

Enfranchisement, although less pervasive than treaties, also struck at the very future of the First Nations' identity. Under the existing Indian Act, the

IAB had the power to forcefully nullify the Indian status of any person or band considered sufficiently advanced and to declare them enfranchised. In practice this was not used, but the fear of its potential drew near-universal condemnation in First Nations submissions to the SJC. For the dominant society, enfranchisement was a good and desirable end, but for Native people it signified only loss: "Enfranchisement to us means that we must surrender everything that we have inherited from our ancestors. We must leave our homes and our people. We become strangers among strangers. From respectable Indians worthy to be granted citizenship, once we are enfranchised, we become outcasts to our people, trespassers and a cause of discord to the tribe if we seek our own friends and relatives on the reserves."[64]

Most were not opposed to the option being voluntary, and some wanted the band to exercise control over the process. But more than anything else, indigenous people answered this point in terms like those of Chief Michael Jack of the Shulus Reserve in British Columbia, who stated, "I do not want to be turned into a white man. I want to be an Indian till the end of the world."[65]

In order to ensure that this would be the case, the overwhelming majority of First Nations band councils and Native-rights organizations wanted a greater degree of control over their own lives and communities. These desires varied widely in scope and rationale. For instance, the bands of the Duck Lake Agency in Saskatchewan were undecided over whether to accept the vote in Dominion elections: "We are not in agreement in regard to accepting the franchise or accepting the responsibilities of voting ... We do not feel that our people are ready to accept the responsibilities in connection with this important matter and we recommend that the right to exercise the franchise by our band be approved only by a majority vote of our band in Council."[66] Quite a few wanted to see control of certain issues transferred to their band councils and leaders, such as the creation of reserve school boards to oversee the administration of local schools.[67] Similarly, most First Nations communities were keen to have some safeguards over band membership.[68]

Hand in hand with increasing their own authority were the demands to curb the powers of Indian Agents and the IAB, which Native people found overbearing, intrusive, and arbitrary.[69] The band from the Lower Kootenay Reserve near Creston, British Columbia, summed up these sentiments clearly: "We want our reserve to have a good chief and councilmen and to have them make rulings on the reserve. We want our chief to stand in front, not next to the Indian Agent. The Indian Agent has too much to say; the Indian Agent has too much power over the chief on our reserve. We want the Indian Agent to be set back a step behind the chief."[70] Many bands, although not all, felt themselves prepared and fully capable of exercising greater authority over their own lands and people and resented what they viewed as the excessive domination of the IAB.

Not everyone was satisfied with a limited transition of power. Indeed, quite a few submissions received by the SJC articulated a more grandiose vision. Some argued for a more coherent and comprehensive scheme of self-government. The most extensive plan for transfers of power to band governments was provided by the Indian Association of Alberta in its main brief, although it did not articulate this in terms of self-government.[71] Nonetheless, amounting to as much were its demands for limitations on the powers of the Indian Agent and Superintendent General, the return of its chiefs and councillors "to the status they enjoyed at the signing of the Treaties," the right to choose its leaders in whatever manner it wished, the freedom to vote on local reserve questions, and full control over band membership, expenditure of band funds, leases on reserve lands, mineral rights, and the granting of permits to band members for sale of agricultural produce.[72] The Union of Ontario Indians wanted to go further and petitioned the government "to consider the advisability of fostering self-administration on Indian reserves by abolishing the office of Indian Agent and permitting the elective Chiefs and Band in Council direct access to the Indian Affairs Branch in all matters affecting the band and its management."[73]

The vast majority of the First Nations did not seek to overthrow the entire system of Indian administration in Canada, but a few groups or bands were prepared to demand outright sovereignty and an independent state of their own within the larger Canadian federation. One such assertion was put forward in a brief from the Nipissing Reserve, which argued that in order to advance the "social and economic Status of the Indian Nation ... we must have our freedom by being Govern [sic] by a National Indian Government with his [sic] own Constitution Law; this is the only way that the Indian Nation will be sure that their rights and privileges will be protected."[74] But the most strident call for a separate sovereign status was put forward by the various representatives of the Hereditary Chiefs of the Six Nations Confederacy. These factions of the Six Nations reserves had always maintained that they had never surrendered their status as independent people and that the Royal Proclamation of 1763 and various treaties confirmed their status as allies, rather than as subjects of the Crown. The brief from the Mohawk on the Lake of Two Mountain (Oka) Reserve stated the position most succinctly: "We hereby resolve not to subject to amendment to the Indian Act. As we are resolved to abolish the Indian Act, by virtue of our ancient treaties; that by virtue of our treaty rights Indians of the Six Nations are not liable to any federal or provincial laws within their territories ... That by virtue of our treaty rights we demand of the Canadian Government the recognition and the respect of our sovereign rights and privileges as a Nation."[75] The erudite case put forward by the Six Nations nationalists bespoke a powerful sense of self, with no doubt as to their future place in the country. This robust and independent identity formed the most distinctive aspect of the Native people's representations of themselves to the SJC.

The SJC's task of determining the best future course for Canadian Indian policy was indeed a difficult one – all the more so because the committee had to negotiate based on the discordant images of the "Indian" presented to them. What Canadians wanted out of the SJC was the immediate amelioration of the poor living conditions among the First Nations and a long-range plan that would make the "Indian problem" go away. Only in this way could the collective shame for the nation's "Shabby Treatment" of its indigenous population be eased and its own house be put in order.[76] In part, this sentiment reflected international shifts in notions of equality, freedom, "race," and tolerance; these principles were embodied in the Atlantic Charter and soon to be enshrined in the United Nations' Universal Declaration of Human Rights. But, arguably, the main wellspring for change was Canadians' homegrown desire to make their country match the values and principles for which they had fought so hard.

Yet a case can be made that the dominant society's newfound generosity of spirit for the plight of the First Nations in the immediate postwar period had no equivalent for other groups in Canada. There was nothing comparable expressed in favour of Canadians of Chinese, East Indian, or African ancestry and certainly no warmth of feeling for enemy aliens. While Canadians might have pitied Jews in the wake of the Holocaust, there was no increased willingness to welcome more to Canada's shores than there had been before the war.[77] Canadians felt a special sense of obligation to the "Indian" perhaps because they, unlike immigrant minorities, had not chosen to become a part of Canada. The ambivalence of these sentiments is revealed in a satirical cartoon from the *Vancouver Sun* (see Figure 6.1). This responsibility, for so long neglected, was dragged to the fore by the high-profile nature of First Nations support for the war effort – as was evident in the frequent association of the "Indian-at-war" with the "Indian victim" in the public discussions. For most Canadians, simply appointing the committee was not sufficient; this was made clear by the intense and continuous media scrutiny of the SJC's activities and reports. When combined with the burgeoning activism and politicization of the First Nations, the result was a supercharged national environment for Indian-policy reform.

What can be construed about the First Nations' sense of themselves from the diverse and disparate material they submitted to the SJC? In the first instance, the sheer range of cultures, economic prospects, political aspirations, degrees of organization, and even linguistic aptitude makes it impossible to reconstruct any definitive image Natives had of themselves. Nevertheless, some broad commonalities emerged. These stood in sharp

6.1 "The forgotten man." *Vancouver Sun,* 1947.

contrast to those evident in the dominant society's constructs of the "Indian" even though they had to function, to some extent, within the lingua franca of the dominant society. At the core of the disparity was the question of whether the First Nations ought to continue to exist as separate and distinct cultural and constitutional collectivities. Overwhelmingly, First Nations peoples declared their legitimate right to be and expressed their desire to maintain their identity in the future. Though they had different and conflicting ideas on many issues, their desire to maintain their distinctive cultures cut through all else. It most certainly went against the grain of the assimilation doctrine that formed the public and official common sense in the country. In this way, indigenous people brought a distinct and unique perspective to the SJC and aired their grievances in an unprecedented fashion. The First Nations had their hearing at last, but whether they would be heard remained an open question.

7
Whither the "Indian"?
The Special Joint Senate and House
of Commons Committee to
Reconsider the Indian Act, 1946-48

J. Allison Glen, during the announcement of his motion to create the Special Joint Committee, justified his actions saying that it was, "in the opinion of the government, highly desirable, one might almost say imperative, before revision of the Indian Act is undertaken, certainly before the revised act is submitted to the house, that existing legislation, together with amendments that may be deemed necessary, be carefully studied not only from the point of view of the government and the taxpayer, but also from the point of view of the Indian, and in light of his present-day needs."[1] In the course of his arguments, the minister claimed that the country had reached a crossroads, where the government would either have to:

(1) purchase at public expense the additional lands and additional hunting and trapping rights for an Indian population of 128,000, increasing at a rate of 1,500 per year; or (2) decide on an educational and welfare program that will fit and equip the Indian to enter into competition with the white man not only in hunting and trapping but in agriculture and in the industrial life of the country ... I feel that we have here the crux of what is usually referred to as the Indian problem. I find it difficult to convince myself that an extending Indian reserve system, imposing controls and wardships and reducing Indian responsibility to a minimum, would be or could be in the interests of these people.[2]

So saying, Glen summarized much of the general feeling among English Canadians and received the support of all parties in the House for the proposed Special Joint Committee.

The twenty-two MPs and twelve senators who would compose the membership for most of the next three sessions of Parliament met for the first time on the 28th of May 1946,[3] chaired by D.F. Brown (Liberal MP, Essex West), and handed down its final report 22 June 1948.

During the fall of 1946, while Parliament was in recess, several members of the SJC were reconstituted as a special commission to tour reserves in eastern Quebec and the Maritimes to see for themselves conditions there. Not counting the results of the commission, the SJC, in the course of its investigations, held 128 meetings, heard 122 witnesses, collected 411 written briefs, and amassed a total of 3,211 pages of evidence.[4] Among the witnesses heard were a large number of First Nations representatives from bands and tribes across the country as well as various Native-rights organizations. This marked the first occasion when the First Nations were asked to give their opinion about Canada's Indian policy and administration. The findings and recommendations in the committee's final report would form the foundation for a new Indian Act, although it would not be enacted until 1951.

Previous chapters have dealt with either the "Public Indian" or the "Administrative Indian" largely in isolation from each other, tracking changes within each image. The methodology in this chapter differs somewhat from that used thus far. The focus will be on the arena in which the various images of the "Indian" competed: the public sessions of the SJC embodied in the committee's "Minutes of Proceedings and Evidence." Before the appointed members of the committee, these images strove for ascendancy to see which would shape the future of Canada's relationship with the First Nations and be enshrined in legislation. The arena itself was not neutral. Obviously, the Parliamentarians who made up the SJC did not emerge from a value-free vacuum, as each MP and senator brought his or her own pet issues, preconceptions, and cultural baggage to the table. Despite their varied backgrounds and interests, most took their task seriously, and as a body they worked diligently to complete their review in order to expedite reforms. The result is a remarkably rich and extensive source that has received surprisingly little attention from historians; as Laurie Meijer Drees states, "to date, specific analyses of either the committee or of First Nations presentations before the committee have yet to be done."[5]

An investigation of the Special Joint Committee and the nature of the competition within this forum raises a number of questions. For instance, how were the various images and their proponents treated by the SJC? How level was the playing field for all those who came before the committee? To what extent were Native representatives able to shape the agenda or image of the SJC? To what extent did factors like the memory of the war or the international movement for the protection of human rights manifest themselves in the debate? Did one distinct "Indian" win out in the end? Or did some new icon emerge? Why, and what can the result tell us about postwar English Canada, its views of the Indian problem, and the nature of the relationship between the dominant society and the First Nations?

The stage was set for a contest to determine the future of the "Indian" in Canada when the thirty-four Parliamentarians named to the SJC sat for the first time on 28 May 1946. They usually sat for two-hour sessions, frequently doing so up to three times a day in order to give witnesses a full hearing. This was a heavy load for senators and MPs in the postwar years, an extremely busy time for legislative and committee work. They spent the 1946 session of Parliament deciding process and procedures and listening, with a few notable exceptions, to briefs from officials of the Indian Affairs Branch and other government agencies.[6] With the close of the session, permission was obtained to set up a travelling commission made up of numerous members of the SJC to visit reserves in the Maritimes and eastern Quebec in order to inquire into conditions there. This first-hand experience was augmented by the individual members of the committee visiting those First Nations bands living in or near their constituencies during the Parliamentary hiatus. During the 1947 session, attention was largely focused on hearing representatives from Indian bands and organizations from Quebec, Ontario, the Prairies, and British Columbia. In addition, the SJC finished listening to any remaining IAB briefs and heard from the various churches and several academic experts. Few witnesses appeared before the SJC during the 1948 sitting of Parliament, the majority of which was spent in unrecorded meetings reworking the Indian Act and drafting the final report, which appeared on 22 June.

From the outset, the Special Joint Committee was in no way a level playing field for the diverse representations of the "Indian" brought to the contest. Its members already held strong opinions on many matters pertaining to the "Indian problem" and generally articulated an image of the "Indian" that conformed with the dominant society's assumptions. These appeared early in the SJC's deliberations while they were still struggling with the form and procedure of such difficult matters as Aboriginal representation before the committee. The member of the Co-operative Commonwealth Federation (CCF) for Yorkton, Saskatchewan, G.H. Castleden, argued that since "the amendment of the Act will establish for years to come the type of control which will determine the standards of life training – perhaps the very existence – of these subordinated human beings to whom democracy is denied," watching briefs for five Aboriginal representatives ought to be provided.[7] Aside from the very real, and probably insurmountable, problems of choosing five leaders who could legitimately represent all First Nations communities, committee members also mentioned other concerns with Castleden's scheme. Thomas Reid (Liberal, New Westminster) claimed to "know enough about Indians to know that they are a very suspicious people."[8] J.H. Blackmore (Social Credit, Lethbridge) believed that "anyone who has sat with a group of Indians all through a long day and endeavoured to get them to come to a unanimity of view on one thing must realize the possible dangers."[9] But more to the point, many SJC members did not want to see a bunch of "Indian representatives plus their papooses plus their squaws" "coming down here and camping in Ottawa."[10] They would be merely wasting their time in Ottawa when the SJC was not sitting and would be an unnecessary expense for the committee. Instead, they decided to retain legal counsel, preferably someone of First Nations descent.[11] This individual could act as a liaison with Native communities and delegations, a notion that Reid supported because he felt "there should be someone to control them."[12] The combination of unflattering and victimized representations of the "Indian" mixed freely with those of the "noble savage" and the "Indian-at-war" in the opinions of committee members.

On a more general level, the members of the committee appear to have overwhelmingly supported assimilation, at least at the beginning of the process. An interesting exchange on 11 June 1946 encapsulated some of the collective common sense about the purpose of Canadian Indian policy. J.L. Gibson (Independent, Comox-Alberni), speaking against continuing to segregate Status Indians on reserves, asked rhetorically, "what is the eventual objective of Indian administration in Canada? Are we trying to absorb the Indians eventually into our population?"[13] J.L. Raymond (Liberal, Wright) said that, in his opinion, the "objective is to make good Canadians out of them," to which Gibson replied, "Yes."[14] The two concepts were indistinguishable, regardless of the order in which they appeared: To become useful, productive citizens, or "good Canadians," First Nations people had to be assimilated, and vice versa. Articulating these views of the "Indian" and the Indian problem put the Parliamentarians on the SJC firmly in line with the majority of English Canadians in this period.

Beyond these broad biases of the SJC, its members brought diverse interests, dedication, experience, and ideas to their task. For instance, Reid proved one of the most active members, but his interventions were marked by his West Coast experience with Japanese Canadians both before and during the war. He was intently concerned with blood fractions as a means of determining identity because in British Columbia "our fear was that the mixture with the Japanese blood would lead to development along one line only. The progeny of a white and Japanese marriage were considered oriental. Our fear was that the Japanese would assimilate us and we would not assimilate them, due to the fact the blood stream was more pure, if I should use that word, mongolian."[15] As a result, he was constantly asking witnesses "how far out on the blood line are we going to go to designate a person an Indian."[16] Other members carried their own torches: Senator Iva C. Fallis, the lone woman on the SJC, took it upon herself to champion the cause of Native women's issues; D.S. Harkness (PC, Calgary East), a member of the Veterans' Affairs Committee, enquired into the treatment accorded to First Nations veterans; CCF MPs W. Bryce (Brandon) and Castleden brought their party's ideological support for society's marginalized and downtrodden; and J.D. MacNicol (PC, Davenport), an honourary chief of the Delawares, was a committed crusader for Indian-policy reform who had visited dozens of reserves from the Mackenzie Delta to Ontario.[17] Some of these particular agendas shaped the debates of the SJC to a marked degree.

Despite a wide range of personal viewpoints, a significant proportion of the committee appear to have been genuinely and even passionately interested in the work of the SJC. They took pains to avoid even the appearance of impropriety or inequity in their dealings and responded heatedly when their integrity was challenged. This was perhaps best demonstrated in the treatment of Castleden's motion, mentioned above, and the reaction to press coverage generated after its defeat. Though the proceedings were usually remarkably free of partisan divisions, when Castleden and Bryce pushed for a recorded vote on the motion on 9 July 1946, they provoked a bitter exchange. MacNicol complained that "the impression is going out all over the country that Mr. Castelden alone is fighting the battle of the Indians."[18] But Reid went further:

> You want a recorded vote for the very purpose of putting us on the spot. Let us be frank about it. It is not putting me on the spot. I am fighting for the Indians just as much as you are. I want the Indians before this committee just as much as you or any other member does. Let that be clear. Do not let us have any threats of a recorded vote, because that is what you are wanting. Those two [Castleden and Bryce] want the impression to go out that they are the champions of the Indians and that the committee would not hear the Indians.
>
> *Mr. Castleden:* I did not think that it had come down to that level. I have just finished saying that I am not questioning anybody's sincerity.
>
> *Mr. Reid:* I am down to that level now.
>
> *Mr. Castleden:* I did not think that jealousies would go that far.
>
> *Mr. Reid:* He does not need to accuse me of anything.
>
> *The Chairman* [Brown]: That is enough of that.[19]

Though the chairman calmed the hot heads on this occasion, when the story of the defeat of the motion came out in the *Toronto Star* under the headline "Defeat Move to Let Indians Give Opinion," he exhibited the depth of his concern for the committee's credibility: "It is my humble opinion that any member of this committee or of any other committee of the Senate and House of Commons who for political purposes or political reasons is trying to pit one class against another or to create unrest among any class of persons in Canada is not being honest with himself, he is not being fair to the Senate or the House of Commons, and he is a traitor to his country."[20] Clearly, the intense public desire to win the peace for the "Indian" did not entirely exclude the realities of partisan politics. Nevertheless, in the wake of this donnybrook, party divisions faded to insignificance as the members of the committee came to recognize a shared sense of commitment to their work and, more important, a convergence of views on the principal matters at hand.

Throughout the tenure of the SJC, officials of the Indian Affairs Branch were given a privileged position and recognized as the voice of authority by most members of the committee. A number of the senior officials managed to impress the SJC with their ability, intelligence, and commitment, particularly R.A. Hoey, the director of the IAB, who attended almost every session. This respect augmented the influence they already wielded through their experience in administering the First Nations. Repeatedly, as the work of the committee progressed, the views of IAB officials were sought to clarify the testimony of indigenous delegates and other witnesses. On numerous occasions they offered the last word on contentious questions.

A good example of this occurred on the afternoon of 2 May 1947, with representatives of British Columbia's First Nations in attendance. After listening to Native testimony in the morning, Reid felt it necessary to "check up on one statement ... with the department," which he believed to be inaccurate.[21] "You see, if those statements are allowed to stand, it might give a wrong impression to the public. I am suggesting to the committee it might, perhaps, be advisable to have Major MacKay [the Indian Commissioner for British Columbia] here later." When D.M. MacKay in fact appeared some days later, he was clearly prepared to assume the mantle of authority, opening his presentation by saying, "I do not propose to take a great deal of time this morning, but having listened to some of the representatives from British Columbia I feel there are one or two things which require clarification."[22] He then presented his view of the facts to members with confidence and certitude that he knew what he was talking about.

Importantly, however, the branch was not held in awe by the SJC. A number of the members were skeptical of the abilities of the Indian Affairs Branch personnel and structure and suspicious of their commitment to reform.[23] The ambivalent nature of the committee's relationship with the IAB, as well as with First Nations representatives, can be glimpsed from an interesting exchange on 6 June 1947 during the presentation by the Manitoba delegation. While questioning Sgt. Thomas Prince about the average income of inhabitants on the Fairford Reserve, J.E. Matthews (Liberal, Brandon) noted some inconsistencies between the veteran's testimony and that of two IAB officials: A.G. Hamilton, the provincial inspector of Indian Agencies, and Hugh Conn, the fur supervisor.

From what I have heard of the evidence given by some of the delegates, I prefer to accept the statement of the inspector rather than the statement of Mr. Prince. I do not want to prolong the discussion, but that is my candid impression of the whole thing. There is one thing I am sorry not to have cleared up a little better and that is the discrepancy in the remarks made by Mr. Prince with regards to permits for trapping and shooting and the facts as given by Mr. Conn. There is still a wide gap between the two. I think for the record that gap should be closed so we would know where we are.[24]

Matthews, in his initial comment, referred to the difference between the estimates of the average family income on the Fairford Reserve, which Prince estimated at $200 and Hamilton claimed was $800. Not all members of the committee were prepared to accept the word of an IAB official as truth. Bryce reacted by saying that "Mr. Matthews wants to take Mr. Hamilton's word for it that the income is $800. I cannot give you any figures, Mr. Matthews or anything like that, but I have lived among the Indians. Where they earn $800 I would not know." To this, J.H. Blackmore exclaimed, "Or even $200." There was certainly a credibility gap between the official line and First Nations claims, but the IAB's view of the world was not unquestioned.

Even at the end of the long process, the degree of unease in the relationship was evident. This broke out in open antagonism when the SJC was renewed in 1948 and several members expressed doubts as to whether the recommendations for administrative changes that had been made in their two interim reports had been acted upon by the Indian Affairs Branch. The pugnacious wording of a motion put forward by D.S. Harkness suggests the tone of the committee: "This present Joint Committee on the Indian Act forthwith call and examine Messrs. H.L. Keenleyside, C.W. Jackson, R.A. Hoey, and C.H. Bland, to ascertain the extent to which the above or any other of our previous recommendations concerning administration and personnel in Indian Affairs have been implemented and, if not, why and by whom the said recommendations were frustrated and thwarted."[25] The questioning, particularly of Keenleyside and Hoey, was intensive and at times curt. For instance, on the question of whether the branch had made any concrete moves to decentralize its administration, increase the power of field and regional personnel, and decrease the workload of Indian Agents (now called Indian Superintendents after the American practice), Harkness pressed Hoey, accusing him of "getting around my question," and complained after several minutes of debate that "we are still not getting at my essential point."[26] Despite the evidence given by government officials, Harkness remained unconvinced:

The whole point is that I have not been satisfied in my own mind, and I am not satisfied yet, that the recommendations we have made in previous years have been carried out. As a matter of fact, the evidence from Dr. Keenleyside indicated that in a considerable number of cases our recommendations have not been implemented; and it seems to me that the department is not taking the steps it should to carry out the recommendations of this committee. I can see no sense in the world of this committee spending months of its time accumulating thousands of pages of evidence on the basis of which we make recommendations if the department is going to set aside those recommendations and in their own wisdom say, "Well, if we like your recommendations we will carry them out, but if we do not, we will not pay attention to them."[27]

Not all members were so skeptical, but the tone of the debate clearly indicates that the IAB did not have things all its own way in the forum of the SJC.

Nevertheless, in some areas the official view of the "Indian," the Indian problem, and its solution came to influence the SJC and its deliberations. Some of the assessments of First Nations people evident in the "Administrative Indian" – for instance, improvidence and a lack of responsibility and initiative – found some agreement among committee members.[28] More significant, the SJC seems to have accepted the branch's prescription of greater supervision and encouragement as the principal cure for the Indian problem, accepting the opinion of Hoey, who asserted that "ours is about two-thirds an administrative problem and, perhaps, about one-third a legislative problem."[29] This had been drilled into the SJC in the testimony of all the major IAB personnel but especially by the provincial inspectors of Indian Agencies.[30] During his questioning, W.S. Arneil, the inspector for Ontario, argued that the answer to "our" difficulties "is supervision, more supervision and close supervision," and he went further, later claiming that "the solution to the Indian problem, if I may refer to it as such, is supervision."[31] J.H. Blackmore replied, "I would be inclined to think that there is much in your suggestion." Nor was he alone on the SJC in accepting the importance of supervision, encouragement, and instruction in any solution to the Indian problem.

The IAB's views were influential for two reasons: first, because its proposals represented the authoritative voice of experience; and, second, because there was overlap in a number of crucial aspects between the official representations of its wards and the "Public Indian" framework. Notions of the irresponsible or improvident "Indian" and the commonsense goal of assimilation resonated with members of the SJC because these already existed in their own image of the "Indian." But perhaps most interestingly, the committee was starting to see the First Nations and the Indian problem through lenses like those of the IAB. They were suddenly faced with a similar vantage point in trying to impose their image of the "Indian" upon First Nations people and Canadian Indian policy and were wrestling with similar obstacles. However, the two perspectives were not precisely identical. Even though the committee supported greater supervision by IAB personnel, it consistently argued against too much power and arbitrary control residing unchecked in these government officials. Nevertheless, all things considered, the IAB and the "Administrative Indian" were in a favoured position in the forum of the SJC relative to other participants.

The committee members were very keen to hear from First Nations representatives during the course of their deliberations. Indeed, given the tenor of the public debate on the Indian problem and the intellectual and cultural milieu of the immediate postwar years, it was unthinkable to conduct a review of the Indian Act except in consultation with First Nations people. This had been evident in the critical press response to the defeat of Castleden's motion for watching briefs as a form of Native participation in 1946. The committee was determined to avoid any impression that it was not giving the "Indian" a fair hearing, but its attentive efforts to provide First Nations delegations adequate time went beyond maintaining appearances. There was no mistaking its genuine interest and desire to listen to Native grievances. Moreover, it seems clear that the First Nations' views and sense of identity did stimulate the debates of the SJC and help to shape both its conceptual framework and its conclusions in important ways. Nevertheless, there were noticeable limitations on the degree of influence First Nations representations were able to exert and on the type of issues for which they succeeded in winning support. Though the forum was open to the First Nations and their sense of self, the preconceptions and agenda of the SJC meant that Natives' views and identity were at a disadvantage relative to those of the IAB and other witnesses.

Whatever their expectations of the "Indian" before the SJC was instituted, the Parliamentarians were impressed by the indigenous delegates they interviewed. Many were very eloquent, forceful speakers. One of the outstanding examples was Matthew Lazare, spokesman for the Hereditary Chiefs and the elected council of the Caughnawaga Mohawk. The brief he read demanded the abolition of the Indian Act and sovereignty for the Six Nations Confederacy, drawing a hostile response from a number of SJC members, who branded it an "ultimatum," disagreed with its contents, and challenged the right of the delegation to represent the Caughnawaga.[32] At the end of the debate, however, the most aggressive of the inquisitors, W.G. Case (PC, Grey North), conceded a grudging respect for Lazare, saying "I should like to compliment this gentleman, as a rather able fellow. We have appreciated your evidence, even though we do not altogether agree with it. You have done a good job."[33] In this instance, the committee was forced to acknowledge competence even though the views expressed flew in the face of its own views and image of the "Indian."

However, more often the admiration expressed by committee members reflected their delight at having their own views bolstered. In the case of Brig. Oliver M. Martin, this respect was due not only to the man's intelligence and views, but also to the fact that he represented the ideal "Indian" for SJC members.[34] He had become enfranchised after returning from the Great War, had left the reserve, and had made good in the wider society as a magistrate in Toronto and as a brigade commander during the Second World War. In effect, he was the symbolic and shining example of what the SJC was trying to accomplish. If nothing else, the ability demonstrated by such spokesmen suggested to the SJC that the "Indian" had the potential for advancement. For instance, at the end of the sessions with the First Nations representatives from Saskatchewan, Castleden personally thanked them for their excellent brief and presentation: "I say that your delegation has impressed the committee with your high purpose, your natural ability, your tolerance and sincerity. I think if the committee had any doubts we have living proof here that the Indians of Canada can make a great contribution."[35] To this W. Gariepy (Liberal, Trois Rivières) added an enthusiastic "hear, hear," and W.G. Case agreed that "It certainly indicates they have made progress."[36] Arguably, one of the most significant outcomes of having First Nations people testify before the SJC was that it confirmed in the minds of its members that the "Indian" had great promise and fostered optimism about eventually solving the Indian problem.

As a result of impressive written briefs and moving presentations, the First Nations were able to force some of their grievances onto centre stage of the SJC's agenda. Issues that were incorporated in the committee's terms, such as treaty rights and obligations, were raised to a higher salience by the passion and anger of Native testimony. At first the SJC members seem to have accepted the official line on treaties from IAB evidence, which portrayed them as obsolete remnants that had been surpassed by services and administration provided to Indian bands far in excess of their terms.[37] But the committee found it hard to ignore both the consistency of the First Nations' indictments against the government for abrogating the terms of the treaties and their obvious emotional significance. Increasingly, consideration was given to creation of a mechanism for airing grievances. After the committee had listened to William Zimmerman, Jr., the assistant commissioner of Indian Affairs in the US, discussion revolved around establishing a Claims Commission similar to that created south of the forty-ninth parallel. There, a commission to hear and adjudicate treaty and land claims had been in the works from the beginnings of the American Indian New

Deal in 1934, with no less than eighteen bills introduced in Congress. Only in 1946 was the commission finally established, with the expectation that all claims would be filed within five years and all settlements completed by 1956.[38] In the SJC's interim report at the end of the 1947 session, the recommendation was made that "a Commission, in the nature of a Claims Commission, be set up with the least possible delay to inquire into the terms of all Indian treaties."[39]

One of the most remarkable indications that the First Nations had made an impact on the collective consciousness of the SJC came on the issue of the federal franchise. Though the Native briefs and representations to the committee were split as to whether Native people would accept the vote if it were awarded, the First Nations were nearly unanimous in their determination to accept the vote only if their existing rights and status were not impinged upon. For members of the committee, it was inconsistent and unpalatable to award the federal franchise, that potent symbol of citizenship, while allowing Native people to retain the benefits, protections, and restrictions of Indian Status. They wrestled long over the issue of differentiated citizenship, having difficulty understanding why the "Indian" would not want to shed the shackles of their status for the greater privileges of full citizenship. A good example occurred during the questioning of the inspector of Indian Agencies for Ontario, W.S. Arneil, when he informed the SJC that even on what he considered the advanced reserves in southern Ontario, the First Nations were strongly opposed to enfranchisement.

> *Mr. Reid:* What do you find is one of the principal reasons given to you by the Indians for not wanting to be enfranchised?
>
> *Mr. Arneil:* They answer my question by asking another one; why should I become enfranchised?
>
> *Mr. Gibson:* To become a good Canadian citizen, I would think.
>
> *Mr. Reid:* I would like to know from the point of view of the Indian why he is reluctant; is it because he would rather be under the state than entirely responsible for himself?
>
> *Mr. Arneil:* He does not feel so much that he is under the state. He wishes to be left alone.
>
> *Mr. Richard:* He does not see any advantage to him through it.
>
> *Mr. Arneil:* That is it, he sees no advantage from it. The number who take enfranchisement in the province of Ontario is negligible.[40]

Yet the committee was determined to grant the vote to Native people because "many Indians ha[d] fought and died for the freedom of Canadians" and because they paid most of the taxes applicable to full citizens.[41] In the end, they finally accepted that for First Nations people the franchise was a nebulous and finite reward compared to the loss of identity, kinship ties, and the security of Indian status. On 29 April 1948, after a brief debate over the form that the franchise should take, the SJC voted unanimously to support a motion recommending to the government that the "Indian" be granted the Dominion franchise "without reservation and with no strings."[42]

In addition to bending the SJC's mandate to their own concerns, Native representatives succeeded in winning support from the members on issues not mentioned under the original terms of reference. A prime example of this was the First Nations' consistent agitation against the oppressive powers and excessive control of Indian Agents and the IAB. This became one of the most significant issues for the committee, emerging again and again in its cross-examination of both indigenous delegates and branch representatives. The MPs and senators pursued the point diligently once it was brought to their attention by Andrew Paull in 1946.[43] However, this point reveals something of the limitations on the effectiveness of First Nations presentations: Their views and sense of identity succeeded in gaining SJC support when they coincided with the beliefs of the Parliamentarians or when they struck a chord. In this case, the committee members were moved by the issue because the lack of avenues to appeal the arbitrary powers of the Indian Agent and the branch offended their democratic sensibilities. When matters did not mesh with SJC proclivities, they ignored or shelved them, as in the case of control over band membership, which concerned the First Nations intensely.

All these elements can be seen most clearly in the way that self-government initiatives appeared and were addressed by the SJC. Nothing in the terms of reference made mention of transferring responsibilities to band councils and chiefs; however, First Nations briefs and delegates hammered away at this point. Once again it was Paull, on behalf of the North American Indian Brotherhood, who first raised the matter:

> The Indians should be given self-government; by that we mean self-government under you; we do not mean a rebellion; do you understand me clearly on that? We mean that there should be an Indian council which would meet, and there would be no Indian agent there when the council meets, and we believe there should be a provincial council, and that the provincial council should be responsible to a central board of governors in Ottawa who are not responsible to the government in power, but who are responsible to the Parliament of Canada.[44]

It would subsequently occupy an increasing proportion of the debate although, interestingly, it was the Indian liaison and SJC counsel, Norman

Lickers, who most consistently pressed the issue.[45] Nonetheless, several members were inspired by the concept to a certain extent, and the committee as a whole explored the idea of conferring more powers on the local councils. The first clear indication that they were inclined to do something along these lines came in a discussion with Caughnawaga nationalists on 12 June 1947, when the chairman, D.F. Brown, assured the witnesses that "I think we are prepared to recommend in due course that you be given a greater degree of self-government."[46] On other occasions committee members pressed IAB officials about their views. On 25 April 1947 Castleden questioned G.H. Gooderham, the inspector of Indian Agencies for Alberta, on the matter quite closely, with both agreeing that "greater autonomy" for Indian band councils was "the only solution to the Indian problem."[47] Even Hoey, under examination by British Columbia Conservative MP Grote Stirling (Yale), agreed that in the expenditure of band funds and in granting permits, the control should devolve to the band.[48]

It seems clear from such evidence that indigenous views wielded significant influence, but the SJC accepted self-government on its own terms and shaped it for its own ends. Self-government appealed to committee members in part because the tight constraints on the power of band councils and leaders did not sit well in a country that touted freedom, democracy, and the right to self-determination. In addition, they believed that the deficiencies they saw in the "Indian," especially lack of responsibility, were the result of "too much paternalism" and of control having been taken from Native people in the past.[49] This could be corrected by reversing the process in a restricted and incremental fashion. Moreover, the committee saw its mission as providing a new administrative and legislative structure in order to facilitate the advancement of the "Indian" to a point where they exercised the rights, and accepted the responsibilities, of citizenship.[50] Therefore, extending limited and graduated measures of self-government was an essential tool of instruction to that end. In no way did this vision accommodate the aspirations of First Nations communities for autonomy and a continuing existence as separate cultural and political entities within the Canadian state and society. Overall, the Native representations to the SJC managed to influence the agenda in important, although constrained, ways and even to convey some of their sense of identity. But, for the most part, the committee members took only what resonated with their own beliefs and purpose and overlooked or resisted what did not fit. Thus the First Nations sense of self was at a distinct disadvantage in the arena relative to either the "Administrative Indian" or "Public Indian" predilections of the committee itself.

Throughout the hundreds of hearings, presentations, and meetings of committees and subcommittees, two prominent themes emerged that require specific attention. The first of the two was a buoyant level of hope among SJC members about the prospects of achieving a magna carta for the "Indian." This perhaps ought not to be surprising, as traditionally each new wave of Canadians who turned their attention to the Indian problem, whether government officials or not, brought renewed faith that its solution was only a generation or two away. The committee's confidence arose from a number of factors, not least the unparalleled status of academic experts and the trust in social engineering that was characteristic of the period. The second phenomenon that permeated almost every debate during the SJC's tenure was the crucial question of what the goal of Canadian Indian policy should be: assimilation or a softer integration approach. The majority of committee members came to the Indian problem and their jobs with strongly assimilationist sentiments. However, as they learned more about First Nations people, there was some flirtation with what would come to be termed a policy of integration: the advancement of the "Indian" to equal status as a full citizen while allowing them to retain vestiges of their culture and even, in some cases, their distinct constitutional and treaty rights. Despite the ambiguity between these two options evident in the discussions of the SJC, the language of the Parliamentarians and their treatment of several key issues suggest that overall they still remained wedded to assimilation as the appropriate solution to the Indian problem. This combination of hope and assimilation/integration is arguably the defining characteristic of the SJC and would have a profound effect on its image of the "Indian" and its final recommendations.

It is not difficult to imagine the reasons for the SJC's hope for the future of Canada's Status Indian population. In this regard the legislative anachronisms, bureaucratic inadequacies, meagre funding, and abject neglect that had characterized Canadian Indian administration over the preceding decades were a boon. Virtually anything the SJC recommended was likely to lead to an improvement in the lives of the country's First Nations population. The Indian Act had not seen a major revision since its inception almost seventy years previously, and subsequent additions and amendments had created a labyrinthine statute full of many defunct, ambiguous, and contradictory clauses. The almost desperate lack of personnel and infrastructure in the IAB was also immediately obvious to the SJC and something they could correct. As for the matter of money, Hoey summarized the unique nature of the late 1940s with his comment that "we have reached a stage in public administration – how it will last I cannot say – where money means very little to us."[51] And the committee members were certainly attuned to the change in the public mood toward the "Indian." For instance, J.H. Blackmore, in defence of a motion he put forward in June 1947 to increase the forthcoming budget of the Indian Affairs Branch to at least $15 million, argued that the "the psychological time" was upon them: "The Indians now have confidence we are really going to do something for them;

the Canadian people as a whole are interested in the problem of the Indians; they have become aware that the country has been negligent in the matter of looking after the Indians and they are anxious to remedy the shortcomings. Parliament and the country are 'human rights' conscious."[52] The time was ripe for a careful and profitable reassessment of the "Indian," Indian administration, and the Indian problem.

The hopeful climate in which the SJC went about its business was reinforced by its own reactions to both the First Nations representatives and branch officials with whom it came into contact. In the first instance, the SJC construed the capabilities of Native delegates and the "Indian-at-war" as evidence of the First Nations' potential for advancement and citizenship. But almost as important for SJC members, the senior officials of the Indian Affairs Branch impressed them both with their apparent ability and with their dedication. Moreover, they viewed the changes in senior management, particularly the rise of Hoey to the directorship, as having ushered in a new and more progressive regime. This was confirmed by the testimony of a number of prominent First Nations delegates, who had also noticed the change.[53] To the SJC this suggested that the timing of this review was favourable not only in the context of the broader social, cultural, and economic environment of the nation, but also among the First Nations people and the bureaucracy that administered them.

Importantly, however, the SJC was more than just fortunate in its timing; it eagerly sought an active and forward-thinking plan for the new Indian Act. Central to any such program in the immediate postwar period was the input and direction of experts in medicine, the social sciences, and education. At no time previously had Canadians seen more promise in the ability of the government to play an active role in shaping the country's society and economy, guided by the authoritative expertise of academics.[54] This faith was evident in the discussions the SJC had with two expert witnesses: Dr. T.F. MacIlwraith, the chair of the Department of Anthropology at the University of Toronto, and Diamond Jenness, the Dominion ethnologist for the Department of Mines and Resources.[55] Most significantly, academic and medical experts provided assurances of a means to come to grips with an Indian problem that appeared, at first glance, to be huge, complex, and amorphous.

Perhaps the best example of the importance of experts to the SJC came in its first session of 1947. The SJC greeted enthusiastically, and agreed to recommend government funding for, a project proposed by nutritionist Dr. Frederick Tisdall and anthropologist Dr. Gordon Brown. They had already examined the bands of Norway House Agency in Northern Manitoba and intended to study the diet, economy, society, and psychology of two other "bush Indian" communities over the course of a full year. They hoped to discover "what makes him [the bush Indian] tick, what motivates him."[56] Fundamentally, however, these two men offered a completely restructured view of the Indian problem, one less exceptional, compartmentalized, and thus more tangible. Such deficiencies in the "Indian" as indolence and a sluggish intellect were blamed by Dr. Tisdall on the fact that "the majority of Indians we saw, according to our present day medical standards were sick."[57] The root of the problem was malnutrition, arising from a diet that drew 85 percent of its calories from white flour, sugar, and lard. Therefore, better funding, a more complete diet, and nutritional education were part of the solution to the Indian problem.

Similarly, Brown proposed to harness the knowledge of social anthropologists, "animocologists and fishery experts and agriculturists" because changing a diet "involved the whole social structure of a people" and because it was essential "to find out what to them makes life worth living, and what are goals for which they strive; because any change again must be related to the particular striving which they have."[58] Here again the analysis struck at a finite, identifiable, and curable aspect of the problem; previous Indian policy had not adequately taken account of the peculiar social psychology of the "Indian." However, programs based on a secure foundation of scientific fact and tailored to match the peculiarities of the "Indian" offered a brighter future. Tisdall argued, "from our studies of the Indian that he is fundamentally a good Canadian and his reactions to his conditions are no different from [what] our reactions would be if we were living under his conditions. If he is given proper surroundings, proper food, we can make him a good Canadian, an asset to the nation."[59] If the "Indian" was reacting just like anyone else would under similar circumstances, then they could reasonably be considered a disadvantaged minority, little different from others in Canadian society. Recasting the "Indian" in this way simplified the Indian problem by rendering it a tangible matter of providing improved services, which was something the government could successfully accomplish.

However, the questions remained of what exactly these services were supposed to accomplish and what the desired goal was. SJC members entered the proceedings strongly favouring assimilation as the appropriate destination for the government, the taxpayer, and the "Indian." However, the definition of the term was open to some diverse interpretations. At times it seemed to imply a social and cultural convergence, a process of acculturation. The heavy emphasis placed on education throughout the proceedings was aimed at this type of result. Moreover, the most encouraging aspect of Dr. T.F. MacIlwraith's presentation to the SJC, for some members, was his confirmation of their own beliefs in the inevitability of such assimilation. He stated that when he thought of the future, "rightly or wrongly I see no possibility whatsoever of different groups of Indians surviving in Canada or indeed of any other small groups anywhere else in the world surviving indefinitely without merging and mixing their traits and other characteristics. That cannot be in this atomic age. Sentimentally I regret, and perhaps otherwise, the fusing of Indian ways of life, but I think those ways are passing and are bound to pass."[60] Later in the day, during a debate about the difficulties of societal racism toward Native people, the anthropologist offered the committee a reassuring explanation of the root cause of this prejudice and its elimination, claiming "that we do not have any inherent race prejudice. The race prejudice occurs where one group or another lives a different mode of life; but once the members of another group are living the same type of life and have the same attitudes you have no problem at all."[61] In essence, if the "Indian" would just act, talk, and think like everyone else, the Indian problem would vanish.

At other times, assimilation was used in a way that suggested simply equalizing the legal, constitutional, and economic differences between Status Indians and their Canadian neighbours. For instance, the chairman, D.F. Brown, in discussion with Brigadier Martin, stated that "it is the purpose of this committee to recommend eventually some means whereby Indians have rights and obligations equal to those of all other Canadians. There should be no difference in my mind, or any body else's mind, as to what we are, because we are all Canadians."[62] The assumption seemed to be that if the legal distinctions were erased then the Indian problem would be largely resolved. However, the committee members recognized that the problem they were addressing was much more complicated than merely constitutional status. Nonetheless, these distinctions in rights and duties were symbolically significant and formed an important element of the doctrine of assimilation.

Most commonly, the word assimilation referred to the absorption of the "Indian" race into the larger Euro-Canadian population, a matter of blood and biology. Thomas Reid articulated this aspect of assimilation most clearly in an exchange on 20 May 1947, when he expressed doubts "as to whether the Indian should be confined and kept on his reserve ... keep him by himself and for the next hundred years or so and call him Indian? I am inclined to the view that these segregations cannot bring about a good influence for the country as a whole. I am inclined to the view that assimilation of the Indians in Canada would be a good thing."

Mr. Matthews: When you speak of assimilation Mr. Reid you do not necessarily mean by way of marriage?

Mr. Reid: I am taking [sic] in the broadest sense. I cannot see how a person can be assimilated unless he becomes one of us. Over the years, say in two hundred years from now, perhaps the difference between the Indian and the White would never be noticed. I am not an anthropologist but when I speak of assimilation I speak of one race and one people which can only be achieved by marriage and intermarriage.[63]

It seems odd that Reid, who had expressed such fear at the prospect of Japanese Canadians assimilating British Columbians of European extraction, could argue that assimilation by the Euro-Canadian population was the most benevolent and benign thing that could happen to the First Nations and not see the contradiction. It was this fundamental aspect of assimilationist sentiment that motivated the SJC against the continuing segregation of the First Nations on reserves and in schools. In practice, the SJC moved back and forth from one meaning of assimilation to another, sometimes combining them and not always knowing what interpretation was being used at any one time.

This degree of confusion extended to the hazy distinction between assimilation and a different approach that would allow Native people to maintain some vestiges of their "Indianness." This was well demonstrated by the SJC's mixed reaction to the IAB's ongoing policy of centralizing all First Nations people in Nova Scotia on two large reserves in Shubenacadie and Eskasoni.[64] For instance, in July 1947, when the committee was questioning Hoey about centralization, Bryce was strongly opposed to what he viewed as driving Native people away from settled areas, such as a small reserve on the edge of Sydney that had been eliminated.

Mr. Bryce: We are trying to assimilate the Indian, why not give them a chance there?

Mr. Hoey: We cannot do that.

Mr. Bryce: That seems to be what is happening all along – you are driving the Indians farther back. We should be trying to bring them forward rather than driving them back.

The Chairman: What do you mean by assimilation?

Mr. Bryce: Bringing them in among the white people.

The Chairman: Do you mean have him marry and take his place in our society?

Mr. Bryce: Yes, take his part in society ...

The Chairman: We must try to assimilate the Indian, and I think your definition is correct; that is, to have them assimilated into our society we do not want them to lose their blood stream by any means, and we want them to assimilate into our society. We cannot assimilate them, as you suggest, by keeping them in the hinterland on reserves, we want to bring them out into the open, into the Canadian body politic.

Mr Bryce: Government regulations to-day are driving them back into the hinterlands.

The Chairman: The reserve should be a training ground for citizenship.

Mr. Bryce: They have been on the training ground for the last eighty years. Have they made a fair job of it?[65]

One of the intriguing things about Bryce's comments was that he had previously indicated his support for a more integrationist approach. After listening to Professor MacIlwraith, Bryce had expressed his enjoyment at the presentation and agreement with MacIlwraith's views, especially on enfranchisement: "I think that we have to show the Indian that we are not trying to take something away from him but we are trying to give him something better than before. When all is said and done, he is only getting $5 a year, and if he wants to hang onto it, let him do so. But we should be able to blend the Indians into the white man's life without making them give up everything that they ever had and of which they are proud as a race."[66] The diffuse understanding of assimilation in the debates of the SJC, combined with the permeable nature of the border between it and integration, makes it difficult to measure precisely how far the SJC moved toward accepting integration.

Despite the ambiguity, there is no doubt that the committee moved this way to some degree, if only to accommodate the opposition of First Nations people to assimilation. The easiest tenet of assimilation to shed was cultural convergence. The SJC, as a result of listening to the presentations of Native representatives, the American Indian Affairs Bureau official, and the academic experts during the 1947 session, was willing to concede that it would be appropriate for First Nations people to maintain their cultural connections for sentimental reasons if they so chose. It took longer before they were willing to surrender the legal element of assimilation, yet by the end of their review, even the desire to erase the symbolic distinctions in status between the Indian and the average Canadian had gone by the board. The SJC recommended awarding First Nations people the Dominion franchise without any impingement on Indian status or treaty rights. Relative to the assumptions of the members at the outset of the review process, this was significantly integrationist.

However, these assumptions were not given up because the SJC had turned its back on the eventual assimilation of the "Indian." The committee members could acquiesce to the First Nations' maintaining a cultural identity and even their constitutional uniqueness because, deep down, they believed that these were temporary conditions. They could afford to relinquish these two pillars of assimilation because, in their minds, the crucial biological assimilation of the "Indian" was inevitable. J.H. Blackmore expressed this assumption rhetorically: "Would not the absorption occur just automatically and spontaneously ... by young people falling in love?"[67] If the Indian problem was bound to disappear eventually, then there was no danger in allowing the First Nations to maintain some elements of their culture. What's more, supporting integrationist policies such as granting the federal vote, fostering self-government, and ending segregation in Native schooling, far from being perceived as retrograde steps away from assimilation, were deemed constructive means to that end.[68]

During the course of the SJC's sittings over more than two years, every existing image of the "Indian" prevalent in the public and official realms, along with the First Nations' diverse sense of identity, were aired in the forum. Each had an influence in different ways on the nature of the proceedings, the attitudes of the committee members, and the eventual recommendations. However, no single image gained a clear ascendency over the others to provide a foundation for the SJC's final report and the future of Canada's Indian policy. A new image was needed to encapsulate the heady mixture of lofty ideals, hope, and assimilation that drove the SJC's agenda and findings. It was this new image, the "potential Indian citizen," that would inform and shape the revision of the Indian Act and the future of Canada's relationship with its indigenous peoples.

The committee members could not fall back on any of the four images of the "Public Indian" with which they had set out at the beginning of their mandate. The "Indian-at-war" demonstrated that First Nations people were deserving of better treatment and had been used in the past as evidence of their capacity for future improvement, but it remained too closely tied to the past event to be applicable for the future. Similarly, the "Indian-victim" was useful to explain the past nature of the First Nations' association with Canada and ideal for motivating sympathy in the present, but it could not accommodate the optimism for what lay ahead. Indeed, the "Indian-victim" was what the SJC, and Canadians in general, hoped to banish from existence. The negative contemporary image, the "drunken criminal," was simply too bleak and hopeless a case to be of any help to the SJC. Finally, the "noble savage" would always remain, both in its positive and trivial manifestations, a prominent element of the public representations of the "Indian." However, neither the SJC nor anyone else really believed it was possible or useful for the First Nations to return to the way they were perceived to have been in their days of greatness. Without the core of the "Public Indian" to aid them in determining the form and substance of a new Indian Act, the SJC members were forced to look elsewhere.

This left either the conceptualization of the "Indian" in use by the government officials who had the most contact with Native people or the sense of identity expressed by the First Nations themselves as likely prospects for a new construct on which to build a better Indian policy. The legislators did draw from the "Administrative Indian" to some degree, accepting the IAB's view that the "Indian" was not yet ready to go it alone and still needed guidance and protection. But the committee, whose dealings with Native people had been largely congenial and constructive, rejected the antagonism inherent in the official image. More particularly, IAB personnel's skepticism about the prospects for assimilation simply did not fit with the hopeful tenor of the SJC and Canadian society as a whole in the immediate postwar years. Nor could the Parliamentarians find an appropriate model in the complex representations made before them by First Nations delegations. Certainly, their impressive performance before the SJC had an influence on the committee, but their collective desire to maintain their communities and culture were fundamentally incompatible with the assimilationist leanings of the dominant society. Neither of these manifestations provided a sufficient way of conceptualizing the "Indian" that encapsulated the committee members' hope for achieving a gradual solution to the Indian problem.

What emerged by the later stages of the SJC's activities was the "potential Indian citizen," an image of indigenous people quite unlike any other existing constructs except for the characteristic ambivalence. This "Indian" was presumed to have many fine qualities and to be mentally the equal of any Canadian.[69] On one occasion D.S. Harkness went even further, mentioning an elder he had met on the Stony reserve who he believed proved "that many of these Indians are at least the equal to the more intelligent of the white people."[70] However, despite accepting the natural abilities of the indigenous population, the SJC members could not shake their doubts about the "Indian's" current limitations. Senator Norman Patterson best captured this uncertainty in his report about his visit to reserves around Kenora, Ontario. He stated confidently that "it will take time, but the Indian by sympathetic handling will be an increasingly useful citizen," only to argue that in most cases the "Indian" "is by no means capable of handling his own affairs at present."[71] This seemingly contradictory assessment of the "potential Indian citizen" would have an impact on the final recommendations of the committee.

What really set the new image of the "Indian" apart from past versions was its encapsulation of both the hopeful aspirations for the future and the dominant society's assimilationist ethos. Thomas Farquhar (Liberal, Algoma East), always a keen and sympathetic participant in the SJC, demonstrated this confidence in the "Indian" in his glowing praise of seven of the reserves in his constituency, whose occupants made their living by mixed farming, held their own fall fair, and frequently bested local non-Native farmers in plowing competitions. He declared that these "Indians are an example of what Indians *will* do if given proper instruction, some encouragement and a little financial assistance."[72] C.T. Richard (Liberal, Gloucester) argued that the "Indians have a far better idea of good citizenship than a good many of our people."[73] This was certainly a novel impression of Native people's civic capabilities. Previously, most Canadians would have agreed with the thoughts expressed in the presentation of the Anglican Church, which still saw three barriers to "Indian" enfranchisement:

1   Inability to comprehend the spirit of service which is at the root of demo-
    cratic government.
2   Lack of a sense of responsibility.
3   Tendency towards indigency.[74]

However, the trend in the discussions of the SJC was best summed up in a
comment by Father J.O. Plourde, the superintendent of Indian Welfare and
Training for the Oblate Commission, a member of the Catholic delegation.
He stated that "the Indian is not a lazy fellow by any means. He will work
for his living. He is not a dissipated man either. He will behave properly if
given a chance, police protection and so forth. He is not an immoral man.
He is a family man. He likes his wife and children. In other words, he is
what I would call, at least in prospect, a very good Canadian citizen."[75] This
"potential Indian citizen," then, was more than just worthy of the trap-
pings of citizenship; he was a person who could be just like everyone else if
given the opportunity. Essentially, the "potential Indian citizen" had some
current, although correctable, flaws; was a forward-looking, positive figure
deserving of aid; and was readily assimilable. This image would form the
construct upon which the SJC would develop its program for a new Canadian Indian policy.
   The final recommendations of the SJC, submitted to Parliament on 22
June 1948 as its "Fourth Report," constitute a remarkable, although hardly
revolutionary, document. Perhaps the most remarkable thing about the
committee's final report was that, despite the high-profile nature of Natives' participation in the process, their views and grievances had had a
negligible impact. It would be uncharitable to suggest that the SJC completely ignored all the concerns of the First Nations, but in most cases where
it did acknowledge "Indian" perspectives, the mostly English Canadian committee did so for reasons of its own. Significantly, on a number of issues of
great importance to the First Nations, the final report was silent. Overall,
the final report in no way acknowledged the First Nations' clear ambition
to maintain their distinct collective identities, and assimilation permeated
the conclusions and suggestions of the Special Joint Committee.
   The representations of the First Nations exerted some influence on the
committee's collective image of the "Indian," but when it came to specific
issues, their ability to sway the SJC was diminished. In three respects, the
Parliamentarians clearly agreed with the wishes of Native delegates and briefs.
The committee supported setting up advisory committees to provide the
First Nations with an avenue to appeal departmental and Indian Agent decisions. They also recommended that aged, blind, and infirm First Nations
people should receive pensions, as did all other Canadians, and respected
the universal desire of Indian bands to "prevent persons other than Indians
from trespassing upon or frequenting Indian Reserves for improper purposes."[76]

The final report recommended policies requested by many First Nations: greater self-government and the federal vote without prejudice to their treaty and legal rights. However, the committee had its own reasons for pushing these two initiatives. And in any event, the recommendation that "greater and more progressive measures of self-government of Reserve and Band affairs be granted to Band Councils," along with the financial assistance "to enable them to undertake, under proper supervision, projects for the physical and economic betterment of the Band members," was, in keeping with the SJC's belief in the contemporary weaknesses of the "potential Indian citizen," rather limited and vague.[77] Nor did the SJC's self-government plan, which called for "such Reserves as are sufficiently advanced [to] be then recommended for incorporation within the terms of the Municipal Acts of the province in which they are situated," encompass the aspirations for local autonomy, let alone sovereignty, expressed in many First Nations submissions. These measures were intended to fit with the dominant society's view of the "Indian" and their place in the nation, not simply to serve as altruistic concessions to the "Indian."

This was perhaps nowhere better seen than in the SJC's recommendation on its first term of reference: treaty rights and obligations. In light of the extensive First Nations complaints about infringement of treaty rights, the committee had already suggested in its 1947 interim report that the government ought to set up a Claims Commission to investigate treaty grievances. However, the different wording of the similar recommendation in the final report suggests the underlying motivation:[78] "Your Committee recommends that a Commission in the nature of a Claims Commission be set up, with the least possible delay, to inquire into the terms of all Indian treaties in order to discover and determine, *definitely* and *finally*, such rights and obligations as are therein involved and, further, to assess and settle *finally* and in a just and equitable manner all claims and grievances which have arisen thereunder."[79]

The repetitive stress on the need for finality was the telling sign. First Nations people maintained a strong collective memory of the intent and spirit of the treaties their ancestors had signed with Crown representatives, an interpretation that conflicted with the strict legalistic reading of the agreements prevalent in the government.[80] The SJC seems to have accepted the view of the IAB that the treaties had become largely obsolete. But it had also witnessed evidence first hand of their importance to the First Nations, who, in many cases, construed their sense of identity and the foundation of their entire relationship with Canada from this vantage point. Allowing Native people to cling to what the committee perceived as misconceptions of their treaty rights was viewed as an impediment to their advancement to citizenship. Thus it was essential to have the issue dealt with conclusively, the misapprehensions corrected, and the whole matter closed as quickly as possible. Though this recommendation was a response to Native concerns, its rationale belonged to the dominant society.

On a host of other issues, the SJC virtually ignored the concerns of the First Nations when formulating its recommendations. For instance, the committee decided that Status Indians should continue to pay all taxes except on land or income derived from reserves. But perhaps the most glaring case was its position on the question of voluntary and compulsory enfranchisement. Despite the almost universal and passionate attacks against enfranchisement in First Nations written briefs and presentations to the SJC, the final report contained only a single sentence under this heading. It suggested that the revised act should "contain provisions to clarify the present rules and regulations regarding enfranchisement."[81] Given the potent feelings on the part of Native people and the fact that the powers to force the enfranchisement of an "Indian" had not been implemented for many years, it seems surprising that the committee did not deal with this issue.

Similarly, the overwhelming majority of First Nations bands and organizations across the country had requested the right to control membership in their bands or tribes. Under this heading, the SJC recommended that a new definition of "Indian" be instituted that was "more in accord with present conditions" and that the IAB undertake a revision of current band membership lists. The committee believed that the combination of these measures with "the amendment of those sections of the Act dealing with Band membership will obviate many problems." At least part of the motivation for ignoring the First Nations' desire to have a say in who would, or would not, be a part of their communities was economic. The report states that the government "annually votes moneys to promote the welfare of the Indians. This money should not be spent for the benefit of persons who are not legally members of the Indian Band."[82] Whittling down the number of legal Indians was the more important in light of the increased expenditures necessary to extend the welfare state to include all First Nations people.

The stated purpose of all the proposed revisions was "to make possible the gradual transition of Indians from wardship to citizenship and to help them advance themselves."[83] Underlying many of the suggestions were democratic and liberal principles that sought to give the "Indian" equality and to provide them with opportunities to make good, rather than with handouts. But the thread that tied all these policy recommendations together was assimilation. When the overall program is examined in the context of the shifting image of the "Indian" and the socio-cultural milieu of the immediate postwar years, it is clear that although the SJC provided Native people a hearing, they were heard only selectively. It is the rationale of assimilation that makes sense of the committee's decision to press for a Claims Commission to attain closure on treaty rights and obligations. This rationale also helps make comprehensible the final report's unwillingness to meet demands for tax exemption. Backing away from the status quo would merely have reinforced the exceptional nature of the "Indian" and removed an instrument for teaching civic responsibility. Assimilation clearly emerges behind the SJC's muteness on enfranchisement and band membership. Inherent in making the Indian problem go away was the power to determine, at some point, that those people were no longer Indians in the legal, as well as cultural and racial, sense – essentially the authority to reconstruct them as "potential Indian citizens." In the words of the final report, Canada needed "to facilitate the Indians to become, in every respect, citizens proud of Canada and the provinces in which they reside."[84] So saying, the Special Joint Committee appointed to examine and consider the Indian Act concluded its activities.

The recommendations resulting from the committee's years of effort would provide the basis for a postwar Canadian Indian policy and administration that were functionally, but not fundamentally, different from their precursors. In the end, the Special Joint Committee wound up recommending the repeal or revision of virtually every section of the existing Indian Act. The program they developed largely, although not completely, ignored Native views and aspirations. Most significantly, the First Nations' desires for a continuing separate existence as distinct cultural entities and the maintenance of their treaty-based relationship with the Crown were not acknowledged in the final report. With the help of academic and medical experts, the Indian problem was reconstructed as a problem of a disadvantaged ethnic minority. In this guise it became a solvable matter for the government, requiring the adequate provision of social, health, and educational services. The image of the "Indian" was optimistically recast as the "potential Indian citizen" during the course of the proceedings. Also critical was the SJC's flirtation with integration, which the committee members casually entertained alongside assimilation as they mulled over the future of Canadian Indian policy. But by and large, assimilation remained for most the proper end goal, and a final solution to the Indian problem formed the overarching theme of the SJC's recommendations.

For Indian Affairs Branch officials, there was some reason to feel sanguine. They had managed to weather the criticisms they faced during the review and effectively conveyed their impressions of their charges while enlightening the committee on the ways they believed the Indian problem ought to be solved. The process had raised the organization's profile both within the government and the wider population, banishing the impression that it inhabited an isolated bureaucratic and political backwater. The agency that had previously been chronically underfunded now had more money than it could feasibly spend given the still-severe shortages of material and labour plaguing the country. True, Indian Affairs personnel were not overly thrilled with recommendations for a Claims Commission to investigate treaty grievances and for external advisory committees, among other measures, which they saw as impediments to their work and threats to their control. However, the branch would be moderately successful in the short term in limiting or impeding their inclusion in legislation. Despite the upheaval of the postwar period, there is nothing to suggest that the IAB had altered its image of the "Indian" as a result of Parliamentary and media scrutiny. The "Administrative Indian" remained a very different construct than its publicly discussed counterpart, and Indian Affairs personnel remained noticeably out of step with the society on whose behalf they laboured.

First Nations people also could take pride in their role in the SJC even though they had not won all of the changes they had sought. They had for the first time found a place at the table where Indian policy was determined, and their spokesmen had acquitted themselves well. The proceedings and the evidence presented before the SJC had done more to circulate their views and grievances than anything previous and had afforded Native leaders and associations experience in handling the media and articulating their cause for the wider population. Perhaps more important for the future, the SJC had proved a catalyst for the political organization of the First Nations and had encouraged the establishment of, if not a collective consciousness, at least a sense of shared experiences. Moreover, Native people were quick to put the concessions they had acquired in the new Indian Act to their own use, regardless of the dominant society's rationale in awarding them. Self-government initiatives proved the most important of these, helping First Nations communities to maintain and foster their cultural identity, rather than providing the assimilation tool intended by the SJC. Overall, however, the greatest consequence of the public and governmental reevaluation of the Indian Act and the Indian problem for the First Nations people was that it established as a precedent their legitimate right to be involved in the development of Canadian Indian policy in the future. As the government would discover to its chagrin, in the future it could no longer determine Canadian Indian policy without soliciting at least a modicum of Native participation.

Finally, the dominant society had reason to be pleased with the outcome, and from its perspective the future of the "Indian" appeared bright. Canadians could feel satisfied that the errors of the past had been exposed and addressed, thereby both alleviating the immediate plight of the indigenous population and removing the roadblocks on the road to assimilation. But perhaps most important for the purposes of this study, the process enabled English Canada to reconstruct the First Nations' public image as the "potential Indian citizen" and thereby to rehabilitate the long-standing goal of assimilation. The dissemination of the "Minutes of Proceedings and Evidence," combined with the continuous media coverage, served to educate

Canadians about the First Nations, their views, and their circumstances. This mass of material augmented the already-prevalent desire among Canadians to do right by the Indian both in appreciation for the actions of the "Indian-at-war" and to atone for the negligent treatment that had characterized the country's past relations with its First Nations people.

Though the hard conceptual retooling had been done in fashioning the "potential Indian citizen," and despite the thorough nature of the review and the extensive recommendations produced, the process of formalizing a new Indian Act proved surprisingly drawn out and contentious. Administrative restructuring, personnel changes, and political considerations, arising from the Catholic Church's anger at proposals to change the provisions for denominational schooling, forced Indian-policy reform onto the back burner until after the federal election of 1949.[85] Only after a Cabinet restructuring in 1949-50 did the process gain any impetus.

The Indian Affairs Branch, now within the new Ministry of Citizenship and Immigration, had yet another new minister, Walter Harris (Liberal, Grey Bruce), take the reins of responsibility. Under his guidance, Bill 267, the embryonic Indian Act, was prepared for submission to the House of Commons in the first half of 1950. John Leslie argues that the inexperienced minister "was captured by his policy and legal advisors and by the superstructure of legislation, administrative practices and constitutional arrangements" that had guided Canadian Indian policy since the nineteenth century.[86] The resulting bill in many instances stepped back from some of the measures contained in the provisional draft of the Act prepared by the SJC, reasserting the "Administrative Indian" and official authority. It denied the federal vote to First Nations people and rejected the recommendations for a Claims Commission or regional advisory boards to provide an external check on Indian administration. Moreover, in some ways the proposed legislation increased the arbitrary powers of the minister and IAB officials to interfere in the economic, social, and moral lives of the First Nations. The bill was introduced on 7 June 1950, sparking an immediate flurry of criticism and political opposition from the press, Native groups and bands, civil-liberty associations, the Catholic Church, former members of the SJC, and the opposition parties. In response to the protest, Harris withdrew Bill 267 two weeks later, promising to resubmit it the following year after further consultation.

This consultation included a November 1950 meeting in Regina with Native leaders from western Canada. More important was the Indian Act Conference at the end of February the following year in Ottawa. Harris presented his substantially revised legislation, Bill 79, to First Nations representatives for their input on 28 February, one day after submitting it to Parliament. Formal sessions continued until 3 March, with nineteen official Native delegates presenting their perspectives on the provisions contained in the bill. How much influence this conference exerted over the final shape of the new Act is debatable, but it was another symbolic victory. This new rendition of the bill brought it more in line with the tenor of the SJC and the "potential Indian citizen," as it contained a number of alterations reducing the powers of the minister and his administrators and reinstated the federal vote, although only if a waiver form was signed surrendering tax exemption status. Also, in place of a Claims Commission, the previous ban on First Nations use of the courts to pursue treaty and land-rights issues was lifted, something legislators also perceived as a useful civics lesson for the "Indian."[87] After second reading, a special Commons committee was struck to give the proposed legislation one more review. This process occupied much of April, and the new Act received final passage on 20 June 1951, almost three years after the SJC's final report.

Following implementation of the Indian Act of 1951, the Indian question receded from the minds of Canadians for several years. But the SJC was not the final word on the Indian problem. Another Parliamentary committee was appointed between 1959 and 1961, with other reevaluations in subsequent years. In all these evaluations, the model established by the SJC was replicated. Indigenous consultation was invited, an increasingly clear First Nations agenda was largely glossed over, and the same liberal-democratic principles legitimized a redefined policy of assimilation. It was not until Pierre Trudeau's Liberal government produced its infamous White Paper in 1969, eliciting an explosion of Native protest, that the pattern was broken.

Conclusion

The red man's on the war path! From the loghouses [sic] of the once mighty Six Nations, ancient allies of the "King George Men"; from the prairie lodges of tall and stately Blackfeet west to the Rocky Mountain haunts of nomad Stonies, and north to the smoke-stained tepees of caribou-hunting Chipewyans and Dog Ribs in the Land of the Little Sticks, the moccasin telegraph has carried word that the children of the Great White Father are threatened by the mad dog Hitler and his iron-hatted braves. That the time has come for the red men to dig up the hatchet and join his paleface brother in his fight to make the world safe for the sacred cause of freedom and democracy. And Canadian Indians, whose forebears fought encroaching palefaces in their conquest of the New World, are rallying around the Great White Father to protect embattled Britain and stop the spread of Naziism to North America.[1]

Only three cases have been so far brought to my notice in this agency of Indians being called to report for medical examination, but that was enough to create a furore and I have been beseiged [sic] by delegations who want me to stretch out a long arm and halt all the functions of government. The Department's circular just received makes it clear that Indians are subject to call the same as other citizens, which I think is no more than right. I have explained at some length to the Indians that there should be no reason why their young men, many of whom have at the moment nothing else to do, should not be willing to put in thirty days of military training to fit them for their part in the defence of Canada which should be just as much their obligation as it is their white brethren. I expect that they will benefit by it both physically and mentally.[2]

And so in the end, we return to where we began. These quotations sparked the intellectual journey that produced this book. In light of the findings throughout the body of this text, the writings of these two men ought now to appear much different to the reader than they did upon first glance. The collective common sense, cultural conceits, historical context, and, in the case of the latter, corporate agenda that combined to inspire these words and make them comprehensible to these writers' fellow English Canadians in the early years of the Second World War are now thrown into relief.

What then can be concluded from this intensive investigation of English Canadians' image of the "Indian" over eighteen years? This depends upon the context in which it is viewed. When we focus narrowly on the "Public" and "Administrative Indian," two dichotomous themes suggest themselves. The first notable aspect of the "Indian" image is the variability and adaptability of its form and meaning. Even the seemingly static "Administrative Indian" proved malleable, accommodating the strains produced by the war, First Nations support for the war effort, and the reform of the postwar years. But this versatility was most obvious in the public discussions of the "Indian," where Canadians revealed a remarkable degree of flexibility in their conceptualizations of indigenous people. The dual images with which Canadians entered the Second World War proved highly elastic in their meaning and applicability. However, when these images no longer sufficed to meet the dominant society's needs, Canadians demonstrated few qualms about crafting new images, what Elizabeth Vibert terms "inventive refashioning," to help them make sense of their rapidly changing world.[3] In this process, external stimuli proved the most important, with major shifts in the "Public Indian" corresponding to prominent, emotional events that had little to do with Native people themselves. Nonetheless, the First Nations were able to exert some influence on the dominant society's construction of the "Indian" at certain times. Their impact was most conspicuous in the response to their support for the war during the crisis years of 1940-41 and then again, following the war, in the effects of their participation in the SJC. Previous studies on the Euro-Canadian constructions of the "Indian" have missed the dynamism and immediate responsiveness of a society's image of the "other" to acute external and internal stresses.

The second important theme to emerge from this analysis is that of continuity. For instance, the gulf separating the "Public Indian" from the "Administrative Indian" remained a constant throughout the 1930s and 1940s. The increase in scrutiny of the "Indian" and the issue of Indian policy and administration among the Canadian public did nothing to bridge the divide; if anything this scrutiny widened it, as the previously positive public image of the Indian Affairs Branch faded under a storm of criticism. Consistency also formed the hallmark of the working image of First Nations people articulated by branch personnel. This persistence had a great deal to do with the disciplined nature of the IAB's corporate language, although the adherence to collective norms was weakening by war's end. Arguably, within the conceptual framework it had constructed over decades of administering to its charges, the branch simply did not have the same room to manoeuvre as did the public. Its raison d'être needed to be framed within an unequivocal sense of superiority if the IAB was to continue to give meaning to its duties on a day-to-day basis. Tampering with the pillars of racial superiority that propped up the IAB's purpose could destabilize the entire structure. Thus the branch really had little choice but to cling to its long-standing "Indian" construct. With the completion of the Special Joint Committee's deliberations, and its reaffirmation of assimilation, the age-old mandate of the Indian Affairs Branch and Canadian Indian policy was renewed. Its effects would be seen throughout the subsequent decades.

The underlying foundation of the "Public Indian" also remained fundamentally unchanged despite the gyrations in the public realm during the 1930s and 1940s. The image of the other, the way the dominant society defined the other, and the characteristics with which the other was endowed were all subject to alteration or addition in response to circumstances. But the essential nature of the relationship between Canadians and the First Nations remained. At the base of this common sense rested the deeply rooted assumption that English Canada's race, society, and way of life were superior to those of the "Indian." However, to formulate and candidly champion assimilation on these grounds in the wake of the war was inconceivable. Such sentiments would have been grossly out of step with the international climate of concern for human rights and tolerance and, at home, might have undermined the profound need to justify the reasons for which the war had been fought and to honour the sacrifices it had required. Through the SJC, Canada found a way to win the peace for the "Indian" – by fusing its ideals with a fundamental confidence in its own virtues. Assimilation, although still founded on a conviction of racial superiority, was legitimized and renewed through liberal-democratic principles and confidence in the promise of scientific social engineering by an interventionist government.

Moving beyond the "Indian" image itself, this study sheds light on other issues, including Canadian Indian policy and the Indian Affairs Branch throughout this transitional period. It provides a look behind the facade of an agency and policies that, although intended to liberate First Nations peoples, oppressed them and sought the removal of all distinctions through differentiating the "Indian" in a host of ways both legal and administrative. These contradictions and others, like the dichotomous role of the IAB in First Nations military service, begin to make sense when viewed through the lens of the "Administrative Indian." Here we see the interplay between the branch's raison d'être and growing skepticism among its personnel that the "Indian" could ever be assimilated. Canadian Indian policy's underlying resiliency and consistency is less surprising than it might otherwise seem because throughout these years it was subject to so little scrutiny. Even the postwar internal policy reviews and external SJC process raised barely a whisper of doubt about the ultimate goal of assimilation. What was questioned, and what really changed, were the means to that end, the principles that rationalized it, and the role of the First Nations in the process.

Given the findings of this study, can we still say that the Second World War marked the end of the "Indian's" "era of irrelevance," as it has been characterized by so much of the historiography on Canada's First Nations?[4] The answer to this is both "yes" and "no." In the first instance, there is no doubting that the SJC marked a new degree of First Nations involvement in Indian policy making. Yet the cavalier use of the war's end to mark the transition to a substantially altered period in relations between the First Nations and the dominant society significantly overstates the extent and immediate impact of these changes. There was far too much continuity within both the public and administrative images of the "Indian," even after the war, to support any claims of a paradigm shift. After the wave of postwar public interest in the plight of the First Nations receded, the degree of difference between 1935 and 1955 was even less marked. Moreover, within official circles, resistance to dramatic change remained pervasive, particularly if it triggered fears that too much power might be transferred to the IAB's charges. Finally, although First Nations people themselves attained a role in Indian-policy formulation, they would remain on the periphery of the process for many years to come.[5]

Nevertheless, the war, First Nations military service, and evolving sociocultural norms within English Canada produced an environment between 1943 and 1950 that yielded the necessary legal-technocratic tools to begin the long journey to relevance. Key among these was the precedent that Native people had a legitimate right to participate in the formulation of policies and legislation affecting their daily lives. Whether this participation was truly influential is another question entirely, but from the formation of the SJC onwards the federal government disregarded First Nations input at its peril. Also significant were the politicization of the First Nations across the country sparked by the SJC and some of the revisions in the new Indian Act, such as greater powers for band government. The new organizations and band leaderships provided the training forum for the leaders who would usher the First Nations through both the dramatic late 1960s and the constitutional dealings of the 1980s and 1990s.

Alongside these tools, the war also brought important intellectual and cultural antecedents that would contribute to the First Nations' increasing relevance. English Canadians' ability to conceptualize contemporary First Nations people in a positive manner, something forced on them by Native contributions to the war effort, was the first step. Without this incremental change, there would have been little room to see these people as human beings, little capacity for empathy, and no interest in reforming Canadian Indian policy. With empathy came pity and, measured against the principled rhetoric of the campaign to win the peace, an acceptance of responsibility and guilt. The last and most important step for the dominant society came in recasting assimilation upon a foundation of citizenship, equality, and democracy. This effectively established the philosophical grounds upon which the Native-rights debate would be fought for the rest of the century and would make it progressively harder to withstand First Nations' demands for greater control and autonomy. The last cultural precursor to note here occurred among the First Nations themselves. This came in the first sparks of a collective consciousness resulting from pride in their wartime accomplishments and more directly through their participation in the Special Joint Committee process. It would be too much to say that an articulate pan-Indian identity appeared suddenly in the wake of the war, but the discovery of shared experiences and grievances during the SJC would, in time, blossom. Overall, then, the Second World War and its immediate aftermath might more precisely be said to mark at least the beginning of the end of the "era of irrelevance" for Canada's First Nations.

Turning to the broader society in English Canada, this project has been, at least partly, an examination of total war's impact on a society and culture, viewed through the window of the image of the "Indian." From this perspective a number of conclusions can be drawn. First, it has been remarkable to see how multidimensional are the tools a society will utilize to cope with acute crisis. This was nowhere clearer than in the surprising correlation between the fall of France and the rising tide of English Canadian interest in the "Indian's" contributions to the war effort. Also striking was how the threat of defeat or imminent victory, the extremes of war's emotional spectrum, seized the collective consciousness of the country. Such times are truly formative periods for societies, kindling intensive reexamination of, and debate about, themselves and the wider world. English Canadians' analysis was initially driven by the need to crystallize and confirm what they were fighting for and against. With this clarification largely complete and with the likelihood of victory growing, the propellant shifted to fear about losing the peace and to justifying the sacrifices that the war had entailed. The First Nations' high-profile role during the conflict presented a challenge to Canadians' sense of themselves, revealing the fallacy of nationalist mythologies touting tolerance, equality, and democracy. This challenge demanded action and rectification and helps to explain why the "Indian problem" was deemed a matter of postwar reconstruction. It is hard to understate the significance of the need to win the war and the fear of losing the peace for the dominant society. Nearly as important was determining who was with them and who was not: who fell within the "we" group, as did First Nations people, and who remained an external other. Unfortunately, this sharpening of distinctions generated intolerance and potentially harsh treatment for those unlucky enough to be left on the outside, as Canadians of Japanese heritage discovered after December 1941. Overall, however, English Canadians' resulting self-awareness and, where necessary, self-delusion strengthened societal cohesion, bolstered morale in the darkest of times, and provided a sense of mission during postwar reconstruction.

This study also provides a useful caution against a tendency within the war-and-society field to assume that war's impact is inevitably profound. The reality, as suggested here, was more equivocal than categorical. Certainly, the Second World War's influences on Canada were far-reaching. If its impact could be felt so strongly in how the dominant society constructed notions of First Nations people, who knows what else it may have affected? Yet, as has been seen, even a war as pervasive as the Second World War can leave continuity in its wake.

Concluding this study in 1948 does not signal an end to the collective discussion to which we have been listening, anymore than 1930 marked a beginning. English Canadians have been talking about the "Indian" for centuries and still do so. Pick up any newspaper in the country or listen to a TV or radio newscast on contemporary First Nations issues, and the "Public Indian" imagery and ideas of today are discernable. Some of these no doubt are different from those of 1948, in no small measure because there are more indigenous voices in this debate than during the Depression and war years. However, echoes of notions prevalent during the Second World War linger; so much common sense about the "Indian" remains embedded. In some senses this is disturbing because today's common sense lacks the clearer sense of self that English Canadians possessed during and after the Second World War. Contemporary Canadians have not suffered the tribulations of their parents and grandparents during the 1930s and 1940s; there has not been that same galvanization of the nation, with its concomitant self-examination and resulting self-awareness. Arguably, therefore, our notions of the "Indian" rest on a less secure foundation today. Such insecurity is potentially dangerous given the complexities of the issues swirling around Canada's relations with its various Aboriginal peoples and the intensity of feelings on both sides. Public discourse always oversimplifies, but such reduction built on a shaky foundation ill prepares Canadians for the complicated and probably painful decisions that lie ahead. In the end, however, this is simply speculation until someone spends the time to listen to the dominant society's conversation through the latter half of the twentieth century.

Notes

Introduction

1   Philip H. Godsell, "Red Men Dig Up the Hatchet," *Winnipeg Free Press*, Magazine Section, 24 May 1941, 5.

2   Samuel Devlin to Secretary, 2 October 1940, National Archives of Canada (hereinafter NAC), Record Group 10 (hereinafter RG 10), vol. 6768, file 452-20, pt. 4.

3   A note about terminology: The term "Indian" in quotations refers to the constructed image of First Nations people in use among English Canadians during the period under investigation. The quotations are not used when referring to a particular title or thing, such as Indian Agent, Indian Affairs Branch, the Indian Act, or Canadian Indian policy, or when specifically discussing Status Indians under the Act. However, I will generally use the terms First Nations, Aboriginal, Native, or indigenous when discussing the peoples themselves.

4   Robert F. Berkhofer, Jr., *The White Man's Indian: Images of the American Indian from Columbus to the Present* (New York: Random House, 1978); Peter Hulme, *Colonial Encounters: Europe and the Native Caribbean, 1492-1787* (London: Methuen, 1986); Richard White, *The Middle Ground: Indians, Empires and Republics in the Great Lakes Region, 1650-1815* (Cambridge: Cambridge University Press, 1991); Colin G. Calloway, *Crown and Calumet: British-Indian Relations, 1783-1815* (Norman, OK: University of Okalahoma Press, 1987); and R.G. Moyles and Doug Owram, *Imperial Dreams and Colonial Realities: British Views of Canada, 1880-1914* (Toronto: University of Toronto Press, 1988).

5   Sherry L. Smith, *Reimagining Indians: Native Americans through Anglo Eyes, 1880-1940* (Oxford and New York: Oxford University Press, 2000), 5-6.

6   The notion that the indigenous peoples of the New World formed a single collective entity was itself a European creation, beginning with Columbus, who introduced it to the Old World lexicon "in an offhand manner as an aside through his oft-reprinted letter of 1493." Berkhofer, *The White Man's Indian*, 5.

7   H.C. Porter, *The Inconstant Savage: England and the North American Indian* (London: Duckworth and Co., 1979).

8   Ibid., 10.

9   Lewis Manke, *Aristotle and the American Indians: A Study in Race Prejudice in the Modern World* (Bloomington, Indiana: Indiana University Press, 1959).

10 Gaile McGregor, *The Noble Savage in the New World Garden: Notes Toward a Syntactics of Place* (Toronto: University of Toronto Press, 1988), 12-19.

11 Berkhofer, *The White Man's Indian*, 44-9, 72-85.

12 Harry Liebersohn, *Aristocratic Encounters: European Travelers and North American Indians* (Cambridge: Cambridge University Press, 1998).

13 White, *The Middle Ground*.

14 Theodore Binnema, *Common and Contested Ground: A Human and Environmental History of the Northwestern Plains* (Norman, OK: University of Oklahoma Press, 2001), 9.

15 Berkhofer, *The White Man's Indian*, 29.

16 Brian W. Dippie, *The Vanishing American: White Attitudes and U.S. Indian Policy* (Middleton, CT: Weslyan University Press, 1982), xii.

17 Numerous articles in Canadian magazines and newspapers during the Depression provided such information but with little evident impact on public awareness. For instance, see James Montagnes, "Our Indians Grow More Numerous," *Saturday Night*, 8 July 1933, 3, which cites a government report announcing the latest Indian census numbers, 30 April 1938, 5. The Indian Affairs Branch census revealed a significant growth of over 9 percent, increasing from 104,000 in 1924 to 114,000 in 1938. Such evidence also appeared in other publications as well: "Indian Population Increase Expected," *Calgary Herald*, 26 June 1939, 2; "Says Indians Not Becoming Extinct," *Halifax Chronicle*, 6 March 1935, 2.

18 To get a sense of the issues and the tenor of the controversy, see Michael Bliss, "Privatising the Mind: The Sundering of Canadian History, the Sundering of Canada," *Journal of Canadian Studies* 26, 4 (Winter 1991-92): 5-17; Veronica Strong-Boag, "Contested Space: The Politics of Canadian Memory," *Journal of the Canadian Historical Association* 5 (1994): 3-17; Bryan Palmer, "On Second Thoughts: Canadian Controversies," *History Today* 44, 11 (Nov. 1994): 44-9; Greg Kealey, "Class in English-Canadian Historical Writing: Neither Privatizing, Nor Sundering," *Journal of Canadian Studies* 27, 2 (Summer 1992): 123-29.

19 J.L. Granatstein, *Who Killed Canadian History?* (Toronto: Harper Collins, 1998).

20 Jonathan F. Vance, *Death So Noble: Memory, Meaning and the First World War* (Vancouver: UBC Press, 1997); and Ian Miller, *Our Glory and Our Grief: Torontonians in the Great War* (Toronto: University of Toronto Press, 2002).

21 James L. Dempsey, *Warriors of the King: Prairie Indians in World War I* (Regina, SK: Canadian Plains Research Centre, 1999); Stephen A. Bell, "The 107th 'Timber Wolf' Battalion at Hill 70," *Canadian Military History* 5, 1 (Spring 1996): 73-8; and James W. St. G. Walker, "Race and Recruitment during World War I: Enlistment of Visible Minorities in the Canadian Expeditionary Force," *Canadian Historical Review* 70, 1 (1989): 1-26.

22 Norman Hillmer et al., eds., *On Guard for Thee: War, Ethnicity, and the Canadian State, 1939-1945* (Ottawa: Canadian Committee for the History of the Second World War, 1988).

23 For example, see James L. Dempsey, "Alberta's Indians and the Second World War," in *For King and Country: Alberta and the Second World War*, edited by Ken Tingley (Edmonton: Provincial Museum of Alberta, 1995), 39-52; Michael D. Stevenson, "The Mobilisation of Native Canadians during the Second World War," *Journal of the Canadian Historical Association* 7 (1996): 205-26; R. Scott Sheffield and Hamar Foster, "Fighting the King's War: Harris Smallfence, Verbal Treaty Promises and the Conscription of Indian Men, 1944," *University of British Columbia Law Review* 33, 1 (1999): 53-74; R. Scott Sheffield, "'Of Pure European Descent and of the White Race': Recruitment Policy and Aboriginal Canadians," *Canadian Military History* 5, 1 (Spring 1996): 8-15; and Hugh Shewell, "Jules Sioui and Indian Political Radicalism in Canada, 1943-44," *Journal of Canadian Studies* 34, 3 (Fall 1999): 211-41.

24 Ken Coates and Robin Fisher, eds., *Out of the Background: Readings on Canadian Native History*, 2nd ed. (Toronto: Copp Clark, 1996), 3. Coates and Fisher might have included the war years in this characterization, but their omission is in keeping with the field's penchant for ignoring the Second World War period.

25 J.R. Miller, *Skyscrapers Hide the Heavens: A History of Indian-White Relations in Canada*, 2nd ed. (Toronto: University of Toronto Press, 1991), 221.

26 For example, see Olive P. Dickason, *Canada's First Nations: A History of Founding Peoples from Earliest Times* (Toronto: McClelland and Stewart, 1992), 328-29; and John L. Tobias, "Protection, Civilization, Assimilation: An Outline History of Canada's Indian Policy," in *As Long as the Sun Shines and the Water Flows: A Reader in Canadian-Native Relations*, edited by Ian A.L. Getty and Antoine S. Lussier (Vancouver: UBC Press, 1983), 39-55. The pervasiveness of this practice is evident in Steven High, "Native Wage Labour and Independent Production during the 'Era of Irrelevance,'" *Labour/Le Travail* 37 (Spring 1996): 243-64. Not only does High's conceptual framework explicitly use this characterization of the war, but he also refers to a number of academics whose work does the same.

27 John Leslie, "Assimilation, Integration or Termination? The Development of Canadian Indian Policy, 1943-1963," PhD dissertation, Carleton University, 1999; and Hugh Shewell, "Origins of Contemporary Indian Social Welfare in the Canadian Liberal State: An Historical Case Study in Social Policy, 1873-1965," PhD dissertation, University of Toronto, 1995.

28 High, "Native Wage Labour," 248.
29 Ibid.
30 Edward Said, *Orientalism* (1978; reprint, New York: Vintage Books, 1994).
31 Kay Anderson, *Vancouver's Chinatown: Racial Discourse in Canada, 1875-1980* (Montreal and Kingston: McGill-Queen's University Press, 1991), 10.
32 James W. St. G. Walker, *"Race," Rights and the Law in the Supreme Court of Canada: Historical Case Studies* (Waterloo and Toronto: Wilfrid Laurier University Press and the Osgoode Society, 1997).
33 Two of the best examples are Sarah Carter, "The Missionaries' Indian: The Publications of John McDougall, John MacLean and Egerton Ryerson Young," *Prairie Forum* 9, 1 (1984): 27-44; and Bruce Trigger's, "The Historians' Indian: Native Americans in Canadian Historical Writing from Charlevoix to the Present," *Canadian Historical Review* 67, 3 (1986): 315-42. A more recent example is Peter Geller, "'Hudson's Bay Company Indians': Images of Native People and the Red River Pageant, 1920," in *Dressing in Feathers: The Construction of the Indian in American Popular Culture*, edited by Elizabeth S. Bird (Boulder, CO: Westview Press, 1996), 65-77. Canadian literature has been gleaned for perceptions of the First Nations in two major works: Leslie Monkman, *A Native Heritage: Images of the Indian in English-Canadian Literature* (Toronto: University of Toronto Press, 1981); and more recently an excellent comparative study by Terry Goldie, *Fear and Temptation: The Image of the Indigene in Canadian, Australian and New Zealand Literatures* (Montreal and Kingston: McGill-Queen's University Press, 1989).
34 The following list is only a selection of the major works in the field: Berkhofer, *The White Man's Indian*; Dippie, *The Vanishing American*; Richard Drinnon, *Facing West: The Metaphysics of Indian-Hating and Empire-Building* (Minneapolis: University of Minnesota Press, 1980); Raymond William Stedman, *Shadows of the Indian: Stereotypes in American Culture* (Norman, OK: University of Okalahoma Press, 1982); Bird, ed., *Dressing in Feathers*; Michael Hilger, *From Savage to Nobleman: Images of Native Americans in Film* (Lanham, Maryland, and London: Scarecrow Press, 1995); and Mary Ann Weston, *Native Americans in the News: Images of Indians in the Twentieth Century Press* (Westport, CT: Greenwood Press, 1996).
35 Elizabeth Vibert, *Trader's Tales: Narratives of Cultural Encounters in the Columbia Plateau, 1797-1846* (Norman, OK: University of Okalahoma Press, 1997).
36 Daniel Francis, *The Imaginary Indian: The Image of the Indian in Canadian Popular Culture* (1992; reprint, Vancouver: Arsenal Pulp Press, 1995).
37 Ronald Graham Haycock, *The Image of the Indian: The Canadian Indian as a Subject and a Concept in a Sampling of the Popular National Magazines Read in Canada, 1900-1970* (Waterloo, ON: Waterloo Lutheran University, 1971).
38 Ibid., vi.
39 Weston, *Native Americans in the News*, 2. Canadian newspapers have been the focus of several works. Their early rise to prominence has been ably tracked in Paul Rutherford, *A Victorian Authority: The Daily Press in Late Nineteenth-Century Canada* (Toronto: University of Toronto Press, 1982). To date, the majority of attention in the early to middle twentieth century has been on their transition from political mouthpieces to profit-driven "modern" publications, as evident in the title of the most recent such work by Minko Sotiron, *From Politics to Profit: The Commercialisation of Canadian Daily Newspapers, 1890-1920* (Montreal and Kingston: McGill-Queen's University Press, 1997). Douglas Fetherling suggests that the transition extended well into the post-Second World War period in his small monograph, *The Rise of the Canadian Newspaper* (Toronto: Oxford University Press, 1990).
40 Hilger's *From Savage to Nobleman* is the best and most recent treatment of Hollywood's "Indian," and Mary Ann Weston has examined journalistic impressions of Native people in *Native Americans in the News*. Canadian literature has been gleaned for perceptions of the First Nations in two major works: Monkman, *A Native Heritage;* and Goldie, *Fear and Temptation*. Thus far there has been no systematic examination of the newsreels of the Canadian Film Board, which sometimes covered indigenous subjects.
41 The following analysis of English Canada's "Public Indian" is drawn from a wide range of publications from across the country. These include prominent urban dailies, specifically the *Globe* (the *Globe and Mail* by the late 1930s), the *Winnipeg Free Press, Halifax Chronicle*,

Calgary Herald, Saskatoon Star-Phoenix, and *Vancouver Sun.* Each of the six boasted a readership that extended beyond its municipal boundary. The papers of four smaller communities were also selected for examination: two dailies, the *Prince Albert Daily Herald* and *Brantford Expositor;* and two weeklies, the *Kamloops Sentinel* and *Cardston News.* In addition to the community-based papers, also consulted were the university journals from Toronto, Queen's, and Dalhousie, the conservative weekly magazine *Saturday Night,* the popular weekly *Maclean's,* and the left-leaning literary monthly the *Canadian Forum.*

Chapter 1: The Image of the "Indian" in English Canada, 1930-39

1 R.R.H Lueger, "A History of Indian Associations in Canada, 1870-1970," MA thesis, Carleton University, 1977; and Donald Whiteside, *Efforts to Develop Aboriginal Political Associations in Canada, 1850-1965* (Ottawa: Aboriginal Institute of Canada, 1974).
2 H. McGill to all Agents and Inspectors, 15 March 1933, NAC, RG 10, vol. 3245, file 600,381, in John Leslie, "Assimilation, Integration or Termination? The Development of Canadian Indian Policy, 1943-1963," PhD dissertation, Carleton University, 1999, 67 n. 113.
3 The department was moved to the Ministry of Mines and Resources in 1936 and downgraded to a branch. To maintain continuity with later chapters, the organization will be referred to as the Indian Affairs Branch, IAB, or branch, unless there is a specific pre-1937 reference.
4 This term has been popularized by anthropologist Noel Dyck in his important study *What Is the Indian "Problem": Tutelage and Resistance in Canadian Indian Administration* (St. John's, NF: Institute of Social and Economic Research, 1991). His use of this theoretical concept has been challenged by Victor Satzewich in "Indian Agents and the 'Indian Problem' in Canada in 1946: Reconsidering the Theory of Coercive Tutelage," *Canadian Journal of Native Studies* 17, 2 (1997): 227-57. Duncan Campbell Scott was born in Ottawa in 1862 and moved regularly around Ontario and Quebec as a boy with his father, a Methodist minister. During these years he gained some knowledge of Native people. In 1879, with the aid of his father's political connections, he was able to obtain a position as a copy clerk in the Department of Indian Affairs. Over the next several decades he made a name for himself in the country's literary circles and climbed the ladder within Indian Affairs. He was appointed deputy superintendent general in 1913 and would lead the department for twenty years. Throughout his tenure, and also revealed in his poetry, Scott retained a potent belief in the assimilative mission of the Department of Indian Affairs, a strong adherence to the civilizing mission of the British Empire, and the doom that awaited the "Indian" without benevolent government aid.
5 Directed civilization was a series of policies that attempted to speed up the process of teaching First Nations people to become assimilable. Among the hallmarks were increasingly arbitrary means of enfranchising the "Indian," the proliferation of residential schools that drew the children away from the negative influence of their parents for more thorough indoctrination, and the alienation of reserve lands without the consent of the band.
6 Olive P. Dickason, *Canada's First Nations: A History of Founding Peoples from Earliest Times* (Toronto: McClelland and Stewart, 1992), 328; John L. Tobias, "Protection, Civilization, Assimilation: An Outline History of Canada's Indian Policy," in *As Long as the Sun Shines and the Water Flows: A Reader in Canadian-Native Relations,* edited by Ian A.L. Getty and Antoine S. Lussier (Vancouver: UBC Press, 1983), 39-55, 51.
7 John Collier (1884-1968) was a dynamic social engineer and passionate reformer. His early work experience was as a social worker in New York City during the Progressive era, before he discovered in the Pueblo peoples of the American Southwest in 1920 the communal harmony of preindustrial society. For Collier, here was an alternative means of human relations that would overcome the failings he saw in social Darwinism and competitive capitalism. Through the 1920s, he became an outspoken critic in a growing wave of discontent about the assimilationist drive of American Indian policy and about the Dawes Allotment Act in particular. Collier instead became a committed crusader for the protection of tribal institutions and collective property rights. He was named commissioner of the Indian Affairs Bureau in 1933 and remained in the post until 1945, making him the longest serving commissioner in American history. After his resignation, he was an advisor

for the American delegation at the first General Assembly of the United Nations, where he pressed the cause of dependent peoples across the globe. He remained a critic of American Indian policy until his death. See Kenneth Philip, *John Collier's Crusade for Indian Reform, 1920-54* (Tucson: University of Arizona Press, 1977); and Lawrence C. Kelly, *John Collier and the Origins of Indian Policy Reform* (Albuquerque: University of New Mexico Press, 1982). Sherry L. Smith has stressed that this movement was founded on much more than one man's efforts. Her work covers a group of "middlebrow purveyors of Indianness" who published material for a popular audience, articulating a sympathetic and tolerant image of Native Americans. See Smith, *Reimagining Indians: Native Americans through Anglo Eyes, 1880-1940* (Oxford and New York: Oxford University Press, 2000), 213.

8 See Philip, *John Collier's Crusade*, as well as Lawrence M. Hauptman, *The Iroquois and the New Deal* (Syracuse, NY: Syracuse University Press, 1981), and Peter Iverson, *The Navajo Nation* (Westport, CT: Greenwood Press, 1981), both of which provide excellent examinations of the impact of the New Deal era on specific groups. More useful for this book was Brian W. Dippie, *The Vanishing American: White Attitudes and U.S. Indian Policy* (Middleton, CT: Weslyan University Press, 1982).

9 Philip, *John Collier's Crusade*, xiv.

10 This cartoon encapsulates many of the conflicting images that marked the "Public Indian."

11 It was also something about which the officials of the branch were concerned; in particular, they did not want to be seen to be wasting taxpayers' money in their programs. Public and press criticism was to be avoided if at all possible.

12 J.W. Burns to J.D. Sutherland, 23 August 1932, NAC, RG 10, vol. 6387, file 806-1, pt. 1.

13 J.W. Burns to unknown, 27 March 1934, NAC, RG 10, vol. 6387, file 806-1, pt. 1.

14 R.W. Frayling to R.A. Hoey, 1 February 1937, NAC, RG 10, vol. 6033, file 150-60, pt. 1.

15 This was not the only form of responsibility, or lack thereof, highlighted in this correspondence. Another that ranked highly was the perceived improvidence and spendthrift nature of the "Administrative Indian."

16 A.O'N. Daunt to Secretary, 15 April 1936, NAC, RG 10, vol. 6387, file 801-1, pt. 1.

17 Indian Agent to Secretary, 26 May 1937, NAC, RG 10, vol. 6033, file 150-60, pt. 1.

18 J.E. Baillargeon to R.A. Hoey, 25 January 1937, NAC, RG 10, vol. 6033, file 150-60, pt. 1.

19 Extract from report by Father F.C. Ryan, 6 June 1930, NAC, RG 10, vol. 6061, file 276-1, pt. 1.

20 Superintendent of Welfare and Training to Dr. McGill, 5 February 1937, NAC, RG 10, vol. 6033, file 150-60, pt. 1. Dr. Harold McGill was a Conservative from Calgary appointed by the R.B. Bennett government in 1933 to replace Duncan Campbell Scott as deputy superintendent general. A fiscal conservative, McGill brought a distinctively pecuniary attitude to an already lean department in the throes of the Depression. Efficient and at times autocratic, McGill remained relatively aloof from First Nations people themselves during much of his tenure. He stepped aside in 1945.

21 Indian Agent to Secretary, 23 April 1934, NAC, RG 10, vol. 6387, file 806-1, pt. 1.

22 Russell T. Ferrier to Edward Pritehard, 22 April 1932, NAC, RG 10, vol. 6031, file 150-9, pt. 1.

23 Oblate Catholic Indian Missions to R.A. Hoey, 10 January 1939, NAC, RG 10, vol. 6016, file 1-1-11, pt. 1; J.D. Sutherland to Walter Mutch, 30 January 1936, NAC, RG 10, vol. 6269, file 581-10.

24 J.W. Burns to J.D. Sutherland, 23 August 1932, NAC, RG 10, vol. 6387, file 806-1, pt. 1.

25 Unsigned from Shubenacadie Residential School, N.S., to Mr. McCutchean, 7 June 1937, NAC, RG 10, vol. 6057, file 265-10, pt. 1.

26 Cynthia Commachio, *The Infinite Bonds of Family: Domesticity in Canada, 1850-1940* (Toronto: University of Toronto Press, 1999), and "Dancing to Perdition: Adolescence and Leisure in Interwar English Canada," *Journal of Canadian Studies* 32, 3 (Fall 1997), 5-35.

27 Oblate Catholic Indian Missions to R.A. Hoey, 10 January 1939, NAC, RG 10, vol. 6016, file 1-1-11, pt. 1.

28 Inspector of Indian Agencies to Secretary, 15 September 1931, NAC, RG 10, vol. 6048, file 255-1, pt. 1.

29 A.O'N. Daunt to Secretary, n.d., NAC, RG 10, vol. 6387, file 806-1, pt. 1. This letter refers to the likely source of resistance and rebelliousness among a local band that had come into contact with men from four government relief camps in the area. Another suggested source

was the dreaded half-breed with access to liquor in H.A.W. Brown to Secretary, 5 April 1938, NAC, RG 10, vol. 6031, file 150-9, pt. 1.

30 C.P. Schmidt to J.E. Pugh, 19 November 1938, NAC, RG 10, vol. 6032, file 150-37, pt. 1.

31 R.A. Hoey to Dr. McGill, 7 November 1938, NAC, RG 10, vol. 6059, file 271-1, pt. 2; N.A. McDougall to Secretary, 8 October 1938, NAC, RG 10, vol. 6059, file 271-1, pt. 2. The dispute was not settled until the new year, when the parents finally allowed their children to return to the school.

32 Indian Agent, N.B. Richibucto, to Secretary, 21 February 1939, NAC, RG 10, vol. 6062, file 277-1, pt. 2.

33 Sutherland to McDougall, 25 September 1936, NAC, RG 10, vol. 6057, file 265-10, pt. 1. Another case of such a lack of faith in "Indians" was a directive to the Indian Agent at Moose Factory to ensure that mixed heritage children were not adopted by a Status Indian "for the sole purpose of being permitted to attend an Indian Residential School." A.F. MacKenzie to W.L. Tyrer, 12 June 1935, NAC, RG 10, vol. 6031, file 150-9, pt. 1.

34 Even when there was no perceived master plan, IAB officials were not inclined to trust that First Nations parents would return their children. Indeed, in one letter from R.A. Hoey to an Indian Agent in Saskatchewan, there was no need to explain the policy "for reasons that will readily suggest themselves to you." R.A. Hoey to E.A.W.R. McKenzie, 29 September 1939, NAC, RG 10, vol. 6032, file 150-37, pt. 1.

35 Schmidt to Pugh, 19 November 1938.

36 Indian Agent to Secretary, 23 June 1939, NAC, RG 10, vol. 6057, file 265-10, pt. 1; Sutherland to Mutch, 30 January 1936. These two schools were located in northern Manitoba and Nova Scotia respectively.

37 H.F. Bury to Dr. McGill, 12 May 1933, NAC, RG 10, vol. 281-1, pt. 2.

38 Hoey to McKenzie, 29 September 1939.

39 Philip Phelan to G. Young, 4 October 1938, NAC, RG 10, vol. 6015, file 1-1-6B-Ont., pt. 3.

40 R.T. Ferrier to All Principals of Indian Residential Schools, 18 March 1931, NAC, RG 10, vol. 6016, file 1-1-11, pt. 1; R.A. Hoey to R.W. Frayling, 29 January 1937, NAC, RG 10, vol. 6033, file 150-60, pt. 1; and R.A. Hoey to Walter Mutch, 30 January 1936, NAC, RG 10, vol. 6269, file 581-10.

41 A.O'N. Daunt to Secretary, 30 June 1932, NAC, RG 10, vol. 6387, file 806-1, pt. 1.

42 Robin Brownlie, "Man on the Spot: John Daly, Indian Agent in Parry Sound, 1922-1939," *Journal of the Canadian Historical Association* 5 (1994): 63-86.

43 Extract from Inspector's Report on the Lake Helen Indian Day School, 10 November 1931, NAC, RG 10, vol. 6032, file 150-40A, pt. 1.

44 A.F. Mackenzie to Frank Edwards, 15 April 1930, NAC, RG 10, vol. 6032, file 150-40A, pt. 1. The letter refers to the section of the Indian Act dealing with compulsory school attendance.

45 Hoey to McGill, 7 November 1938.

46 Director to Deputy Minister, 12 November 1938, NAC, RG 10, vol. 6059, file 270-1, pt. 2.

47 The analysis that follows is based on wide reading of the papers and magazines chosen for analysis. For the *Globe* (*and Mail*) each day of three years of the decade (1930, 1935, and 1939 up to the outbreak of war) was read carefully, as I looked at the news stories and editorials, and scanned for advertising. These years were chosen in order to ascertain whether there was any change during the decade. However, while this method provided enormous quantities of material, it proved highly time-consuming. To speed up my research, two months were chosen arbitrarily from each of 1930, 1935, and 1939 for the other dailies. The rural dailies were examined in the same fashion as the large urban papers, while every edition of the weeklies was canvassed for each of the three years. In the case of *Saturday Night,* a subject index existed for the years up to 1937, and the stories on First Nations topics were located accordingly. I read issues from 1930 and 1935 for advertising and from 1938 to 1939 for stories and ads to complete the decade. Each issue of *Maclean's* was examined in the three years. Finally, I read every monthly issue of the *Canadian Forum* and the university journals for the decade up to the outbreak of war.

48 The debates on Indian Affairs during the 1930s found in *Hansard* rarely broke down along partisan lines. Occasionally, the committee or House debates did divide along party lines,

but these were over issues of protocol or procedure rather than substantive differences. The discussions suggest that the goal of speedy assimilation was believed to be logical and right by all parties regardless of their political stripe.

49   *Saturday Night,* 24 August 1935, 5.

50   *Cardston News,* 3 July 1930, 2; *Saturday Night,* 10 May 1930, 8; 20 May 1939, 9; and 22 July 1939, 8; *Prince Albert Daily Herald,* 5 July 1930, 15. Such advertisements appeared in most Canadian publications with regularity during the decade.

51   Marius Barbeau, "The Thunder Bird of the Mountains," *The University of Toronto Quarterly* 2, 1 (1932): 92-110; "The Indians of the Prairies and the Rockies: A Theme for Modern Painters," *The University of Toronto Quarterly* 1, 2 (1931): 197-206; "Our Indians: Their Disappearance," *Queen's Quarterly* 30, 4 (1931): 691-707; "Indian Eloquence," *Queen's Quarterly* 39, 3 (1932): 451-64; and "How Totem Poles Originated," *Queen's Quarterly* 46, 3 (1939): 304-11.

52   Barbeau, "The Indians of the Prairies and the Rockies," 197.

53   Barbeau, "On the Way to Asia," *Canadian Forum* 15, 178 (November 1935): 366-67.

54   Barbeau, ibid.; "Our Indians: Their Disappearance"; and "The Indians of the Prairies and the Rockies," 199. The Orient and all things Asian were viewed by Canadians as highly exotic and mystical during the early part of the twentieth century. See Kay Anderson, *Vancouver's Chinatown: Racial Discourse in Canada, 1875-1980* (Montreal and Kingston: McGill-Queen's University Press, 1991).

55   Barbeau, "Our Indians: Their Disappearance," 703.

56   "Indian Ceremony Adds Color to Exhibition," *Winnipeg Free Press,* 11 August 1930, 3; "Sun Dance at Blood Reserve Sees Gathering of U.S. and Canadian Tribesmen," *Cardston News,* 27 July 1939, 5.

57   "God Save the King Is Chanted in Cree before Their Majesties," *Winnipeg Free Press,* 3 June 1939, 2; "Silk-Stockinged Indians," *Vancouver Sun,* 3 June 1939, 4; "Iroquois Clan Cheers as King and Queen Pass," *Globe and Mail,* 19 May 1939, 19; "'Indian Welcome' for King, Queen," *Saskatoon Star-Phoenix,* 13 January 1939, 7; "Indians Honor Their Majesties," *Halifax Chronicle,* 1 June 1939, 1; "Indians to Stage Show for Monarch," *Kamloops Sentinel,* 12 May 1939, 11; "Royal Visitors Enjoyed Calgary Indian Display Mayor Tells Convention," *Calgary Herald,* 14 June 1939, 20; "Squaws Become Style Conscious," *Prince Albert Daily Herald,* 7 August 1939, 4; "Crees Chant National Anthem in Tongue Strange to Royalty," *Brantford Expositor,* 3 June 1939, 2.

58   "They Wanted Papooses Too," *Halifax Chronicle,* 12 June 1939, 27; "Iroquois Clan Cheers" and "Six Nations at Kitchener," *Brantford Expositor,* 7 June 1939, 3.

59   "Os-Ke-Non-Ton Pleases Crowd," *Globe,* 6 September 1935, 11. Chief Os-Ke-Non-Ton was a prominent Six Nations baritone who performed widely across North America and Europe to wide acclaim. He often mixed Aboriginal songs and subjects into his repertoire and performed in "all the glory of his native attire." This juxtaposition of the primitive "Indian" with the complexities of modernity was a common theme; for instance, see "Natives Bring Furs, Enjoy Modern Cafes," *Prince Albert Daily Herald,* 4 January 1939, 4.

60   "The Red Man Tries the Pipes," *Cardston News,* 16 October 1930. A portion of the background of the photo has been cut out around the two men and a hand-drawn tepee added to complete the picture.

61   "Crees Chant National Anthem," *Globe and Mail,* 3 June 1939, 1.

62   John C. Ewers, "The Emergence of the Plains Indian as the Symbol of the North American Indian," in *American Indian Stereotypes in the World of Children: A Reader and Bibliography,* edited by Arlene B. Hirschfelder (Metuchen, NJ: The Scarecrow Press, 1982), 16-32.

63   *Globe,* 18 March 1930, 5, and 2 April 1930, 5; *Brantford Expositor,* 14 April 1930, 11, and 28 April 1930, 2. A multitude of commodities were sold using "Indian" logos or themes in advertising, almost always with Plains "Indian" attributes. For instance, Consumer's Gas ran an ad for their refrigerator that claimed it ran as "Silent as a Stalking Indian." This was visualized with a vague picture of two Indian warriors bearing tomahawks and creeping, presumably quietly, through some bushes. *Saturday Night,* 3 September 1938, 10. Even such mundane products as Big Chief Beer, Donnacona Insulating Lumber, Windsor Salt, and Arrowhead Flour drew on "the Romance of the Plains" and "Indian" imagery to help sell

their products: *Saskatoon Star-Phoenix*, 10 January 1930, 10; *Globe*, 27 May 1930, 5; *Saturday Night*, 25 May 1935, 20; *Prince Albert Daily Herald*, 7 June 1939, 5.

64 "Chief Jimmy Has Courage," *Kamloops Sentinel*, 25 November 1930, 1.

65 "The Silent Enemy," *Calgary Herald*, 25 September 1930, 5.

66 *Saturday Night*, 25 May 1935, 10, and 29 June 1935, 4; *Globe*, 23 May 1935, 7, and 4 July 1935, 7.

67 Dippie, *The Vanishing American*, 18-21.

68 "Let the Indian Hunt," *Globe*, 13 May 1930, 4.

69 Inconstant Reader, "Preferences section," *Canadian Forum* 12, 133 (October 1931): 22. In this particular case, the novel referred to an Inuit man. However, the reviewer's commentary on the "noble savage" and its personification in the principal character are relevant to discussions of the "Indian." There were differences between the way that Canadians constructed the "Eskimo" and the "Indian," but in this regard they were virtually identical.

70 The best biography is Donald B. Smith, *From the Land of Shadows: The Making of Grey Owl* (Saskatoon: Western Producer Prairie Books, 1990).

71 "Grey Owl to Lecture," *Halifax Chronicle*, 30 October 1935, 9.

72 An interesting example of his eloquence can be seen in the text of a speech he was to make on the BBC in Great Britain in early 1938. The conservation themes he argued so strenuously were not always deemed acceptable to a British listening public, whose sport-hunting interests were still immensely powerful. "Grey Owl's Silencing," *Saturday Night*, 29 January 1938.

73 Smith, *From the Land of Shadows*, 214-15.

74 This is evident in a well-written piece by Frederick Niven, a man who published regularly on "Indian" historical topics and his own acquaintances among the Blackfoot. "Amerindian," *Dalhousie Review* 19, 2: 143-46.

75 Mary Weeks, "Gone Is the Old Trail," *Saturday Night*, 2 January 1937, 1, 3.

76 "The Red Man's Way," *Globe*, 9 February 1935, 4.

77 "The Indian's Lost Hunting," *Globe*, 10 November 1930, 4.

78 One example was the Toronto dance craze of early 1939 called "The Injun," developed by a well-known local dance pair and described at length with photos in *Saturday Night*, "Pale-faces Follow in the Steps of the Red Men," 7 January 1939. The principal steps, titled "the Injun," "the Tomahawk," "the Tepee," and the "Ki-Yi, Ki-Yay," unwittingly caricatured Euro-Canadian perceptions of indigenous forms of dance and their supposedly warlike nature.

79 "Chiefs Use Wives' Lipstick as 'War Paint' to Meet King," *Globe and Mail*, 7 June 1939, 1.

80 "Indians Honor Their Majesties," *Halifax Chronicle*, 1 June 1939, 1.

81 "Six Nations at Kitchener," *Brantford Expositor*, 7 June 1939, 3.

82 "Modern Indian Love Call," *Vancouver Sun*, 3 June 1939, 4.

83 "Indians Halt Fight to Battle Constable," *Calgary Herald*, 4 January 1930, 22. The article finished with a witty reference to the men being intoxicated, saying "regretfully they glanced behind as they left the courtroom, where two jugs of wine and a can of 'heat' occupied a prominent position on the centre table."

84 Examples of this abound, including: "Indian Kills Police Constable During Chase," *Prince Albert Daily Herald*, 28 August 1939, 2; "Indian Arrested on C.N.R. Train," *Halifax Chronicle*, 15 September 1930, 4; "Indian Woman Gets 20 Years," *Calgary Herald*, 2 February 1935, 2; "Four Years for Indian," *Kamloops Sentinel*, 18 February 1930, 1; "Two Indians Held for Theft of Car," *Brantford Expositor*, 10 April 1930, 15; and "Fear Foul Play in Indian's Death," *Globe*, 14 December 1935, 2.

85 For instance, see "MicMac Chief Fined in Court," *Halifax Chronicle*, 16 September 1930, 3.

86 "Sumas Chief Fearful of Farm Dykes, Prophecy Fulfilled When Big Valley Inundated," *Calgary Herald*, 25 February 1935, 15.

87 "Indian Took Fire Water," *Brantford Expositor*, 18 February 1935, 6. According to the secondary headlines, the man was "Tamed by Night in Cells."

88 "They Wanted Papooses Too," *Halifax Chronicle*, 12 June 1939, 27.

89 "One Feather Not Enough," *Cardston News*, 20 February 1930, 4.

90 "Indian Problems," *Kamloops Sentinel*, 8 February 1935, 2. This editorial recognized that the general public was largely indifferent to the circumstances of the local Indian bands, claiming that "the continuous apathy certainly indicates too that among us white people the attitude is too much of 'It's only an Indian after all.'" Only rarely was such sentiment expressed during the decade.

91 "Protect the Indian," *Kamloops Sentinel*, 21 February 1939, 2.

92 Tina Loo, "Dan Cramner's Potlatch: Law as Coercion, Symbol and Rhetoric in British Columbia, 1884-1951," *Canadian Historical Review* 73, 2 (1992): 125-65; J.R. Miller, "Owen Glendower, Hotspur and Canadian Indian Policy," *Ethnohistory* 37, 4 (1990): 386-415. Both of these look at the attempts to suppress the potlatch ceremonies of the Pacific Coast peoples, but the subject of Native resistance is receiving wider attention. See, for example, Katherine Pettipas, *Severing the Ties that Bind: Government Repression of Indigenous Religious Ceremonies on the Prairies* (Winnipeg: University of Manitoba Press, 1994); and F. Laurie Barron, "The Indian Pass System in the Canadian West, 1882-1935," *Prairie Forum* 13, 1 (1988): 25-42.

93 Brian Titley, *A Narrow Vision: Duncan Campbell Scott and the Administration of Indian Affairs in Canada* (Toronto: UBC Press, 1986).

94 Harold Hawthorn, ed., *A Survey of the Contemporary Indians of Canada: A Report on Economic, Political, Educational Needs and Policies*, vol. 1 (Ottawa: Queen's Printer, 1966 and 1967), 369.

95 Each of these individuals served long careers in the department. For instance, Robert A. Hoey was born in Ireland in 1883, educated in Winnipeg, and served as a Methodist minister in Manitoba before becoming associated with the agrarian political movement of the interwar years. He served as a Progressive MP from 1921 to 1925 before turning to provincial politics, where he served as minister of education. His close friend, T.A. Crerar, brought him into Indian Affairs as superintendent of Indian education (later welfare and training). He became acting director after Dr. Harold McGill retired in 1945, serving as such until 1948, when he accepted a posting at the United Nations. T.R.L. MacInnes was born in Victoria, BC, and educated at McGill University before entering the service of Indian Affairs in 1913. After a long career as an Indian Agent, he became branch secretary in 1935 and held this position until the 1950s. G.H. Gooderham's grass roots went deeper than any other's, as he grew up on the Blackfoot Reserve, where his father served as an agent, and virtually inherited the position from him. He would rise to the position of provincial inspector of Indian Agencies for Alberta in 1946, after twenty-five years of work with the branch. William Morris Graham, born in Ontario in 1867, began employment as a clerk with the Department of Indian Affairs in 1885. But he was a capable and ambitious man and rose to become an Indian Agent at the File Hills Agency in Saskatchewan by 1896. He would go on to become the leading Indian Affairs administrative figure in western Canada during the early decades of the twentieth century. He gained support from Ottawa to launch the experimental File Hills colony, where residential-school graduates were given aid to begin farming in a model settlement largely cut off from other elements of the local indigenous community. He was promoted again to Indian commissioner for the Prairie provinces in 1918, but never attained his ultimate goal of becoming head of Indian Affairs. Increasingly, he clashed with Duncan Campbell Scott and the Ottawa administration and was forcibly retired in 1932, just as Scott himself was preparing to vacate the post of deputy superintendent general of Indian Affairs. Graham faded into retirement a bitter man. See Brian Titley, "W.M. Graham: Indian Agent Extraordinaire," *Prairie Forum* 8, 1 (1983): 25-41. Daly served almost twenty years as the Indian Agent in Parry Sound and is the subject of Robin Brownlie's interesting article, "Man on the Spot."

96 Duncan Campbell Scott is also well known for his poetry, much of which contained "Indian" themes and characters. The "Indian" of Scott's poems descended from a wild and romantic past, but there was a clear division between the wild, "savage," historical "Indian" and the degraded and declining remnants that he was forced to deal with in his position as deputy superintendent general. He repeatedly portrayed struggles between the energetic old ways and the new realities of civilization for indigenous people. Controlling the flickers of this wild energy of the past was the essence of the civilizing mission, particu-

larly as he emphasized the infantile nature of First Nations people and viewed the assimilation process as one of maturing and weaning the Indian from his primitive state. See Leslie Monkman, *A Native Heritage: Images of the Indian in English-Canadian Literature* (Toronto: University of Toronto Press, 1981); and Terry Goldie, *Fear and Temptation: The Image of the Indigene in Canadian, Australian and New Zealand Literatures* (Montreal and Kingston: McGill-Queen's University Press, 1989).

97 Philip H. Godsell, "Indians on Relief," *Saturday Night*, 12 December 1936, 5. Only rarely did commentators directly attack Canada for its role. One example that went against this general rule was written by a former superintendent of the Six Nations Indians, Lt.-Col. C.E. Morgan, who challenged his readers to "ask yourself who is better off, the Negroes in the United States who were slaves, with nothing, and are now free citizens, or the Indians, who owned Canada and are now but little better off than were the Negroes before emancipation." "Lo, the Poor Indian," *Saturday Night*, 2 April 1938, 2.

Chapter 2: The "Administrative Indian" as Soldier and Conscript, 1939-45

1 These events have been outlined in R. Scott Sheffield, "'... in the same manner as other people': Government Policy and the Military Service of Canada's First Nations People, 1939-1945," MA thesis, University of Victoria, 1995; and Michael D. Stevenson, "The Mobilisation of Native Canadians during the Second World War," *Journal of the Canadian Historical Association* 7 (1996): 205-26.

2 Alison Bernstein, *American Indians and World War II: Toward a New Era in Indian Affairs* (Norman, OK: University of Oklahoma Press, 1991); Tom Holm, "Fighting a White Man's War: The Extent and Legacy of American Indian Participation in World War II," *The Journal of Ethnic Studies* 9, 2 (1981): 69-81; Thomas A. Britten, *American Indians in World War I: At Home and at War* (Albuquerque, NM: University of New Mexico Press, 1997); Jeré Bishop Franco, *Crossing the Pond: The Native American Effort in World War II* (Denton, TX: University of North Texas Press, 1999); and Kenneth William Townsend, *World War II and the American Indian* (Albuquerque, NM: University of New Mexico Press, 2000).

3 After the Great War, Canada made a similar but much more limited gesture by granting the vote to First Nations veterans without negating their Indian status. Full citizenship was not extended, nor was the privilege of the franchise given to those who had not enlisted.

4 Hayes was a Pima Indian from the American Southwest. He served a capable but relatively inconspicuous term in the US Marine Corps in the Pacific theatre. This all changed when, during the battle of Iwo Jima, Hayes was one of the soldiers to raise the American flag captured in the famous photo for *Life* magazine. The entire flag-raising party was returned to the United States for promotional tours in aid of recruiting and boosting home-front morale. The spotlight shone especially brightly on Hayes, who was increasingly uncomfortable with the attention and perhaps never fully recovered. After the war, a broke and broken man, he drank himself to death in relative obscurity in 1955. For more information, see Albert Hemingway, *Ira Hayes: Pima Indian* (New York: University Press of America, 1988).

5 Holm, "Fighting a White Man's War," 78-9. This interpretation is best articulated by Holm and Clayton R. Koppes, "From New Deal to Termination: Liberalism and Indian Policy, 1933-1953," *Pacific Historical Review* 46, 3 (1977): 543-66. Also worth a look is Donald L. Fixico, *Termination and Relocation: Federal Indian Policy, 1945-60* (Albuquerque, NM: University of New Mexico Press, 1986), especially Chapter 1, "Warriors in World War II and New Attitudes." Though showing its age, this orthodox interpretation has not been significantly altered to date. Motivated by similar liberal democratic principles of individualism and equality, Pierre Trudeau and Jean Chrétien developed the 1969 White Paper on Indian Affairs, which in many ways mirrored the American policy of termination. It called for nullification of Indian status, abolition of the Indian Act, and the granting of full citizenship. The storm of protest from Aboriginal groups in response to the measure and the later withdrawal of the White Paper effectively marked the end of assimilation as government policy and the political resurgence of Aboriginal people in Canada.

6 Holm, "Fighting a White Man's War," 79.

7 Jonathan F. Vance, *Death So Noble: Memory, Meaning and the First World War* (Vancouver: UBC Press, 1997).

8 Ian Miller, *Our Glory and Our Grief: Torontonians in the Great War* (Toronto: University of Toronto Press, 2002).
9 Maclachlan to Camsell, 18 March 1941, DND, DHist 112.3H1.009/D293. In fact, several Native men did manage to enlist prior to 1943, but their numbers were very small as a proportion of overall enlistment.
10 Hollies to OIC, RCAF Recruiting Centre, Montreal, NAC, RG 24, vol.3307, file H.Q. 282-1-2 v.2. The motivation for this decision is uncertain. The memo cited contains no explanation for the decision, and no mention of it was found elsewhere.
11 Jean Barman, Yvonne Hébert, and Don McCaskill, eds., *Indian Education in Canada,* Volume 1: *The Legacy* (Vancouver: UBC Press, 1986), 18.
12 Nor does this tell the whole story, as well over half of Native recruits were rejected due to health or education restrictions or as a result of "racist" recruiters and policies. For more information on this issue, see R. Scott Sheffield, "'Of Pure European Descent and of the White Race': Recruitment Policy and Aboriginal Canadians," *Canadian Military History* 5, 1 (Spring 1996): 8-15; and Stevenson, "The Mobilisation of Native Canadians."
13 Michael D. Stevenson, *Canada's Greatest Wartime Muddle: National Selective Service and the Mobilization of Human Resources during World War II* (Montreal and Kingston: McGill-Queen's University Press, 2001), 4.
14 Director to Cory, 24 September 1940, NAC, RG 10, vol. 6768, file 452-20, pt. 4.
15 Cory to McGill, 26 September 1940, NAC, RG 10, vol. 6768, file 452-20, pt. 4.
16 This is evident in a number of works on those First Nations leaders and organizations that were prominent during this era, including: E.P. Patterson, "Andrew Paull and Canadian Indian Resurgence," PhD dissertation, University of Washington, 1962; Hugh Shewell, "Jules Sioui and Indian Political Radicalism in Canada, 1943-44," *Journal of Canadian Studies* 34, 3 (Fall 1999): 211-41; Paul Tennant, *Aboriginal Peoples and Politics: The Indian Land Question in British Columbia, 1849-1989* (Vancouver: UBC Press, 1990); Jean Goodwill and Norma Sluman, *John Tootoosis* (1982; reprint, Winnipeg: Pemmican Publications, 1984); and Alan Morley, *Roar of the Breakers: A Biography of Peter Kelly* (Toronto: Ryerson Press, 1967).
17 Jules Sioui (1906-90), a Huron from Loretteville, Quebec, was among the more radical indigenous leaders of this era. He proved instrumental in organizing two national Native conferences in 1943 and 1944, which brought indigenous grievances over conscription and taxation to national attention. However, his radicalism combined with his abrasive style to make him a pariah with government officials of all stripes, and he was out of step with other Native leaders of the day, minimizing his initially high profile. As a result, he was quickly marginalized from the burgeoning new politicization of First Nations people and would remain an outsider in the postwar years. John Tootoosis was a prominent Plains Cree political leader from Saskatchewan. He played a critical role along with Sioui in organizing the wartime Native conferences, was somewhat active in the early life of the North American Indian Brotherhood (NAIB), and eventually helped to create and lead the primary provincial native organization set up after the war. Andrew Paull was a Squamish man who became a prominent advocate for Native rights from the 1920s to the 1950s. He first came to prominence when he became involved as an interpreter for the McKenna-McBride Commission in British Columbia in the 1920s. Paull also had been active within various indigenous political organizations from the Allied Tribes in 1916. He later gained prominence as a sports writer for the *Vancouver Province* newspaper and as a promoter of Native events and sporting teams. He joined and helped to organize and build the Native Brotherhood of British Columbia (NBBC) in 1942, a long-lived and effective Native rights group with strong representation up and down the Pacific Coast. But he had his own vision of things and left the NBBC in 1943 to help found the NAIB as a truly national organization. He remained among the most high-profile and eloquent postwar activists until his death in 1960. See Tennant, *Aboriginal Peoples and Politics*, 89, 99, 118-21, 129.
18 These included the Union of Ontario Indians (a branch of the NAIB) in 1946-47; the Manitoba Indian Brotherhood in 1946; the Union of Saskatchewan Indians, formed in 1946 with the help of the provincial Co-operative Commonwealth Federation (CCF) and G.H. Castelden, the federal CCF member for Yorkton, effectively amalgamating the three previous provincial organizations under one structure; and the Confederation of Interior Tribes of BC (loosely affiliated with Paull's NAIB) in 1947.

19 Stevenson, "The Mobilisation of Native Canadians."
20 Alexander Morris, *The Treaties of Canada with the Indians of Manitoba, the North West Territories and Kee-wa-tin* (Saskatoon: Fifth House, 1880), 218, 234. See also Memorandum for T.R.L. MacInnes, by R. Grenier, 13 June 1941, NAC, RG 10, vol. 8594, file 1/1-11, pt. 1. For a more involved discussion of these limited exemptions, the treaty promises, and the legal issues raised, see R. Scott Sheffield and Hamar Foster, "Fighting the King's War: Harris Smallfence, Verbal Treaty Promises and the Conscription of Indian Men, 1944," *University of British Columbia Law Review* 33, 1 (1999): 53-74.
21 T.A. Crerar (1876-1975) was the product of a Scots heritage and a rural Manitoba upbringing. He served in public life from 1917 until his retirement in 1966. He was the only man to serve in two wartime Cabinets, as minister of agriculture under Sir Robert Borden and as minister of mines and resources under William Lyon Mackenzie King. In between he briefly led the Progressive Party in its meteoric rise in the early 1920s. He served as minister of mines and resources from 1935 until 1945, during which he was titular head of the Indian Affairs Branch. Crerar remained aloof from the day-to-day running of Indian Affairs during this decade and proved autocratic when he did become involved in administering Canada's Status Indian population. For more information, see J.E. Rea, *T.A. Crerar: A Political Life* (Montreal and Kingston: McGill-Queen's University Press, 1997).
22 J. Ostrander to Secretary, 11 September 1941, NAC, RG 10, vol. 6764, file 452-6, pt. 2.
23 I was first struck by the parallels while reading the first-hand accounts of Native children who had experienced residential schools in Celia Haig-Brown's, *Resistance and Renewal: Surviving the Indian Residential School* (Vancouver: Tillacum Library, 1988). J.R. Miller's *Shingwuak's Vision: A History of Native Residential Schools* (Toronto: University of Toronto Press, 1996), based on extensive archival and oral research, is the best survey of the residential experience in Canada to date. His monograph provides ample examples of this pattern, the dominant-society beliefs upon which it was based, and some painful examples of its impact on First Nations children.
24 Samuel Devlin to Secretary, 2 October 1940, NAC, RG 10, vol. 6768, file 452-20, pt. 4.
25 J. Thibault to Secretary, 21 April 1942, NAC, RG 10, vol. 6768, file 452-20, pt. 4.
26 Circular Letter from T.R.L. MacInnes, 13 September 1939, NAC, RG 10, vol. 6764, file 452-6, pt. 2.
27 T.R.L. MacInnes to M. Christianson, Esq., 2 July 1941, NAC, RG 10, vol. 6764, file 452-6, pt. 2.
28 Director – Circular Letter, 31 July 1943, NAC, RG 10 vol. 6768, file 452-20, pt. 4.
29 Agent's Report for March 1940, 6 April 1940, NAC, RG 10, vol. 6765, file 452-6-56.
30 M.S. Todd to Secretary, 2 April 1942, NAC, RG 10, vol. 6768, file 452-20, pt. 4.
31 See Sheffield, "'... in the same manner as other people,'" Chapters 3 and 4.
32 For instance, see James W. St. G. Walker, "Race and Recruitment during World War I: Enlistment of Visible Minorities in the Canadian Expeditionary Force," *Canadian Historical Review* 70, 1 (1989): 1-26; and Stephen A. Bell, "The 107th 'Timber Wolf' Battalion at Hill 70," *Canadian Military History* 5, 1 (Spring 1996): 73-8.
33 Director to Col. C.R. Hill, 19 August 1942, NAC, RG 10, vol. 6764, file 452-6, pt. 2.
34 Report of Kwawkewlth Agency, March 1944, NAC, RG 10, vol. 6769, file 452-20-3. The First Nations of this agency were especially involved in the fishing industry after the removal of the Japanese from the Pacific Coast. The number of deferrals was also due to the intransigence of the National Selective Service authorities who were not keen to accept Native conscripts by this stage of the war; see Stevenson, "The Mobilisation of Native Canadians."
35 Victor Webb to Secretary, 22 October 1940, NAC, RG 10, vol. 6768, file 452-20, pt. 4.
36 Memorandum from Director to Mr. Cory, 24 September 1940, NAC, RG 10, vol. 6768, file 452-20, pt. 4.
37 W. Cory to the Director, 26 September 1940, NAC, RG 10, vol. 6770, file 452-26, pt. 2.
38 The IAB and DNWS repeatedly referred the question to the Department of Justice in 1940, 1941, 1942, and twice in 1944, and the courts had their say in *Le Roi v. Harris Smallfence*, a test case in Montreal during 1943. See *Le Roi v. Harris Smallfence*, Court of the King's Bench in Montreal, Quebec, 21 June 1943 [unreported]; and NAC, RG 10, vol. 6769, file 452-20-10, pt. 2.

39 Sheffield, "'... in the same manner as other people,'" and Stevenson, "Mobilising Native Canadians," detail Native protests and resistence to registration and conscription.

40 Director to Deputy Minister, 7 February 1941, NAC, RG 10, vol. 6770, file 452-26, pt. 2, mentions the IAB's concerns regarding the issue of how the Six Nations would record their nationality on the National registration form. The dismissal of the 1918 precedent of exempting Native people from conscription was already mentioned. See Cory to the Director, 26 September 1940, NAC, RG 10, vol. 6770, file 452-26, pt. 2.

41 Frank Edwards to Secretary, 26 September 1940, NAC, RG 10, vol. 6770, file 452-26, pt. 2.

42 Devlin to Secretary, 2 October 1940.

43 Sheffield, "'... in the same manner as other people,'" 98, quoting Director to Randle, 5 November 1940, NAC, RG 10, vol. 6770, file 452-26, pt. 2

44 The Status Indian population of the four treaty areas was 22,450 according to a departmental census in 1939, when the total Status Indian population was 118,378. By 1944 the total Status Indian population had risen to 125,686. See Canada, Parliament, *Special Joint Committee of the Senate and the House of Commons appointed to examine and consider the Indian Act*, Minutes of Proceedings and Evidence, No. 1, 28 and 30 May 1946, 8.

45 Circular letter from MacInnes, 13 September 1939.

46 Secretary to Inspectors of Indian Agencies and the Indian Commissioner of BC – Strictly Confidential, 17 April 1942, NAC, RG 10, vol. 6768, file 452-20, pt. 4. The letter concerned problems encountered in ensuring that Native men who were located in remote areas responded to calls for medical exams and military training. If the RCMP was sent to apprehend these individuals, the expense was often great, and even if the "Indian" was located, the chances of his passing the medical exam were not high.

47 Ibid. The IAB was so worried about the appearance of equality that the secretary closed this circular with an extra admonishment to maintain secrecy and avoid leakage of such information. If word had gotten out, it would have had the consequence of establishing an unwanted precedent of special treatment for the "Indian."

48 This was noted by John L. Tobias in his landmark article, "Protection, Civilization, Assimilation: An Outline History of Canada's Indian Policy," in *As Long as the Sun Shines and the Water Flows: A Reader in Canadian-Native Relations*, edited by Ian A.L. Getty and Antoine S. Lussier (Vancouver: UBC Press, 1983), 39-55.

49 D.M. MacKay to C.G. Pennock, 16 January 1942, NAC, RG 10, vol. 6768, file 452-20, pt. 4.

50 D.M. McKay to Secretary, 24 April 1942, NAC, RG 10, vol. 6768, file 452-20, pt. 4.

51 A. Hoey – Circular to all Indian Agents, Inspectors of Indian Agencies and the Indian Commissioner of British Columbia, 12 February 1945, NAC, RG 10, vol. 6769, file 452-20, pt. 6.

52 Many of these protests arrived at the IAB via the Indian Agents' reports – for example: Brisebois to Indian Affairs Branch, 5 October 1940; T.W. Webb to Secretary, 22 October 1940; A.G. Smith to Secretary, 30 October 1940; Blackfoot Council Meeting – Minutes, 30 May 1941; W.P.B. Pugh to Secretary, 1 October 1941, NAC, RG 10, vol. 6768, file 452-20, pt. 4; Randle to Indian Affairs, 15 March 1943; and Blackfoot Council Meeting – Minutes, 21 February 1945, NAC, RG 10, vol. 6769, file 452-20, pt. 6. Frustrated by the lack of action on the part of Indian Affairs, however, many Natives sent their protests to the prime minister, the minister of defence, and even the British high commisioner. See, for example, Shot Both Sides, Frank Red Crow, Percey Creighton, Fred T. Feathers and Cross Child to Minister of Defence, 3 September 1942, NAC RG 10, vol. 6769, file 452-20, pt. 5; "Jas S. Hill" Oshweken to W.L.M. King, 21 September 1940; and Arthur Anderson to Malcolm MacDonald, High Commissioner for the United Kingdom, 22 February 1941, NAC, RG 10, vol. 6770, file 452-26, pt. 2.

53 Brisebois to McGill, 2 December 1943, NAC, RG 10, vol. 6768, file 452-20, pt. 4. The agent attributed the outbreak in part to the tensions created by the conscription issue.

54 Secretary to Inspectors of Indian Agencies and the Indian Commissioner of BC, 17 April 1942.

55 C. Schmidt to Secretary, 26 May 1942, NAC, RG 10, vol. 6768, file 452-20, pt. 4.

56 A.G. Hamilton to Secretary, 10 November 1942, NAC, RG 10, vol. 6769, file 452-20, pt. 5.

57 Director – Circular to all Indian Agents, Inspectors and the Indian Commissioner of BC, 31 July 1943, NAC, RG 10, vol. 6768, file 452-20, pt. 4.

58 Smith to Secretary, 30 October 1940.

59 Director to T.L Bonnah, 5 April 1944, NAC, RG 10, vol. 6769, file 452-20-10, pt. 1.

60 Much of the opposition to conscription among Native groups up and down the Pacific Coast was attributed to the activities of the "Native Brotherhood," although it is not clear whether the agents were referring to the Native Brotherhood of British Columbia or to the North American Indian Brotherhood, led by Andy Paull. W. Christie to Secretary, 11 October 1941, NAC, RG 10, vol. 6768, file 452-20, pt. 4; F. Earl Anfield – Report for December 1943, Bella Coola Agency, NAC, RG 10, vol. 6769, file 452-20-3; and Chief Executive Assistant to S.H. MacLaren, 31 July 1943, NAC, RG 10, vol. 6769, file 452-20, pt. 6. Robin Brownlie has demonstrated the tendency for IAB correspondence to blame agitators during the interwar years in her article, "Man on the Spot: John Daly, Indian Agent in Parry Sound, 1922-1939," *Journal of the Canadian Historical Association* 5 (1994): 63-86.

61 D.M. MacKay to Secretary, 13 November 1941, NAC, RG 10, vol. 11 288, file 139-44.

62 Alfred Barber – Agent's Reports, 1 November 1940, 30 November 1940, and Barber to Secretary, 21 March 1941, NAC, RG 10, vol. 6770, file 452-26, pt. 2. Barber was more patient than most Indian Agents in this regard. Few would have waited so long or tried so often to persuade the individual before informing the authorities and initiating legal action.

63 Barber to Secretary, 21 March 1941.

64 Usually the agent would try to isolate the principal "agitators" and first persuade them in the hopes of diffusing the opposition within a community. If this failed, these individuals were then made an example of and prosecuted.

65 Director – Circular to all Indian Agents, Inspectors and the Indian Commissioner of BC, 31 July 1943.

66 D.J. Allen to the Director, 25 September 1940, NAC, RG 10, vol. 6770, file 452-26, pt. 2.

67 Ibid. Similar difficulties to those experienced in Brantford were experienced by the IAB as a result of the activities of affiliated groups on other Iroquois reserves, such as St. Regis, Caughnawaga, Tyendinaga, and others. D.J. Allen was a part of what John Leslie has identified as a "Manitoba mafia" in Indian Affairs during these years, along with Crerar, Hoey, and Crerar's assistant, C.W. Jackson, as well as Crerar's eventual successor, J.A. Glen. Leslie, "Assimilation, Integration or Termination? The Development of Canadian Indian Policy, 1943-1963," PhD dissertation, Carleton University, 1999.

68 Director to the Deputy Minister, 7 February 1941.

69 T.C. Davis to McGill, 2 May 1941, NAC, RG 10, vol. 6770, file 452-26, pt. 2.

70 C.W. Jackson to McGill, 14 February 1941; T.C. Davis to C.W. Jackson, 12 February 1941, NAC, RG 10, file 452-26, pt. 2.

71 Jackson to McGill, 14 February 1941.

72 McGill to T.C. Davis, 6 May 1941, RCMP Division file 40 T 172/73, 30 March 1943, NAC, RG 10, vol. 6770, file 452-26, pt. 2.

Chapter 3: The "Public Indian" Goes to War, September 1939-December 1941

1 Of the papers surveyed, the *Vancouver Sun, Winnipeg Free Press, Halifax Chronicle, Brantford Expositor, Saskatoon Star-Phoenix, Kamloops Sentinel, Cardston News,* and *Prince Albert Daily Herald* all carried a substantial number of "Indian" stories, relative to the pre-war years, with some showing a slight increase. Only the *Globe and Mail* significantly reduced its previously large number of Native human-interest stories.

2 The most widely reported and brutal of the cases was that of Nelson Sammy, a Cree of the White Bear Reserve in Saskatchewan, who was eventually executed for the murder of his wife, her parents, and an RCMP constable in August 1939. "Indian Accused of Murdering Four Persons," *Prince Albert Daily Herald,* 28 September 1939, 8. Another case was that of a Blood man named Round Nose, or in some stories Big Nose, who was charged with the murder of his wife in September 1939. The *Calgary Herald* noted the incident on 23 September 1939, 4, and the trial in "Charge Indian Murdered Wife," 12 October 1939, 1. The *Cardston News* carried extensive coverage of the death and the subsequent trial. See "Blood Indian Held at Lethbridge Jail as Wife Near Death at Local Hospital," 21 September 1939, 1; "Blood Indian Faces Murder Charge," 12 October 1939, 3; "Round Nose Confined for Trial," 19 October 1939, 1.

3   "The Indian List: Alberta Roll of Interdictions Tragic Record of Drinkers," *Calgary Herald*, 2 September 1939, 24.
4   *Cardston News*, 19 October 1939, 2. This disclaimer was at the end of a short editorial assuring Cardstonians that, despite the recent spate of crime stories involving people from the nearby Blood Reserve, the Blood "Indians" were really a peace-loving and law-abiding people. The editors went further, noting "the wonderful progress in adopting the ways and manners of living of their neighbours."
5   "Six Sarcees Had Income of $2,500 in '38," *Calgary Herald*, 30 January 1940, 10.
6   "Clever Display By B.C. Indians," *Vancouver Sun*, 17 September 1939, 18; "Museum Show Stresses Beauty of Indian Art," *Globe and Mail*, 11 January 1940, 5; "Indian Fair to Start Tuesday," *Brantford Expositor*, 5 October 1939, 6.
7   "High Death Rate: Federal Authorities Fight Tuberculosis among Indians," *Winnipeg Free Press*, 9 September 1939, 5; "The Vanishing American Isn't Vanishing," *Halifax Chronicle*, 5 January 1940, 4; "Indians Not Vanishing," *Brantford Expositor*, 5 September 1939, 6. The greater publicity given to the growth of the Indian population still seems not to have fully penetrated the myth of the decline and inevitable extinction of the "Indian" race. See, for instance, "Injun Summer," *Winnipeg Free Press*, Magazine Section, 14 October 1939, 1. The poem describes an old-timer telling a young boy about the "Indian Summer" and the "Injuns" of days gone by. He assures the boy that although there were once "heaps of Injuns around here – thousands – millions, I reckon," there was no reason to be frightened, as there "hain't none around here now, leastways no live ones. They been gone this many a year. They all went away and died, so they ain't no more left."
8   One article made light of legends among the Cree of northern Manitoba regarding an aquatic moose, which the papers dubbed "A Moose of the Ogopogo Class" and a "submeroose." "Here's Moose of the Ogopogo Class," *Saskatoon Star-Phoenix*, 8 September 1939, 6. Ogopogo was the name of a famous mythical creature that First Nations people claim inhabited Lake Okanagan in British Columbia. The story garnered wide circulation through the practice of printing articles from other papers and reached the *Halifax Chronicle*, via the *Montreal Gazette*, by the end of September as "Amphibious," 30 September 1939, 4.
9   Philip H. Godsell, "Today Is Indian Day," *Winnipeg Free Press*, Magazine Section, 30 September 1939, 6.
10   "Three Squaws," *Vancouver Sun*, 10 October 1939, 4.
11   "Hitler Fated for Hot Place Now British Angry," *Prince Albert Daily Herald*, 15 September 1939, 8.
12   "An Indian Chief," *Halifax Chronicle*, 11 October 1939, 4.
13   "Indians Did Not Believe War On," *Calgary Herald*, 15 September 1939, 11.
14   "Indians' Discover Conflict's Effect," *Halifax Chronicle*, 15 September 1939, 2.
15   "Andy Ned," *Vancouver Sun*, 26 October 1939, 4.
16   "First Local Volunteers for Army Service Leave Here for Training," *Cardston News*, 14 September 1939, 1.
17   "Eighteen Mistawasis Indians Join Infantry," *Saskatoon Star-Phoenix*, 14 October 1939, 3.
18   Two photos were included with the story, one taken of the eighteen recruits, the other showing Chief Dreaver in full regalia, complete with eagle-feather headdress and heavily beaded buckskin clothing. Joe Dreaver had enlisted as a sapper in the First World War, earning a Military Medal in Belgium while serving with the Royal Canadian Engineers. Though he lost two brothers in the Great War, he served again in the Veterans' Guard during the Second World War, watching German POWs in Medicine Hat, Alberta. Now chief of the Mistawassis Cree, he strongly encouraged Native service in the military, including that of his three sons and two daughters. He would remain a driving force in the politicization of Saskatchewan First Nations after the Second World War.
19   The prevalence of scientific racism, eugenics, and a belief in the fixed nature of racial categories and attributes in Canada during the first half of the twentieth century is evident in James W. St. G. Walker, *"Race," Rights and the Law in the Supreme Court of Canada: Historical Case Studies* (Waterloo and Toronto: Wilfrid Laurier University Press and the Osgoode Society, 1997); Angus McLaren, *Our Own Master Race: Eugenics in Canada, 1885-1945* (Toronto: McClelland and Stewart, 1990); Howard Palmer, *Patterns of Prejudice: A History of Nativism*

in Alberta (Toronto: McClelland and Stewart, 1982); W. Peter Ward, *White Canada Forever: Popular Attitudes and Public Policies Towards Orientals in British Columbia,* 2nd ed. (Montreal and Kingston: McGill-Queen's University Press, 1990); and Kay Anderson, *Vancouver's Chinatown: Racial Discourse in Canada, 1875-1980* (Montreal and Kingston: McGill-Queen's University Press, 1991).

20 According to the story, if each of the eighteen passed his medical exam (eleven had already passed), then there would be twenty men enlisted out of a reserve population of about 225.

21 "Indians Did Not Believe War On," *Calgary Herald,* 15 September 1939, 11.

22 "Cree Indians Given Thanks of Canada," *Brantford Expositor,* 27 January 1940, 7.

23 "Honor Where Due," *Winnipeg Free Press,* 18 January 1940, 11.

24 On 6 January 1940, the Canadian Press released a story from Canada House in London based on selected clippings from British papers' treatment of the arrival of the first soldiers from Canada. The amusing story belittled the naivety and ignorance of the British journalists, who paid particular attention to the Native and black soldiers. One of the terms coined by the *Glasgow Evening News* that was singled out for particular derision was "Maginot Mohicans." See *Saskatoon Star-Phoenix,* 6 January 1940, 2; *Prince Albert Daily Herald,* 6 January 1940, 5; "Canucks Chuckle at Press Reports," *Halifax Chronicle,* 6 January 1940, 1-2; "Without Their Tomahawks," *Brantford Expositor,* 10 January 1940, 4. Most carried the Canadian Press story verbatim, but the *Expositor* printed an editorial that went far beyond the bemused tone of the original piece. It was more darkly sarcastic and caustic in its assessment of the British press.

25 "Honor Where Due," *Winnipeg Free Press,* 18 January 1940, 11.

26 Robert H. Keyserlingk, "Breaking the Nazi Pact: Canadian Government Attitudes Towards German Canadians, 1939-1945," in *On Guard for Thee: War, Ethnicity, and the Canadian State, 1939-1945,* edited by Norman Hillmer et al. (Ottawa: Canadian Committee for the History of the Second World War, 1988), 53-69, 60.

27 "Nazis Seeking to Rouse Indians," *Winnipeg Free Press,* 5 June 1940, 3. The story was also carried in "Reports of 'Fifth Column' Operation Among U.S. Indians," *Brantford Expositor,* 5 June 1940, 12; and in a different format in "Hitler Includes American Indian," *Saskatoon Star-Phoenix,* 7 June 1940, 7.

28 See Kenneth William Townsend, *World War II and the American Indian* (Albuquerque, NM: University of New Mexico Press, 2000), Chapter 2; and Jeré Bishop Franco, *Crossing the Pond: The Native American Effort in World War II* (Denton, TX: University of North Texas Press, 1999), Chapter 1. There is no evidence that a similar attempt was ever made in Canada.

29 "Indians Are Loyal," *Calgary Herald,* 4 July 1940, 4.

30 Only about one-sixth of the Indian population was exempted due to explicit, verbal treaty promises that had been made during the negotiation of Treaties 3, 6, 8, and 11 between 1876 and 1921. These treaty areas covered northeastern British Columbia, a large portion of the Prairies, parts of northwestern Ontario, and the Territories.

31 "Indians Are Loyal," *Calgary Herald,* 4 July 1940, 4.

32 "Indian Generous to War Causes," *Saturday Night,* 10 August 1940, 17. The piece opened claiming, "Assuredly to be counted among the most patriotic of Canada's citizens are Saskatchewan Indians who have given generously of their money, and in one case have donated an ambulance, to help the Empire war cause."

33 "Indians Display Loyalty in Gift of Treaty Money," *Saskatoon Star-Phoenix,* 17 June 1940, 4. An abbreviated version of the story also appeared both in the *Winnipeg Free Press,* "Indian Aid: Give Treaty Money to Help Win War," 17 June 1940, 10, and a few weeks later, via the *Windsor Star,* in the *Halifax Chronicle,* "Three Cheers for the Crees," 3 July 1940, 8.

34 "Indian Children Assist Red Cross," *Vancouver Sun,* 6 July 1940, 16.

35 This was also the case in a similar article in Winnipeg, "Aid from Indians: Residents of Manitoba Do Bit in Filling Red Cross Coffers," *Winnipeg Free Press,* 7 August 1940, 3.

36 This was not uniformly the case. The paper in Saskatoon assured its readers that the Fishing Lake Band had made the decision to donate $1,000 to the government for war costs entirely of its own initiative but went on to claim that "the articles published in the *Star-Phoenix* concerning the recent donations from other Indian bands in the Province were

more or less responsible for the decision of this particular band." "Indian Band Donates $1,000 to War Effort," *Saskatoon Star-Phoenix*, 25 July 1940, 10.

37 "Stonies at Ceremonial Sun Dance Pray for Victory for Britain," *Calgary Herald*, 20 June 1940, 1-2. The *Herald* actually ran two stories about the Sun Dance that day, the other being "Tom-Toms of Stonies Beat Time for Tribesmen's Sun Dance Ritual," *Calgary Herald*, 20 June 1940, 1, 5.

38 "Stonies at Ceremonial Sun Dance Pray for Victory for Britain," *Calgary Herald*, 20 June 1940, 1-2.

39 "Tom-Toms of Stonies Beat Time for Tribesmen's Sun Dance Ritual," *Calgary Herald*, 20 June 1940, 1, 5.

40 "Stonies at Ceremonial Sun Dance Pray for Victory for Britain," *Calgary Herald*, 20 June 1940, 1-2.

41 "Men of Tough Northern Breed with Grey and Simcoe Foresters at Camp Borden," *Globe and Mail*, 1 July 1940, 5. This was a brief photo essay, but the largest picture was of "Private Jack Kahbejee, Chippewa Indian from Southampton district, [who] laughs broadly as he starts to fill his palliasse with straw."

42 "Indians Donate $2,080 to Purchase Ambulance," *Saskatoon Star-Phoenix*, 19 September 1940, 11. A similar story about several Alberta Cree communities who gave an ambulance to the Royal Canadian Army Medical Corps ran on the front page in Brantford a week later, "Cree Indians Give R.C.A.M.C. Ambulance," *Brantford Expositor*, 25 June 1940, 1.

43 "Metis Pledge Their Support," *Saskatoon Star-Phoenix*, 2 July 1940, 3; "All-Indian Battalion Suggested," *Saskatoon Star-Phoenix*, 5 July 1940, 4; "Indian Band Donates $1,000 to War Effort," *Saskatoon Star-Phoenix*, 25 July 1940, 4. Chief Dreaver's call for an "all-Indian" unit also appeared in "Indians May Form Battalion," *Prince Albert Daily Herald*, 5 July 1940, 3; and "All-Indian Battalion," *Winnipeg Free Press*, 5 July 1940, 7.

44 This subject remains poorly documented by historians and anthropologists in Canada. However, a sense of the diversity of motivation and response can be gleaned from R. Scott Sheffield, "'... in the same manner as other people': Government Policy and the Military Service of Canada's First Nations People, 1939-1945," MA thesis, University of Victoria, 1995; Janice Summerby, *Native Soldiers Foreign Battlefields* (Ottawa: Ministry of Supply and Services Canada, 1993); James L. Dempsey, "Alberta's Indians and the Second World War," in *For King and Country: Alberta and the Second World War*, edited by Ken Tingley (Edmonton: Provincial Museum of Alberta, 1995), 39-52; Fred Gaffen, *Forgotten Soldiers* (Penticton, BC: Theytus Books, 1985); and Janet F. Davison, "We Shall Remember Them: Canadian Indians and World War II," MA thesis, Trent University, 1992.

45 James L. Dempsey, *Warriors of the King: Prairie Indians in World War I* (Regina, SK: Canadian Plains Research Centre, 1999). Dempsey argues that this was one of the primary reasons for enlistment among Plains First Nations. He effectively details the survival of cultural forms and meaning among these groups up to the outbreak of war in 1914. He infers from this that the warrior ethic remained alive and a primary rationale for Prairie Native recruits, but he provides very little evidence in support of this claim.

46 "Indians Display Loyalty in Gift of Treaty Money," *Saskatoon Star-Phoenix*, 17 June 1940, 4.

47 "Three Cheers for the Crees," *Halifax Chronicle*, 3 July 1940, 8.

48 Dempsey, *Warriors of the King*, 34-5.

49 Ibid., 35.

50 "Worshipped by Indians," *Vancouver Sun*, 7 June 1940, 10; "Kamloops Gale Kills Indian," *Vancouver Sun*, 13 July 1940, 16; "Artistry of B.C. Indians Feature of Exhibition," *Vancouver Sun*, 29 August 1940, 13. Traditional images still abounded in the following articles: "Canada Has Wealth of Folklore and Handicraft," *Prince Albert Daily Herald*, 1 June 1940, 4; "Indian Pays With His Life for Murder," *Prince Albert Daily Herald*, 5 July 1940, 2; "Survived All Progeny, Big Wind Dies at 101," *Globe and Mail*, 13 July 1940, 5; and "Kilted Indians Arrive, Dumfound Scot Writers," *Globe and Mail*, 3 August 1940, 3.

51 "Indians Celebrate Their Treaty Day," *Saskatoon Star-Phoenix*, 22 June 1940, 8.

52 "Fifteen Stony Tepees for Fair Indian Camp," *Calgary Herald*, 2 July 1940, 10; "Indians Seek Prize Last Won 28 years Ago," *Calgary Herald*, 8 July 1940, 9; "Braves, Squaws Thrill Crowds at Street Show," *Calgary Herald*, 9 July 1940, 9; "Sarcees in Finery Thrill City Visitors,"

Calgary Herald, 10 July 1940, 10; "Indians Display Best Wigwam Competition," *Calgary Herald*, 15 July 1940, 10. The coverage of "Indian" material also appeared in a number of other Stampede articles during the week and in numerous pictorials.

53 For 1941 every issue of the weekly publications was examined and, among the dailies, those papers for all of January, 27 April to 6 June, 22 June to 30 July, and all of December. These time periods covered the British winter victories in the Western Desert as well as the German conquest of Greece and Crete, Erwin Rommel's entry into the African theatre, Germany's invasion of the Soviet Union, and the Japanese offensives of December, notably Pearl Harbor and the invasion of Hong Kong, which marked the first time Canadian ground forces fought in pitched battle.

54 Of course, there were wide variations among the papers consulted, most noticeably in the virtual disappearance of the "Indian" from the *Halifax Chronicle*. Only three articles involving "Indian" subject matter or imagery appeared in the time periods searched, less than half the number that had appeared in September 1939 alone. The *Globe and Mail* and *Prince Albert Daily Herald* also significantly decreased their coverage of "Indian" stories. However, only slight declines were evident in the *Brantford Expositor*, *Saskatoon Star-Phoenix*, and *Winnipeg Free Press*, and there was no decline at all in the *Calgary Herald*, *Cardston News*, and *Vancouver Sun*. Remarkably, the *Kamloops Sentinel*, which had previously given only minimal attention to the "Indian," significantly increased its coverage in 1941, printing twenty-seven stories about "Indians" as opposed to the two they had printed in 1940. Numbers themselves are crude indicators, but they do provide a general sense of waxing and waning interest.

55 "Six Nations Indians With the Dufferin and Haldimand Rifles," *Brantford Expositor*, 4 January 1941, 2. Other stories about enlistment of Native soldiers include: "Indian Soldier Writes School from England," *Kamloops Sentinel*, 27 November 1941, 11; "Six Recruits from Cardston," *Cardston News*, 3 June 1941; "Crees Enlist When Chief Calls," *Calgary Herald*, 26 June 1941, 3; "Seven Sons Serving," *Prince Albert Daily Herald*, 5 December 1941, 3; "Proud of Warrior, Now at Hong Kong," *Saskatoon Star-Phoenix*, 17 December 1941, 3; "29 Enlisted from the Pas District," *Winnipeg Free Press*, 30 June 1941, 6; "Indians Serve in War Units," *Brantford Expositor*, 31 January 1941, 3; and "Saskatchewan Has Platoon of Full-Blooded Indians," *Globe and Mail*, 4 July 1941, 13.

56 "Natives Value Civilization, Aid War Fund," *Globe and Mail*, 8 July 1941, 3; "Indian Trappers Buy Certificates," *Brantford Expositor*, 28 January 1941, 14; "Indians Contribute to Red Cross from Treaty Money," *Prince Albert Daily Herald*, 21 July 1941, 4; "Indians Have Come Here Annually for 60 Years," *Saskatoon Star-Phoenix*, 26 July 1941, 3, 6; "London Fund Aided By Cree Indians," *Winnipeg Free Press*, 2 June 1941, 4; "Indian Girls Help Park Spitfire Fund," *Calgary Herald*, 30 May 1941, 18; "Sun Dance Helps Red Cross," *Cardston News*, 22 July 1941, 1; "Indians Win Prizes," *Kamloops Sentinel*, 5 June 1941, 7; "Indian Woman First to Buy War Bond," *Vancouver Sun*, 31 May 1941, 37.

57 "Blood Indians Generous to War Service Fund," *Cardston News*, 29 April 1941, 1, 2.

58 "Racial Prejudice," *Winnipeg Free Press*, 16 July 1941, 13. The paper had previously reported the comments of the Indian Agent from Birtle, Manitoba, that Native men were being refused the opportunity to enlist. "Agent Says Indians Unsuccessfully Tried to Enlist," *Winnipeg Free Press*, 8 July 1941, 4.

59 The reality was that policies affecting the eligibility of First Nations men for enlistment were not uniform across the country. At this time, the district recruiting officer for Manitoba (Military District 10), Major M. Garton, was encouraging his subordinates to inhibit Aboriginal recruits. See Sheffield, "'... in the same manner as other people,'" and Michael D. Stevenson, "The Mobilisation of Native Canadians during the Second World War," *Journal of the Canadian Historical Association* 7 (1996): 205-26.

60 "Red Men Dig Up the Hatchet," *Winnipeg Free Press*, Magazine Section, 24 May 1941, 5.

61 The *Calgary Herald*, *Cardston News*, *Saskatoon Star-Phoenix*, *Prince Albert Daily Herald*, *Winnipeg Free Press*, *Brantford Expositor*, and *Halifax Chronicle* all demonstrated this decline in negative or demeaning portrayals of Native people during 1941.

62 An example of this more balanced treatment can be seen in "Saw Indian Hit Woman," *Saskatoon Star-Phoenix*, 17 December 1941.

63 "An Indian Legend," *Kamloops Sentinel*, 24 April 1941, 12; "Peaceful Indian Village Con-
    ceals Secret Woe," *Calgary Herald*, 9 July 1941, 10; "Address By Chief Mike Mountain
    Horse," *Cardston News*, 4 February 1941; "Indian Women Sees Family Die of Hunger,"
    Winnipeg Free Press, 30 January 1941, 4; "The Final Frontier," *Prince Albert Daily Herald*, 14
    January 1941, 2.
64 "Chief Proud of Daughter," *Calgary Herald*, 22 July 1941, 16.
65 See "Hitler Fated for Hot Place Now British Angry," *Prince Albert Daily Herald*, 15 September
    1939, 8; and "An Indian Chief," *Halifax Chronicle*, 11 October 1939, 4.

Chapter 4: Winning the War Only to Lose the Peace?

 1 This discussion is based on an intensive examination of the daily newspapers from Octo-
    ber 1943; May, September, and December 1944; and April and May 1945; as well as every
    issue of the weeklies from 1943 to May 1945. Also consulted was an Indian Affairs file on
    Indian Act reform, 1940-44, containing, among other things, letters from interested pri-
    vate citizens, clippings from newspapers, and much of the text of the sessions of the House
    Committee on Reconstruction and Re-establishment that were dedicated to the "Indian
    problem" in the postwar years.
 2 Grant Dexter, "Liberals and the C.C.F. Challenge," *Winnipeg Free Press*, 8 October 1943, 11.
 3 Ibid.
 4 J.L. Granatstein, *Canada's War: The Policies of the Mackenzie King Government, 1939-1945*
    (Toronto: Oxford University Press, 1975), 264-65.
 5 Dexter, "Liberals and the C.C.F. Challenge."
 6 Ibid.
 7 G. Cairns, "What of New Order? Soldiers Want to Know," *Globe and Mail*, 7 October 1943,
    6. This article also appeared as "War Veterans and the New Order," *Calgary Herald*, 9 Octo-
    ber 1943, 4, and curiously under the name of A. Riddell in the *Saskatoon Star-Phoenix*, 9
    October 1943, 10.
 8 Peter Neary, "Introduction," in *The Veterans Charter and Post-World War II Canada*, edited
    by Peter Neary and J.L. Granatstein (Montreal and Kingston: McGill-Queen's University
    Press, 1998), 3-14, 6.
 9 Leonard C. Marsh was a young economist who had worked at the London School of Eco-
    nomics for Sir William Beveridge before coming to McGill University. A member of the
    League for Social Reconstruction, the left-wing brain trust of the Cooperative Common-
    wealth Federation during the thirties, he was made the research director of the Committee
    on Reconstruction, and his name would become the label for the committee's main work:
    the Report on Social Security for Canada.
10 Peter S. MacInnis, "Planning Prosperity: Canadians Debate Postwar Reconstruction," in
    Uncertain Horizons: Canadians and Their World in 1945, edited by Greg Donaghy (Canadian
    Committee for the History of the Second World War, 1997), 231-59, 241. This report was
    Canada's answer to the famous Beveridge Report produced in Britain just prior to the Marsh
    Report.
11 Reference Papers, Wartime Information Board, *Post-War Planning in Canada – No. 1*, 30 July
    1943, NAC, RG 38, vol. 211, file 6468.
12 J.L. Granatstein and Desmond Morton, *A Nation Forged in Fire: Canadians and the Second
    World War 1939-1945* (Toronto: Lester and Orpen Dennys, 1989), 168.
13 *Public Opinion Quarterly* 7, 4 (1943): 748. Interestingly, this figure was much higher in Canada
    than was the case in either the United States or Great Britain, where the corresponding
    figures were 32 percent and 57 percent respectively.
14 "Rotarian K.L. Lee Addresses Club on the Subject of Post War Reconstruction," *Cardston
    News*, 4 March 1943, 1.
15 "Dangers of Prejudice Pointed Out by Drew," *Globe and Mail*, 15 October 1943, 15.
16 Certainly, this emerges strongly from a speech by K.L. Lee to the Cardston Rotary Club, as
    he suggests that government controls on prices and wages ought to continue in peacetime.
    "Rotarian K.L. Lee Addresses Club on the Subject of Post War Reconstruction," *Cardston
    News*, 4 March 1943, 1. This becomes even more evident in opinion polls the following
    year. In one poll conducted in October 1944, 49 percent of Canadians thought that the

federal government should take the lead in promoting postwar employment, a further 16 percent favoured provincial and municipal governments taking the lead, and only 23 percent believed that industry and business should fill this role. *Public Opinion Quarterly* 9, 4 (1944-45): 601.

17 "Alberta Indian Wins in Army Sports in Italy," *Calgary Herald*, 26 October 1943, 15. There was no attempt to make this story colourful or quaint; it merely noted with pride that Pte. Gordon Yellowfly, an Indian from Gleichen, Alberta, had excelled in competitive sports in the army, as he had before going overseas. Yellowfly had captured third place in the Calgary Herald Road Race a year previously, just before being shipped overseas. The article also noted that the soldier had seen active service in Africa, Sicily, and Italy with the "famous 8th Army." For another example of this type of story, see "Three Cree Indians Join Active Army," *Winnipeg Free Press*, 5 October 1943, 4.

18 "Brant Descendant Shows Stamina in Campaign in Italy," *Brantford Expositor*, 9 October 1943, 1. This more colourful article highlighted heredity in the exceptional service performed by Pte. William Brant, great-grandson of famed Chief Joseph Brant, as a runner in the rugged hills of Italy.

19 Jack Hambleton, "Their Braves Gone to War, Cape Croker's Indian Women and Children Carry On," photo collection, *Globe and Mail*, 23 October 1943, 15, and "Bruce Peninsula Reserve Does Bit to Put Every Victory Loan Over Top," *Globe and Mail*, 23 October 1943, 15.

20 This is evident in a number of works on prominent First Nations leaders and organizations in this era, including E.P. Patterson, "Andrew Paull and Canadian Indian Resurgence," PhD dissertation, University of Washington, 1962; Paul Tennant, *Aboriginal Peoples and Politics: The Indian Land Question in British Columbia, 1849-1989* (Vancouver: UBC Press, 1990); Jean Goodwill and Norma Sluman, *John Tootoosis* (1982; reprint, Winnipeg: Pemmican Publications, 1984); and Alan Morley, *Roar of the Breakers: A Biography of Peter Kelly* (Toronto: Ryerson Press, 1967).

21 The North American Indian Brotherhood, which arose from these wartime meetings in Ottawa, would become one of the more prominent of many associations arising among First Nations communities. See Chapter 2, n. 18.

22 "Indians Ask Exemptions," *Prince Albert Daily Herald*, 23 October 1943, 8; "Indians Ask Tax Exemptions," *Vancouver Sun*, 21 October 1943, 11; "Indians Ask Tax, Army Exemptions," *Vancouver Sun*, 22 October 1943, 25; "Indian Petition Was Presented," *Brantford Expositor*, 23 October 1943, 4; "Indians Press Gov't to Grant Exemptions," *Calgary Herald*, 23 October 1943, 7; "Indian Deputation Preparing Written Argument in Museum," *Globe and Mail*, 21 October 1943, 13; "Indians Ask for Army, Tax Exemptions," *Globe and Mail*, 22 October 1943, 7.

23 "Indians Plead for Exemption from Income Tax, Army Service," *Globe and Mail*, 21 October 1943, 4; "Indians Present Petition," *Globe and Mail*, 23 October 1943, 2; "Canadian Hero Drops in on Parliament Hill," *Vancouver Sun*, 25 October 1943, 13. The latter *Globe and Mail* article was accompanied by a dramatic photo of a number of "Indian" chiefs in "full regalia" standing on the steps of the Parliament buildings, where they were received by M.J. Coldwell, the leader of the Co-operative Commonwealth Federation (CCF). Evidently, the CCF, which had other concerns prior to the war, had begun, like many Canadians, to develop an empathetic position on the conditions of the First Nations. Indeed, during the postwar era the CCF (later the National Democratic Party) would become an outspoken champion for Native issues. However, this did not mean that the party's vision, when translated into policy, did not include its own brand of well-meaning but patronizing paternalism, as James Pitsula demonstrated in "The Saskatchewan CCF Government and Treaty Indians, 1944-1964," *Canadian Historical Review* 75, 1 (March 1994): 21-52.

24 "Indians Ask Tax Exemptions," *Vancouver Sun*, 21 October 1943, 11; "Indians Ask for Army, Tax Exemptions," *Globe and Mail*, 22 October 1943, 7.

25 "Indians Ask Exemptions," *Prince Albert Daily Herald*, 23 October 1943, 8.

26 "Indians Have Fine Harvest," *Saskatoon Star-Phoenix*, 23 October 1943, 13.

27 "Canadian Hero Drops in on Parliament Hill," *Vancouver Sun*, 25 October 1943, 13.

28 Francis Pegahmagabow was an Ojibwa from the Parry Island Band in Ontario who enlisted in August 1914. He served throughout the Great War as a sniper, earning the Military

Medal with two bars for courage in the field. He was invalided home in 1919, where he went on to serve in the Algonquin Regiment of the peacetime militia and as chief and councillor for his band. He died in 1952. Fred Gaffen states that his reported number of kills varied, the highest estimate being 378, which seems extraordinarily high. *Forgotten Soldiers* (Penticton, BC: Theytus Books, 1985), 28. This is the number quoted as well by the *Vancouver Sun* in "Canadian Hero Drops in on Parliament Hill," 25 October 1943, 13. The official number of confirmed kills by Pegahmagabow could not be ascertained.

29   "MacNicol Made Indian Chief," *Globe and Mail,* 12 October 1943, 21. Interestingly, J.D. MacNicol (PC, Davenport) was becoming a keen critic of Canadian Indian policy. He sat on the Reconstruction Committee that briefly examined Indian Affairs in 1944 and would be appointed to the Special Joint Parliamentary Committee to examine the Indian Act in 1946.

30   "Outlines Program for B.C. Indians," *Kamloops Sentinel,* 8 December 1943, 13. MacKay had always been one of the more progressive and sympathetic of the senior officials in the Indian Affairs Branch.

31   *Public Opinion Quarterly* 9, 3 (1945): 375.

32   *Public Opinion Quarterly* 8, 4 (1944-45): 601.

33   Interestingly, several of the MPs sitting on this committee would later become outspoken and active members of the Special Joint Committee on the Indian Act in 1946. See Canada, House of Commons, *Special Committee on Reconstruction and Re-establishment, Minutes of Proceedings and Evidence,* 18 and 24 May 1944.

34   Ibid., 24 May 1944, 313.

35   "Canada's Indians Nobly Upholding Traditions," *Kamloops Sentinel,* 12 April 1944, 6; "50 Kamloops Indians Wearing Uniform," *Kamloops Sentinel,* 12 April 1944, 6; "Many Indians in Canada's Forces; Brave Fighters," *Kamloops Sentinel,* 12 April 1944, 6; "Indian Chief's Son Killed in Action, France," *Kamloops Sentinel,* 19 July 1944, 1; "Dies of Wounds," *Kamloops Sentinel,* 17 January 1945, 1; "Two Indians Become Casualties," *Kamloops Sentinel,* 21 March 1945, 4.

36   "Legislature Urges Dominion to Better Conditions for Indians," *Kamloops Sentinel,* 22 March 1944, 12; "Greater Emphasis Being Placed at Indian School on Technical Training; Boys Learn Farming, Mechanics; Girls, Home Arts," *Kamloops Sentinel,* 12 April 1944, 1-2; "1000 Indians Visit Children at School; Enjoy Concert," *Kamloops Sentinel,* 12 April 1944, 1-2; "500 At Indian School Concert," *Kamloops Sentinel,* 28 February 1945, 6; "1000 Indians Visit Children at School, Attend Concert," *Kamloops Sentinel,* 4 April 1945, 5; "More than 250 Indians Busy on Hop Harvest," *Kamloops Sentinel,* 20 September 1944, 12; "Indian Land near Lytton Put Under Irrigation," *Kamloops Sentinel,* 4 April 1945, 11.

37   "Pictures and Stories on Work of Indians," *Kamloops Sentinel,* 8 March 1944, 1; "Indian Agent Exposes White Man's False Ideas About Natives," *Kamloops Sentinel,* 21 June 1944, 1, 3; "Bracken Club Gains Better Understanding of Indian Problem," *Kamloops Sentinel,* 4 April 1945, 1. This last story drew a passionate letter to the editor in response from an individual who warned that the information provided to the Bracken Club by H.E. Taylor, the Kamloops Indian Agent, was not to be fully trusted, particularly with regard to the intelligence of the "Indians" and his lack of understanding of "Indian sociology." C.G. Wallace, "For the Indians," *Kamloops Sentinel,* 11 April 1945, 11.

38   "A Reproach to All of Us," *Kamloops Sentinel,* 4 April 1945, 2. This page also contained a response to the *Vancouver Sun* from the highly sympathetic president of the Okanagan Society for the Revival of Indian Arts and Crafts, Albert Millar, "Champions Native Indians," *Kamloops Sentinel,* 4 April 1945, 2.

39   "The Canadian Indian," *Saskatoon Star-Phoenix,* 25 September 1944, 9.

40   Winifred Paris to the Committee on Reconstruction and Re-establishment, 6 August 1944, NAC, RG 10, vol. 8585, file 1/1-2-17.

41   "East Indians and the Vote," *Kamloops Sentinel,* 29 March 1944, 2.

42   Patricia E. Roy, "The Soldiers Canada Didn't Want: Her Chinese and Japanese Citizens," *Canadian Historical Review* 59, 3 (1978): 343. See also Marjorie Wong, *The Dragon and the Maple Leaf: Chinese Canadians and World War II* (London, ON: Pirie Publishing, 1994).

43   John J. Honigmann, "Canada's Human Resources," *Canadian Forum* 26, 282 (July 1944): 84.

44 For material on this subject, see Mona Gleason, "Psychology and the Construction of the 'Normal' Family in Postwar Canada, 1945-60," *Canadian Historical Review* 78, 3 (September 1997): 442-77; and Terry Copp and Bill McAndrew, *Battle Exhaustion: Soldiers and Psychiatrists in the Canadian Army, 1939-1945* (Montreal: McGill-Queen's University Press, 1990). The growth in stature of the social sciences and specifically sociology during the interwar years is examined in Marlene Shore, *The Science of Social Redemption: McGill, the Chicago School and the Origins of Social Research in Canada* (Toronto: University of Toronto Press, 1987), and in Harry H. Hiller, *Society and Change: S.D. Clark and the Development of Canadian Sociology* (Toronto: University of Toronto Press, 1982).

45 "Legislature Urges Dominion to Better Conditions for Indians," *Kamloops Sentinel*, 22 March 1944, 12.

46 *Native Canadians: A Plan for the Rehabilitation of Indians*, the Okanagan Society for the Revival of Indian Arts and Crafts, 1944, NAC, RG 10, vol. 6811, file 470-3-6, pt. 1. This brief strongly advocated that Canada imitate the American Indian New Deal legislation in any reform process. In a letter published in the *Kamloops Sentinel* on 4 April 1945 ("Champions Native Indians," 2), the president of this organization, Albert Millar, claimed to have received "nearly three hundred letters" since the distribution of its brief to the Committee on Reconstruction and Re-establishment.

47 Miriam Chapin, "New Deal in Order for Indians of Canada," *Saturday Night*, 23 September 1944.

48 *Native Canadians: A Plan for the Rehabilitation of Indians*, the Okanagan Society for the Revival of Indian Arts and Crafts, 1944, NAC, RG 10, vol. 6811, file 470-3-6, pt. 1.

49 "Indians, West and East," *Saturday Night*, 11 November 1944, 2.

50 "The Canadian Indian," *Saskatoon Star-Phoenix*, 25 September 1944, 9.

51 Millar, "Champions Native Indians," *Kamloops Sentinel*.

52 B.T. Richardson, "The Indians' Need," *Calgary Albertan*, 22 August 1944, NAC, RG 10, vol. 8585, file 1/1-2-17.

53 "Where Rivers Run North," *Winnipeg Free Press*, 19 April 1945, 13. The report quoted in this story was by Dr. Andrew Moore "for the Canadian Social Science Research Council," yet another indication of the growing interest of academics in the social conditions of the First Nations at the close of the Second World War.

54 "A Reproach to All of Us," *Kamloops Sentinel*, 4 April 1945, 2.

55 Ibid. This was quoted from the *Vernon News*.

56 "The Canadian Indian," *Saskatoon Star-Phoenix*, 25 September 1944, 9.

57 Kathleen Coburn, "The Red Man's Burden," *Canadian Forum* 24, 285 (October 1944): 153.

58 "Must Close Indian Hospitals Unless More Nurses Found," *Globe and Mail*, 2 September 1944, 13.

59 "Indian Hospitals of Manitoba Face Desperate Need for Help," *Winnipeg Free Press*, 7 September 1944, 1.

60 "Question Medical Care Given to Indians in North," *Globe and Mail*, 17 April 1945, 4. A brief Canadian Press version of this story was also carried in the *Saskatoon Star-Phoenix*, "Says Indians in Bad Way," 17 April 1945, 2.

61 Ibid.

62 Chapin, "New Deal in Order," *Saturday Night*.

63 Frederic Niven, "Canada's Indians Are Helping with Tons of Old Buffalo Bones," *Saturday Night*, 10 June 1944, 37.

64 Millar, "Champions Native Indians," *Kamloops Sentinel*. This was also clearly expressed in Honigmann, "Canada's Human Resources," and in "Bracken Club Gains Better Understanding of Indian Problem," *Kamloops Sentinel*, 4 April 1945, 1.

65 Millar, "Champions Native Indians," *Kamloops Sentinel*.

66 B.T. Richardson, "The Indians' Need," *Calgary Albertan*, 22 August 1944, NAC, RG 10, vol. 8585, file 1/1-2-17.

67 *Hansard*, 17 July 1944, 4935. Quoted in James W. St. G. Walker, *"Race," Rights and the Law in the Supreme Court of Canada: Historical Case Studies* (Waterloo and Toronto: Wilfrid Laurier University Press and the Osgoode Society, 1997), 20.

68 *Vancouver Sun*, 3 May 1944, 9, emphasis in the original.

69   Wallace Havelock Robb, "Indian Leaders Encouraged to Press Claims for Justice," *Globe and Mail*, 7 June 1944, NAC, RG 10, 8585, file 1/1-2-17.

70   "Legislature Urges Dominion to Better Conditions for Indians," *Kamloops Sentinel*, 22 March 1944, 12; Coburn, "The Red Man's Burden," 154; "Indians, West and East," *Saturday Night*, 11 November 1944, 2.

71   Ibid.; "Legislature Urges Dominion to Better Conditions for Indians," *Kamloops Sentinel*, 22 March 1944, 12.

72   Ibid.

73   "The Canadian Indian," *Saskatoon Star-Phoenix*, 25 September 1944, 9.

74   B.T. Richardson, "The Indians' Need," *Calgary Albertan*, 22 August 1944, NAC, RG 10, vol. 8585, file 1/1-2-17; Chapin, "New Deal in Order," *Saturday Night*.

75   "Survey of Indian Problems Asked," *Globe and Mail*, 14 April 1945, 4. This story reported on the decision of the United Church Board of Home Missions to request a Royal Commission to study the relations between First Nations people and the Dominion.

76   Coburn, "The Red Man's Burden," 154. Rev. E.E.M. Johlin, editor of the periodical *Wampum*, also called for a thorough study, preferably a Royal Commission, in "Native Canadians: A Plan for the Rehabilitation of Indians," *Wampum* 5, 3 (July 1944).

77   The one exception to this had been the large conference in 1941, under the joint auspices of the University of Toronto and Yale University, which brought together academics and senior officials from the United States and Canada to discuss the Indian problem and its administration in both countries. A number of the papers presented at the conference were subsequently published in C.T. Loram and T.F. MacIlwraith, eds., *The North American Indian Today: University of Toronto-Yale University Seminar Conference, Toronto, September 4-16, 1939* (Toronto: University of Toronto Press, 1943).

78   "The Canadian Indian," *Saskatoon Star-Phoenix*, 25 September 1944, 9.

79   *Vancouver Sun*, 26 May 1944, 6.

80   Honigmann, "Canada's Human Resources," 84.

81   *Native Canadians: A Plan for the Rehabilitation of Indians*, the Okanagan Society for the Revival of Indian Arts and Crafts, 1944, NAC, RG 10, vol. 6811, file 470-3-6, pt. 1.

82   Chapin, "New Deal in Order," *Saturday Night*; B.T. Richardson, "The Indians' Need," *Calgary Albertan*, 22 August 1944, NAC, RG 10, vol. 8585, file 1/1-2-17.

83   Coburn, "The Red Man's Burden," 154.

84   Winifred Paris to the Committee on Reconstruction and Re-establishment, 6 August 1944, NAC, RG 10, vol. 8585, file 1/1-2-17.

85   "Legislature Urges Dominion to Better Conditions for Indians," *Kamloops Sentinel*, 22 March 1944, 12; "Indians, West and East," *Saturday Night*, 11 November 1944, 2.

86   "The Canadian Indian," *Saskatoon Star-Phoenix*, 25 September 1944, 9; "Survey of Indian Problems Asked," *Globe and Mail*, 14 April 1945, 4.

87   Mary Berdey and J.N.W. Booth to Mr. Harold W. McGill, 15 November 1944, NAC, RG 10, vol. 8585, file 1/1-2-17.

88   "Legislature Urges Dominion to Better Conditions for Indians," *Kamloops Sentinel*, 22 March 1944, 12.

89   Coburn, "The Red Man's Burden," 154.

90   Wallace, "For the Indians," *Kamloops Sentinel*.

91   For instance, see an editorial response to MacInnes's comments before the Reconstruction Committee in the *Brantford Expositor*, which argued that if "the reservation system were to be discarded, it could scarcely be without the consent of the Indians," NAC, RG 10, vol. 8585, file 1/1-2/17.

92   "The Canadian Indian," *Saskatoon Star-Phoenix*, 25 September 1944, 9; "A Reproach to All of Us," *Kamloops Sentinel*, 4 April 1945, 2.

93   Ibid.; Millar, "Champions Native Indians," *Kamloops Sentinel*.

94   "A Reproach to All of Us," *Kamloops Sentinel*, 4 April 1945, 2.

95   Ibid.

96   Ibid.

97   Millar, "Champions Native Indians," *Kamloops Sentinel*.

98   Chapin, "New Deal in Order," *Saturday Night*.

99 Winifred Paris to the Committee on Reconstruction and Re-establishment, 6 August 1944, NAC, RG 10, vol. 8585, file 1/1-2-17; Coburn, "The Red Man's Burden."

100 Chapin, "New Deal in Order," *Saturday Night*.

101 "The Canadian Indian," *Saskatoon Star-Phoenix*, 25 September 1944, 9.

Chapter 5: The "Administrative Indian" at the Threshold of Peace, January-March 1946

1 Peter Neary, "Introduction," in *The Veterans Charter and Post-World War II Canada*, edited by Peter Neary and J.L. Granatstein, (Montreal and Kingston: McGill-Queen's University Press, 1998) 10.

2 T.A. Crerar's voluminous personnel papers held at Queen's University contain less than a handful of minor references to Indians or the Indian Affairs Branch, providing an emphatic demonstration of how little involved the minister was with the IAB's affairs or its charges during his nine years as superintendent general of Indian Affairs. J. Allison Glen was, like so many officials in the Indian Affairs Branch, a Scotsman. He was elected as a Liberal MP for Marquette, Manitoba, in 1926 and served consistently in the House from 1935 through to his taking on the portfolio of Mines and Resources on 18 April 1945. He had previously served as the Speaker of the House of Commons. His tenure as minister was brief, however, as Walter Harris took over in 1948.

3 Draft of Glen Circular letter, 7 January 1946, NAC, RG 10, vol. 6811, file 470-2-8, pt. 1.

4 Ibid. Almost all responses to Glen's letter are contained in NAC, RG 10, vol. 6810, file 470-2-3, pt. 10.

5 This file is mentioned by John Leslie, "Assimilation, Integration or Termination? The Development of Canadian Indian Policy, 1943-1963," PhD dissertation, Carleton University, 1999, 108; and by Victor Satzewich, "Indians Agents and the 'Indian Problem' in Canada in 1946: Reconsidering the Theory of Coercive Tutelage," *Canadian Journal of Native Studies* 17, 2 (1997): 232. Satzewich sets the number of responses at thirty-eight, whereas Leslie claims only thirty-five responses. Presumably, Leslie was counting only those letters from agents who included substantive answers to the minister's requests. In addition to the thirty-eight responses in the Glen correspondence file, I found another response from T.L. Bonnah, Indian Agent at St. Regis, near Cornwall, Ontario. This letter was written in May 1946 and began by saying, "some time ago, comments were asked for with a view to any changes that might be beneficial insofar as a revision of the Indian Act is concerned." Bonnah is almost certainly referring to the minister's letter of January, but because he wrote so late and framed his response in the context of Indian Act revision, it was misfiled in a file containing correspondence about revision of the Act. T.L. Bonnah to the Indian Affairs Branch, 14 May 1946, NAC, RG 10, vol. 6811, file 470-2-3, p. 11.

6 Satzewich, "Indian Agents and the 'Indian Problem' in Canada in 1946," 233. See also the contents of NAC, RG 10, vol. 6811, file 470-2-8, pt. 1, which contains Glen's letter and all but one of the responses received from the field personnel.

7 This particular body of documents has recently received a detailed analysis by sociologist Victor Satzewich, "Indian Agents and the 'Indian Problem' in Canada in 1946." He used the letters to test the application of the theory of coercive tutelage to Indian Agents by anthropologist Noel Dyck in his thought-provoking book *What Is the Indian "Problem": Tutelage and Resistance in Canadian Indian Administration* (St. John's, NF: Institute of Social and Economic Research, 1991). Satzewich's conclusions provide qualified support for the coercive-tutelage model but with the caveat that "the attitudes of Indian Agents towards Indian people, their work, and the branch of the federal government they worked for, were somewhat more complex than what is suggested by Dyck," (256-67). This is accurate, as the coercive-tutelage model (at least as Dyck applies it) is too rigid a conceptual tool to accommodate the complexities in the relationship between the Canadian state and First Nations people. Nonetheless, Satzewich's reading of the Glen correspondence is not fully convincing for two reasons. First, in extracting the responses of the Indian Agents from the context of their letters for statistical analysis, Satzewich misses a crucial component of the agents' language: specifically, the intense concern with their own authority. Second, he measures the progressiveness of the agents in 1946 Canada by the yardstick of late-1990s

"correct-thinking," perspectives on Aboriginal issues, and Canadian Indian administration. His surprise at the agents' sophisticated responses amplified the significance of what he called "relational" explanations for the "Indian problem" to a degree not warranted by the evidence.

8   Draft of Glen Circular letter, 7 January 1946, NAC, RG 10, vol. 6811, file 470-2-8, pt. 1.

9   The language of conflict and armies was a common element in IAB discourse, as first noted in Chapter 1. That this comment struck a chord with several of the agents, who mentioned it specifically in their responses, suggests that the branch's relationship with the "Indian" was still conceived of as a long, ongoing war to civilize and assimilate their charges. Glen was then in a very real sense preparing his soldiers to renew the fight with fresh conviction and élan in the wake of the Second World War.

10   Draft of Glen Circular letter, 7 January 1946, NAC, RG 10, vol. 6811, file 470-2-8, pt. 1.

11   Ibid.

12   Norman Paterson to Minister of Mines and Resources, 4 February 1946; H.E. Taylor to J. Allison Glen, 1 February 1946; R. Howe to Glen, 4 February 1946, NAC, RG 10, vol. 6811, file 470-2-8, pt. 1.

13   F. Earl Anfield to Mr. Glen, 30 January 1946, NAC, RG 10, vol. 6811, file 470-2-8, pt. 1. Nor was Anfield the only agent to request the aid of psychology in the effort to further the cause, as A.G. Smith in Birtle, Manitoba, also asked whether a psychologist could give them some advice. A.G. Smith to the Hon. J. Allison Glen, 23 January 1946, NAC, RG 10, vol. 6811, file 470-2-8, pt. 1.

14   Ibid.; H. Lariviere to the Hon. J. Allison Glen, 19 January 1946, NAC, RG 10, vol. 6811, file 470-2-8, pt. 1.

15   J.E. Daly to Mr. Glen, 19 February 1946, NAC, RG 10, vol. 6811, file 470-2-8, pt. 1.

16   J.L. Bryant to the Honourable J. Allison Glen, 26 January 1946, NAC, RG 10, vol. 6811, file 470-2-8, pt. 1. Bryant generalized this to all reserves, making the obvious point that "of course on all reserves there is always the odd Indian who is inclined to oppose anything one tries to do." See also T.L. Bonnah to the Indian Affairs Branch, 14 May 1946, NAC, RG 10, vol. 6811, file 470-2-3, pt. 11.

17   Geo. W. Down to Mr. Glen, 18 January 1946, NAC, RG 10, vol. 6811, file 470-2-8, pt. 1.

18   J.P.B. Ostrander to the Honourable J.A. Glen, 4 February 1946, NAC, RG 10, vol. 6811, file 470-2-8, pt. 1.

19   Taylor to Glen, 1 February 1946; Ostrander to Glen, 4 February 1946; Howe to Glen, 4 February 1946; N.J. McLeod to Honourable J. Alvin [sic] Glen, 20 January 1946; Indian Agent, Peigan Agency, to Mr. Glen, 3 February 1946, NAC, RG 10, vol. 6811, file 470-2-8, pt. 1.

20   E. McPherson to Mr Glen, 30 January 1946, NAC, RG 10, vol. 6811, file 470-2-8, pt. 1.

21   Samuel Devlin to the Honourable J. Allison Glen, 22 January 1946, NAC, RG 10, vol. 6811, file 470-2-8, pt. 1.

22   S.H. Simpson to the Honourable J.A. Glen, 19 January 1946, NAC, RG 10, vol. 6811, file 470-2-8, pt. 1. Simpson claimed that the "Indian" not only was lacking in responsibilities, but "in so many cases refuses to accept" them even if offered.

23   Indian Agent, Peigan Agency, to Glen, 3 February 1946, NAC, RG 10, vol. 6811, file 470-2-8, pt. 1.

24   Smith to Glen, 23 January 1946, NAC, RG 10, vol. 6811, file 470-2-8, pt. 1.

25   Robert Lamothe to the Honourable J. Allison Glen, 21 January 1946, NAC, RG 10, vol. 6811, file 470-2-8, pt. 1.

26   W. Young to the Hon. J.A. Glen, 6 February 1946, NAC, RG 10, vol. 6811, file 470-2-8, pt. 1.

27   A.D. Moore to the Honourable J. Allison Glen, 28 January 1946, NAC, RG 10, vol. 6811, file 470-2-8, pt. 1.

28   Ibid.

29   Anfield to Glen, 30 January 1946, NAC, RG 10, vol. 6811, file 470-2-8, pt. 1.

30   J. Waite to the Honourable J. Allison Glen, 29 January 1946; A.D. Moore to Glen, 28 January 1946; Stuart Spence to the Minister's Office, 28 January 1946; R.G. Lazenby to Glen, 21 January 1946; Taylor to Glen, 1 February 1946; J.M. Barre to Glen, 23 January 1946; Howe to Glen, 4 February 1946; J. Gillet to Minister, 26 February 1946; Bryant to Glen, 26 January 1946, NAC, RG 10, vol. 6811, file 470-2-8, pt. 1.

31 F.J.C. Ball to the Honourable J. Allison Glen, M.P., 30 January 1946, NAC, RG 10, vol. 6811, file 470-2-8, pt. 1.
32 Bryant to Glen, 26 January 1946, NAC, RG 10, vol. 6811, file 470-2-8, pt. 1.
33 Daly to Glen, 19 February 1946; J.E. Gendron to Glen, 29 January 1946; McLeod to Glen, 20 January 1946; J.G. Burke to Glen, 23 March 1946; Howe to Glen, 4 February 1946, NAC, RG 10, vol. 6811, file 470-2-8, pt. 1.
34 R.S. Davis to J. Allison Glen Esq., 4 February 1946, NAC, RG 10, vol. 6811, file 470-2-8, pt. 1.
35 Gifford Swartman to the Hon. J.A. Glen, 4 February 1946, NAC, RG 10, vol. 6811, file 470-2-8, pt. 1.
36 Paterson to the Minister, 4 February 1946, NAC, RG 10, vol. 6811, file 470-2-8, pt. 1.
37 Simpson to Glen, 19 January 1946, NAC, RG 10, vol. 6811, file 470-2-8, pt. 1. The issue of treaty promises, especially verbal ones not written into the texts of the treaties, and the disparity between the official record of the negotiations and the First Nations' oral record of the spirit of the agreements has generated a large body of case law as well as a growing historiography. For instance, see the important book by the Treaty 7 Elders and Tribal Council, *The True Spirit and Original Intent of Treaty 7* (Montreal and Kingston: McGill-Queen's University Press, 1996).
38 F. Matters to the Hon. Mr. J. A. Glen, 15 January 1946, NAC, RG 10, vol. 6811, file 470-2-8, pt. 1.
39 Lazenby to Glen, 21 January 1946, NAC, RG 10, vol. 6811, file 470-2-8, pt. 1.
40 Taylor to Glen, 1 February 1946, NAC, RG 10, vol. 6811, file 470-2-8, pt. 1.
41 Dr. T.J. Orford to the Hon. J Allison Glen, 1 February 1946, NAC, RG 10, vol. 6811, file 470-2-8, pt. 1.
42 Ball to Glen, 30 January 1946, NAC, RG 10, vol. 6811, file 470-2-8, pt. 1.
43 Taylor to Glen, 1 February 1946, NAC, RG 10, vol. 6811, file 470-2-8, pt. 1.
44 Burke to Glen, 23 March 1946, NAC, RG 10, vol. 6811, file 470-2-8, pt. 1.
45 Moore to Glen, 28 January 1946, NAC, RG 10, vol. 6811, file 470-2-8, pt. 1. Presumably Moore means that too much *intra*marriage was a bad thing and that intermarriage with non-Aboriginal people would be positive.
46 J.A. Marleau to the Honourable J. Allison Glen, 26 January 1946, NAC, RG 10, vol. 6811, file 470-2-8, pt. 1.
47 They were not the only such letters; see Moore to Glen, 28 January 1946, NAC, RG 10, vol. 6811, file 470-2-8, pt. 1., to be discussed below, which advocated a clear and strong call for termination.
48 Waite to Glen, 29 January 1946, NAC, RG 10, vol. 6811, file 470-2-8, pt. 1.
49 Presumably Ball is referring in part to the antipotlatch laws enacted by the government on the west coast of British Columbia from 1885 and perhaps also to the regulations against the Sun and Thirst Dances and other ceremonial events among the Plains peoples. See Ball to Glen, 30 January 1946, NAC, RG 10, vol. 6811, file 470-2-8, pt. 1.
50 Simpson to Glen, 19 January 1946, NAC, RG 10, vol. 6811, file 470-2-8, pt. 1.
51 Anfield to Glen, 30 January 1946, NAC, RG 10, vol. 6811, file 470-2-8, pt. 1, emphasis in the original.
52 Ibid.
53 Bryant to Glen, 26 January 1946; Howe to Glen, 4 February 1946; Wm. Christie to Glen, 5 February 1946; Swartman to Glen, 23 January 1946; Lazenby to Glen, 21 January 1946; Waite to Glen, 29 January 1946; A.D. Moore to Mr. Glen, 28 January 1946; G.E. Hurle to Mr. Glen, 24 January 1946, NAC, RG 10, vol. 6811, file 470-2-8, pt. 1. Only J.G. Burke, from Port Arthur, Ontario, mentioned a negative impact from the war. Apparently, at his agency the agricultural activity had suffered because so many of the people had joined in war activities. Burke to Glen, 23 March 1946, NAC, RG 10, vol. 6811, file 470-2-8, pt. 1.
54 McPherson to Glen, 30 January 1930, NAC, RG 10, vol. 6811, file 470-2-8, pt. 1.
55 Daly to Glen, 19 February 1946, NAC, RG 10, vol. 6811, file 470-2-8, pt. 1.
56 Bryant to Glen, 26 January 1946, NAC, RG 10, vol. 6811, file 470-2-8, pt. 1.
57 Anfield to Glen, 30 January 1946, NAC, RG 10, vol. 6811, file 470-2-8, pt. 1.
58 Moore to Glen, 28 January 1946, NAC, RG 10, vol. 6811, file 470-2-8, pt. 1.
59 W.J.D. Kerley to Hon. J. Allison Glen, 16 February 1946; Devlin to Glen, 22 January 1946, NAC, RG 10, vol. 6811, file 470-2-8, pt. 1.

60 Gendron to Glen, 29 January 1946, NAC, RG 10, vol. 6811, file 470-2-8, pt. 1. J.E. Daly expressed the hope to the minister that "we shall all do our utmost to treat the Indian as a rational creature, capable of attaining the status of ordinary working people, and in so doing we may rest assured that many of our most difficult problems will in time disappear." Daly to Glen, 19 February 1946, NAC, RG 10, vol. 6811, file 470-2-8, pt. 1.

61 Moore to Glen, 28 January 1946, NAC, RG 10, vol. 6811, file 470-2-8, pt. 1.

62 Canada, House of Commons, Minutes of the Special Committee on Reconstruction and Re-establishment, 18 May 1944, 312-19. MacInnes was apparently unapologetic, as he published similar sentiments in the article "History of Indian Administration in Canada," *Canadian Journal of Economic and Political Science* 12, 3 (1946): 387-94.

63 Down to Glen, 18 January 1946; Ostrander to Glen, 4 February 1946; Lazenby to Glen, 21 January 1946; Taylor to Glen, 1 February 1946. See also Daly to Glen, 19 February 1946, and J.M. Barre to Glen, 23 January 1946, NAC, RG 10, vol. 6811, file 470-2-8, pt. 1.

64 Howe to the Glen, 4 February 1946, NAC, RG 10, vol. 6811, file 470-2-8, pt. 1. J.A. Marleau pressed for a similar policy for exactly the same reasons, believing this would be "a step towards progress." Marleau to Glen, 26 January 1946, NAC, RG 10, vol. 6811, file 470-2-8, pt. 1.

65 Bryant to Glen, 26 January 1946, NAC, RG 10, vol. 6811, file 470-2-8, pt. 1.

66 Lariviere to Glen, 19 January 1946, NAC, RG 10, vol. 6811, file 470-2-8, pt. 1.

67 McLeod to Glen, 20 January 1946, NAC, RG 10, vol. 6811, file 470-2-8, pt. 1. McLeod's final comment refers to the Co-operative Commonwealth Federation (CCF) in Saskatchewan and to other white agitators, who were actively encouraging the First Nations of that province to organize and take their concerns to the premier, Tommy Douglas, who would aid them in their cause. For more on this subject, see James Pitsula, "The Saskatchewan CCF Government and Treaty Indians, 1944-1964," *Canadian Historical Review* 75, 1 (March 1994): 21-52, and the more recent book by F. Laurie Barron, *Walking in Indian Moccasins: The Native Policies of Tommy Douglas and the CCF* (Vancouver: UBC Press, 1997).

68 Simpson to Glen, 19 January 1946, NAC, RG 10, vol. 6811, file 470-2-8, pt. 1. Dr. T.J. Orford also mentioned the difficulty of maintaining morale when slow progress was made. Orford to Glen, 1 February 1946, NAC, RG 10, vol. 6811, file 470-2-8, pt. 1. Norman Paterson and Samuel Devlin, the agents in Kenora and Parry Sound respectively, both predicted that their work was a "long term proposition" "since it involves a gradual change of character." Paterson to the Minister, 4 February 1946; Devlin to Glen, 22 January 1946, NAC, RG 10, vol. 6811, file 470-2-8, pt. 1. The following agents all spoke of the need for hard work, patience, and perseverance: Bryant to Glen, 26 January 1946; Gendron to Glen, 29 January 1946; and Ball to Glen, 30 January 1946, NAC, RG 10, vol. 6811, file 470-2-8, pt. 1.

69 Lazenby to Glen, 21 January 1946, NAC, RG 10, vol. 6811, file 470-2-8, pt. 1.

70 Matters to Glen, 15 January 1946, NAC, RG 10, vol. 6811, file 470-2-8, pt. 1.

71 W. Young to the Hon. J.A. Glen, 6 February 1946, NAC, RG 10, vol. 6811, file 470-2-8, pt. 1. Education was usually seen as a panacea for the Indian problem in this era, regardless of the proponent's agenda. The content and aim of this education was a different matter.

72 McLeod to Glen, 20 January 1946, NAC, RG 10, vol. 6811, file 470-2-8, pt. 1.

73 Taylor to Glen, 1 February 1946, NAC, RG 10, vol. 6811, file 470-2-8, pt. 1.

74 Gillett to the Minister, 26 February 1946, NAC, RG 10, vol. 6811, file 470-2-8, pt. 1.

75 McLeod to Glen, 20 January 1946, NAC, RG 10, vol. 6811, file 470-2-8, pt. 1.

76 Only three agents advocated setting up advisory boards: Anfield to Glen, 30 January 1946; Lazenby to Glen, 21 January 1946; and Stuart Spence to the Minister's Office, 28 January 1946, NAC, RG 10, vol. 6811, file 470-2-8, pt. 1. And just a single agent believed that the politicization of the First Nations was a "healthy sign" without expressing some reservations (Christie to Glen, 5 February 1946, NAC, RG 10, vol. 6811, file 470-2-8, pt. 1.) or was willing to recommend hiring "Indian" employees without qualification (Howe to Glen, 4 February 1946, NAC, RG 10, vol. 6811, file 470-2-8, pt. 1.).

77 Gillett to the Minister, 26 February 1946, NAC, RG 10, vol. 6811, file 470-2-8, pt. 1.

78 W. Young to the Hon. J.A. Glen, 6 February 1946, NAC, RG 10, vol. 6811, file 470-2-8, pt. 1.

79 Lazenby to Glen, 21 January 1946, NAC, RG 10, vol. 6811, file 470-2-8, pt. 1.

80 Ball to Glen, 30 January 1946, NAC, RG 10, vol. 6811, file 470-2-8, pt. 1.

81 Bryant to Glen, 26 January 1946, NAC, RG 10, vol. 6811, file 470-2-8, pt. 1. Another agent argued that First Nations war veterans would be ideally suited to receive positions in the IAB bureaucracy. G.E. Hurl to Mr. Glen, 24 January 1946, NAC, RG 10, vol. 6811, file 470-2-8, pt. 1.

82 MacPherson to Glen, 30 January 1946, NAC, RG 10, vol. 6811, file 470-2-8, pt. 1.

83 Taylor to Glen, 1 February 1946, NAC, RG 10, vol. 6811, file 470-2-8, pt. 1.

84 Ball to Glen, 30 January 1946, NAC, RG 10, vol. 6811, file 470-2-8, pt. 1.

85 Smith to Glen, 23 January 1946, NAC, RG 10, vol. 6811, file 470-2-8, pt. 1.

86 Waite to Glen, 29 January 1946, NAC, RG 10, vol. 6811, file 470-2-8, pt. 1.

87 Ostrander to Glen, 4 February 1946, NAC, RG 10, vol. 6811, file 470-2-8, pt. 1.

88 Lariviere to Glen, 19 January 1946, NAC, RG 10, vol. 6811, file 470-2-8, pt. 1. This policy was also advocated by N.J. McLeod, who disliked the interference of provincial-education inspectors, whom he held responsible for giving First Nations children the same curriculum as "White" children, which was, in his opinion, "definitely beyond the capabilities of Indian children at this time." McLeod to Glen, 20 January 1946, NAC, RG 10, vol. 6811, file 470-2-8, pt. 1. In addition, Dr. T.J. Orford, from Moose Factory, Ontario, believed that the use of provincial extension services should be kept only to an advisory capacity because "the health and welfare of Indians is essentially the responsibility of a Department set up for that purpose and we must assume it in entirety." Orford to Glen, 1 February 1946, NAC, RG 10, vol. 6811, file 470-2-8, pt. 1.

89 W. Young to the Hon. J.A. Glen, 6 February 1946, NAC, RG 10, vol. 6811, file 470-2-8, pt. 1. Young also believed that the restrictions that prohibited the sale of cattle by "Indians" should be maintained because "if close supervision and restrictions on the sale of stock were lifted, I think the cattle would disappear by half within a year."

90 See, for instance, R. Scott Sheffield, *A Search for Equity: A Study of the Treatment Accorded to First Nations Veterans and Dependants of the Second World War and Korea* (Ottawa: The Final Report of the National Round Table on First Nations Veterans' Issues, May 2000).

91 Ostrander to Glen, 4 February 1946, NAC, RG 10, vol. 6811, file 470-2-8, pt. 1. The inspector assured the minister that "Farming Instructors and other employees who are in daily contact with the Indians will use the payment of family allowances to advise and encourage the Indian women in the proper preparation of meals and the proper use which can be made of children's clothing to get the most out of the expenditure." The family allowances were greeted with some suspicion by many First Nations people, who feared that they might undermine their treaty rights. However, by 1946 many had agreed to accept the payments, which significantly improved the basic standard of living on reserves across the country.

92 Kerley to Glen, 16 February 1946, NAC, RG 10, vol. 6811, file 470-2-8, pt. 1.

93 Daly to Glen, 19 February 1946, NAC, RG 10, vol. 6811, file 470-2-8, pt. 1.

94 Indian Agent, Peigan Agency, to Glen, 3 February 1946, NAC, RG 10, vol. 6811, file 470-2-8, pt. 1.

95 Marleau to Glen, 26 January 1946, NAC, RG 10, vol. 6811, file 470-2-8, pt. 1. It is ironic that the designation of legal minority was placed on Native people because they were not believed capable of making their own decisions, whereas this official turned that rationale on its head to argue that the legal definition determined the "Indians'" ability. Often common sense about the inferiority of a minority group and the legal and legislative structures that formalize the power relationship serve to reinforce each other in a vicious circle. This has been ably revealed in James W. St. G. Walker, *"Race," Rights and the Law in the Supreme Court of Canada: Historical Case Studies* (Waterloo and Toronto: Wilfrid Laurier University Press and the Osgoode Society, 1997). It has also found a prominent place in the debates about European and American racism, New World slavery, and which came first, the institution of slavery or the racism that deemed it right. David B. Davis, *The Problem of Slavery in Western Culture* (Ithaca, NY: Cornell University Press, 1966); Winthrop D. Jordan, *The White Man's Burden: Historical Origins of Racism in the United States* (New York: Oxford University Press, 1974); Edmund S. Morgan, *American Slavery, American Freedom: The Ordeal of Colonial Virginia* (New York: W.W. Norton and Co., 1975); Barbara J. Fields, "Slavery, Race and Ideology in the United States of America," *New Left Review* 18 (1990): 95-118; George L. Mosse,

Toward the Final Solution: A History of European Racism (New York: Howard Fertig, 1978); and Eric Williams, *Capitalism and Slavery* (1944; reprint, London: Andre Deutsch, 1964).

96 For instance, see John L. Tobias, "Protection, Civilization, Assimilation: An Outline History of Canada's Indian Policy," in *As Long as the Sun Shines and the Water Flows: A Reader in Canadian-Native Relations*, edited by Ian A.L. Getty and Antoine S. Lussier (Vancouver: UBC Press, 1983), 39-55; and Robin Brownlie, "Man on the Spot: John Daly, Indian Agent in Parry Sound, 1922-1939," *Journal of the Canadian Historical Association* 5 (1994): 63-86.

97 Previously, the IAB had done little to foster good relations with the media or to promote itself, its actions, or the activities of Status Indians. But branch officials had always gladly provided information to reporters and had even permitted some officers to present material in radio talks. However, Indian Agents were not encouraged to develop relationships with local press agencies, and the departmental collection of photographs and motion picture material was, to use Hoey's phrase, "almost non-existant [sic]." Memorandum, Director to the Deputy Minister, 24 April 1947, NAC, RG 10, vol. 6815, file 482-1-1, pt. 1.

Chapter 6: Into the Arena

1 Canada, House of Commons, *Debates*, 13 May 1946, 1446.

2 Nearly half of the 411 submissions to the SJC were received from Native sources.

3 W.J. Robson to Prime Minister Mackenzie King, 15 October 1945, NAC, RG 10, vol. 6811, file 470-2-3, pt. 11.

4 Reta G. Rowan to R.A. Hoey, 10 October 1945; W.J.S. Hatter to the Indian Affairs Branch, 6 December 1945; C. Willmott Maddison to the Minister, Department of Indian Affairs, 7 March 1946; H.P. McKeown to R.A. Hoey, 6 March 1946; Resolution of Sault Ste. Marie City Council Passed 25 February 1946; Mrs. K.G. Kern to R.A. Hoey, Esq., 23 April 1946; M. MacCulloch to J.A. Glen, 28 January 1946, NAC, RG 10, vol. 6811, file 470-2-3, pt. 11.

5 C.W.M. Hart et al. to the Rt. Hon. W.L. Mackenzie King, 23 April 1946, NAC, RG 10, vol. 6811, file 470-2-3, pt. 11. Both Hart, a sociologist, and MacIlwraith, an anthropologist, were from the University of Toronto, and the latter would be one of two academics to appear before the SJC to present expert evidence. Brigadier Martin was an enfranchised Six Nations man. He had served in the militia from 1909 and in 1915, at the age of twenty-two, took leave from a teaching career to enlist for military service overseas. He was promoted to lieutenant, serving seven months on the Western Front before transferring to the Royal Flying Corps in 1917 and eventually qualifying as a pilot. He returned to teaching, became principal of a school in Toronto, and rose to command of the Haldimand Rifles militia regiment in 1930. During the Second World War, he would become the highest ranking indigenous officer in the Canadian Armed Forces as a brigadier commanding the 14th and later 16th Canadian Infantry Brigades guarding the Pacific Coast. He retired from active duty in 1944 to become a magistrate in southern Ontario, the first Native man to do so, serving as such until 1957. Unfortunately, little could be found on Mrs. McCay.

6 [Illegible] to R.A. Hoey, 3 December 1946; Gogama Board of Trade to the Department of Mines and Resources, 1 April 1946, NAC, RG 10, vol. 6811, file 450-3-6, pt. 1.

7 Rev. C.D. Powers to the Department of Indian Affairs, 11 June 1946; Rev. W.A. Cameron to the Minister of Mines and Resources, 17 May 1946; Clerical Secretary, LeR. Mooers to R.A. Hoey, 12 November 1946; R.W. Mayhew, M.P., to R.A. Hoey, Esq., 13 March 1947; Secretary, Edmonton Teachers' Local Association to the Hon. J.A. Glen, 15 June 1946, NAC, RG 10, vol. 6811, file 470-3-6, pt. 1; Canadian Legion of the British Empire Service League, Resolution Submitted, *SJC*, Minutes and Proceedings no. 5, 20 March 1947, 162; Agnes L. Rean to the Hon. J.A. Glen, K.C., 16 February 1948, NAC, RG 10, vol. 8583, file 1/1-2-16, pt. 3; Helen E. Thyne to the Hon. H. [sic] A. Glen, 7 April 1947, NAC, RG 10, vol. 6811, file 470-3-6, pt. 1; Ramona C. Strong to the Dept. of Indian Affairs, 6 March 1948, NAC, RG 10, vol. 8583, file 1/1-2-16, pt. 3; *SJC*, Minutes and Proceedings no. 5, 20 March 1947, 199. The preceding is a representative sample of the types of sources mentioned but is only a small fraction of the total received by the IAB and SJC.

8 For example, the Western Canada-Yukon Fish and Game Council, although expressing sympathy with the difficult circumstances of Native life, was eager to amend the Indian Act to ensure that "Indians" abide by provincial and territorial game laws, as "it is incom-

patible with conservation that any section of the community shall be permitted to kill big game, game birds or fish during the breeding and spawning season." *SJC*, Minutes and Proceedings no. 14, 18 July 1946, 605.

9 J.E. Fry to the Hon. James A. Glen, 1 January 1948 , NAC, RG 10, vol. 8583, file 1/1-2-16, pt. 3.

10 "Indian Buys Wine to Oblige RCMP," *Vancouver Sun*, 15 May 1946, 6; "Indian Stabs Another As Dance Ends," *Kamloops Sentinel*, 9 January 1946, 1; "Border Liquor is Attraction to Indians of Saulte [sic] Ste. Marie," *Brantford Chronicle*, 17 November 1945, 1; "Indians' View on the Virtues of Firewater," *Flin Flon Miner*, 10 May 1947. In its brief to the SJC, the Board of Trade from Cochrane, Ontario, quoted from two late-seventeenth-century French documents commenting on the horrors of brandy among the "Indians" before declaring that "modern students of the problem ["Indians" and alcohol] see little to correct in such reports. Whatever degree of equality in economic, political and social spheres may be attained for the Indian population, it would seem that they are even less capable than their white neighbours of using liquor with discretion." *SJC*, Minutes and Proceedings no. 14, 18 July 1946, 643.

11 "Ottawa Pow-Wow May Net Brand New Deal for Indians," *Prince Albert Daily Herald*, 28 July 1947; "Unruffled Ottawa Stops to Stare at Indian Braves," *Prince Albert Daily Herald*, 26 May 1947; "Indians on Warpath Over Bingo, Jesuits," *Globe and Mail*, 14 June 1947; "B.C. Indians Stalk MP's in Their Lair," *Vancouver Sun*, 27 June 1946; "Caughnawaga Verbal Tomahawks Aimed at Government, Jesuits," *Montreal Gazette*, 13 June 1947.

12 *SJC*, Minutes and Proceedings no. 5, 20 March 1947, 179.

13 "Indian War Hero Heads New Battle," *Winnipeg Tribune*, 4 December 1946, 1, 5, 13; "Indians Find Champion in World War Hero," *Winnipeg Tribune*, 7 December 1946. Thomas Prince was from the Broken Head Band of Salteaux, near Scantebury Manitoba. Prince enlisted in 1940 at the age of twenty-four, originally as a sapper. By 1942 he had transferred to an elite combined Canadian-American special forces unit officially titled the 1st Special Service Force. Serving with this unit in Italy and France, he would become one of the most highly decorated Canadian soldiers of the Second World War, earning a Military Medal, and an American Silver Star with ribbon. He would later act as spokesperson for the Manitoba delegation to the SJC in 1947 before serving again with Canadian troops in Korea. His later life was an often difficult one, as he lived in poverty in Winnipeg estranged from his family and band. His sad story has come to symbolize the inherent bitterness and contradictions of First Nations war service, much as the case of Ira Hayes did in the United States.

14 "Indian War Hero Heads New Battle," *Winnipeg Tribune*, 4 December 1946, 1, 5, 13.

15 "Cowichan Indians Request New Deal from Government," *Victoria Daily Colonist*, undated clipping, NAC, RG 10, vol. 6811, file 470-3-7.

16 *SJC*, Minutes and Proceedings no. 41, 9 July 1947, 2017.

17 "Deplores Canada's Attitude to Indians," *Winnipeg Free Press*, 18 May 1946, 18.

18 "The Original Canadians," *Saint John Telegraph Journal*, 15 July 1946. In fact, the TB death rate was 732 per *hundred* thousand, but the difference in the rates between First Nations people and the general Canadian population was still stunning.

19 *SJC*, Minutes and Proceedings no. 5, 20 March 1947, 155.

20 For instance, see the column by Elmore Philpott, "Native Voices," *Vancouver Sun*, 4 September 1946. Philpott argued that "In two world wars, and in a thousand walks of peacetime life, the Indian people have shown that they have capacities, developed or latent, quite as high as those of any other people on earth."

21 "'Vanishing Indian' Myth," *Saint John Telegraph Journal*, date illegible, NAC RG 10, vol. 6811, file 470-3-7.

22 "The Case for the Indian," *Saint John Telegraph Journal*, 18 July 1946. Canadians' "eagerness" to spring to the defence of minorities in Canada, such as Japanese Canadians, or of Jews in other lands was doubtful if the historiography on race and racism in Canada is any indication. See Irving Abella and Harold Troper, *None Is Too Many: Canada and the Jew of Europe, 1933-38* (Toronto: Lester and Orpen Dennys, 1982); Singh B. Bolaria and Peter S. Li., eds., *Racial Oppression in Canada: Enlarged Second Edition* (Toronto: Garamond Press, 1988); Norman Hillmer et al., eds., *On Guard for Thee: War, Ethnicity, and the Canadian State,*

1939-1945 (Ottawa: Canadian Committee for the History of the Second World War, 1988); Angus McLaren, *Our Own Master Race: Eugenics in Canada, 1885-1945* (Toronto: McClelland and Stewart, 1990); Howard Palmer, *Patterns of Prejudice: A History of Nativism in Alberta* (Toronto: McClelland and Stewart, 1982); James W. St. G. Walker, "Race and Recruitment during World War I: Enlistment of Visible Minorities in the Canadian Expeditionary Force," *Canadian Historical Review* 70, 1 (1989): 1-26; James W. St. G. Walker, *"Race," Rights and the Law in the Supreme Court of Canada: Historical Case Studies* (Waterloo and Toronto: Wilfrid Laurier University Press and the Osgoode Society, 1997); and W. Peter Ward, *White Canada Forever: Popular Attitudes and Public Policies Towards Orientals in British Columbia,* 2nd ed. (Montreal and Kingston: McGill-Queen's University Press, 1990).

23 "A plea for Indians," *Regina Leader-Post,* 4 February 1947.

24 *SJC,* Minutes and Proceedings no. 41, 9 July 1947, 2015.

25 "The Original Canadians," *Saint John Telegraph Journal,* 15 July 1946; Maddison to the Minister, 7 March 1946, NAC, RG 10, vol. 6811, file 470-2-3, pt. 11; "Lo, the Poor Indian," *Vancouver Sun,* 16 May 1946, 4.

26 "CCYM Asks Indians Get Full Rights," *Vancouver Sun,* 22 April 1946; Rean to Glen, 16 February 1948, NAC, RG 10, vol. 8583, file 1/1-2-16, pt. 3; Mayhew to Hoey, 13 March 1947, NAC, RG 10, vol. 6811, file 470-3-6, pt. 1; "Support Indian Status Appeal Request at Baptist Convention," *Victoria Daily Colonist,* 28 June 1946.

27 Maddison to the Minister, 7 March 1946, NAC, RG 10, vol. 6811, file 470-2-3, pt. 11.

28 "Status of Indians Neglected," editorial from unknown periodical, NAC, RG 10, vol. 6811, file 470-3-7.

29 Roy F. Fleming, "A Word for the Indians," *Saturday Night,* 27 July 1947, emphasis in the original.

30 *SJC,* Minutes and Proceedings no. 5, 20 March 1947, 155.

31 *SJC,* Minutes and Proceedings no. 5, 13 and 21 April 1948, 199. This was the first resolution in a seven-point plan submitted by the Graduate Student Christian Movement at the University of British Columbia.

32 *SJC,* Minutes and Proceedings no. 41, 9 July 1947, 2020.

33 Ibid.

34 "Indians to Seek Changes in Law," *Calgary Albertan,* 19 April 1947.

35 Quarterly Report of the Agent for Period Ending June 30th 1946, Bella Coola Indian Agency, B.C.; T.L. Bonnah to the Indian Affairs Branch, 28 May 1946, NAC, RG 10, vol. 6811, file 470-3-6, pt, 1. Indian Agent Bonnah forwarded a petition from the Hereditary Chiefs of the Caughnawaga and the St. Regis Reserves to Ottawa along with an attached letter stating that "it is regretted that some of our Indians should have nothing else to do but entertain themselves in such a manner."

36 Agent's Confidential Report, Walpole Island Agency, James W. Daley, Indian Agent, 15 July 1946; Report for the Quarter Ending Dec. 31 1946, J.F. Lockhart, Indian Agent, NAC, RG 10, vol. 8583, file 1/1-2-16, pt. 1. Daley was particularly concerned with the newly elected band council, which was in his estimation radical and impossible to deal with "until they cool down."

37 Agent's Report for the Quarter ending December 31, 1945, A.D. Moore, Indian Agent, NAC RG 10, vol. 6811, file 470-2-3, pt. 11.

38 The surge in the formation of First Nations political organizations during the 1940s is visible in a chart printed in Donald Whiteside, *Historical Development of Aboriginal Political Associations in Canada: Documentation,* vol. 1 (Ottawa: Reference Aids – Indexes 1973), 38. The chart tracked the number of major organizations formed in each decade: seven during the 1920s, a further seven during the 1930s, and a jump to twelve during the 1940s. Importantly, most of those formed during the 1920s and 1930s folded prior to the Second World War. In the wake of the postwar policy-reform activity, several organizations shut down, and the number of new organisations shrank to nine before the explosion of First Nations nationalism and politicization in the late 1960s and early 1970s (thirty-three organizations during the 1960s and forty-one between 1970 and 1973).

39 The secondary literature on Native organization during this period agrees on this point and has been ably summarized by John Leslie, "Assimilation, Integration or Termination?

The Development of Canadian Indian Policy, 1943-1963," PhD dissertation, Carleton University, 1999, 83-7.

40   For instance, John Laurie was instrumental in the establishment of the Indian Association of Alberta in 1939 and served as its secretary until 1959. See Don Smith, "John Laurie: A Good Samaritan," in *Citymakers: Calgarians After the Frontier,* edited by Max Foran and S. Jameson (Calgary: Historical Society of Alberta, 1987), 263-74. Similarly, in Saskatchewan, the merging of several distinct Indian organizations into the Union of Saskatchewan Indians owed much to the efforts of left-leaning lawyer Morris Shumiachter, CCF Member of Parliament G.H. Castleden, and Premier Tommy Douglas. See James Pitsula, "The Saskatchewan CCF Government and Treaty Indians, 1944-1964," *Canadian Historical Review* 75, 1 (March 1994): 21-52, and F. Laurie Barron, *Walking in Indian Moccasins: The Native Policies of Tommy Douglas and the CCF* (Vancouver: UBC Press, 1997).

41   Peter Kulchyski has argued that the this moderation was due to many Native leaders having "internalized" the Indian Act and thus the hegemonic practices and culture of Canadian society in "Aboriginal People and Hegemony in Canada," *Journal of Canadian Studies* 30, 1 (Spring 1995): 60-8. As will be seen, the exceptions to this rule were to be found among the traditional elements of the various Six Nations reserves in Ontario and Quebec, such as the Hereditary Chiefs, who viewed themselves as allies of the British Crown rather than British subjects under the Indian Act. The other exception was Jules Sioui from Loretteville, Quebec, who had been instrumental in setting up major wartime conferences in Ottawa that led to the formation of the North American Indian Brotherhood. However, Sioui's aggressive and radical ideas do not seem to have found a warm reception among the majority of indigenous leaders, and he had been marginalized by the end of the war.

42   The Protestant-dominated Native Brotherhood of British Columbia (NBBC) was formed in the early 1930s on the north coast of British Columbia and, although it carried out political activities and agitated for Native rights, functioned primarily as a union for Aboriginal fisherman on the coast. Peter Kelly, a Methodist minister and member of the Haida Nation, was the NBBC's principal spokesperson for Indian-policy reform, making ten trips to Ottawa between 1936 and 1946 to lobby and petition on behalf of the brotherhood. Both he and the organization were moderates and accepting of assimilation as inevitable and perhaps even positive for their people. Some of its other leading figures, including Arthur Adams, Chief William Scow, Guy Williams, and Andrew Paull, had already been political activists for decades, and a few would achieve very high profiles as advocates for Native rights over the next several decades. See Alan Morley, *Roar of the Breakers: A Biography of Peter Kelly* (Toronto: Ryerson Press, 1967), 144-47, and E.P. Patterson, "Andrew Paull and Canadian Indian Resurgence," PhD dissertation, University of Washington, 1962, Chapter 8. The Indian Association of Alberta formed in 1939, was reorganized in 1944, and claimed the support of almost every band in the province. On the Indian Association of Alberta, see Laurie Meijer Drees, "Citizenship and Treaty Rights: The Indian Association of Alberta and the Canadian Indian Act, 1946-1948," *Great Plains Quarterly* 20 (Spring 2000): 141-58.

43   In Saskatchewan three organizations were formed during the war: the Association of Saskatchewan Indians, formed in 1943 under the leadership of Chief Joe Dreaver from the Mistawasis Reserve; the Saskatchewan Branch of the North American Indian Brotherhood, formed by John Tootoosis in 1944; and the Protective Association for Indians and their Treaties, formed in the Qu'Appele area. In Quebec the most radical of all the Native leaders during this period, Jules Sioui, from the Loretteville Reserve, led the Protection Committee of the Indian Tribes of Quebec from 1943 until 1944, when he became active in setting up the North American Indian Brotherhood. Finally, on Cape Breton Island the Grand General Council of Cape Breton was formed in 1944 and lasted until the emergence of the new Indian Act in 1951.

44   Paull had been a sports promoter in Vancouver, running lacrosse and baseball teams for many years, and had maintained a high profile in the local and provincial media. Patterson, "Andrew Paul and Canadian Indian Resurgence," 191-92. He would later use his image as a colourful character to further his ends as leader of the NAIB.

45   These included the Union of Ontario Indians (a branch of the NAIB) in 1946-47; the Manitoba Indian Brotherhood in 1946; the Union of Saskatchewan Indians, formed in

1946 with the help of the provincial Co-operative Commonwealth Federation (CCF) party and G.H. Castelden, federal CCF member for Yorkton, effectively amalgamating the three previous provincial organizations under one structure; and the Confederation of Interior Tribes of BC (loosely affiliated with Paull's NAIB) in 1947.

46 Norman Lickers, an articulate Brantford barrister and member of the Six Nations, was the first indigenous person to become a lawyer in Ontario. He was part of the Indian delegation at the conference on the North American Indian hosted in Toronto in 1939. He was the sole Native person directly affiliated with the process. He served in this capacity during each of the three sessions of Parliament in which the SJC sat, corresponding with First Nations groups to organize their attendance during the 1947 hearings. However, he also frequently questioned those presenting briefs before the committee and provided an indigenous perspective for SJC members when other Native people were absent.

47 *SJC*, Minutes and Proceedings no. 5, 20 March 1947, 164.

48 *SJC*, Minutes and Proceedings no. 12, 21 April 1947, 571-653, and no. 41, 9 July 1947, 2094-95. Laurie Meijer Drees, in her article "Citizenship and Treaty Rights," does a good job of summarizing the complex and impressive submission of the Indian Association of Alberta (IAA). She correctly notes that the IAA saw no contradiction between citizenship and treaty rights but unfortunately overemphasizes the degree of congruence between the IAA's views and those of the members of the SJC. For the government members involved, citizenship was almost a synonym for assimilation and was seen not so much as an end unto itself, but rather as a means toward achieving assimilation. Moreover, her focus on one sophisticated organization blinded her to the substantial divisions within and between First Nations groups on many issues, including those of citizenship and treaty rights.

49 The remarkable similarity of wording in these letters is immediately evident. John Leslie mentions vaguely that evidence has been uncovered at the Archives Deschâtelets in the records of the Oblate Indian and Eskimo Welfare Commission indicating that this was done; see Leslie, "Assimilation, Integration or Termination?" 162, n. 116. The Catholic hierarchy was particularly concerned with the question of denominational schooling, which all these letters strongly supported. According to Leslie, they distrusted the Protestant-dominated Indian Affairs Branch and SJC, and the IAB, in turn, viewed with cynicism these "inspired briefs."

50 *SJC*, Minutes and Proceedings no. 5, 13 April to 21 June 1948, 215. This was taken from a brief submitted by chiefs and councillors of the Carrier First Nation from north central British Columbia.

51 *SJC*, Minutes and Proceedings no. 41, 9 July 1947, 2075.

52 John Leslie counted twenty-nine briefs in favour of better-funded religious instruction and thirty-three desiring an overhauled system of nondenominational schools; see Leslie, "Assimilation, Integration or Termination?" 162, n. 115.

53 *SJC*, Minutes and Proceedings no. 25, 22 May 1947, 1338. This quotation was drawn from the brief submitted by the Veterans' Association of Wikwemikong, Manitoulin Island, Ontario.

54 *SJC*, Minutes and Proceedings no. 19, 8 May 1947, 979.

55 *SJC*, Minutes and Proceedings no. 26, 23 May 1947, 1426.

56 Ian V.B. Johnson, *Helping Indians to Help Themselves – A Committee to Investigate Itself: The 1951 Indian Act Consultation Process* (Treaties and Historical Research Centre, Indian and Northern Affairs Canada, 1984), 17. See also D.F. Brown's speech to the SJC membership at its opening session in 1948. *SJC*, Minutes and Proceedings no. 1, 19 February 1948, 9.

57 *SJC*, Minutes and Proceedings no. 2, 11 March 1947, 52.

58 An example of this use can be found in the brief submitted on behalf of the Millbrook Band near Truro, Nova Scotia, by their legal counsel. *SJC*, Minutes and Proceedings no. 21, 13 August 1946, 854-55. While traditionally this phrase is associated with efforts to win the right of representation, as in the revolt of the Thirteen Colonies, in the case of many of Canada's First Nations, most of whom did not desire the franchise, the phrase was turned around to read, "no taxation because we have and want no representation." A significant minority did feel that they deserved the federal vote because they were paying taxes and performing military service, such as in the brief from the band on Georgina Island, Ontario.

SJC, Minutes and Proceedings no. 26, 23 May 1947, 1440. Typically, in their briefs the First Nations did not even bother to defend their opposition to paying taxes, but most who did based their argument on their rights under treaty.

59 *SJC*, Minutes and Proceedings no. 33, 12 June 1947, 1796.

60 This quotation is taken from the brief submitted by the United Native Farmers' Organisation of the Stó:lô Tribe in Sardis, British Columbia. *SJC*, Minutes and Proceedings no. 21, 13 August 1946, 848. This argument was also forwarded by the Aboriginal Natives of the Fraser Valley and the Interior Tribes of the Interior of British Columbia. *SJC*, Minutes and Proceedings no. 2, 11 March 1947, 57. The similarity in wording suggests that there was some overlap in the membership of these two organizations.

61 An example of this appeared in the submission from the Lake Constance Band in Ontario. *SJC*, Minutes and Proceedings no. 21, 13 August 1946, 862-63. More can be found in the briefs from the Six Nations reserves in St. Regis, Caughnawaga, and Oka, including the briefs both from those parts of the communities that supported the elected council and from those that declared their allegiance to the Six Nations Confederacy and their Hereditary Chiefs. *SJC*, Minutes and Proceedings no. 33, 12 June 1947 and no. 34, 13 June 1947.

62 *SJC*, Minutes and Proceedings no. 21, 13 August 1946, 829.

63 Ibid., 830.

64 This quotation was taken from the brief submitted by the Native Brotherhood of British Columbia. *SJC*, Minutes and Proceedings no. 41, 9 July 1947, 2046.

65 *SJC*, Minutes and Proceedings no. 41, 9 July 1947, 2039.

66 Ibid., 2075.

67 This was a request from the Red Bank Band in New Brunswick. *SJC*, Minutes and Proceedings no. 21, 13 August 1946, 882.

68 The Mississauga of the Credit River felt that cases ought to require a majority vote of the entire band. *SJC*, Minutes and Proceedings no. 41, 9 July 1947, 2094.

69 Even in this case there was an exception in the form of a dissenting brief from the Moose Woods Band in Saskatchewan, which actually requested that the powers of their Indian Agent be increased. *SJC*, Minutes and Proceedings no. 5, 20 March 1947, 218. This desire ran directly against that of the other bands of Sioux [Dakota] represented in their joint brief, to which the Moose Woods brief was attached, who argued for a degree of self-determination. *SJC*, Minutes and Proceedings no. 5, 20 March 1947, 215.

70 *SJC*, Minutes and Proceedings no. 21, 13 August 1946, 865.

71 *SJC*, Minutes and Proceedings no. 12, 21 April 1947, 571-653.

72 *SJC*, Minutes and Proceedings no. 12, 21 April 1947, 576-77, 587, 588-96.

73 *SJC*, Minutes and Proceedings no. 41, 9 July 1947, 2083.

74 *SJC*, Minutes and Proceedings no. 26, 23 May 1947, 1439.

75 *SJC*, Minutes and Proceedings no. 33, 12 June 1947, 1794-95. The wording was different, but the nature of the demands was similar in the submission from the same faction on the St. Regis Reserve. *SJC*, Minutes and Proceedings no. 5, 13 April to 21 June 1947, 209.

76 "Shabby Treatment," *Montreal Gazette*, 18 July 1947. This editorial was originally produced by the *Toronto Star*.

77 This is not to say that there was no gain for these groups as a result of their war service. The franchise was finally granted in British Columbia to Chinese and Japanese veterans, but in a host of other ways they remained discriminated against; see Patricia E. Roy, "The Soldiers Canada Didn't Want: Her Chinese and Japanese Citizens," *Canadian Historical Review* 59, 3 (1978): 356-57; and Patricia E. Roy, *The Oriental Question: Consolidating a White Man's Province, 1914-41* (Vancouver: UBC Press, 2003). On attitudes to Jews, see Walker, *"Race," Rights and the Law in the Supreme Court of Canada*, especially Chapter 4; Abella and Troper, *None Is Too Many*; and Paula Jean Draper, "Fragmented Loyalties: Canadian Jewry, the King Government and the Refugee Dilemma," in *On Guard for Thee: War, Ethnicity, and the Canadian State, 1939-1945*, edited by Norman Hillmer et al. (Ottawa: Canadian Committee for the History of the Second World War, 1988), 151-77.

Chapter 7: Whither the "Indian"?

1 Canada, House of Commons, *Debates*, 13 May 1946, 1446.

2 Ibid.
3 The MPs were: Messrs. B. Arsenault, J.H. Blackmore, D.F. Brown, H.E. Brunelle, W. Bryce, W.G. Case, G.H. Castleden, J.A. Charlton (PC, Brantford-Wentworth), T. Farquhar, W. Gariepy, J.L. Gibson, J.A. Glen, D.S. Harkness, W. Little, J.D. MacNicol, J.E. Matthews, M. McLean, J.L. Raymond, T. Reid, C.T. Richard, F.T. Stanfield, and G. Stirling. The Senate appointed as its representatives on the SJC: A. Blais, V. Dupuis, Iva C. Fallis, C.E. Ferland, R.B. Horner, J.F. Johnston, G.B. Jones, J.A. MacDonald, D. MacLennan, J. Nicol, N. McI. Patterson (who was replaced by J.J. Stevenson), and W.H. Taylor. Canada, Parliament, *Special Joint Committee of the Senate and the House of Commons appointed to examine and consider the Indian Act* (hereinafter the *SJC*), Minutes and Proceedings no. 1, 28 and 30 May 1946, ii. Over the more than two years that the committee sat, there were only minor changes in personnel beyond the replacement of Patterson, which were due to the retirement of MP Grote Stirling and the death of Senator Johnston.
4 *SJC*, Minutes and Proceedings no. 5, April-June, 1948, 186. The total number of pages is taken from John Leslie, "Assimilation, Integration or Termination? The Development of Canadian Indian Policy, 1943-1963," PhD dissertation, Carleton University, 1999, 177.
5 Laurie Meijer Drees, "Citizenship and Treaty Rights: The Indian Association of Alberta and the Canadian Indian Act, 1946-1948," *Great Plains Quarterly* 20 (Spring 2000): 142.
6 In the estimation of Ian V.B. Johnson, the committee "spent almost as much time debating form, process and other matters unrelated to Indian concerns as they did examining evidence and discussing substantive issues." *Helping Indians to Help Themselves – A Committee to Investigate Itself: The 1951 Indian Act Consultation Process* (Treaties and Historical Research Centre, Indian and Northern Affairs Canada, 1984), 17. This is a bit uncharitable; the SJC did spend a great deal of time on such procedural matters, but this was not uncommon in Parliamentary committees.
7 *SJC*, Minutes and Proceedings no. 1, 28 and 30 May 1946, 29.
8 *SJC*, Minutes and Proceedings no. 1, 28 and 30 May 1946, 44.
9 *SJC*, Minutes and Proceedings no. 1, 28 and 30 May 1946, 52.
10 *SJC*, Minutes and Proceedings no. 1, 28 and 30 May 1946, 45, 50. The first comment was provided by the chairman, D.F. Brown (Liberal, Essex West), and the second by J.A. Charlton.
11 Norman Lickers was more than just symbolically important to the SJC; he was also important in helping the committee to rework the Act for its final report.
12 *SJC*, Minutes and Proceedings no. 1, 28 and 30 May 1946, 40.
13 *SJC*, Minutes and Proceedings no. 4, 11 June 1946, 153.
14 Ibid.
15 *SJC*, Minutes and Proceedings no. 29, 3 June 1947, 1538.
16 *SJC*, Minutes and Proceedings no. 9, 28 March 1947, 422.
17 Senator Fallis spoke about her desire to examine Native women's issues in *SJC*, Minutes and Proceedings no. 3, 14 March 1947, 72. Reference to MacNicol's concern for the Indian question can be found in *SJC*, Minutes and Proceedings no. 4, 18 March 1947, 134.
18 *SJC*, Minutes and Proceedings no. 11, 9 July 1946, 490.
19 *SJC*, Minutes and Proceedings no. 11, 9 July 1946, 491.
20 *SJC*, Minutes and Proceedings no. 12, 11 July 1947, 511.
21 *SJC*, Minutes and Proceedings no. 17, 2 May 1947, 807.
22 *SJC*, Minutes and Proceedings no. 19, 8 May 1947, 922.
23 Castleden, MacNicol, Brunelle, Richard, and Matthews had been members of the Committee of Reconstruction and Reestablishment in 1944, when the uninspiring testimony of IAB personnel had led that special committee to recommend a thorough review of Canadian Indian policy and administration.
24 *SJC*, Minutes and Proceedings no. 31, 6 June 1947, 1658. The language used by Matthews is striking. He refers in the latter part of the quotation to a discrepancy between the testimony of Prince and Conn, but whereas the information offered by the Native representative was termed "remarks," the branch official had given the "facts."
25 *SJC*, Minutes and Proceedings no. 1, 19 February 1948, 11. H.L. Keenleyside was the deputy minister of mines and resources, who was responsible for Indian Affairs. C.W. Jackson was a senior ministerial aid, Hoey was the superintendent general of Indian Affairs, and C.H. Bland was the chairman of the Civil Service Commission.

26 *SJC*, Minutes and Proceedings no. 2, 2 and 4 March 1948, 59.
27 *SJC*, Minutes and Proceedings no. 4, 23 March and 6, 8, and 9 April 1948, 159.
28 In a debate over the lack of good roads built on Indian reserves, W.G. Case complained that "if these people will develop a little initiative, they will build their roads as our grandparents did." *SJC*, Minutes and Proceedings no. 3, 14 March 1947, 79. For an example of a discussion about the spendthrift nature of the "Indian," see *SJC*, Minutes and Proceedings no. 8, 24 June 1946, 378-80.
29 *SJC*, Minutes and Proceedings no. 38, 24 June 1947, 1942.
30 For instance, see the testimony of D.M. MacKay in *SJC*, Minutes and Proceedings no. 4, 11 June 1946, 124, or the testimony of G.H. Gooderham in *SJC*, Minutes and Proceedings no. 15, 25 and 28 April 1947, 747. Gooderham, however, was more willing to grant powers and responsibilities to Native people and communities than were many of his IAB colleagues. *SJC*, Minutes and Proceedings no. 15, 25 and 28 April 1947, 748-49.
31 *SJC*, Minutes and Proceedings no. 8, 24 June 1946, 383.
32 *SJC*, Minutes and Proceedings no. 33, 12 June 1947, 1706-12, 1756-72.
33 *SJC*, Minutes and Proceedings no. 33, 12 June 1947, 1769.
34 *SJC*, Minutes and Proceedings no. 17, 30 July 1946, 715; no. 19, 6 August 1946, 744-66.
35 *SJC*, Minutes and Proceedings no. 20, 9 May 1947, 1056.
36 Ibid.
37 The evidence supplied by Hugh Conn, the fur supervisor, was particularly noteworthy in this respect, as he argued that the treaties had been "almost legislated out of existence." *SJC*, Minutes and Proceedings no. 16, 25 July 1947, 685. Gooderham argued that the government was giving more than the treaties required. *SJC*, Minutes and Proceedings no. 15, 25 and 28 April 1947, 748. MacKay and MacInnes similarly argued that the lack of treaties for British Columbia's First Nations made no difference because they were treated the same anyway, which further undermined the significance of treaties in the minds of the SJC membership; see *SJC*, Minutes and Proceedings no. 3, 6 June 1946, 86.
38 Brian W. Dippie, *The Vanishing American: White Attitudes and U.S. Indian Policy* (Middleton, CT: Weslyan University Press, 1982), 332-33.
39 *SJC*, Minutes and Proceedings no. 41, 9 July 1947, 2004.
40 *SJC*, Minutes and Proceedings no. 8, 24 June 1946, 377-78.
41 *SJC*, Minutes and Proceedings no. 5, 13 April to 21 June 1948, 183.
42 Ibid., 181-84.
43 *SJC*, Minutes and Proceedings no. 9, 27 June 1946, 426, 450.
44 *SJC*, Minutes and Proceedings no. 9, 27 June 1946, 427.
45 For example, Lickers led the discussion of the issue with the Saskatchewan delegation, which consisted of John Tootoosis, president of the Union of Saskatchewan Indians; Chief John Gambler; Chief Joe Dreaver; and the Reverend Ahab Spence, a Cree teacher. Committee members MacNicol, Case, and Blackmore joined the debate; see *SJC*, Minutes and Proceedings no. 20, 9 May 1947, 1061-65.
46 *SJC*, Minutes and Proceedings no. 33, 12 June 1947, 1771.
47 *SJC*, Minutes and Proceedings no. 15, 25 and 28 April 1947, 748.
48 *SJC*, Minutes and Proceedings no. 38, 24 June 1947, 1951-52.
49 *SJC*, Minutes and Proceedings no. 15, 25 and 28 April 1947, 748. Castleden stated, "I think that there is general agreement that there has been too much paternalism." Thomas Reid used the same words several days earlier in the surprising comment that "In assimilation there is too much paternalism." *SJC*, Minutes and Proceedings no. 13, 22 April 1947, 692. The term "paternalism" seems to have been a bad word for committee members symbolizing all that had been wrong with Canada's Indian policy and administration in the past.
50 *SJC*, Minutes and Proceedings no. 19, 6 August 1946, 744.
51 *SJC*, Minutes and Proceedings no. 38, 24 June 1947, 1941.
52 *SJC*, Minutes and Proceedings no. 32, 10 June 1947, 1673. This figure of $15 million was taken from testimony of Hoey in 1946 that in order for the branch to begin a worthwhile program for Indian advancement, the appropriations would need to be approximately $14 million per year; see *SJC*, Minutes and Proceedings no. 1, 28 and 30 May 1946, 27. This was approximately double the estimate for the fiscal year 1946-47.

53 For instance, Andrew Paull admitted that there had been a general improvement in relations with the branch since Hoey took the reins of office. *SJC*, Minutes and Proceedings no. 18, 5 and 6 May 1947, 892.

54 See J.L. Granatstein, *The Ottawa Men: The Civil Service Mandarins, 1935-57* (Toronto: Oxford University Press, 1982), and Doug Owram, *The Government Generation: Canadian Intellectuals and the State, 1900-1945* (Toronto: University of Toronto Press, 1986).

55 *SJC*, Minutes and Proceedings no. 29, 3 June 1947, 1521-56. MacIlwraith's presentation to the SJC and the subsequent debate are some of the most interesting pages in the entire "Minutes of Proceedings and Evidence" of the committee. Diamond Jenness, a New Zealander, began his long and illustrious scholarly career in Canada in 1913 after completing his anthropological education at Oxford University. He conducted field research among many indigenous societies and through his publications and post as chief anthropologist of the National Museum of Canada became the doyen of the discipline in the country. His testimony would prove influential during the SJC hearings partly because of his academic and official stature. For more on Jenness's contributions to the SJC, see Peter Kulchyski, "Anthropology in the Service of the State: Diamond Jenness and Canadian Indian Policy," *Journal of Canadian Studies* 28, 2 (Summer 1993): 21-50.

56 *SJC*, Minutes and Proceedings no. 1, 5 and 6 March 1947, 7-25.

57 *SJC*, Minutes and Proceedings no. 1, 5 and 6 March 1947, 8.

58 Ibid., 16-17.

59 Ibid., 10.

60 *SJC*, Minutes and Proceedings no. 29, 3 June 1947, 1538.

61 *SJC*, Minutes and Proceedings no. 29, 3 June 1947, 1548.

62 *SJC*, Minutes and Proceedings no. 19, 6 August 1946, 744.

63 *SJC*, Minutes and Proceedings no. 24, 20 May 1947, 1259.

64 Under the centralization scheme developed by the IAB in the early to mid-1940s and instituted in the face of significant opposition from Mi'Kmaq communities across the province, dozens of small scattered reserves were sold off and their populations encouraged to move to two large central reserves. Technically, the residents of these smaller defunct reserves were not forced to move, but in effect they were deprived of government services unless they did so. The primary reason for the plan was administrative, as it had been costly and extremely difficult to adequately provide health, education, and welfare services to so widely scattered a population. From the perspective of the SJC, centralization merely encouraged "Indians" to move back to the reserve in order to gain adequate services, which Harkness called a "backward step"; see *SJC*, Minutes and Proceedings no. 38, 24 June 1947, 1954.

65 *SJC*, Minutes and Proceedings no. 40, 2 July 1947, 1990.

66 *SJC*, Minutes and Proceedings no. 29, 3 June 1947, 1549. Bryce's reference to five dollars per year alluded to the annual treaty payment made to some First Nations people under a number of treaties. His glib tone, which dismissed the First Nations' fervent faith in the importance of their treaties as a matter of five dollars, suggests that even a sympathetic individual like Bryce thought little of treaties or indigenous culture and certainly perceived no threat in allowing annuity payments to continue.

67 *SJC*, Minutes and Proceedings no. 4, 11 June 1946, 153.

68 For instance, in the debate about awarding the Dominion franchise to "Indians," D.F. Brown explained that part of the rationale for doing so was that "we cannot instil in the Indians a knowledge of our democratic principles and forms of government unless we give them the privilege of participating." *SJC*, Minutes and Proceedings no. 5, 13 April to 21 June 1948, 183.

69 For example, see the debates with the delegates from the Catholic Church, during which J.A. Charlton (PC, Brantford-Wentworth) challenged them, saying "Would you not say that, if given the same opportunity the Indian child is just as capable as the white?" *SJC*, Minutes and Proceedings no. 27, 27 May 1947, 1490.

70 *SJC*, Minutes and Proceedings no. 4, 18 March 1947, 118. In a similar vein, Senator R.B. Horner, in complimenting Chief Joe Dreaver and the other members of the Saskatchewan delegation for their fine presentation, was only sorry that they did not recommend

enfranchisement "because I can picture some wonderful orators coming from their race." *SJC*, Minutes and Proceedings no. 20, 9 May 1947, 1056.
71 *SJC*, Minutes and Proceedings no. 3, 14 March 1947, 88.
72 *SJC*, Minutes and Proceedings no. 4, 18 March 1947, 125, emphasis added.
73 *SJC*, Minutes and Proceedings no. 17, 30 July 1946, 715.
74 *SJC*, Minutes and Proceedings no. 9, 28 March 1947, 405.
75 *SJC*, Minutes and Proceedings no. 27, 27 May 1947, 1484.
76 *SJC*, Minutes and Proceedings no. 5, 13 April to 21 June 1948, 188.
77 *SJC*, Minutes and Proceedings no. 5, 13 April to 21 June 1948, 187.
78 The wording of the recommendation in the 1947 interim report can be found on page 154.
79 *SJC*, Minutes and Proceedings no. 5, 13 April to 21 June 1948, 187, emphasis added.
80 This conflict between the letter and the spirit of the treaties continues at the end of the twentieth century in the nation's courts, in its academic texts, and in the media.
81 *SJC*, Minutes and Proceedings no. 5, 13 April to 21 June 1948, 188.
82 *SJC*, Minutes and Proceedings no. 5, 13 April to 21 June 1948, 187.
83 *SJC*, Minutes and Proceedings no. 5, 13 April to 21 June 1948, 187.
84 *SJC*, Minutes and Proceedings no. 5, 13 April to 21 June 1948, 190.
85 The Catholic Church was more wedded to maintaining denominational schooling than were any of the other churches involved in Aboriginal education. The SJC had been inclined to more secular instruction, preferably in day schools and ideally with the indigenous children integrated into neighbouring provincial school systems. The staunch opposition that the Catholic Church was mounting made the Liberal government nervous about pressing the issue and appearing anti-Catholic before a federal election.
86 Leslie, "Assimilation, Integration or Termination?" 211.
87 Ibid., 232-33.

Conclusion
1 Philip H. Godsell, "Red Men Dig Up the Hatchet," *Winnipeg Free Press*, Magazine Section, 24 May 1941, 5.
2 Samuel Devlin to Secretary, 2 October 1940, NAC, RG 10, vol. 6768, file 452-20, pt. 4.
3 Elizabeth Vibert, *Trader's Tales: Narratives of Cultural Encounters in the Columbia Plateau, 1797-1846* (Norman, OK: University of Okalahoma Press, 1997), 277.
4 J.R. Miller, *Skyscrapers Hide the Heavens: A History of Indian-White Relations in Canada*, 2nd ed. (Toronto: University of Toronto Press, 1991), 221.
5 John Leslie, "Assimilation, Integration or Termination? The Development of Canadian Indian Policy, 1943-1963," PhD dissertation, Carleton University, 1999.

Bibliography

Primary Sources

Newspapers and Other Periodicals
Brantford Expositor
Calgary Herald
Canadian Forum
Cardston News
Dalhousie Review
The Globe (and Mail)
Halifax Chronicle
Kamloops Sentinel
Prince Albert Daily Herald
Public Opinion Quarterly
Queen's Quarterly
Saskatoon Star-Phoenix
Saturday Night
University of Toronto Quarterly
Vancouver Sun
Winnipeg Free Press

Government Records
The Aboriginal Soldier after the Wars. Report of the Standing Senate Committee on Aboriginal Peoples, 1995.
Canada. *Report of the Royal Commission on Aboriginal Peoples*. Vol. 1, *Looking Forward, Looking Back*. Ottawa: Canada Communication Group, 1996.
Hansard
Minutes of Proceedings and Evidence of the Special Joint Senate and House of Commons Committee on the Indian Act, 1946-1948.
National Archives of Canada
  Record Group 10, Indian Affairs
  Record Group 24, Department of National Defence
  Record Group 27, Department of Labour
  Record Group 36/18, Dependants' Allowance Board
  Record Group 36/31, Wartime Information Board
  Record Group 38, Department of Veterans' Affairs
  Record Group 41, Canadian Broadcasting Corporation
  Record Group 44, National War Services

Other
Social Planning for Canada. Research Committee for the League for Social Reconstruction. Toronto: Thomas Nelson and Sons, 1935.

Secondary Sources
Abel, Kerry. *Drum Songs: Glimpse of Dene History*. Montreal and Kingston: McGill-Queen's University Press, 1993.
–. "Tangled, Lost and Bitter? Current Directions in the Writing of Native History in Canada." *Acadiensis* 26, 1 (Autumn 1996): 92-101.
Abella, Irving, and Harold Troper. *None Is Too Many: Canada and the Jew of Europe, 1933-38*. Toronto: Lester and Orpen Dennys, 1982.
Adair, John, and Evon Vogt. "Navajo and Zuni Veterans: A Study of Contrasting Modes of Cultural Change." *American Anthropologist* 51, 4 (1949): 547-68.
Anderson, Kay. *Vancouver's Chinatown: Racial Discourse in Canada, 1875-1980*. Montreal and Kingston: McGill-Queen's University Press, 1991.
Armour, Leslie, and Elizabeth Trott. *The Faces of Reason: An Essay on Philosophy and Culture in English Canada, 1850-1950*. Waterloo, ON: Wilfrid Laurier University Press, 1981.
Barbeau, Marius. "The Thunder Bird of the Mountains." *The University of Toronto Quarterly* 2, 1 (1932): 92-110
Barman, Jean, Yvonne Hébert, and Don McCaskill, eds. *Indian Education in Canada*. Vol. 1, *The Legacy*. Vancouver: UBC Press, 1986.
Barnes, Trevor J., and James S. Duncan, eds. *Writing Worlds: Discourse, Text and Metaphor in the Representation of Landscape*. London and New York: Routledge, 1992.
Barron, F. Laurie. "The Indian Pass System in the Canadian West, 1882-1935." *Prairie Forum* 13, 1 (1988): 25-42.
–. *Walking in Indian Moccasins: The Native Policies of Tommy Douglas and the CCF*. Vancouver: UBC Press, 1997.
Bell, Stephen A. "The 107th 'Timber Wolf' Battalion at Hill 70." *Canadian Military History* 5, 1 (Spring 1996): 73-8.
Berkhofer, Robert F., Jr. *The White Man's Indian: Images of the American Indian from Columbus to the Present*. New York: Random House, 1978.
Bernstein, Alison R. *American Indians and World War II: Toward a New Era in Indian Affairs*. Norman, OK: University of Oklahoma Press, 1991.
Binnema, Theodore. *Common and Contested Ground: A Human and Environmental History of the Northwestern Plains*. Norman, OK: University of Oklahoma Press, 2001.
Bird, Elizabeth S., ed. *Dressing in Feathers: The Construction of the Indian in American Popular Culture*. Boulder, CO: Westview Press, 1996.
Blake, Raymond B., and Jeffrey Keshen, eds. *Social Welfare Policy in Canada: Historical Readings*. Toronto: Copp Clark, 1995.
Bliss, Michael. "Privatising the Mind: The Sundering of Canadian History, the Sundering of Canada." *Journal of Canadian Studies* 26, 4 (Winter 1991-92): 5-17.
Bolaria, B. Singh, and Peter S. Li., eds. *Racial Oppression in Canada: Enlarged Second Edition*. Toronto: Garamond Press, 1988.
Bothwell, Robert, and Norman Hillmer, eds. *The In-Between Time: Canadian External Policy in the 1930s*. Toronto: Copp Clark, 1975.
Britten, Thomas A. *American Indians in World War I: At Home and at War*. Albuquerque, NM: University of New Mexico Press, 1997.
Broadfoot, Barry. *The Veterans' Years: Coming Home from the War*. Vancouver and Toronto: Douglas and McIntyre, 1985.
Brownlie, Robin. "Man on the Spot: John Daly, Indian Agent in Parry Sound, 1922-1939." *Journal of the Canadian Historical Association* 5 (1994): 63-86.
Bushnell, John H. "From American Indian to Indian American: The Changing Identity of the Hupa." *American Anthropologist* 70 (1968): 1108-16.
Calloway, Colin. *Crown and Calumet: British-Indian Relations, 1783-1815*. Norman, OK: University of Oklahoma Press, 1987.

Campbell, Robert Malcolm. *Grand Illusions: The Politics of the Keynesian Experience in Canada, 1945-1975*. Peterborough: Broadview Press, 1987.

Carter, Sarah. "The Missionaries' Indian: The Publications of John McDougall, John Maclean and Egerton Ryerson Young." *Prairie Forum* 9, 1 (1984): 27-44.

–. *Lost Harvests: Prairie Indian Reserve Farmers and Government Policy*. Montreal and Kingston: McGill-Queen's University Press, 1991.

–. *Capturing Women: The Manipulation of Cultural Imagery in Canada's Prairie West*. Montreal and Kingston: McGill-Queen's University Press, 1997.

Coates, Ken. *Best Left as Indians: Native-White Relations in the Yukon Territory, 1840-1973*. Montreal and Kingston: McGill-Queen's University Press, 1991.

–, and Robin Fisher, eds. *Out of the Background: Readings on Canadian Native History*. 2nd ed. Toronto: Copp Clark, 1996.

Cole, D., and Ira Chaikin. *An Iron Hand Upon the People: The Law against the Potlatch on the Northwest Coast*. Vancouver: Douglas and McIntyre, 1990.

Commachio, Cynthia. "Dancing to Perdition: Adolescence and Leisure in Interwar English-Canada." *Journal of Canadian Studies* 32, 3 (Fall 1997): 5-35.

–. *The Infinite Bonds of Family: Domesticity in Canada, 1850-1940*. Toronto: University of Toronto Press, 1999.

Copp, Terry, and Bill McAndrew. *Battle Exhaustion: Soldiers and Psychiatrists in the Canadian Army, 1939-1945*. Montreal: McGill-Queen's University Press, 1990.

–. "Ontario, 1939: The Decision for War." *Ontario History* 86, 3 (September 1994): 269-78.

Curtin, Philip D. *The Image of Africa: British Ideas and Action, 1780-1850*. Madison, WI: University of Wisconsin Press, 1964.

Davis, David B. *The Problem of Slavery in Western Culture*. Ithaca, NY: Cornell University Press, 1966.

Davison, Janet F. "We Shall Remember Them: Canadian Indians and World War II." MA thesis, Trent University, 1992.

Deloria, Vine, Jr., ed. *American Indian Policy in the Twentieth Century*. Norman, OK: University of Oklahoma Press, 1985.

Dempsey, James L. "Alberta Indians and the Second World War." In *For King and Country: Alberta and the Second World War,* edited by Ken Tingley, 39-52. Edmonton: Provincial Museum of Alberta, 1995.

–. *Warriors of the King: Prairie Indians in World War I*. Regina: Canadian Plains Research Centre, 1999.

Dickason, Olive P. *Canada's First Nations: A History of Founding Peoples from Earliest Times*. Toronto: McClelland and Stewart, 1992.

Dippie, Brian W. *The Vanishing American: White Attitudes and U.S. Indian Policy*. Middleton, CT: Wesleyan University Press, 1982.

Donaghy, Greg, ed. *Uncertain Horizons: Canadians and Their World in 1945*. Canadian Committee for the History of the Second World War, 1997.

Draper, Paula Jean. "Fragmented Loyalties: Canadian Jewry, the King Government and the Refugee Dilemma." In *On Guard for Thee: War, Ethnicity, and the Canadian State, 1939-1945,* edited by Norman Hillmer, Bohdan S. Kordan, and Lubomyr Y. Luciuk, 151-77. Ottawa: Canadian Committee for the History of the Second World War, 1988.

Drinnon, Richard, *Facing West: The Metaphysics of Indian-Hating and Empire-Building*. Minneapolis: University of Minnesota Press, 1980.

Dyck, Noel. *What Is the Indian "Problem": Tutelage and Resistance in Canadian Indian Administration*. St. John's, NF: Institute of Social and Economic Research, 1991.

–. *Differing Visions: Administering Indian Residential Schooling in Prince Albert 1867-1995*. Halifax: Fernwood Publishing, 1997.

Evans, Gary. *John Grierson and the National Film Board: The Politics of Propaganda*. Toronto: University of Toronto Press, 1984.

Ewers, John C. "The Emergence of the Plains Indian as the Symbol of the North American Indian." In *American Indian Stereotypes in the World of Children: A Reader and Bibliography,* edited by Arlene B. Hirshfelder, 16-32. Metuchen, NJ: Scarecrow Press, 1982.

Fetherling, Douglas. *The Rise of the Canadian Newspaper*. Toronto: Oxford University Press, 1990.

Fields, Barbara J. "Slavery, Race and Ideology in the United States of America." *New Left Review* 18 (1990): 95-118.

Finger, John R. "Conscription, Citizenship, and 'Civilization': World War I and the Eastern Band of Cherokee." *North Carolina Historical Review* 63, 3 (1986): 283-308.

Fisher, Robin. *Contact and Conflict: Indian-European Relations in British Columbia, 1774-1890.* Vancouver: UBC Press, 1977.

Fixico, Donald L. *Termination and Relocation: Federal Indian Policy, 1945-1960.* Albuquerque: University of New Mexico Press, 1986.

Francis, Daniel. *The Imaginary Indian: The Image of the Indian in Canadian Popular Culture.* 1992. Reprint, Vancouver: Arsenal Pulp Press, 1995.

Franco, Jeré Bishop. *Crossing the Pond: The Native American Effort in World War II.* Denton, TX: University of North Texas Press, 1999.

Friar, Ralph E., and Natasha A. Friar. *The Only Good Indian ... The Hollywood Gospel.* New York: Drama Book Specialists, 1972.

Gaffen, Fred. *Forgotten Soldier*. Penticton, BC: Theytus Books, 1985.

Geller, Peter, "'Hudson's Bay Company Indians': Images of Native People and the Red River Pageant, 1920." In *Dressing in Feathers: The Construction of the Indian in American Popular Culture,* edited by Elizabeth S. Bird, 65-77. Boulder, CO: Westview Press, 1996.

Gleason, Mona. "Psychology and the Construction of the 'Normal' Family in Postwar Canada, 1945-60." *Canadian Historical Review* 78, 3 (September 1997): 442-77.

Goldie, Terry. *Fear and Temptation: The Image of the Indigene in Canadian, Australian, and New Zealand Literatures.* Kingston and Montreal: McGill-Queen's University Press, 1989.

Goodwill, Jean, and Norma Sluman. *John Tootoosis*. 1982. Reprint, Winnipeg: Pemmican Publications, 1984.

Granatstein, Jack L. *Canada's War: The Policies of the Mackenzie King Government, 1939-1945.* Toronto: Oxford University Press, 1975.

–. *The Ottawa Men: The Civil Service Mandarins, 1935-57.* Toronto: Oxford University Press, 1982.

–. *Who Killed Canadian History?* Toronto: Harper Collins, 1998.

–, and Desmond Morton. *A Nation Forged in Fire: Canadians and the Second World War 1939-1945.* Toronto: Lester and Orpen Dennys, 1989.

Guest, Dennis. *The Emergence of Social Security in Canada*. Vancouver: UBC Press, 1980.

Haig-Brown, Celia. *Resistance and Renewal: Surviving the Indian Residential School.* Vancouver: Tillacum Library, 1988.

Harris, Cole. *Making Native Space: Colonialism, Resistance, and Reserves in British Columbia.* Vancouver: UBC Press, 2002.

Harrison, Dick. *Unnamed Country: The Struggle for a Canadian Prairie Fiction.* Edmonton: The University of Alberta Press, 1977.

Hauptman, Lawrence P. *The Iroquois and the New Deal.* Syracuse, NY: Syracuse University Press, 1981.

—. "Africa View: John Collier, the British Colonial Service and American Indian Policy, 1933-1945." *The Historian* 48 (May 1986): 359-74.

Hawthorn, Harold, ed. *A Survey of the Contemporary Indians of Canada: A Report on Economic, Political, Educational Needs and Policies.* Vol. 1. Ottawa: Queen's Printer, 1966 and 1967.

Haycock, Ronald Graham. *The Image of the Indian: The Canadian Indian as a subject and a concept in a sampling of the popular national magazines read in Canada 1900-1970.* Waterloo, ON: Waterloo Lutheran University, 1971.

Hemingway, Albert. *Ira Hayes: Pima Indian*. New York: University Press of America, 1988.

High, Steven. "Native Wage Labour and Independent Production during the 'Era of Irrelevance,'" *Labour/Le Travail* 37 (Spring 1996): 243-64.

Hilger, Michael. *From Savage to Nobleman: Images of Native Americans in Film.* Lanham, MD: Scarecrow Press, 1995.

Hiller, Harry H. *Society and Change: S.D. Clark and the Development of Canadian Sociology.* Toronto: University of Toronto Press, 1982.

Hillmer, Norman, Bohdan S. Kordan, and Lubomyr Y. Luciuk, eds. *On Guard for Thee: War, Ethnicity, and the Canadian State, 1939-1945.* Ottawa: Canadian Committee for the History of the Second World War, 1988.

Hirschfelder, Arlene B., ed. *American Indian Stereotypes in the World of Children: A Reader and Bibliography.* Metuchen, NJ: Scarecrow Press, 1982.

Holm, Tom. "Fighting a White Man's War: The Extent and Legacy of American Indian Participation in World War II." *The Journal of Ethnic Studies* 9, 2 (1981): 69-81.

Hulme, Peter. *Colonial Encounters: Europe and the Native Caribbean, 1492-1787.* London: Methuen, 1986.

Huttenback, Robert A. *Racism and Empire: White Settlers and Colored Immigrants in the British Self-Governing Colonies, 1830-1910.* Ithaca, NY: Cornell University Press, 1976.

Innis, Harold. *The Fur Trade in Canada: An Introduction to Canadian Economic History.* 1936. Reprint, Toronto: University of Toronto Press, 1970.

Iverson, Peter. *The Navajo Nation.* Westport, CT: Greenwood Press, 1981.

–. "Building Toward Self-Determination: Plains and Southwestern Indians in the 1940s and 1950s." *The Western Historical Quarterly* 16 (1985): 163-73.

Ives, Don. "The Veterans Charter: The Compensation Principle and the Principle of Recognition of Service." In *The Veterans Charter and Post-World War II Canada,* edited by Peter Neary and J.L. Granatstein, 85-94. Montreal and Kingston: McGill-Queen's University Press, 1998.

Jenness, Diamond. *The Indians of Canada.* 1932. Reprint, Ottawa: Queen's Printer, 1967.

–. "Canada's Indians Yesterday. What of Today?" *Canadian Journal of Economics and Political Science* 20 (1954): 95-100.

Johlin, Rev. E.E.M. "Native Canadians: A Plan for the Rehabilitation of Indians." *Wampum* 5, 3 (July 1944).

Johnson, Charles M. "The Children's War: The Mobilisation of Ontario Youth during the Second World War." In *Patterns of the Past: Interpreting Ontario's History,* edited by Roger Hall, William Westfall, and Laurel Sefton McDowell, 365-66. Toronto: Dundurn Press, 1988.

Johnson, Ian V.B. *Helping Indians to Help Themselves – A Committee to Investigate Itself: The 1951 Indian Act Consultation Process.* Ottawa: Treaties and Historical Research Centre, 1984.

Jordan, Winthrop D. *The White Man's Burden: Historical Origins of Racism in the United States.* New York: Oxford University Press, 1974.

Kealey, Greg. "Class in English-Canadian Historical Writing: Neither Privatizing, Nor Sundering." *Journal of Canadian Studies* 27, 2 (Summer 1992): 123-29.

Kelly, Lawrence C. *John Collier and the Origins of Indian Policy Reform.* Albuquerque: University of New Mexico Press, 1982.

Keshen, Jeff. "Getting It Right the Second Time Around: The Reintegration of Canadian Veterans of World War II." In *The Veterans Charter and Post-World War II Canada,* edited by Peter Neary and J.L. Granatstein, 62-84. Montreal and Kingston: McGill-Queen's University Press, 1998.

Keyserlingk, Robert H. "Breaking the Nazi Pact: Canadian Government Attitudes Towards German Canadians, 1939-1945." In *On Guard for Thee: War, Ethnicity, and the Canadian State, 1939-1945,* edited by Norman Hillmer, Bohdan S. Kordan, and Lubomyr Y. Luciuk. Ottawa: Canadian Committee for the History of the Second World War, 1988.

Koppes, Clayton R. "From New Deal to Termination: Liberalism and Indian Policy, 1933-1953." *Pacific Historical Review* 46, 3 (1977): 543-66.

Kulchyski, Peter. "A Considerable Unrest: F.O. Loft and the League of Indians." *Native Studies Review* 1, 1-2 (1988): 95-117.

–. "Anthropology in the Service of the State: Diamond Jenness and Canadian Indian Policy." *Journal of Canadian Studies* 28, 2 (Summer 1993): 21-50.

–. "Aboriginal People and Hegemony in Canada." *Journal of Canadian Studies* 30, 1 (Spring 1995): 60-8.

Lackenbauer, P. Whitney. "Vanishing Indian to Vanishing Military: Military Training and Aboriginal Lands in Twentieth Century Canada." PhD dissertation, University of Calgary, 2003.

Leslie, John. "Assimilation, Integration or Termination? The Development of Canadian Indian Policy, 1943-1963." PhD dissertation, Carleton University, 1999.

Liebersohn, Harry. *Aristocratic Encounters: European Travelers and North American Indians.* Cambridge: Cambridge University Press, 1998.

Loo, Tina. "Dan Cramner's Potlatch: Law as Coercion, Symbol and Rhetoric in British Columbia, 1884-1951." *Canadian Historical Review* 73, 2 (1992): 125-65.

Loram, C.T., and T.F. MacIlwraith, eds. *The North American Indian Today: University of Toronto-Yale University Seminar Conference, Toronto, September 4-16, 1939.* Toronto: University of Toronto Press, 1943.

Lueger, R.R.H. "A History of Indian Associations in Canada, 1870-1970." MA thesis, Carleton University, 1977.

Lyman, Christopher M. *The Vanishing Race and Other Illusions: Photographs of Indians by Edward S. Curtis.* New York: Pantheon Books/Smithsonian Institute, 1982.

MacInnes, T.R.L. "History of Indian Administration in Canada." *Canadian Journal of Economic and Political Science* 12, 3 (1946): 387-94.

MacInnis, Peter S. "Planning Prosperity: Canadians Debate Postwar Reconstruction." In *Uncertain Horizons: Canadians and Their World in 1945,* edited by Greg Donaghy, 231-59. Ottawa: Canadian Committee for the History of the Second World War, 1997.

Manke, Lewis. *Aristotle and the American Indians: A Study in Race Prejudice in the Modern World.* Bloomington, IN: Indiana University Press, 1959.

McGregor, Gaile. *The Noble Savage in the New World Garden: Notes Toward a Syntactics of Place.* Toronto: University of Toronto Press, 1988.

McLaren, Angus. *Our Own Master Race: Eugenics in Canada, 1885-1945.* Toronto: McClelland and Stewart, 1990.

Meijer Drees, Laurie. "Citizenship and Treaty Rights: The Indian Association of Alberta and the Canadian Indian Act, 1946-1948." *Great Plains Quarterly* 20 (Spring 2000): 141-58.

Miller, Ian. *Our Glory and Our Grief: Torontonians in the Great War.* Toronto: University of Toronto Press, 2002.

Miller, J.R. "Owen Glendower, Hotspur and Canadian Indian Policy." *Ethnohistory* 37, 4 (1990): 386-415.

–. *Skyscrapers Hide the Heavens: A History of Indian-White Relations in Canada,* 2nd ed. Toronto: University of Toronto Press, 1991.

–. *Shingwauk's Vision: A History of Native Residential Schools.* Toronto: University of Toronto Press, 1996.

Milloy, John S. *A National Crime: The Canadian Government and the Residential School System, 1879 to 1986.* Winnipeg: University of Manitoba Press, 1999.

Monkman, Leslie. *A Native Heritage: Images of the Indian in English Canadian Literature.* Toronto: University of Toronto Press, 1981.

Morgan, Edmund S. *American Slavery, American Freedom: The Ordeal of Colonial Virginia.* New York: W.W. Norton and Co., 1975.

Morley, Alan. *Roar of the Breakers: A Biography of Peter Kelly.* Toronto: Ryerson Press, 1967.

Morris, Alexander. *The Treaties of Canada with the Indians of Manitoba, the North West Territories and Kee-wa-tin.* Saskatoon: Fifth House, 1880.

Morton, Desmond. *The Last War Drum: The North West Campaign of 1885.* Toronto: Hakkert, 1972.

–. "The Canadian Veterans' Heritage from the Great War." In *The Veterans Charter and Post-World War II Canada,* edited by Peter Neary and J.L. Granatstein, 15-31. Montreal and Kingston: McGill-Queen's University Press, 1998.

–, and Glenn T. Wright. *Winning the Second Battle: Canadian Veterans and the Return to Civilian Life, 1915-1930.* Toronto: University of Toronto Press, 1987.

–, and J.L. Granatstein. *Victory 1945: Canadians from War to Peace.* Toronto: Harper Collins, 1995.

Mosse, George L. *Toward the Final Solution: A History of European Racism*. New York: Howard Fertig, 1978.

Moyles, R.G., and Doug Owram. *Imperial Dreams and Colonial Realities: British Views of Canada, 1880-1914*. Toronto: University of Toronto Press, 1988.

Murray, Paul T. "Who Is an Indian? Who Is a Negro? Virginia Indians in the World War II Draft." *Virginia Magazine of History and Biography* 95, 2 (1987): 215-31.

Nash, Gerald A. *The American West Transformed: The Impact of the Second World War*. Bloomington, IN: Indiana University Press, 1985.

Neary, Peter, and J.L. Granatstein, eds. *The Veterans Charter and Post-World War II Canada*. Montreal and Kingston: McGill-Queen's University Press, 1998.

Nock, David A. *A Victorian Missionary and Canadian Indian Policy: Cultural Synthesis vs. Cultural Replacement*. Waterloo, ON: Wilfrid Laurier University Press, 1988.

Owram, Douglas. *The Government Generation: Canadian Intellectuals and the State, 1900-1945*. Toronto: University of Toronto Press, 1986.

–. "Canadian Domesticity in the Postwar Era." In *The Veterans Charter and Post-World War II Canada*, edited by Peter Neary and J.L. Granatstein, 205-23. Montreal and Kingston: McGill-Queen's University Press, 1998.

Palmer, Bryan. "On Second Thoughts: Canadian Controversies." *History Today* 44, 11 (November 1994): 44-49.

Palmer, Howard. "Patterns of Racism: Attitudes Towards Chinese and Japanese in Alberta, 1920-1950." *Social History* 8 (1980): 137-60.

–. *Patterns of Prejudice: A History of Nativism in Alberta*. Toronto: McClelland and Stewart, 1982.

Patterson, E.P. "Andrew Paull and Canadian Indian Resurgence." PhD dissertation, University of Washington, 1962.

Pettipas, Katherine. *Severing the Ties that Bind: Government Repression of Indigenous Religious Ceremonies on the Prairies*. Winnipeg: University of Manitoba Press, 1994.

Philip, Kenneth R. *John Collier's Crusade for Indian Reform, 1920-1954*. Tucson, AZ: University of Arizona Press, 1977.

–. "Stride Toward Freedom: The Relocation of Indians to Cities, 1952-1960." *The Western Historical Quarterly* 16 (1985): 175-90.

Pierson, Ruth Roach. *"They're Still Women After All": The Second World War and Canadian Womanhood*. Toronto: McClelland and Stewart, 1986.

Pitsula, James. "The Saskatchewan CCF Government and Treaty Indians, 1944-1964." *Canadian Historical Review* 75, 1 (March 1994): 21-52.

Porter, H.C. *The Inconstant Savage: England and the North American Indian*. London: Duckworth, 1979.

Rea, J.E. *T.A. Crerar: A Political Life*. Montreal and Kingston: McGill-Queen's University Press, 1997.

Roy, Patricia E. "The Soldiers Canada Didn't Want: Her Chinese and Japanese Citizens." *Canadian Historical Review* 59, 3 (1978): 341-58.

–. *The Oriental Question: Consolidating a White Man's Province, 1914-41*. Vancouver: UBC Press, 2003.

Rutherford, Paul. *A Victorian Authority: The Daily Press in Late Nineteenth-Century Canada*. Toronto: University of Toronto Press, 1982.

Said, Edward. *Orientalism*. 1978. Reprint, New York: Vintage Books, 1994.

Satzewich, Victor, and Linda Mahood. "Indian Agents and Band Governance: Deposing Indian Chiefs in Western Canada." *Canadian Ethnic Studies* 26 (1994): 40-58.

–. "Indian Agents and the 'Indian Problem' in Canada in 1946: Reconsidering the Theory of Coercive Tutelage." *Canadian Journal of Native Studies* 17, 2 (1997): 227-57.

Sheffield, R. Scott. "'... in the same manner as other people': Government Policy and the Military Service of Canada's First Nations People, 1939-1945." MA thesis, University of Victoria, 1995.

–. "'Of Pure European Decent and of the White Race': Recruitment Policy and Aboriginal Canadians." *Canadian Military History* 5, 1 (Spring 1996): 8-15.

–. *A Search for Equity: A Study of the Treatment Accorded to First Nations Veterans and Dependants of the Second World War and Korea*. Ottawa: The Final Report of the National Round Table on First Nations Veterans' Issues, May 2000.

–, and Hamar Foster. "Fighting the King's War: Harris Smallfence, Verbal Treaty Promises and the Conscription of Indian Men, 1944." *University of British Columbia Law Review* 33, 1 (1999): 53-74.

Shewell, Hugh. "Origins of Contemporary Indian Social Welfare in the Canadian Liberal State: An Historical Case Study in Social Policy, 1873-1965." PhD dissertation, University of Toronto, 1995.

–. "Jules Sioui and Indian Political Radicalism in Canada, 1943-44." *Journal of Canadian Studies* 34, 3 (Fall 1999): 211-41.

Shore, Marlene. *The Social Science of Redemption: McGill, the Chicago School and the Origins of Social Research in Canada*. Toronto: University of Toronto Press, 1987.

Slater, David W. *Finance and Reconstruction: The Role of Canada's Department of Finance, 1939-1946*. Ottawa: Privately published, 1996.

Smith, Donald B. "John Laurie: A Good Samaritan." In *Citymakers: Calgarians After the Frontier*, edited by Max Foran and S. Jameson, 263-74. Calgary: Historical Society of Alberta, 1987.

–. *From the Land of Shadows: The Making of Grey Owl*. Saskatoon: Western Producer Prairie Books, 1990.

Smith, Sherry L. *Reimagining Indians: Native Americans through Anglo Eyes, 1880-1940*. Oxford and New York: Oxford University Press, 2000.

Sotiron, Minko. *From Politics to Profit: The Commercialisation of Canadian Daily Newspapers, 1890-1920*. Montreal and Kingston: McGill-Queen's University Press, 1997.

Stacey, C.P. *Arms, Men and Governments: The War Politics of Canada, 1939-1945*. Ottawa: Queen's Printer, 1970.

–. *Canada and the Age of Conflict*. Vol. 2, *1921-1948: The Mackenzie King Era*. Toronto: University of Toronto Press, 1981.

Stedman, William. *Shadows of the Indian: Stereotypes in American Culture*. Norman, OK: University of Oklahoma Press, 1982.

Stevenson, Michael D. "The Mobilisation of Native Canadians during the Second World War." *Journal of the Canadian Historical Association* 7 (1996): 205-26.

–. "National Selective Service and Employment and Seniority Rights for Veterans, 1943-46." In *The Veterans Charter and Post-World War II Canada*, edited by Peter Neary and J.L. Granatstein, 95-109. Montreal and Kingston: McGill-Queen's University Press, 1998.

–. *Canada's Greatest Wartime Muddle: National Selective Service and the Mobilization of Human Resources during World War II*. Montreal and Kingston: McGill-Queen's University Press, 2001.

Strong-Boag, Veronica. "Home Dreams: Women and the Suburban Experiment in Canada, 1945-1960." *Canadian Historical Review* 72, 4 (1991): 471-504.

–. "Contested Space: The Politics of Canadian Memory." *Journal of the Canadian Historical Association* 5 (1994): 3-17.

Struthers, James. *The Limits of Affluence: Welfare in Ontario, 1920-1970*. Toronto: University of Toronto Press, 1994.

–. "Family Allowances, Old Age Security, and the Construction of Entitlement in the Canadian Welfare State, 1943-1951." In *The Veterans Charter and Post-World War II Canada*, edited by Peter Neary and J.L. Granatstein, 179-204. Montreal and Kingston: McGill-Queen's University Press, 1998.

Summerby, Janice. *Native Soldiers Foreign Battlefields*. Ottawa: Ministry of Supply and Services Canada, 1993.

Tate, Michael L. "From Scout to Doughboy: The National Debate over Integrating American Indians into the Military, 1891-1918." *The Western Historical Quarterly* 17, 4 (1986): 417-37.

Taylor, John Leonard. *Canadian Indian Policy During the Interwar Years, 1918-1939*. Ottawa: Treaties and Historical Research Centre, 1984.

Tennant, Paul. *Aboriginal People and Politics: The Indian Land Question in British Columbia, 1848-1989.* Vancouver: UBC Press, 1990.

Thompson, John, and Alan Seager. *Canada, 1922-1939: Decades of Discord.* Toronto: McClelland and Stewart, 1985.

Titley, Brian. "W.M. Graham: Indian Agent Extraordinaire." *Prairie Forum* 1 (1983): 25-41.

–. *A Narrow Vision: Duncan Campbell Scott and the Administration of Indian Affairs in Canada.* Toronto: Butterworths, 1986.

Tobias, John L. "Protection, Civilization, Assimilation: An Outline History of Canada's Indian Policy." In *As Long as the Sun Shines and the Water Flows: A Reader in Canadian-Native Relations,* edited by Ian A.L. Getty and Antoine S. Lussier, 39-55. Vancouver: UBC Press, 1983.

Townsend, Kenneth William. *World War II and the American Indian.* Albuquerque: University of New Mexico Press, 2000.

Treaty 7 Elders and Tribal Council. *The True Spirit and Original Intent of Treaty 7.* Montreal and Kingston: McGill-Queen's University Press, 1996.

Trigger, Bruce. *Natives and Newcomers: Canada's "Heroic Age" Reconsidered.* Montreal and Kingston: McGill-Queen's Press, 1985.

–. "The Historians' Indian: Native Americans in Canadian Historical Writing from Charlevoix to the Present." *Canadian Historical Review* 67, 3 (1986): 315-42.

Troper, Harold. "Canada's Immigration Policy since 1945." *International Journal* 48, 2 (1993): 255-81.

Vance, Jonathan F. *Death So Noble: Memory, Meaning, and the First World War.* Vancouver: UBC Press, 1997.

Veatch, Richard. *Canada and the League of Nations.* Toronto: McClelland and Stewart, 1975.

Vibert, Elizabeth. *Trader's Tales: Narratives of Cultural Encounters in the Columbia Plateau, 1797-1846.* Norman, OK: University of Oklahoma Press, 1997.

Vogt, Evon Z. *Navaho Veterans: A Study of Changing Values.* 1951. Reprint, Millwood, NY: Kraus, 1973.

Walker, James W. St. G. "Race and Recruitment during World War I: Enlistment of Visible Minorities in the Canadian Expeditionary Force." *Canadian Historical Review* 70, 1 (1989): 1-26.

–. *"Race," Rights and the Law in the Supreme Court of Canada: Historical Case Studies.* Waterloo and Toronto: Wilfrid Laurier University Press and the Osgoode Society, 1997.

Ward, W. Peter. *White Canada Forever: Popular Attitudes and Public Policies Towards Orientals in British Columbia,* 2nd ed. Montreal and Kingston: McGill-Queen's University Press, 1990.

Washburn, Wilcomb E. *Red Man's Land – White Man's Law: The Past and Present Status of the American Indian.* 1971. Reprint, Norman, OK: University of Oklahoma Press, 1995.

Weston, Mary Ann. *Native Americans in the News: Images of Indians in the Twentieth Century Press.* Westport, CT: Greenwood Press, 1996.

Whitaker, Reg, and Gary Marcuse. *Cold War Canada: The Making of a National Insecurity State, 1945-1957.* Toronto: University of Toronto Press, 1994.

White, Richard. *The Middle Ground: Indians, Empires, and Republics in the Great Lakes Region, 1650-1850.* Cambridge: Cambridge University Press, 1991.

White, W. Bruce. "The American Indian as Soldier, 1890-1919." *Canadian Review of American Studies* 7 (Spring 1976): 15-25.

Whiteside, Donald. *Historical Development of Aboriginal Political Associations in Canada: Documentation.* Vol. 1. Ottawa: Reference Aids – Indexes, 1973.

–. *Efforts to Develop Aboriginal Political Associations in Canada, 1850-1965.* Ottawa: Aboriginal Institute of Canada, 1974.

Williams, Eric. *Capitalism and Slavery.* 1944. Reprint, London: Andre Deutsch, 1964.

Wong, Marjorie. *The Dragon and the Maple Leaf: Chinese Canadians and World War II.* London, ON: Pirie Publishing, 1994.

Zissu, Eric M. "Conscription, Sovereignty, and Land: American Indian Resistance during World War I." *Pacific Historical Review* 64, 4 (1995): 537-66.

Index

"**A**dministrative Indian," 11, 174, 177-78; characteristics of, 20-24, 49, 112, 116, 123, 186n15; favoured position before SJC, 156, 167; infantile nature of, 23, 113; in postwar, 112, 118, 125-26; resistance to change, 60-61, 118-19, 126-27, 177; sources, 12, 20; and undermining Native opposition, 57, 61, 113

alcohol, 37, 64, 132, 140, 211n10

Allen, D.J., 59

Anderson, Arthur, 59

Army, Canadian, 45, 48

assimilation, 20, 41, 49, 104, 147, 165, 214n48; as appropriate solution to "Indian problem," 101, 106, 119, 126, 136, 151, 161, 172, 179; confidence in, 102, 119-20, 136, 173; different definitions of, 163-66; lack of success, 23, 50, 61, 96, 126; Native resistance to, 39, 120, 166; need for supervision to achieve, 122; non-partisan agreement upon, 153, 188n48; postwar reaffirmation of, 169, 171, 173, 178, 180; role of military service, 47-48, 50, 60-61

Atlantic Charter, 96, 99, 131, 146

Barbeau, Marius, 26

Bill 79, 174

Bill 267, 174

Blackfoot, 27, 98

Blackmore, J.H., 150, 154, 161, 166

Blood, 68, 73, 80, 196n4

Brantford Expositor, 36, 197n24

Brown, D.F., 148, 152, 160, 164, 218n68

Bryce, W., 151, 154, 165-66, 218n66

Calgary Herald, 72-73

Calgary Stampede, 78

Canadian Forum, 187n47

Canadian Pacific Railway, 33-35

Cardston News, 13, 27, 38, 64

Case, W.G., 156

Castelden, G.H., 150-52, 157, 160, 213n40, 214n45, 216n23, 217n49

Caughnawaga, 98, 156, 160, 212n35, 215n61

Chippewa, 88

citizenship, 96, 120, 160, 170, 180, 214n48; desire to grant to First Nations, 136, 162, 168; as goal of Indian policy, 101-2, 119, 165, 171; Native demands for, 141; obligations of, 44, 51, 134, 176; resistance to special rights in addition to, 101-2, 136-37, 158; rights of, 51, 134

Claims Commission. *See* Special Joint Committee, Claims Commission

Collier, John, 17-18, 185n7

Committee of Friends of the Indians, 131

Committee on Reconstruction and Re-establishment, 92, 94, 101, 120, 200n1, 216n23

conscription: administration of Natives, 43, 45, 47, 52-53; as catalyst to Native politicization, 89, 139; exemption for Status Indians, 47, 51, 55; home defence, 46, 62; military training, 1-2, 46, 49, 176; and national unity, 42; Native resistance to, 46, 52, 55-56, 58; symbolic meaning of, 51-52, 60, 112

Co-operative Commonwealth Federation (CCF), 16, 86, 200n9, 201n23, 208n67, 214n45

Cree, 27, 97, 196n18, 198n42; reluctant involvement in Northwest Rebellion, 5; support for war effort, 68-70

Crerar, Thomas A., 47, 109, 112, 190n95, 205n2

assimilation, 117, 165; standard of living on, 98-99, 121
"Indian victim," 130, 132, 146; characteristics of, 105, 133; emergence of, 90, 99; integration, 137, 161, 166, 172; lack of blame for, 91; as rhetorical tool, 106, 134, 167

Japan, 63, 79, 85, 108
Japanese Canadians, 151, 165, 181, 211n22; internment of, 7
Jenness, Diamond, 162, 218n55
Jews, 90, 135, 146, 211n22, 215n77
Jones, Thomas, 89

Kamloops Sentinel, 38, 93, 103
Keenleyside, H.L., 154-55, 216n25
Kelley, Peter, 213n42
King, William Lyon Mackenzie, 42, 62, 87
Kwawkewlth Agency, 50

LaFlèche, L.R., 52
Laurie, John, 213n40
Lazare, Matthew, 156
Liberal Party, 86-87, 92
Lickers, Norman, 139, 159, 214n46, 216n11, 217n45

MacIlwraith, T.F., 131, 162-63, 166, 210n5
MacInnes, T.R.L., 40, 92, 101, 120, 190n95, 208n62
MacKay, D.M., 54-55, 91, 153, 202n30
Maclean's, 187n47
MacNicol, J.D., 91, 152, 202n29, 216n23
Marsh Report, the, 87
Martin, Oliver M., 131, 157, 164, 210n5
McColl-Frontenac Oil Company, 27-31
McGill, Harold, 21, 46, 50, 109-10, 186n20, 190n95
Métis, 5
Mi'Kmaq, 218n64
Millar, Albert, 103-4, 203n46

national registration, 42, 44, 46, 48, 56
National Resources Mobilization Act (NRMA), 42, 45-46, 52, 62
Native Brotherhood of British Columbia (NBBC), 131, 139, 213n42
New Deal, Indian, 18, 157; Canadian advocates of, 102, 104, 203n46; decline of, 43; influence on Canadian debate, 101. *See also* Indian policy, American
new order: characteristics of, 87; desire for, 85, 105; and fear of losing the peace, 85, 87; and interventionist government, 88; place of First Nations in, 86; threat

of "Indian problem" to, 100, 105. *See also* reconstruction, postwar
"noble savage," 39, 68, 93; association with Rousseau, 4; characteristics of, 36, 105; nostalgic romanticization of, 5, 31-32; object of humour, 38; in postwar, 132, 167; tool of social criticism, 4, 67, 78
North American Indian Brotherhood (NAIB), 46, 138-39, 143, 201n21, 213n41
Northwest Rebellion, 5

Ojibwa (Anishnabe), 90
Oka, 142, 145, 215n61
Okanagan Society for the Revival of Indian Arts and Crafts, 96, 98, 101, 103-4

Paull, Andrew, 46, 89, 139, 143, 159, 213n42, 213n44, 218n53
Pegahmagabow, Francis, 90, 201n28
Peigan, 50, 97, 125
"potential Indian citizen," 167, 172-73, 174-75; characteristics of, 168-70
potlatch, 74, 190n92
Prince Albert Daily Herald, 78, 93, 94
Prince, Thomas, 133, 153-54, 211n13
Progressive Conservative Party, 86
"Public Indian." *See* "drunken criminal," "Indian-at-war," "Indian victim," "noble savage," and vanishing "Indian"

RCAF (Royal Canadian Air Force), 45
RCN (Royal Canadian Navy), 45
reconstruction, postwar, 10, 87, 108, 127, 181; dominating public agenda, 86; government unwilling to discuss (1939-43), 86; inclusion of Indian policy in, 91, 94, 180; planning for, 87. *See also* new order
recruitment, 2, 45. *See also* enlistment
Reid, Thomas, 150-53, 158, 164, 217n49
reserves. *See* Indian reserves
residential schools. *See* education
Royal Canadian Air Force, 45
Royal Canadian Mounted Police (RCMP), 24, 50, 56, 72
Royal Canadian Navy, 45

Saint John Telegraph Journal, 134
Saturday Night, 187n47
Scott, Duncan Campbell, 17, 39-40, 41, 185n4, 186n20, 190n95, 190n96
self-government, 145, 159, 167, 170
Shumiachter, Morris, 213n40
Sioui, Jules, 46, 89, 213n41, 213n43
Six Nations Iroquois, 156, 176, 215n61; military service of, 79; nationalists and